KILL-CAVALRY

General Hugh Judson Kilpatrick. Courtesy of the Library of Congress.

KILL-CAVALRY

The Life of Union General Hugh Judson Kilpatrick

by Samuel J. Martin

STACKPOLE BOOKS

Published by
STACKPOLE BOOKS
5067 Ritter Road
Mechanicsburg PA 17055
www.stackpolebooks.com

Printed in the United States of America

10 9 8 7 6 5 4 3 2 1

FIRST EDITION

Library in Congress Cataloging-in-Publication Data

Martin, Samuel J.
    Kill-Cavalry : the Life of Union General Hugh Judson Kilpatrick / by Samuel J. Martin.
        p. cm.
    Originally published: Madison, NJ : Fairleigh Dickinson University Press, 1996.
    Includes bibliographical references and index.
    ISBN 0-8117-0887-X
        1. Kilpatrick, Judson, 1836–1881. 2. Generals—United States—Biography.
3. United States. Army—Biography. 4. United States—History—Civil War,
1861–1865—Cavalry operations. 5. United States—History—Civil War,
1861–1865—Campaigns. I. Title.

E467.1.K345 M37 2000
973.7'41'092—dc21
[B]
                                     99-047528

Contents

Acknowledgments

Kilpatrick left no personal letters or diaries (all of this material was destroyed by his daughter, Laura, just before her death in 1955), so ascertaining the details of his life was a challenge, a puzzle that had to be compiled a piece at a time. Many people were of much help, and I want to acknowledge those who contributed to my research.

Mike Miers and Kathy DiCastro led me through the musty records of the National Archives in Washington, D.C.

Edward Skipworth of Rutgers University provided a number of key bits of information about Kilpatrick's life.

Daniel Jones of the New Jersey State Archives supplied the microfilm of the Sussex Independent.

Carolyn A. Davis of Syracuse University found a letter shedding light on Kilpatrick's lecture career.

Susan A. Walker, Alicia Mauldin, and Judith Sibley of the United States Military Academy at West Point researched details on Kilpatrick's cadet life.

Therese A. Erskine, Reference Librarian for the Sussex (New Jersey) County Library, provided information on Kilpatrick's family.

Elsa Meyers of the New Jersey Historical Society found an interesting letter on Kilpatrick for me and made a number of good suggestions as to where I might find material on my subject.

Jan Flores of the Georgia (Savannah) Historical Society found details about Kilpatrick's time in Georgia.

Harriett Kenny was a wonderful host during my visit to Barnwell, South Carolina.

Kathy Hartley was kind enough to invite me to her home in Barnwell, South Carolina, where Kilpatrick held his "Nero Dance" in 1865.

Joyanne Hawkins from the Indiana University Library in Bloomington, Indiana, supplied information about Kilpatrick from their files.

Otis Amason presented interesting detail about Kilpatrick's 1864/1865 headquarters at Midway Church in Georgia.

8 ACKNOWLEDGMENTS

Margaret M. Sherry with Princeton University libraries in New Jersey, guided me to various sources on Kilpatrick.

My frequent visits to the rare book collections at the Thomas Cooper and Carolinian libraries at the University of South Carolina were always fruitful.

And the people at the Chatham County (Georgia) Library, Hinesville County (Georgia) Library, Beaufort County (South Carolina) libraries, Armstrong State College (Savannah, Georgia) Library, and Barnwell County (South Carolina) Library, could not have been more helpful.

I want to especially acknowledge James Mack Adams, who carefully read my manuscript and corrected my innumerable errors in grammar.

I am very grateful to Dr. Alan C. Downs, Assistant Professor, Department of History at Georgia Southern University, who not only perused the book for factual accuracy but also made many valuable suggestions on style.

Lisa Kosanke prepared the many excellent maps found in the book.

KILL-CAVALRY

Prologue

It was a dark and stormy night. It really was! "Cold, raw and rainy," Federal captain James H. Kidd recalled. "The atmosphere [was] full of moisture, which gradually turned into an icy sheet."[1]

Three thousand Union cavalrymen under Brigadier General Hugh Judson Kilpatrick were headed toward Richmond where they hoped to dart into the Confederate capital to free their compatriots held captive at Belle Isle and Libby Prisons. They had slipped past the Rebel pickets posted along the banks of the Rapidan River and were now riding deep into Southern territory.

"Into the dark night . . . a darkness that could be felt . . . rode the brave troops," Kidd recorded. "On and on, for hours and hours, facing the biting storm, feeling the pelting rain, staring with straining eyes into the black night, striving to see when nothing was visible to the keenest vision, listening with perked ears for the sound of hoofs [ahead] which with a rhythmical tread signaled the way."[2]

On Tuesday, 1 March 1864, about 10:00 A.M., the column finally came to a numbed halt. The Union force had ridden to within a mile of Richmond, so close one could "look into the streets and count the spires on the churches."[3]

It was time. Kilpatrick was on schedule, ready for the sprint into the city that would free his imprisoned comrades. The men waited for his order to go. "Each . . . had screwed his courage to the sticking point," Kidd wrote, "to follow wherever our gallant commander led."[4]

Kilpatrick issued an order, but it was not what his men had anticipated. "In case any . . . should be wounded," he said, "[unit commanders] will be obliged to make their own arrangements for the transportation and care of them, since no ambulances are available."[5]

"From that moment," Kidd declared, "the mental attitude of [even] the bravest was one of apathetic indifference."[6]

Every man felt that Kilpatrick had lost his nerve, that he would never give the order to charge the old men and young boys bravely manning the earthen forts outside of the Confederate capital. And they were right. He soon turned his column east, away from Richmond, toward the Peninsula where the haven of Union ports on the sea beckoned to him.

Kilpatrick's friends (and he had many) were shocked to learn that he had been unable to summon the courage to carry out his assault on Richmond. They considered him a gallant leader, a man so eager for action that Kilpatrick had earned the nickname "Kill-Cavalry" because he never spared himself, his troops, or their horses in his determination to confront the Rebels.

Kilpatrick's enemies (and he had many) had anticipated his failure to attack Richmond. They were convinced that he was a coward—an egotistical, lying, sadistic, philandering, thieving miscreant whose lofty reputation had been gained by words, not deeds. The South certainly agreed with this description. Had they won their independence, and captured him in the process, they probably would have hung Kilpatrick as a war criminal.

Although both views can be supported by facts, the latter is no doubt closer to the truth. Kilpatrick's exploits were more often contemptible than commendable.

He did, however, play a leading role in both theaters of the war. He was one of the young Turks who led the Union cavalry to equality in the east with Southern general James Ewell Brown (Jeb) Stuart's cavaliers, and Kilpatrick was the commander of the western horsemen who took part in Sherman's March to the Sea. He achieved a major general's rank, and he could never be considered "dull." His life story follows, the biography of an antihero.

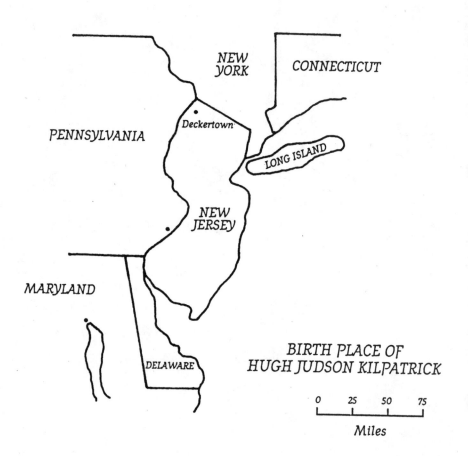

NEW
YORK

CONNECTICUT

PENNSYLVANIA

Deckertown

LONG ISLAND

NEW
JERSEY

MARYLAND

DELAWARE

BIRTH PLACE OF
HUGH JUDSON KILPATRICK

0   25   50   75

Miles

1

Antebellum

Northwestern New Jersey is mountainous country, part of the piedmont whose rolling, wooded knolls precede the soaring Appalachians that stretch from Maine to Alabama. Deckertown (now Sussex), the principal village in the area known as "The Valley of the Cloves," was circled by pleasant farms back in 1836, one of which was owned by Simon Kilpatrick. He and his wife, the former Julia Wickham, were especially nervous that winter. She was pregnant with their fourth child, a "caboose baby" coming in their twentieth year of marriage. The other children—a son, Wickham, and daughters, Adeline and Charity—were already approaching adulthood.[1]

Snow capped the peaks surrounding Deckertown on 14 January 1836 when Hugh Judson Kilpatrick was born, and the family fears turned to joy with the arrival of a healthy second boy. Judson had mixed ancestry: his paternal grandfather, Ephram Kilpatrick, was an Irishman who had settled the two hundred acres the family now farmed; William Wickham, his mother's father, was a Dutchman from Massachusetts. During the Revolutionary War, when William was a child, a British soldier entered his house and slashed his head with a saber while he lay in his cradle. He carried that scar to his grave [2]

Judson's aging parents considered him special, which is typical for a late-coming child. "[They] grow up in a different family world from that of their older siblings," experts Pamela Daniels and Kathy Weingarten state. "Parents . . . [are] better, more involved and relaxed with 'caboose' children."[3]

The special involvement that Judson shared with his parents no doubt included his attending the parades of the state militia. Simon Kilpatrick was a colonel, and he presented an inspiring sight to his son, who watched with awe as his father, in a resplendent uniform, shouted orders to troops.[4] He, too, would be a soldier.

His parents made sure that Judson received the best education available, sending him first to Liberty Hill School and then Mt. Retirement Seminary.[5] As soon as he learned to read, Judson concentrated on military men. "The great conquerors of the world and their deeds filled his youthful breast with military ardor," James Moore, an early biographer, recorded, "and the . . .

15

laurels that decked the brows of heroes like Alexander, Caesar, Charlemagne, or Napoleon, made him wish for a field . . . to emulate their prowess and valor."[6]

As he grew older, Judson's dreams expanded. He would still be a military man, but after gaining fame on the field of battle, he would be elected governor of New Jersey, then president of the United States.[7] His parents' excessive pride in their late-arriving son no doubt swelled his confidence, and he proceeded to pursue his bold plan.

The first stage, to be a soldier, an officer in the U.S. Army, required that he be appointed by his congressman to West Point. Judson applied for the nomination in 1855 but was rejected. Favoritism counted more than ability, and he was only a farmer's son who had no sway with a politician.[8] Undaunted, Judson set out to solve this problem. He would simply help in reelecting the congressman, who would then show his gratitude by granting Judson an appointment to the academy. George Vail was the candidate that Judson campaigned for in the fall of 1855. "He went from village to village haranguing the electors," the Comte de Paris reported. "The people were impressed with his speeches and his youth. The member was reelected and Kilpatrick entered West Point."[9]

His mother at first had been thrilled with Judson's gaining entry to West Point, but she soon missed her son, and much to his distress, she besieged the academy with letters asking that he be discharged. His father was ill; Judson was needed on the farm. The superintendent contacted a doctor in Sussex County to check into the matter, and found that although Judson's father was indeed incapacitated, he had been ill for twelve or more years. Given this evidence the superintendent sent Mrs. Kilpatrick a stiff letter, advising her that Judson must remain at West Point.[10]

Although Judson had gained his first objective, the members of the academy were not too impressed with their newest plebe. Kilpatrick stood only five feet five inches tall, weighed 140 pounds, and "his self-confident air, strongly marked face, and consequential walk at once marked [him] among his fellows, and called forth all the talent of the older cadets in making him an object of their amusement and discipline."[11] They made fun of his wide mouth with perfectly formed teeth, his large nose, and his thinning, sandy hair. Judson reacted to these vicious taunts with good nature, sharp repartee, and if necessary, his fists. He fought often, most times against boys who were bigger and stronger than he. And he generally won, including an epic forty-minute bout with an adversary twice his size, which gained him the esteem and wary respect of his fellow cadets.[12]

Judson's class included fifty-nine plebes. With his goal to be the best of soldiers, he had to do well in comparison to his compatriots, and he did so. He ranked fifteenth in mathematics and twentieth in English studies his first year. Although the high rankings he achieved might have been anticipated, no one could have foreseen Judson's record for demerits. None![13] Among his future Civil War contemporaries, Adelbert Ames drew eleven, Emery Upton sixty-five, and Thomas Rosser ninety-nine. Judson capped off a good start by being promoted to lance corporal.[14]

When the 1857 plebe class reported to West Point, Judson Kilpatrick was there to greet them. "His favorite diversion," George King wrote, "was 'running it' on new cadets."[15] He had endured harassment, and he would make sure that these neophytes suffered, too. He showed a sadistic urge that would reach unconscionable levels during the Civil War. One recruit remembered his first encounter with Judson. "He buttoned up my citizen's coat, turned up the collar, advised me not to become too fond of ladies' society, told me to get my hair cut, and invited me to bring him a bucket of water."[16]

During his second year at the academy, Judson joined the Dialectic Society, playing major roles in the different dramas that the club presented. "He distinguished himself as an amateur actor," James Wilson declared.[17] This activity, however, did not detract from his performance as a student. He ranked twenty-second in his class of fifty-two in mathematics, tenth in English studies, and thirty-second in French.[18] Although he did accumulate twenty-five demerits, this was only a few more than that recorded for the class's best performer. Kilpatrick was rewarded for his good effort with a promotion to corporal at the end of the year.[19]

By 1858 the issue of slavery had inflamed the nation and threatened civil war. Among the key tinder kegs were the Dred Scott decision by the Supreme Court, denying status as citizens to Blacks;[20] the Lecompton Constitution in Kansas, which first promised the South a slave state, then was rejected by voters in a questionable election;[21] and the Lincoln/Douglas debates over slavery in general.[22] The cadets at West Point were not immune to arguing their position, and Judson Kilpatrick was in the forefront of the antislavery group. "He was a most blatant and interminable talker," said Morris Schaff.[23] Wilson stated, "He was distinctly unpopular with the Southerners."[24] Interestingly, Judson was not an abolitionist; he simply did not like the boys from below the Mason-Dixon line, who bore an air of superiority that he would not acknowledge. Kilpatrick was involved in a host of confrontations, and he displayed unflinching courage by taking on all comers.

Despite his many bellicose encounters, Judson managed to end the term with only fifteen demerits plus promotion to sergeant.[25] He continued to excel in class (now fifty members) by ranking fifteenth in philosophy, thirty-fourth in drawing, and nineteenth in Spanish.[26]

In his fourth year, Judson suddenly became less involved in the debates that tore at the very fabric of both the nation and the academy. His ardor had not diminished; it had taken a different bent: love. He had met a girl in New York City, Alice Shailer, the niece of F. H. Allen, an important politician, so

Cadet Hugh Judson Kilpatrick. Courtesy of the Special Collections Division of the United States Military Academy Library.

instead of spending his weekends arguing with the other cadets, he took leave to visit his new sweetheart. "The Post Orders detail numerous instances," Susan P. Walker of the United States Military Academy Archives notes, "in which [Kilpatrick] was granted extended limits for a Saturday afternoon of his choosing."[27] Judson had to stay out of trouble because the privilege of leaving the grounds was only accorded to one who had accumulated no demerits over a three-month period.

Kilpatrick ended the year with no demerits and a promotion to lieuten-ant.[28] He ranked twenty-first in ethics, twentieth in chemistry, twenty-seventh in infantry tactics, twelfth in drawing, twelfth in cavalry tactics, and twenty-first in artillery tactics.[29] His class remained at fifty members.

In the fall of 1860, Judson began his final year at West Point. He was careful to keep his record clear of demerits so he could continue to call on Alice in New York City; they planned to marry in August after his graduation from the academy.[30] National events, however, threatened their romance.

The November presidential election found four candidates vying for the office. The Republican Party, made up of former Whigs plus the abolitionists, named Abraham Lincoln; Stephen A. Douglas was the Northern Democratic nominee; Southern Democrats supported John C. Breckinridge; and John Bell was the Constitutional Union entrant, running as a compromise between the various factions. When Lincoln won (despite polling only about 40 percent of the vote), the seeds for disunion were sown.[31]

South Carolina seceded on 20 December 1860. Six states (Mississippi, Florida, Alabama, Georgia, Louisiana, and Texas) quickly followed, and the nation stood at a crossroads. When Lincoln refused to surrender Fort Sumter in Charleston Harbor, the South bombarded the bastion, forcing Lincoln's hand. His response was to call for seventy-five thousand volunteers to suppress the rebellion. Rather than bear arms against their sister Southern states, Virginia, North Carolina, Tennessee, and Arkansas left the Union and the Civil War began.[32]

Judson "went wild with excitement" over the fall of Fort Sumter, and his outspoken criticism of the South led to a fist fight with William W. Dunlap of Kentucky. The cadets were entering the mess hall when the brawl erupted. A few continued inside to eat a bad meal; most skipped supper that evening to stay outside and watch a good bout.[33]

As volunteers rushed to enlist at the recruiting centers, Judson took steps to join them. He called his classmates to a meeting to sign a petition to the secretary of war, asking him to allow them to graduate early so they could enter the army.[34] The request was granted, and on 6 May 1861 commencement ceremonies took place in the Cadet Chapel. Judson's final year record (seven-teenth in engineering, twentieth in minerals and geology, thirteenth in ord-nance and gunnery, twenty-first in ethics)[35] placed him seventeenth in a class of forty-five, but because of his ability as a speaker, he was chosen to give the valedictory address.[36]

Alice had come to see the bars of a second lieutenant of artillery pinned to Judson's shoulders. When the ceremony was over, they went to a reception at a local hotel. A friend of Judson's approached them. "Kill is going to the field and may not return," he slyly suggested. "Better get married now."[37]

Judson thought this was a great idea, and when Alice said she was willing, the Reverend J. W. French was summoned to the hotel to conduct the wedding rites.[38] All but ten cadets from Judson's class attended the hurried ceremony. After a honeymoon of one night, he left Alice for Washington and the war.

Judson Kilpatrick, recent graduate of West Point, was a bright, well-spoken lad who was intensely interested in all subjects and people that he encountered. Although he was not "one of the boys" (his lack of demerits demonstrates that he was probably a loner), he was respected by his classmates, as evidenced by their selecting him to speak at their graduation exercises.

He showed signs, however, of a flawed character. Although Judson was eloquent, he talked too much. He tended to be intolerant in his interests—one whose views were always right—and if words could not persuade, then his fists continued the argument. He seemed to be more "noticeable" than "notable."

These faults could have been just the signs of youthful immaturity. The army, however, was expecting him to lead men into battle, and if he did not age quickly, his future would be at best controversial.

2

Big Bethel

When Judson and his classmates reached Washington, they were greeted in person by the army commander, General Winfield Scott. He was weak from age and infirmity, and his aides had to hold him erect as he shook hands with each of the newly commissioned lieutenants. "I wish there were five hundred of you instead of only forty-five," he lamented.[1]

The class retired to Willard's Hotel that night. In the early dawn they were wakened to help douse a fire to the house next to the hotel. Colonel Elmer Ellsworth's Zouaves, a regiment composed of firemen from New York City, joined in putting out the flames. Judson must have observed these soldiers upon his arrival in Washington and envied their colorful uniforms—white gaiters, baggy red pantaloons, short blue jackets decorated with shiny brass buttons, and red kepis.[2] He could never have guessed that in only a week he would be similarly dressed

Judson had taken a careful look at the opportunities for rank in the army, and he recognized at once that the best chances lay with the volunteer force. He had taken steps toward gaining such an assignment, writing on 21 April to the governor of New Jersey for a post with the state militia,[3] and asking his mathematics professor at the academy, Governeur K. Warren, to suggest him for a captaincy with a New York regiment.[4] Warren must have come through, because on 9 May Kilpatrick learned that he was to leave immediately for Fort Schuyler, located on Staten Island in New York Harbor. He had been commissioned as captain of Company H, Fifth New York Infantry.[5]

When Lincoln had asked for seventy-five thousand volunteers to put down the rebellion, he had given each state a quota for their share of the total. Abram Duryee, a wealthy importer from New York City who had been active in the state militia for over twenty-five years and who rose to the rank of colonel before resigning in 1859,[6] quickly moved to recruit the Fifth New York, one of the seventeen regiments from that state. He filled his ranks in just four days, dressed his men in Zouave uniforms, and began drills at Fort Schuyler.[7] Only two weeks after Kilpatrick had joined the unit, the regiment was ordered to Fortress Monroe on the Virginia Peninsula. The troops were loaded on three tugs

(*Satellite, Only Son,* and *C. P. Smith*) and shipped into the city where they paraded down Broadway to the plaudits of dignitaries and thousands of spectators. The columns then went back to the East Fifteenth Street pier to board the *Alabama* for the sea voyage south.[8]

Upon reaching Fortress Monroe, Kilpatrick began to train his men. He emphasized military drill but also made sure the troops enjoyed themselves. He knew the men would work harder for officers they liked, and he sought means to endear himself to his command. For example he challenged his privates to a mule cart race. The contest was comical, with Judson standing up in his wagon, chasing after the enlisted team, and yelling, "Halt! Halt!" as he tried to keep them in sight.[9] He lost the race but gained rapport with his troops.

Kilpatrick's men also liked his contempt for the orders forbidding theft from the nearby farmers. Although Major General Benjamin F. Butler, a former politician from Massachusetts in charge of the camp, had prohibited foraging, Judson looked the other way as his men helped themselves. "It was a well-known fact," Colonel Joseph B. Carr, Second New York, related, "that the Zouaves' rations [were augmented with] chicken, roast pig, ham, corn and other first class foods."[10] Kilpatrick saw from the start that his enemy included the citizens of the South.

In his training of the men, Judson concentrated on skirmishing, and by 22 May he felt that they were ready to take the field. He led a patrol of forty soldiers up the Peninsula to Hampton, forded the water there, then moved along the Yorktown Road to Newmarket where he found the Rebels destroying a bridge. A volley sent the enemy scampering northward. Judson then returned to Hampton, gathering booty (one horse, a harness, three mules, four drums, some grain, and a few arms) along the way.[11] Kilpatrick celebrated his "victory" by raising the Union flag and making a speech, directed more toward a newspaper reporter than to his men. He was soon rewarded when a favorable story appeared on the front page of the *New York Times*. It was a most auspicious start in promoting his military career.[12]

The forays by Kilpatrick and other company captains convinced Butler that he could successfully assault the Rebels at Big Bethel. He laid out a plan. Because of the skill he had shown in skirmishing, Kilpatrick was assigned a lead role. He would leave camp at 9:30 P.M. on 9 June to clear the path to Big Bethel. To prevent anyone from alerting the Rebels of the imminent attack, Kilpatrick would make captives of local citizens he found along the way.[13] The rest of the Fifth New York under Colonel Duryee would leave Hampton at midnight, followed by the Third New York under Colonel Frederick Townsend at 1:00 A.M. To the left a second column would advance north out of Newport News. The First Vermont, headed by Lieutenant Colonel Peter T. Washburn, would lead the way, followed by the Seventh New York under Colonel John E. Bendix. The First and Second New York and the Fourth Massachusetts would

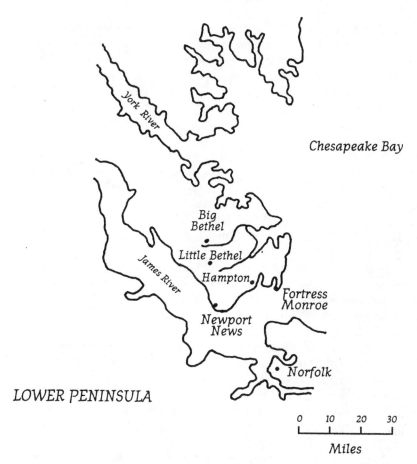

act in reserve. Brigadier General Ebenezer W. Pierce held overall command of the attack.[14]

Butler's plan called for the two columns to march in the form of an inverted *V* as they advanced. They would merge below Little Bethel, the initial point of attack. To avoid confusion when they met in the darkness, the men should challenge any unknown troops with the password, "Boston."[15]

Kilpatrick left on schedule and arrived at Little Bethel without incident about 1:00 A.M. Two hours later as the Fifth New York and First Vermont came into Judson's view, the sound of muskets exploded to the rear. Colonels Washburn and Duryee conferred and deduced that the Rebels had assaulted the Union soldiers following them, and they hastily marched back to confront the enemy.[16]

When they arrived at the point of fighting, they found a fiasco had occurred in the Northern ranks. Colonel Townsend's pickets, upon encountering

Colonel Bendix's merging men, gave the password, "Boston." The Seventh New York troops, however, had not been advised of this code, and they responded by opening fire. "Boston!" the ranks of the Third New York cried, and the Seventh New York answered with an artillery salvo. As he approached the confused chaos from the north, Colonel Washburn suspected that the fray was between friends, and he took steps to halt the melee. "I immediately formed my [whole] command," he wrote, "and caused [them] to shout 'Boston' four times."[17] Colonel Washburn's arrival broke up the skirmish, and the Yankees finally discovered that they were fighting each other. Twenty-one casualties had been suffered.[18] The sounds of the skirmish had obviously warned the Confederates that the Union was approaching (from Boston?), and in a hurried conference of officers, Colonels Duryee and Washburn argued that the attack should be canceled. General Pierce, however, decided to proceed with an assault. The regiments at hand were formed, and with Kilpatrick's company in the lead, the Federals headed for Big Bethel.

Approaching a small bridge, Kilpatrick spotted a blazing campfire up ahead. He gathered twenty men and crept silently toward the Confederate outpost.

"Who comes there?" a Southern sentry challenged.[19]

"Who stands there?" Judson replied.

"A Virginian!"

"Charge!" Kilpatrick bellowed, and his men fired as they raced into the clearing to capture all of the Confederates before they could warn their compatriots of the coming Federals.

Passing through Little Bethel the Union columns came to a brief halt to burn the lone building at the crossroads. The advance then continued to Big Bethel where the Rebels were ensconced in earthen forts along a sluggish stream. There was a breastwork on each side of the road beyond the creek; a third bulwark had been raised in front of the run, west of the road. The Confederate flanks were protected by marshland. The only solid ground available for a charge was the open field left of the bridge that spanned the stream. Kilpatrick placed his men in some woods on the left. He estimated the enemy strength at two to three thousand troops.[20]

The Confederates awaiting the Federals' assault actually totaled only about fourteen hundred men under the overall command of Colonel John Magruder. They included the First North Carolina led by Colonel Daniel H. Hill, who occupied the works above the water, and the Third Virginia under Colonel William D. Stuart, who manned the western bastion in front of the run.[21]

Pierce deployed his troops for battle, placing the Fifth New York, supported by an artillery battery, in the woods left of the road. The Seventh New York gathered in a forest to the right. The other three regiments were in echelon in reserve. The fray began when the Union cannons fired at 9:40 A.M.[22]

Given the order to charge, the Fifth New York started to advance through

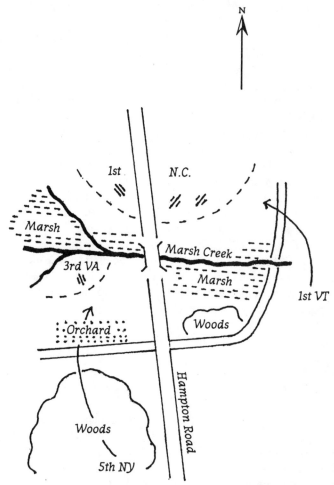

BATTLE AT BIG BETHEL
JUNE 10, 1861

the woods. The thick growth, however, quickly broke up their line, and when the Rebel guns responded to the Federal barrage, sending shells whizzing overhead, the Zouaves fell to the ground, still within the confines of the glen.[23]

Ignoring the inaccurate fire by the Rebels from the fort across the field, Colonel Duryee and his staff (including Kilpatrick) stepped out from under the trees to get a better view of the enemy position. Spotting the Union officers, the Rebel gunners sent a gust of grapeshot toward the assembly, and one of the pellets sliced into Judson's left buttock. "Are we going to stay here and be shot down, and do nothing?" he groaned as he clutched his bleeding posterior.[24]

Duryee's reply was an order to fall back into the woods, but Lieutenant Jacob Duryee, his son, refused to retire. "Who will follow me?" he cried, "I will charge the batteries!"[25] A group of 250 men joined him as he dashed out into the open into a peach orchard short of the creek. Judson limped forward, too, but his wounded rump hurt so bad that he soon slumped to the ground. As a comrade helped him hobble to the rear, he was joined by Lieutenant Duryee and his chargers, who had found the enemy's fire too fierce to withstand.

On the right Colonel Washburn sent his regiment forward to flank the Confederate barricade. "The attack by my men was very spirited," he wrote, "[but] the enemy's fire appeared to be concentrated on us. . . . About twenty minutes [later, when] the enemy brought their artillery to bear on us . . . I ceased firing and withdrew my men . . . under the cover of the woods."[26] Seeing that he could not repel the Rebels from their strong position, General Pierce ordered a general retreat. The Fifth New York led the way, followed by the other regiments who had been deployed at the front. The First New York under Colonel William H. Allen and the Second New York led by Colonel Carr, who had been held back at New Market in reserve, hurried up to protect the Yankee rear, and they repelled a feeble pursuit by the enemy.[27] Kilpatrick rode home on a white mule.[28]

"Everything was utterly mismanaged," General Butler conceded in his memoirs.[29] The Union lost seventy-six men in the skirmish (twenty-one of whom fell under the fire of their own comrades), and Pierce was so vilified for his failure to drive the Rebels from their works that he was forced to give up his commission.[30]

Kilpatrick, however, was judged a hero by the newspapers. They falsely reported him being shot while "gallantly" leading a Federal charge, the first Union officer to be wounded in the war.[31] The editors failed to notice the comic significance of his being hit in the posterior while supposedly facing the enemy. His wound, "more painful and humiliating than serious—a bullet across the butt,"[32] caused Alice to scamper to his side to nurse Kilpatrick back to health. She brought him a gift, a battle flag that she had embroidered for her husband. The design had a circle round "two eagles engaged in combat, the one crushing the other in his talons." The motto, "Tuebor" (meaning "I will defend"), was written beneath the birds, and above were two streamers with their names, "Alice" and "Kilpatrick."[33] Judson would carry that flag throughout the rest of the war.

Alice became the darling of the camp, and when the Union decided to strengthen their position near Hampton with earthen breastworks, she dug the first shovelful of dirt.[34]

"Tuebor" Flag. Courtesy of the Library of Congress.

She also wrote down at Kilpatrick's dictation his report of the battle. "We found the enemy with about from three to five thousand men posted in a strong position," he asserted, a gross exaggeration of the Confederate force. "Captains Winslow, Bartlett, and myself charged with our commands in front. The enemy were forced out of the first battery, all the forces were rapidly advancing . . . everything promised a speedy victory, when we were ordered to fall back. Where this order came from I do not know."[35] His description of the skirmish was untrue, but the lies could have been even worse. Alice deleted claims that Judson offered about his own bravery, "less injustice be done to others."[36]

By recording blatant falsehoods about his performance in battle, Kilpatrick showed his raw greed for fame as a soldier. He then compounded his deception by sending a copy of this report to the *New York Times,* which published the entire narrative on 14 June 1861.[37] While Colonel Duryee must have been upset with his subordinate's audacity, he recognized the value that Judson's name now held, and when asked to return an officer to New York City to sign up additional recruits for the regiment, he sent Kilpatrick.[38]

The enlistments mounted rapidly, and Judson sent the new men down to Fortress Monroe as soon as they could be equipped. He also kept himself in the spotlight. On 18 July he took part in a ceremony where the ladies of New York City presented him with a new regimental flag. The event was covered by the newspapers, and Kilpatrick again saw his name in print.[39]

Just when Judson was about to rejoin his command, bringing the last of the recruits with him, he was told to hold for possible new orders. The men might be needed in Washington.

The reason why Kilpatrick was detained lay in the wooded and rolling ground along Bull Run, a narrow, meandering stream that flowed west of Washington, D.C. Early in the morning of 21 July a Federal army of thirty-five thousand men under Brigadier General Irwin McDowell attacked the Rebels entrenched behind Bull Run. The Union assault, a flanking maneuver against the Confederate left, succeeded at first, but General Pierre G. T. Beauregard's troops from the South made a determined stand on top of Henry Hill. Later that day, reinforcements led by General Joseph E. Johnston arrived via trains from the Shenandoah Valley. They joined in driving the Federals from the field, and the Yankees fled in disarray back to Washington.[40]

Kilpatrick's recruits were hurried to Washington to help protect the capital from possible Confederate attack. Judson, however, received orders to return to Fortress Monroe where Colonel Duryee was impatiently awaiting his resuming command of his infantry company. He did not go. Instead of obeying Duryee's call to duty, on 1 August Kilpatrick applied for sick leave so he could stay in New York City. His wound no longer bothered him; he was involved in a perfidious scheme to gain a promotion for himself.

While recruiting soldiers for Duryee's infantry in New York City, Judson found he was competing for volunteers with J. Mansfield Davies, who was signing up men for a cavalry regiment that he hoped to head. Davies offered Kilpatrick a deal: if Judson would send recruits to the cavalry instead of the infantry, Davies would put him second in command with the rank of lieutenant colonel. Kilpatrick quickly agreed.[41]

Thousands of men volunteered after the Union defeat at Bull Run, and when Kilpatrick saw the new cavalry regiment's ranks about full, he offered his resignation from the Fifth New York. "He has not been . . . with his command since the latter part of June," Duryee wrote coldly on 14 August, "and allowing an appointment to be made in his place will relieve us from what has been . . . an embarrassment."[42]

After serving Davies for six weeks without an official rank, Kilpatrick was finally commissioned lieutenant colonel of the Second New York Cavalry on 25 September 1861.[43]

Kilpatrick's first experience as a military officer in the field was promising. He displayed a knack for organization and an ability to lead. Especially noteworthy was his talent for gaining the confidence and devotion of the troops in his command. His enormous ego, however, presented a problem. Instead of accepting praise (or criticism) as was his due, Kilpatrick insisted on embellishing his accomplishments almost beyond belief. He seemed oblivious to the fact that such falsehoods diminished his laurels. And he was selfish, putting personal goals above those of the army. This would soon result in creating animosity from his peers.

3

Drills and Misdeeds

Recruits joining the Second New York, named "The Harris Light Cavalry" because New York Senator Ira Harris bought the men uniforms and equipment, were sent to Scarsdale, New York, for training.[1] Kilpatrick, however, went to New Jersey where he enlisted troops from his home area for the regiment. Two companies were enrolled. On 5 August 1861 after a swearing in ceremony at Newton, New Jersey, he put his new recruits on the train for Scarsdale.[2] They spent the following few weeks drilling under Kilpatrick's tutelage.

The Harris Light Cavalry soon received orders to report for duty in Washington, D.C., and Kilpatrick was put in charge of moving several companies (284 men/51 horses) to the Union capital. He met with the Northern Central Railroad, arranged for a special train, and on 7 September, the men and mounts boarded in New York City for the trip southwest.

Because Kilpatrick had insisted that there be no change of cars en route, the train was forced to follow a roundabout path. The locomotive chugged into the station at Harrisburg, Pennsylvania, about 6:00 A.M. on 8 September. Not expecting a detour and probably too arrogant to question the long route, Judson suspected Rebel sabotage, a plot to prevent his reaching the capital.[3] The engine and its cars sat motionless for hours, and by 11:00 A.M., Kilpatrick was convinced he was the target of a Southern conspiracy. He decided to take steps to thwart the Confederates. He sent five men, led by Lieutenant Samuel Milligan, to seize control of the locomotive and start the train south.

When the soldiers attempted to take over the train, the engineer called for help. James C. Clarke, the yard superintendent, rushed to the scene where he learned that the Union troops had been sent by Kilpatrick. He went to see Judson to ask why he had issued instructions to commandeer the engine, but instead of an explanation, Clarke was threatened with his own arrest if he tried to stop the seizure of the train. He managed to calm Kilpatrick by convincing him that no Rebel plot was underway and that the engineer should be allowed to stay in place; by 11:30 A.M. the locomotive had started south toward Washington.[4]

Although Kilpatrick had been mollified, the engineer he had threatened seethed with indignation, and as he approached Cockeysville (a hamlet twenty-one miles north of Baltimore), the engineer suddenly decided to get even. He turned on the steam, and as the accelerating train hit a sharp curve, three cars were spun off the track. Kilpatrick was not hurt, but seven of his men died in the accident. Jumping to the ground, Judson ran toward the engine, which had ground to a halt. He arrived too late to prevent the crazed engineer from uncoupling the locomotive and then climbing back into his cab. As he sped away the engineer shouted defiantly to Kilpatrick, "There are your goddamn cars in a pile!"[5]

The engineer was arrested when he arrived in Baltimore. Although the engineer was responsible for the accident, the *New York Times* also blamed Kilpatrick for his role in the fiasco. "Flushed with a little brief authority," it stated , "[he] doubtless went beyond the limits of his duty to overcome the delay." The *Times* continued, "The detention excited [his] impatience and prompted the misguided and unwarrantable attempt to take possession of the locomotives."[6] The incident revealed an ominous character defect in Kilpatrick: he would act both blindly and violently under pressure.

When Judson finally reached Washington, he took his men to Ball's Crossroads, east of the capital, where the regiment was in training. The Second New York Cavalry was undergoing intensive drills, part of a comprehensive organizational program conceived by the new commander of the Union Army of the Potomac, Major General George B. McClellan.

After graduating second in his 1846 class at West Point, McClellan was assigned to the staff of General Scott, who was leading the U.S. Army in the war against Mexico. He did well, earning two brevet promotions. McClellan remained in the army until 1857 when he resigned to join the Illinois Central Railroad. He was a division president for the Ohio and Mississippi line when the Civil War erupted. He immediately rejoined the service, assuming command of the Ohio volunteers, and he led the force that drove the Confederates out of western Virginia in July 1861.[7]

President Lincoln had summoned McClellan to the capital the day after the Rebels had routed the Yankees at Bull Run.[8] His initial task had been to take charge of the panicked men who had fled from the battlefield, but when Congress authorized recruitment of thousands of additional troops to coerce the Southern states back into the Union, McClellan took these volunteers under his wing, too. He was a brilliant administrator, and with his guidance, the men improved rapidly, soon becoming proud and disciplined soldiers.[9]

Most of the new troops were trained as infantry because General Scott, commander in chief of the army, was opposed to recruiting cavalry. "The war will be short and over long before . . . volunteer cavalry could be [ready] to take the field," he claimed.[10] Those who visited the camps where the troopers

General George B. McClellan. Courtesy of the Library of Congress.

trained could readily understand Scott's aversion to cavalry. "Everybody from the . . . officers on down had first to learn how to get on a horse," Bruce Catton wrote, "and then how to stay on once the brute began to move."[11]

Kilpatrick's regiment had few problems with horses, however, because most were without mounts. The troopers, who also lacked uniforms, were forced to practice their formations on foot until 1 October, when their animals finally arrived.[12]

Colonel Davies had almost no cavalry experience, and so he put Kilpatrick in charge of training the men. Having been reared on a working farm, Judson was a competent rider. "[He has] the appearance of an eagle pouncing on a prey," declared Willard Glazier, a private in the Harris regiment. "We have seen him leap over barriers where only few could follow him."[13] Other men were less impressed by Kilpatrick's riding ability. "He looked more like a monkey than a man on horseback," wrote Major James A. Connolly.[14] Colonel Theodore Lyman contended, "It was hard to look at him without laughing."[15]

Although Kilpatrick's riding skill may have been debatable, he was adept at training men. General William W. Averell said that Judson was "[One of] the most efficient . . . colonels . . . who assisted with energy and zeal in the . . . creation [of the Yankee cavalry]."[16] He held practices first on the open fields east of the capital, then moved his camp to Arlington, Virginia, to the grounds of Robert E. Lee's confiscated estate.

The regiment was attached to the infantry division under General McDowell.[17] A career army officer, a graduate of West Point in 1838, McDowell taught tactics at the academy, served in the artillery during the Mexican War, and then was involved with the adjutant general's office up to the beginning of the Civil War. He had led the Union force routed at Bull Run and was demoted to his current command because of that defeat.[18]

McClellan had concluded that the Union horsemen were incapable of independent command because during one of his first reviews, he had had to recall the First New York Cavalry from the parade field due to "so much confusion and the officers so wanting in ability to quietly restore order."[19] The cavalry's role was further diluted by the infantry division leaders, who generally divided their horse regiments into squadrons so that each brigade commander would have his own troop.[20] So instead of mounting fierce charges against enemy lines, the cavalry's duties were limited to delivering messages, picketing the perimeters of the infantry camps, and attending to their brigade commander at parades.[21]

Kilpatrick must have been disgusted at performing these menial tasks. And though he worked diligently at training his men, he would not live with them, bunking instead at a hotel in downtown Washington. Other officers resented his affluent lifestyle. "He gives orders like a Satrap," a former class mate groaned, "and while I defend him . . . from attacks by those who do not know him, I do not agree with his conduct."[22]

Rooming in a fancy hotel cost a lot of money, more than Kilpatrick could afford on his military pay, and he foolishly sought means to augment his income. He soon found a willing source, the regimental sutler.

When they saw a chance to make a fortune from the Civil War, Hiram C. Hull and William D. McPherson formed a partnership as sutlers for the Harris Light Cavalry. Hull would be the on-site manager; McPherson supplied the money. Their initial venture was a contract, negotiated with Kilpatrick, to sell the regiment one hundred horses. "I paid Lieut. Colonel Kilpatrick twenty dollars in gold," Hull admitted later, "as a present . . . for his influence in procuring . . . the contract."[23] This illicit pact, no doubt demanded by Kilpatrick, was only the first of many that would eventually send him to jail.

On 20 November1861 McClellan conducted a grand review of his army for Lincoln, members of his cabinet, and assorted dignitaries. Kilpatrick's regiment, judged the best trained in all the cavalry, was given the prime role—to mount a mock charge at the end of the program. After seventy thousand infantry had paraded past the podium, Kilpatrick's cavalry made a spirited dash down the field.[24] Everyone was most impressed with the zealous demonstration, and Kilpatrick was placed on the Board for Examination of Officers of Volunteer Cavalry as a reward for his efforts.[25] The members met to weed out officers they judged incapable of their rank. In addition to winning this honor, he also was named provost marshall, then the inspector general for McDowell's Division.[26]

Kilpatrick was fortunate that these honors were granted before he conducted his second review, which turned out to be a disaster. The Harris Light received their colors early in December, and a large number of dignitaries, including Lincoln, were present for the occasion. The banner was presented and accepted, appropriate speeches were given, and then the regiment started to perform. Their maneuvers were brought to an untimely end when some infantry in the rear fired a volley of shots. The salvo "instantly broke up the squadrons," according to William Howard Russell, an English reporter, "and sent them kicking, plunging, and falling [all] over the field, to the great amusement of the crowd."[27]

Greatly embarrassed by the fiasco, Kilpatrick must have been driven to seek another field for his future, and he made his move 1 January 1862 when he accepted an appointment to McClellan's personal staff.[28] This post, however, was only a subterfuge. Kilpatrick would not serve under McClellan; he would function as the chief of artillery for Senator James H. Lane, who was seeking a military commission as the head of a force that would invade the South out of Kansas.[29]

Lane, described as being "gaunt, tattered, uncombed and unshorn,"[30] was a lawyer who had led the Fifth Indiana during the Mexican War. After serving a term in Congress, he moved to Kansas where he became a violent antislavery advocate, one of John Brown's associates. He was elected to the Senate in 1861 when Kansas was admitted to the Union, and he became one of Lincoln's close friends.[31] He had used this relationship to advance an absurd scheme to take thirty thousand men (fifteen thousand cavalry, ten thousand infantry, four thousand Indians, plus other specialists) south from Kansas toward New Orleans. He planned to drive the Confederates out of Missouri and Arkansas, then veer into Texas.[32]

Senator Lane left the capital for Kansas on 19 January 1862. His accompanying staff included Kilpatrick.[33] When he reached Fort Leavenworth, however, Lane learned that General David Hunter, the local department commander, planned to lead the expedition. He appealed to Lincoln to put him in charge, but the president backed Hunter's contention that the command was rightfully his.[34] When Lane refused to serve as a subordinate, the campaign was abandoned. Kilpatrick had no choice but to return home and rejoin his regiment.

When he got back to Washington, Kilpatrick learned that the dull days of winter had come to an end. Action had begun on both the eastern and western fronts. In Kentucky General Ulysses S. Grant had assaulted the Rebel battlements blocking passage down the Tennessee and Cumberland Rivers. Both Forts Henry and Donelson surrendered unconditionally to Grant. The waterways into the heart of Tennessee lay open to the Union.[35]

In the east the Southern forces had also retreated, but in this case, they had withdrawn on their own. Johnston, who commanded the troops below Washington, saw that his line was vulnerable so far forward. On 9 March 1862, he retired to a stronger position along the Rappahannock River in Virginia.[36]

The Rebel retreat allowed McClellan to advance into Virginia, and Kilpatrick was among the first to camp on Southern soil. He quickly took advantage of the situation to enhance his pocketbook. Under the laws of war, private property that could be useful to the enemy was called "contraband," and it could be seized without renumeration. This included farmers' horses. As Kilpatrick roamed the fields south of Washington, the Virginia plantations along the Potomac River, he gathered as many as he could find. He branded most with a "U.S.," signifying army property, but kept the choicest mounts for himself, which he sent to stables in Washington. The sutlers, acting as Kilpatrick's agent, sold them for him. A large gray mare went for $100; a dapple gray brought $100; and a dark chestnut mare was priced at $50.[37]

While Kilpatrick was busy filling his wallet, McClellan was resisting what he considered premature pleas to march his army on Richmond. Lincoln, the Congress, and the newspapers all harangued him to move. Lincoln, in fact, issued an order to McClellan to seize and occupy Manassas Junction "on or before February 22, 1862."[38] His intent was to start the army on an overland campaign against the Rebel capital. McClellan, however, wanted to avoid a series of bloody battles to reach the gates of Richmond. He hoped instead to put his troops on boats, sail to Fortress Monroe, and then march up the peninsula between the James and York Rivers to capture the Rebels' principal city via a siege.[39]

Early in March as McClellan stalled Lincoln, his plans were almost upset by a Southern innovation. The Confederates had seized the Northern warship *Merrimack,* covered it with iron plates, renamed it *Virginia,* and attacked the Union's fleet in Hampton Roads. The Yankee's wooden ships proved no match for the armored Southern vessel, and it seemed that nothing could stop the

Virginia from steaming up the Potomac to shell Washington. Moving an army south by water past this behemoth would be impossible.

On 9 March, however, the same day that Johnston withdrew from Manassas, the Yankees unveiled an ironclad of their own. The *Monitor,* a tiny ship armed with twin guns mounted on a revolving turret, faced the *Virginia,* and in a thrilling two-hour duel, the adversaries fired shell after shell at the other. The missiles only bounced off the iron plates attached to the sides of each ship, and the battle ended in a stalemate. But with the *Monitor* now available as a buffer, the sea route to Richmond opened for McClellan.[40]

The Federal army started embarking for the Peninsula on 17 March. Kilpatrick, however, was destined to march south through Virginia. In agreeing to McClellan's tactic to take Richmond via the sea, Lincoln insisted on maintaining a force on land between Washington and the Rebel army emplaced along the Rappahannock River. McDowell, promoted to corps command and put in charge of thirty thousand soldiers (including the regiment led by Kilpatrick), was detached from McClellan for this role.[41]

Kilpatrick was placed in command of the regiment due to Colonel Davies being ill, and he led his men south from their camp on 4 April 1861.[42] Clearing the path for the infantry, they rode toward Fredericksburg, Virginia, a point that would allow McDowell either to defend Washington if Johnston chose to come north or to continue south to unite with McClellan in his siege of the Confederate capital. Kilpatrick moved past Fairfax Court House, Centreville, and into Bristoe Station on schedule without encountering Rebel resistance.

Going to war did not impede Kilpatrick in his financial projects. Prior to leaving Washington, the sutler approached him to ask for help in collecting the monies owed by the men for past purchases. Kilpatrick ordered his troops to pay off their IOUs, and he received $20.00 from McPherson as a kickback for bringing in the cash.[43] At Bristoe Station, he saw another means to augment his income. "Hull and myself met Lieut. Colonel Kilpatrick," McPherson related. "He remarked that he was Provost Marshal . . . there was a large quantity of tobacco in the neighborhood which could be 'bought,' and that he . . . would render us all the assistance in his power, either officially or otherwise [to acquire that tobacco]." For his share in the plan, Kilpatrick expected to "receive one-third of all monies accrued from the sale of the tobacco."[44] Forty bales were seized as "contraband," and Kilpatrick was granted a $100.00 credit to his unpaid account with the sutler. This outstanding balance included money loaned Kilpatrick by Hull and McPherson, yet another impropriety.[45]

Continuing his push south, Kilpatrick finally met Rebel pickets at Catlett's Station. He easily routed them and rode on toward Falmouth, a few miles above Fredericksburg. As he approached Spotted Tavern on the afternoon of 17 April, the Confederate cavalry under Colonel William H. F. "Rooney" Lee loomed to his front. Kilpatrick assaulted the Rebel troopers, first with just a company, then a full battalion, and finally with his entire regiment. The out-numbered Southerners withdrew to the south. Kilpatrick claimed that the enemy resistance was feeble and "in a moment, he was fleeing in all directions."[46]

The incident fired Kilpatrick's ardor for battle, and he could not wait to lock horns with Lee's cavalry again. Acting with typical haste, when he returned to camp, Kilpatrick met with Colonel George D. Bayard, head of the First Pennsylvania Cavalry, to plan a midnight assault on the Rebels.

During this time Kilpatrick continued to display strong ability as a leader. He was zealous in training his troopers, and superiors recognized both his skills and the considerable energy that he brought to his assigned duties.

Kilpatrick's character flaws, however, were also evident. He reacted rashly under pressure, striking out blindly against adversaries (e.g., the train engineer) without thinking of the possible consequences. He was not a man that one would want to follow into battle.

Another shortcoming was his arrogance, his feeling that he was not subject to the same rules as others, that he could steal, take bribes, or use his office for personal advantage with impunity.

And as noted earlier, Kilpatrick had no loyalty for his command. He was quick to abandon his responsibilities if he saw a brighter future looming elsewhere.

4

McClellan

Kilpatrick was not the only Union commander seeking to confront the Rebels in April 1862. After Grant's victories at Fort Henry and Fort Donelson had opened water passage into central and western Tennessee, General Don Carlos Buell's Army of the Ohio had moved up the Cumberland River to seize Nashville. Grant had taken his Army of the Tennessee up the Tennessee River to Pittsburg Landing, just above the Mississippi border, where he planned on assaulting the Confederate defenders of the area, the Southern Army of the Mississippi led by General Albert Sidney Johnston. He would wait, however, until Buell had come cross-country to join him before launching his attack.

Knowing that the imminent combination of the two Union forces would give the Yankees overwhelming numbers to oppose him, Johnston decided to attack Grant before reinforcements arrived, and on 3 April he headed his troops north out of Corinth, Mississippi. Their assault on 6 April surprised Grant, and in a bloody fray, he was driven back to the banks of the Tennessee River. Johnston was mortally wounded during the battle, however, leaving the Rebels disorganized and confused by their success. Buell's advance element reached the scene that evening, and in the morning, they joined with Grant's troops in a massive counterattack that sent the Confederates reeling in retreat to Corinth. The two-day affair resulted in over thirteen thousand casualties for the Yankees and more than ten thousand for the South, an appalling number that signaled the horrors of war to come.[1]

Further south a Union force consisting of the Army of the Gulf under General Benjamin Butler, who had relinquished his post at Fortress Monroe, and the navy's Western Gulf Blockading Squadron under Admiral David G. Farragut were starting their campaign to capture New Orleans. The South considered the metropolis impregnable because Fort Jackson and Fort St. Philip blocked passage up the Mississippi River. The night of 24 April, however, under a fierce bombardment, Farragut sailed safely past the bastions and anchored off the city's docks. The small Rebel army under General Mansfield Lovell charged with defending New Orleans fled, and Farragut walked ashore the next morning to take control of the port.[2]

Other Federal successes during April included the fall of Fort Pulaski outside of Savannah, Georgia; the defeat of a Confederate advance at Pea Ridge,
Arkansas; and the capture of Island Number 10 on the Mississippi River just
above Memphis, Tennessee. The Yankees were winning every confrontation,
and with the end of the war in view, Kilpatrick had to move quickly if he
wanted to share in the glory.

The objective for Kilpatrick's and Bayard's early morning assault on 18
April was to capture the bridge over the Rappahannock at Falmouth. Their
force was composed of four companies from the First Pennsylvania Cavalry
and seven companies from the Harris Light. They followed a circular path to
the front, led by a local Union sympathizer who had come into camp to warn
the Federals that the Rebels lay in ambush up ahead. He took the troopers
along a country lane around the trap, but when the Yankees reentered the
Warrenton Road at Greeve's Chapel, they discovered the enemy positioned for

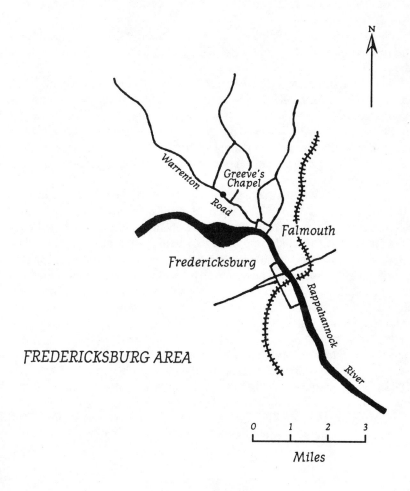

battle.[3] The Ninth Virginia Infantry lay behind a barricade blocking the road where it peaked on a knoll; Rooney Lee's cavalry was posted in the brush on both sides of the pike.[4]

Bayard formed his four companies and charged, but when the Rebels fired a deadly volley, his troopers broke and ran for the rear. Bayard bitterly wrote that two companies were so frightened, they "fled back to camp without having either horse or man injured."[5]

Kilpatrick had led several of his companies left, down a wooded path on the Rebels' flank. He was looking to enter the fray after Bayard had smashed through the Confederate's line. But when Bayard's assault was thrown back, Kilpatrick saw that he lay open to an enemy counterattack. He reacted by bluffing that he had a superior force on hand. "Bring up your artillery in the centre!" he cried loud enough so that the Rebels could hear him. "Infantry on the left!"[6]

"But, Colonel," a naïve Federal captain responded. "We haven't got any inf——."

"Silence in the ranks!" Kilpatrick interrupted angrily, afraid that the Rebels would discover his bluff. "Artillery in the centre," he yelled again. "Infantry on the left."

The Rebels may have been fooled, because they stayed in place, awaiting the Yankees' next move. Kilpatrick remained in the bushes, but Bayard decided to attempt another charge. He took four of Kilpatrick's companies and raced up the hill to within twenty-five yards of the barricades, but a second volley by the Confederates forced him to retreat again. "As I knew nothing of the enemy's force," Bayard later reported, "I decided to withdraw my command."[7]

Kilpatrick's only role in the skirmish was to bring up the rear as Bayard led the way back to camp. He depicted to friends, however, that he had attacked the barricade and broken through the enemy's line, but that the Pennsylvania troopers had failed to follow him, forcing Kilpatrick to ram his way back through the Rebels to rejoin Bayard.[8] This lie was not listed by Kilpatrick in an official report of the skirmish, which he obstinately refused to submit. "I have called upon him for it frequently," General Christopher C. Auger complained to headquarters, "but as he is not under my command, I have no means of enforcing the requests."[9]

Given Kilpatrick's thirst for glory plus his practical political sense, it is strange that he would so deliberately antagonize a superior officer, particularly one who wielded considerable influence. Auger had graduated from West Point in 1843, fought creditably during the Mexican War, and then served on the frontier prior to the start of the Civil War.[10] He had a host of friends in the army, many important to Kilpatrick's future (nine of his classmates would become Union generals), and gaining his displeasure could only hinder the young colonel's chances for success. Kilpatrick seemed not to care, however. He often felt contempt for his superiors, and he would find reason to snub other prominent men in the future.

As morning broke the leading columns of McDowell's infantry came up, and Kilpatrick led them into Falmouth. They found that the Rebels had retired across the river. To prevent Union pursuit, they had burned the bridges spanning the water. McDowell established a camp along the stream across from Fredericksburg, a position that the Federals would hold throughout the rest of the war.

While McDowell moved overland toward Richmond, keeping his force between the Confederates and Washington to protect the Yankee capital, McClellan's army had sailed to Fortress Monroe, landed, and started up the Peninsula. He was moving slowly, maneuvering instead of fighting, hoping for a bloodless campaign in capturing the city.[11]

At first the Federal plan worked well. McClellan laid siege to Yorktown, and after a month's wait, entered the old village on 4 May. "[My] success," he reported to Lincoln, "is brilliant."[12] The next day his men attacked the Rebels at Williamsburg and drove them from their line, which fronted the colonial capital. McClellan continued his push west, and by17 May was so close to Richmond that when he pleaded for reinforcements, Lincoln, seeing the Confederates consumed by the defense of their capital and unlikely to attack Washington, agreed to release McDowell from Falmouth, to come south to join with McClellan in the final assault on Richmond.[13]

Kilpatrick and his cavalry prepared to ride south, but before they could start, their orders were canceled. Washington was endangered! Southern general Thomas "Stonewall" Jackson had attacked the Union force under General Nathaniel Banks in the Shenandoah Valley. After routing the Federals at Front Royal on 23 May, Jackson moved on Winchester. He shattered Banks's defensive lines there, driving the Yankees across the Potomac River, clearing the path for an attack on the nation's capital.[14]

Lincoln ordered McDowell to the Valley to confront the victorious Jackson. "A question of legs," he said. "Put in all the speed you can."[15] His urgency was derived from the opportunity to catch Jackson in a pincer: McDowell from the east; General John C. Frémont coming from the west. While troops from McDowell rushed to the Valley (a division led by General James Shields), Kilpatrick, still commanding the regiment during Colonel Davies's absence, rode for Thoroughfare Gap in the Bull Run Mountains to block any attempt by Jackson to escape the snare.[16]

Jackson did run, but he scurried south, not east where Kilpatrick lay awaiting. When it became obvious that he was of no use in the mountains, Kilpatrick was recalled back to Falmouth, then sent toward Richmond to obtain information on Confederate troop movements. He returned on 28 May to report that the Rebels had dispatched fifteen thousand men to the Valley to reinforce Jackson. "They had no intention of abandoning their position in our front till last Saturday," he related, "when sudden orders were received from Richmond to march at once."[17] Kilpatrick was not aware that he had been misled, that loyal Southerners, posing as Federal sympathizers, had sought him out to give him false information. No troops had gone to the Valley. Their intent was to convince the Union that Jackson posed a threat to Washington and that McDowell was needed to protect the capital and could not risk taking his corps to Richmond to join McClellan. They succeeded because Kilpatrick fell for the ruse.

As McDowell looked west, the Rebels suddenly assaulted McClellan's line outside of Richmond. Johnston launched his attack on 31 May, but while the Yankees held their ground, not only repelling the ferocious Confederate charge but also severely wounding Johnston during the Battle of Seven Pines, their victory resulted in the elevation of General Robert E. Lee to the head of the Southern army defending the capital.[18] This change in command would prove disastrous to the Yankee cause through the coming years.

Kilpatrick could only watch from Falmouth as events unfolded rapidly. Jackson escaped the Federals' pincer in the Valley by retreating south on the macadamized pike. When he reached Harrisonburg, Jackson swung east, off the main road, and offered battle. He first defeated Frémont at Cross Keys on 8 June, then routed Shields near Port Republic the next day.[19] Jackson then brought his forces to Richmond where he and Lee attacked McClellan. In the Seven Days battles, 25 June through 1 July, they forced McClellan to withdraw his force to Harrison's Landing along the James River. Richmond had withstood the Union challenge.[20]

Although Kilpatrick was no doubt disappointed at having had essentially no role in this first attempt to capture the Southern capital, McClellan's failure created an opportunity for expanded cavalry operations. Kilpatrick would soon take advantage of this opening.

During this frustrating campaign, Kilpatrick continued to offer a mixed view of his potential as a military leader. Although he did not fight during the skirmish near Falmouth, Kilpatrick displayed a clever presence of mind by deceiving the Rebels as to the strength of his position. He possibly saved his command.

Not content, however, with just receiving plaudits for his quick thinking, Kilpatrick boasted that his force fought the battle. This disparaged his compatriot, Colonel Bayard. When General Auger ordered Kilpatrick to write up his false claims, Judson recognized that this was a trap, meant to expose his lies.

He refused to file the report, but this did not prevent his superiors from learning that his words could not be trusted.

In his only role in the Seven Days Battles, Kilpatrick was asked to scout the enemy's movements. He conducted only a timid probe, and when Rebel sympathizers told him Lee was shipping troops to the Valley, Kilpatrick submitted this inaccurate report. This resulted in McDowell's being pinned at Fredericksburg, which contributed to the Union defeat.

5

John Pope

Disappointed in McClellan's performance, Lincoln tried a different strategy for capturing Richmond, a land campaign from the north. General John Pope was called from the west to lead the invading force, the new Army of Virginia, formed from the commands of Banks, Frémont, and McDowell.[1]

Pope, who was born in Kentucky, was raised in Illinois, where his father was a federal judge. He went to West Point and graduated in 1842. After four years of survey duty, he fought in the Mexican War, winning two brevet promotions for bravery. He returned to the topographical engineers, where he was serving when the Civil War erupted. Pope had won two victories (New Madrid and Island Number Ten) in the Union's ongoing efforts to open the Mississippi River and was considered a most promising general.[2]

Upon taking command, Pope issued a bombastic statement, intended to lift the confidence of his men. "I have come to you from the West," he said, "where we have always seen the backs of our enemies."[3] The Rebels scoffed at this arrogant assertion, and the veterans of the Army of the Potomac scowled over Pope's impugning their fighting ability. Both soon learned that Pope was a man of action as well as words. He quickly organized his army, then marched south, crossing the Rappahannock River to assume a threatening position. Banks's and Franz Sigels's corps, plus James B. Rickett's Division of McDowell's Corps, set up camp near Culpeper Court House; Rufus King's Division remained to the east by Fredericksburg.[4]

Kilpatrick's regiment was assigned to King's Division. An 1833 graduate of West Point, King resigned his commission after only three years of army service to start a career as a civil engineer. He then became a newspaper editor, and in 1861 he had just been made a delegate to the Vatican when the Civil War started. He refused the post to take command of a brigade in McDowell's Division. When McDowell was promoted to lead a corps, King (who had yet to see action) was raised to division level.[5]

Pope's first objective was to sever the communications between Richmond and the Shenandoah Valley, and he ordered a two-point assault on the Virginia Central Railroad, the key link between these areas. General John P. Hatch,

General John Pope. Courtesy of the Library of Congress.

who headed the only cavalry brigade in the army, would lead a force to destroy the tracks near Gordonsville; Kilpatrick would take his men south to tear up the rails at Beaver Dam Station.[6]

Kilpatrick headed south out of Falmouth about 7:00 P.M. on 19 July. "[After] a forced march through the night," a trooper recalled, "we descended upon Beaver Dam depot on the Virginia Central, like so many ravenous wolves."[7] The railroad station was undefended. A solitary Rebel captain, John S. Mosby (later to earn fame as a partisan), was standing on the platform, waiting for the train to Gordonsville, where he hoped to join the recently arrived Stonewall

Jackson.[8] After capturing Mosby, Kilpatrick began ripping up the tracks and tearing down the telegraph lines several miles to either side of the station. He then burned the depot. The result was a tremendous explosion, as forty thousand rounds of ammunition and one hundred barrels of flour had been stored in the wood building.[9]

With his prisoner in hand, Kilpatrick headed for home. He pushed the troopers hard, not halting to rest despite the fact that most had been up for thirty-six hours. Those who slept in the saddle, trusting their mount to keep going, had some strange experiences. One awoke "to find himself alone with his horse, who was grazing [in an] unknown field."[10] A second rider with a fast-moving horse was borne through the ranks "until the poor fellow [awoke to find] himself . . . passing . . . the colonel and his staff at the head of the column."[11]

Kilpatrick arrived at Falmouth just before midnight on 20 July, having ridden eighty miles in thirty hours. Pope himself lauded the effort. "The affair was most successful, and reflects high credit upon the commanding officer and his troops," he stated to Washington.[12] Unfortunately for Kilpatrick, however, Pope did not know that leader's name. "As soon as full particulars are received [on the raid]," he reported to Edwin M. Stanton, secretary of war, "I will [send] the name of the commanding officer."

Pope did remember Hatch, the cavalry chief he had sent to rip up the Virginia Central track at Gordonsville. Hatch had assembled a strike force combining infantry and cavalry, including a complete baggage train, and headed south on 18 July. When Pope heard about this odd blend of troops for a raid, he exclaimed, "I never dreamed of such a thing. . . . Send forward at once and stop [him]!"[13]

No one had to stop Hatch. His movement, slowed by the muddy roads, ground to a halt before he reached Orange Court House, and on 21 July he returned on his own without having accomplished his objective. His dismal performance made Kilpatrick's star shine all the brighter.

At Falmouth, Mosby, the prisoner of war, found himself the center of the Yankees' attention. "Colonel [Kilpatrick] . . . treated me with the greatest courtesy," he stated in his memoirs. "General King . . . ordered my arms . . . restored. . . . Colonel Davis, who captured me, offered to lend me . . . money. I thanked him, but declined."[14] After ten days, Mosby was exchanged for Lieutenant C. A. Bayard, Fifth Wisconsin.

The Harris Light was exhausted by their foray to Beaver Dam, but Kilpatrick was so pumped by the praise of Pope and King, he immediately set out on another raid on the Virginia Central Railroad. His command, plus troopers from the Third Indiana and Fourteenth Brooklyn, rode out of Falmouth at 4:00 P.M. on 22 July, headed for Hanover Junction. The horsemen crossed the Massaponax River at 8:00 P.M. where they lay at rest until 2:00 A.M. "I commenced a

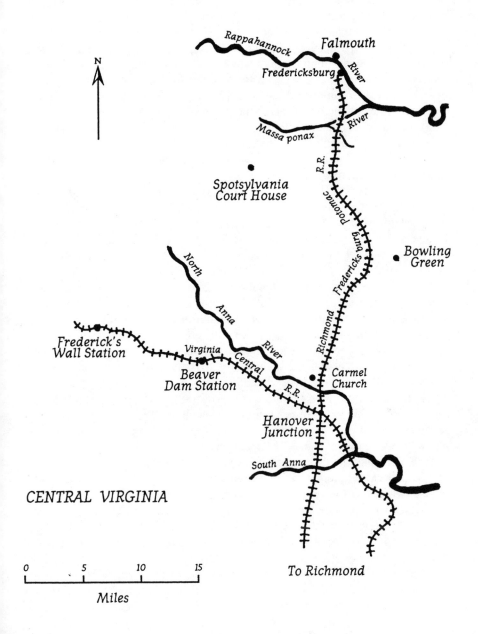

N

Rappahannock   Falmouth

Fredericksburg   River

Massaponax   River

R.R.

Spotsylvania
Court House

Potomac

Bowling
Green

North

Fredericks

Anna

Richmond

Frederick's
Wall Station

Virginia   River

Central

Beaver
Dam Station   R.R.

Carmel
Church

Hanover
Junction

South Anna

CENTRAL VIRGINIA

0   5   10   15

Miles

To Richmond

rapid march for [a] rebel camp, supposed to be at Carmel Church," Kilpatrick reported.[15] When he reached the North Anna River at daybreak, Kilpatrick encountered a woman who told him that the Rebels had withdrawn below the river, but that every morning about 7:00 A.M., they sent scouts north to man the church. He decided to ambush the enemy patrol. A company was placed out in the open; the Confederates came up and prepared to attack the Yankees, whereupon Kilpatrick led a mounted charge that scattered their numbers. "The Rebels were whipped, pursued, and driven into the river," Kilpatrick declared.[16]

Lieutenant William A. Kimball followed the fleeing enemy soldiers, and he soon returned to report that their camp was along the road just below the stream, atop a knoll that sloped gently toward the water. The ground was level to the rear, perfect for a cavalry charge.[17]

Kilpatrick was determined to attack the Rebels, and he prepared his force: the Harris Light was deployed along the sides of the road; the Third Indiana under Major George H. Chapman held the center. The latter would mount a charge on the road, while the Harris Light would assault the enemy's flanks. The troopers moved forward at a gallop. When the Rebels saw the Yankees coming, they fled southward. Kilpatrick chased them for five miles to within sight of Hanover Junction. He then returned to destroy their camp, burning tents, stores, and six railroad cars filled with grain.[18]

Just as they had finished their devastation of the Confederate camp, Kilpatrick's band was attacked by General Jeb Stuart's troopers. Kilpatrick claimed that he repelled the Southern charge, "forcing them back in great confusion," but since Stuart had assaulted with two thousand men, Kilpatrick more likely ran to the river, crossed, and fled to Falmouth.[19]

Kilpatrick again received the plaudits of both King and Pope, neither of whom doubted his report of performing "a march of 70 miles and the encounter and defeat of two bodies of Confederate cavalry . . . in twenty-nine hours and without the loss of a man."[20] Pope, however, again did not know the name of "the commanding officer . . . who [has] distinguished [himself."[21]

Kilpatrick's exploits were once more enhanced by a sad performance by Hatch. He headed toward Gordonsville on 23 July, carrying "two days' cooked rations, and nothing else" per strict instructions from Pope.[22] He returned after only thirty hours of travel, never coming close to his objective. "The utter breaking up of my horses, the state of the roads, and the storms" were reasons Hatch listed for failing to execute his mission.[23]

Perhaps influenced by Kilpatrick's success, Pope moved on 2 August to give his cavalry more freedom of operation. The scattered regiments were organized into three brigades, each allocated to an infantry corps commander. Colonel John Beardsley headed five regiments assigned to the First Corps; Brigadier General John Buford (replacing Hatch) led four regiments serving the Second Corps; and Bayard took charge of five regiments allotted to the

Third Corps.[24] Their orders would be issued by only the corps leaders or Pope himself.[25] Kilpatrick reported to Bayard.

Having joined with Bayard in the attack at Falmouth on 18 April, Kilpatrick was already familiar with his leader. After graduating from West Point in 1856, Bayard had served on the western frontier prior to the start of Civil War. He led the First Pennsylvania in the Shenandoah Valley against Jackson, then brought his regiment east to join Pope's army. He was a brigadier general, his promotion dated 28 April, serving in an administrative post as chief of cavalry to the Third Army Corps.[26]

On 4 August Kilpatrick headed out on his third raid in two weeks. This time, however, he was a part of an armed reconnaissance, led by Colonel Lysander Cutler of the Fifth Wisconsin Infantry. The expedition left Falmouth about 2:00 A.M. and advanced throughout the night, arriving at Spotsylvania Court House the following morning. After resting most of the day, they started marching again about 5:00 P.M. and reached Mount Pleasant at sunset, where they bivouacked that night.[27]

Warned of enemy troops in the area, Cutler decided his best chance to avoid an unwanted confrontation lay in moving in the dark, so at 2:00 A.M. on 6 August, he took his men south. Cutler hoped to arrive at his objective, Frederick's Hall Station, by morning, but he took a wrong turn and lost his way. Daylight revealed his force farther from the railroad than when they had started out. As the sun climbed in the sky, the heat became intense, and Cutler saw that he had to rest his men for awhile. They began marching again about 1:30 P.M. and finally reached Frederick's Hall at 4:30 P.M.

Kilpatrick's troopers immediately spread out and began to tear down telegraph lines and rip up track. As they performed their destruction, the infantry was busy in the town, wrecking the railroad turntable, burning a wooden warehouse that contained one thousand bushels of corn and several tierces of whiskey, and torching the other buildings owned by the railroad. Everyone had completed their work by 6:00 P.M.[28]

Marching north through gathering darkness, Cutler came to a halt at Waller's Tavern. He had expected to camp there for the night, but upon receiving word that the Rebels were approaching his position, Cutler woke his force at 4:30 A.M. and headed for Spotsylvania Court House. When they reached their destination, "the men laid down from pure exhaustion," Cutler stated. "The only murmurs I heard," he added, "were those of disappointment at not meeting the enemy."[29]

Although Cutler and Kilpatrick could take pride in having successfully achieved their mission, they had pushed the men too hard. Kilpatrick's troops in particular were exhausted. "Many were confined to their tents on their return to camp," Henry Meyer recollected, "[suffering] saddle boils and lameness."[30] For the first time, Kilpatrick heard men muttering his name as "Kill-Cavalry."

The South under Robert E. Lee could have contested the cavalry raids by Kilpatrick, but Lee had other, more crucial concerns than just protecting railroad depots. His Army of Northern Virginia, totaling seventy-five thousand men, was faced with holding McClellan's force of one hundred thousand at bay at Harrison Landing on the James River while at the same time he confronted Pope and his forty-five thousand troops along the Rapidan River. Lee had two corps, one commanded by General James Longstreet, the second led by Jackson. Longstreet was at Richmond, keeping an eye on McClellan; Jackson had come north to deal with Pope.

While Lee was justifiably worried about having to deal with two Federal armies, Lincoln was just as uneasy with his situation. Lee held the option of assaulting either of the Yankee forces in the field, but they were positioned so that neither could reinforce the other. Lincoln decided that he had to consolidate his armies, and on 3 August he ordered McClellan to come north.[31]

When Lee learned of the Northern plan, he saw that his only chance to defeat the Union was to lure Pope into battle before McClellan's force reached the field. Jackson opened the campaign by assaulting Pope's van, Banks's Division, near Cedar Mountain on 10 August. Banks held the upper hand at first, but when Southern general Ambrose P. Hill's division entered the fray, the balance swung to Jackson, and he drove Banks from the field.[32] Pope with Sigel's Division reached the area the next morning. The Union now held the advantage in numbers, and Jackson prudently retired to Gordonsville to await the arrival of Longstreet's Corps from Richmond.

Pope, of course, had no desire to attack Lee until his reinforcements from McClellan arrived. He decided to set up his lines above the Rappahannock River where he would be impregnable because of the wide and deep waters. As Banks and Sigel withdrew from their positions along the Rapidan River, King's Division (and Kilpatrick) moved west to join the rest of the army.

Kilpatrick reached the front just in time to take part in protecting the rear of Pope's army as it crossed over the Rappahannock. Five regiments of cavalry (the First Pennsylvania, the First Maine, the First New Jersey, the Second New York, and the First Rhode Island) under Bayard screened the infantry as they forded the stream at Beverly Ford by Brandy Station. On 20 August, just after the First Maine and the First Rhode Island had waded the water, Confederate horsemen led by Jeb Stuart appeared in the distance. They apparently meant to attack their Union counterparts.[33]

Bayard quickly assumed a defensive posture. He placed Kilpatrick's Second New York in the center on the road; the First New Jersey led by Colonel Joseph Karge was positioned west, six hundred yards behind Kilpatrick; and Colonel Owen Jones's First Pennsylvania was also posted to the rear, in a woods to Kilpatrick's left.[34]

"Down came the enemy, charging along the road," one of the First New

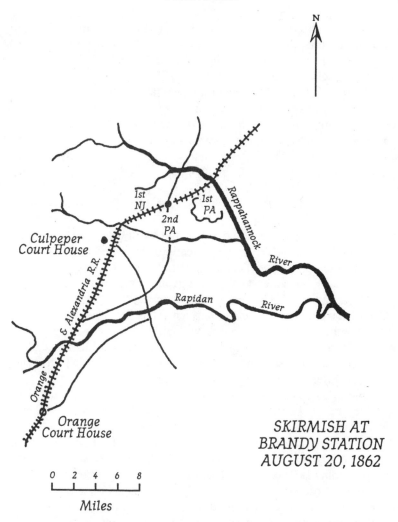

N

SKIRMISH AT
BRANDY STATION
AUGUST 20, 1862

0   2   4   6   8

Miles

Jersey troopers wrote, "and Kilpatrick was ordered to meet them."[35] The Rebels approached in a cloud of dust; the Second New York moved forward at a uniform gallop in a column of platoons. Although Kilpatrick should have been bravely leading his regiment, he rode alongside the columns, cowering perhaps but better positioned "to give the men personal encouragement while keeping their ranks aligned."[36]

Just as Kilpatrick's bugler was set to blow "Charge," the leader of the front platoon suddenly pulled on the reins of his horse, halting the animal, backing him right through the following ranks. The nervous riders behind also came to a stop, and the regiment faltered in confusion. Kilpatrick started for the head of the columns to regain control of his men, but before he could put them back into line, the enemy (the Confederate Twelfth Virginia) smashed into his wavering troops, sending them flying off the field.[37] Continuing to charge, the Rebels poured through the broken Union center.

As Kilpatrick and his frightened troopers fled for the rear, the Confederates swerved left to assault the First New Jersey. Karge tried to change front to receive the charge, but as he wheeled his men, three Rebel regiments—the Sixth, Seventh, and Seventeenth Virginia—roared from the west and crashed into his right and rear. The fray was fierce, hand-to-hand, as adversaries first emptied pistols at each other, then swung sabers. The onslaught proved too savage for the First New Jersey, who "spurred as rapidly as possible to the rear," according to Henry Pyne, "fighting . . . as they did so, with the foremost of their pursuers."[38]

The First New Jersey retreated toward the forest where the First Pennsylvania lay hidden in reserve. As the retreating troops fled through the trees, their compatriots opened fire on the pursuing Confederates, and the salvo brought the Rebel horsemen to a halt. "I gathered together all the men to be found," Bayard admitted in his report of the skirmish, "[and] crossed the river."[39]

Despite the embarrassing rout of his men in this first face-to-face encounter with the Southern cavalry, Kilpatrick was not censured for his poor performance. "[He] displayed [his] usual . . . coolness," Bayard inexplicably concluded later when advising army headquarters about the affair. "Lieutenant Colonel Kilpatrick was always active and brave."[40]

Unable to mount a direct charge against Pope across the water, Lee attempted to turn the Federal flank by sidling to his left. Each time he moved, however, Pope countered with a corresponding maneuver that kept his troops in position to check any attempt by the Confederates to ford the river and bring him to battle. Lee was forced to commence a desperate strategy. He divided his army, sending Jackson's Corps off on a wide swing around Pope's right, headed for the Northern supply depot at Manassas Junction in the Union rear. Stonewall reached Bristoe Station the evening of 26 August. He tore up the tracks there, then turned north and roared into Manassas Junction, where he proceeded to burn the buildings, cars, and tents filled with provisions.[41]

Pope was shocked to learn that Jackson was deep in his rear, between his troops and Washington, D.C. He reacted by retreating rapidly, looking not only to protect the capital from a Rebel attack but also to fall on Stonewall before Lee could come north with Longstreet's Corps to unite his army. In his frantic effort to "bag" Jackson, Pope sent all of his corps toward Manassas Junction (which Stonewall had already abandoned), opening Thoroughfare Gap for Lee's use in hurrying Longstreet's force to the scene. On 27 August after he belatedly realized his error, Pope sent the cavalry (Kilpatrick's horsemen) and Rickett's infantry division into the gap to block Longstreet's approach. These

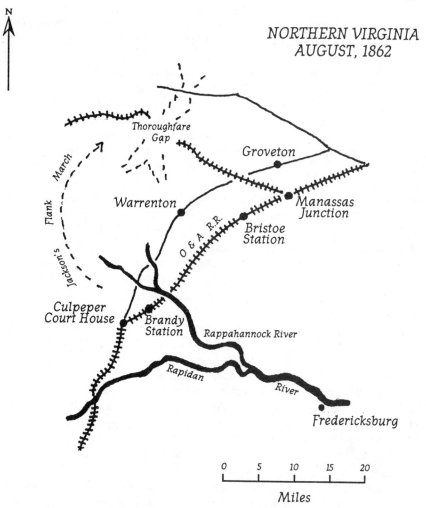

*NORTHERN VIRGINIA
AUGUST, 1862*

Thoroughfare
Gap

Groveton

Flank March

Jackson's

Warrenton

Manassas
Junction

O & A. R.R.

Bristoe
Station

Culpeper
Court House

Brandy
Station

Rappahannock River

Rapidan

River

Fredericksburg

0   5   10   15   20

Miles

troops proved too few, and the Rebels easily pushed past them and on toward
a reunion with Jackson. During the uneven skirmish, a few of Kilpatrick's
troopers were wounded.[42]

The evening of 28 August, the Federals finally found Jackson at Groveton,
Virginia. General John Gibbon's "Iron" Brigade" was attacked by the Rebels
as he marched along the Warrenton Turnpike. Gibbon fought back, and the
bloody fray ended in a draw.[43] Pope faced two options. He could delay any
action until the rest of McClellan's force arrived (four divisions, two each
from the Third and Ninth Corps totaling eighteen thousand men, were already
on hand, and the Fifth Corps led by General Fitz John Porter, ten thousand
additional troops, was now approaching from the east).[44] This would allow

Lee the time he needed to merge his army. Pope's alternative was to move against Jackson at once, before the Confederates could join their forces. He decided to attack.

Pope commenced his assault at daybreak on 29 August. Jackson, however, was entrenched in an impregnable position, so despite the Union's superior numbers, he managed to hold his ground against repeated charges throughout the day. And that afternoon, Longstreet arrived on the field, assuming a post to Stonewall's right. When Pope resumed his attack the next morning, he exposed his flank to Longstreet, who threw his entire corps into the fray. Pope was routed, sent reeling back toward Washington.[45]

Kilpatrick had a passive role in the battle. His regiment was split up, some serving as escorts for McDowell, the rest acting as couriers, carrying messages from Pope's headquarters to the infantry generals on the front line.[46]

When the retreat began, the Harris Light was reformed and given the job of maintaining order, keeping the panicked Northern soldiers in line, preventing anyone from deserting their ranks. As General Abner Doubleday's brigade stumbled in the dark past Kilpatrick's mounted men toward the rear, a Rebel artillery battery hurried up and started to shell the fleeing Federals. Kilpatrick, no doubt frustrated by having had only a minimum role in the battle, made a snap decision. "General McDowell wants the Harris Light to take [that] battery," he called as he galloped down his line. "Draw [your] sabres!"[47]

The men formed in a column of squadrons in a field off the pike, then wheeled onto the road. Kilpatrick watched as they cantered toward the enemy gunners. "[It was] too dark to see any distance ahead" was how one of the riders explained their slow pace.[48] Suddenly sheets of flame from both the front and flank tore into troopers, toppling many from their mounts. The charge disintegrated into a terrified melee of man and beast trying to escape the hail of lead that whizzed out of the night. "Wheel and retire!" an officer yelled as he led the survivors to the rear and safety.

The infantry was appreciative of Kilpatrick's efforts. "We were obliged to fall back, the enemy following, until checked by a daring charge of the Harris Light Cavalry," Doubleday wrote admiringly in his official report.[49] Those involved, however, held a different view. "The charge was a blunder," Henry Meyer declared. "[We] were subjected to not only the fire of the enemy but also from our infantry on the right of the road, who, hearing the clatter of the horses . . . and unable to see . . . assumed it to be a charge of the enemy's cavalry . . . Kilpatrick was severely criticized in the regiment for it."[50] "Kill-Cavalry" no longer meant just the wear and tear of hard marches on mounts and men.

Following their victory at Second Manassas, the Rebels under Lee moved north into Maryland. The Union, led by McClellan, followed his route; Pope had been relieved from duty because of his defeat. Kilpatrick did not accompany

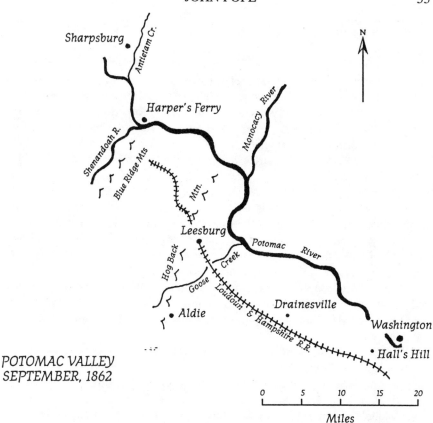

POTOMAC VALLEY
SEPTEMBER, 1862

the infantry. His casualties during the recent campaign had been high, 83 men killed, wounded, or captured, leaving him with only 152 available for duty.[51] The regiment needed rest and reinforcements. He set up camp at Hall's Hill, about eight miles south of the capital, and spent the next few weeks training the fresh troopers who had been added to his force.[52]

On 16 September Kilpatrick embarked on a mission to ascertain the enemy's strength around Leesburg. He took ten companies (six from the Second New York and two each of the First New Jersey and Ninth Pennsylvania) of cavalry with him out of Washington. He spent the night at Dranesville.[53] He crossed Goose Creek the following morning, reaching Leesburg that afternoon. When he rode into town at the van of his column, Kilpatrick spotted a small band of enemy cavalry massed on the main street. "See the rascals!" he yelled. "Go for 'em, boys!"[54]

The Rebels fled west, out of town, before the oncoming Yankee troopers. Their flight, however, was planned, because they had set up an ambush behind a fence just beyond the village. When the Union riders galloped by this point, the bushwhackers opened fire, wounding seven and capturing another of Kilpatrick's horsemen.[55]

The foolish charge added to Kilpatrick's reputation as "Kill-Cavalry," but he was unperturbed at taking unnecessary casualties. He proceeded to strip the town of weapons, destroying about two hundred muskets and appropriating a twelve-pound howitzer. And upon his return to camp, Kilpatrick received praise for his effort from Colonel Davies, who wrote, "The expedition [was] conducted with spirit and judgment."[56]

The same day that Kilpatrick skirmished with the enemy at Leesburg, McClellan attacked Lee's army, entrenched along Antietam Creek near Sharpsburg, Maryland. He assaulted the Rebel left, then the center, and finally the right, allowing Lee to shift his troops across the front and compensate for having fewer numbers. The combined casualties in the battle exceeded twenty-six thousand, an appalling total, particularly because the fight ended in a draw. After holding the field for a day to prove he had not been defeated, Lee withdrew his force back across the Potomac into Virginia."[57]

The shock of the huge losses at the Battle of Antietam brought an end to fighting in the fall of 1862. Kilpatrick, confined to his camp south of Washington, turned to exploiting the local citizens as his enemy. His troops foraged for supplies, confiscating virtually every hen and pig in sight.

People's complaints over the cavalry's activities grew vociferous, especially against the Tenth New York (who could be identified by the "10" on their hats). Kilpatrick demonstrated his gall by referring to this sister regiment as nothing but "an aggregation of chicken-thieves."[58]

Colonel William I. Irvine, chief of the Tenth New York, was incensed over Kilpatrick's accusation, and he set out to prove it wrong. He ordered every man in his command to take the figure "10" off their hats; a few days later he went on patrol, looking for troopers displaying a "10" on their cap.

"A good crop of 'Tenth New York men' were brought in," Noble Preston stated, "all loaded with 'farm products.' But every man . . . [belonged] to the Harris Light."[59]

Irvine took the culprits to Kilpatrick's headquarters, where he confronted him by saying, "Here . . . are some of those Tenth New York thieves; do with them as you please."[60]

Pretending to be shocked, Kilpatrick put the men under arrest. But as soon as Irvine left, he let the troopers go. "Kilpatrick admired too much such enterprise," Preston said, "to punish [them]."[61]

Even Kilpatrick, however, had a limit to his depravity. When an old lady came crying to his headquarters, to say that the men in his command had stolen everything she had to live on, he posted an aide at her doorstep to solicit "contributions" from the troopers as they rode past her house. She soon had "poultry and provisions sufficient to supply a . . . division of hungry Yankees," Preston recalled.[62]

While the men were gathering hens and hogs, Kilpatrick had his eye on bigger game. Mules! On the way to Leesburg, he encountered a farmhand hauling manure in a wagon, pulled by two mules. He immediately confiscated the team. "I need them at the present," Judson explained to George W. Jackson, the angry owner, who had rushed to the scene, "but they will be returned to you."[63]

A few days later, when Jackson went to the Harris Light camp to recover his mules, he found that Kilpatrick had sold the team to a sutler for seventy-five dollars. Unlike other locals, who simply accepted their loss, Jackson filed a formal complaint with the provost marshall.[64]

In the subsequent investigation, Kilpatrick's dealings with the sutler (his sale of confiscated horses and tobacco, borrowing money, taking bribes, etc.) came to light. When Kilpatrick, who had gone to New York City to recruit men for the regiment, returned to camp, he was arrested, taken into Washington, and thrown into Old Capitol Prison.[65]

"The affidavits . . . taken in the case of Colonel Kilpatrick leave little question of his guilt," Stanton, secretary of war, concluded.[66] One of Kilpatrick's aides, Lieutenant George Burnham, and both Hull and McPherson, the regimental sutlers, had each signed a sworn statement attesting to his misdeeds.

Fortunately for Kilpatrick, the Federal army was short of daring cavalry leaders, so Captain Theophilus Gaines, who was in charge of building a case for his prosecution, tried instead to clear him for further duty. General King wrote a letter claiming that he had ordered the tobacco confiscated, that Kilpatrick had not sold it but distributed it among the men; Private Theodore Northrup, Kilpatrick's orderly, said that Kilpatrick had never sold a captured horse; and Gaines concluded that since the mules were still in camp when Kilpatrick left for New York City to sign up recruits, he could not possibly have sold them. Hull's sworn testimony was ignored because he was "not reliable for truth and veracity."[67]

"The examination I have made," Gaines reported, "fully justifies [my] conclusion that he is guilty of no offenses."[68]

William Whiting, the solicitor in the case, noted that Gaines's evidence was made "orally and not under oath . . . yet they render it proper to give the accused the benefit of the doubt. . . . I therefore recommend his discharge from arrest."[69]

After spending three months in Old Capitol Prison, Kilpatrick was released on 21 January 1863. He was in a hurry to return to camp because Davies had officially retired while he was incarcerated. Kilpatrick had been named to take his place as colonel in command of the Harris Light.[70] But before going back to his regiment, he probably rode to West Point to call on Alice. She was pregnant, a result of conjugal visits to Kilpatrick when he was in jail.

During that summer of 1862, Kilpatrick found his niche in the Civil War. He proved to be an intrepid raider, eager and able to slip behind enemy lines to disrupt their routes of supply and communications. His growing fame was enhanced in two ways: there were no peers or superiors on the scene to dispute his exorbitant claims for success; and the other cavalry leaders failed miserably in similar assignments.

Kilpatrick was certainly courageous in leading his men deep into Rebel territory, but he was not so brave when personally confronting the Confederates. He avoided riding at the van, the point of greatest danger, in the skirmish along the Rappahannock, which led to his regiment being routed.

And although he was not willing to expose his own life in battle, Kilpatrick had little compunction about ordering his men to certain death. Time and again he sent troopers into charges that resulted in inordinate casualties. His epithet "Kill-Cavalry" was well earned.

Kilpatrick, of course, was not the only Yankee officer to use his position for personal gain. He was certainly one of the first, however, and his release from prison, despite valid charges pending against him, must have encouraged both Kilpatrick and others in their later devastation of the Confederacy.

6

Descriptions

"General Kilpatrick was . . . very insignificant looking . . . small, with ugly, reddish hair."[1]

Although Mrs. J. H. Foster (a Southern lady) was certainly not an admirer of Kilpatrick, her description of him matched that of one of his advocates, Federal major Charles B. Loop, who said, "He is the most insignificant looking whelp I most ever saw.[2] Lloyd Lewis, Sherman's biographer, stated that Kilpatrick was "a bristling little man with a long red nose and longer and redder sideburns."[3] Kilpatrick seemed to be even shorter because, as Burke Davis alleged, he was "hunchbacked . . . [having] a . . . habit of thrusting his head downward, like a restless horse."[4]

Kilpatrick's short height, however, did not mean that he was physically weak. "Though . . . slender in form and delicate in mould," Glazier related, "yet it would seem as [if] his bones were [made of] iron and his sinews steel. . . . He had a wonderful power of endurance."[5] Meyer stated, "He was incapable of fatigue."[6] Kidd recalled that Kilpatrick was as "supple and agile as an athlete."[7]

Kidd went on to state, "His face was . . . marked . . . showing . . . individuality in every line. [He had] a prominent nose, a wide mouth, a firm jaw, thin cheeks set off by side whiskers rather light in color. . . . [His] eyes . . . were cold and lustrous, but searching . . . a countenance that once seen, was never forgotten."[8]

Although many officers neglected their dress in the field, Kilpatrick always looked sharp. He wore a "close-fitting and natty suit of blue," Kidd wrote, "[and] a black hat with the brim turned down on one side, up on the other . . . which gave to the style his own name."[9]

His associates recalled Kilpatrick as outgoing, always cheerful. He was "good natured, approachable," Meyer wrote.[10] His biographer at West Point stated, "He had unwavering good nature. . . . We recall his frank smile."[11] Wilson related that Judson was "full of enthusiasm."[12] We all liked his bright face," General Oliver O. Howard recalled.[13]

Although Kilpatrick was a pleasant individual, he also was overly zealous,

Union general Hugh Judson Kilpatrick, from *The Photographic History of the Civil War,* edited by Francis Trevelyan Miller. 10 vols. New York: The Review of Reviews Company, 1911.

being "highly excitable and [of] nervous temperament," according to Meyer. "Whenever we reached camp and everyone else seemed to think that men and horses should have a rest, Kilpatrick was writing letters [to his superior] asking for authority . . . to start out on a . . . .raid or to give him a chance to get into a fight."[14] Mary Elizabeth Sergent wrote that Kilpatrick was "terribly in earnest."[15] Wilson said he showed "a fiery temper."[16] "He has an indomitable will that cannot brook defeat," Glazier declared.[17]

Kilpatrick passed his personal intensity on to his men through frequent and fervid speeches. He was "a blatant and interminable talker," Morris Schaff recounted.[18] "He would harangue the men," Meyer stated.[19] "What [Kilpatrick] has to say," Glazier said, "he says with such perspicuity that no one doubts his meaning."[20] "His voice had a peculiar, piercing quality," Kidd related. "He was a ready and fluent speaker . . . who could charm his audience with his insinuating tongue."[21]

Others, who paid more attention to what Kilpatrick said instead of his elocution, were less impressed with his speaking ability. He was profane. "It is 'By God' and 'Goddamn' all the time with Kilpatrick," Confederate Colonel J. F. Waring rejoined.[22] Because he repeatedly boasted about his own exploits, many found Kilpatrick disgusting. "He was the most vain, conceited, egotistical little poppyjay I ever saw," declared Union Major Connolly.[23] Charles Francis Adams remarked that Kilpatrick was "given to much blowing."[24] Union colonel Lyman pictured him as a "frothy braggart without brains, who gets . . . his reputation by newspapers."[25]

One of the reasons for the antagonism toward Kilpatrick was his lack of veracity. "His accounts of battles were . . . boastful and unreliable," Lewis concluded.[26] "[A] man would hardly be a cavalry officer if he did not talk big," Colonel Charles S. Wainwright declared, "but a dispatch bearing Kilpatrick's name leads to . . . doubt of its accuracy."[27] Friends posed excuses for Kilpatrick's trouble with the truth. "His memory and imagination," General Howard related, "were often in conflict."[28]

Kilpatrick's lies were meant to enhance his reputation, not only in what he achieved but also how he performed during confrontations. He proclaimed his own bravery so many times that even his enemies granted him this quality. Wilson wrote that "Kilpatrick always [showed] unflinching courage,"[29] and Kidd said, "He was brave to rashness."[30] A close examination of his battles, however, proves that Kilpatrick was no hero. When facing only token resistance, he willingly led a charge, but when opposing a competitive force, Kilpatrick always put another in front of his columns. He stayed out of the fight, waiting to "ride to glory over the graves of his men."[31]

The only exception to this practice was when the Rebels lured him into ambush by offering a seemingly weak front. He fell into this trap often because he was a poor military tactician. "Kilpatrick's standing order," a newspaper

reporter quoted Lieutenant S. H. Ballard, "was 'Charge, God damn them,'
whether they were five or five thousand."[32] Kidd noted that he was called "Kill-
Cavalry" because "so many lives were sacrificed by him for no good purpose
whatever."[33] "Kilpatrick mingled so much besotted rashness," according to
Frederick Whittaker, "that his greatest successes were always marred by unnecessary slaughter, while he suffered more than one mortifying and humiliating defeat."[34]

In addition to his lying about being heroic, Kilpatrick falsely claimed high
morals. He convinced Wilson (a resolute teetotaler) that he "neither drank nor
gambled."[35] This was untrue; he kept liquor in his tent, which he shared with a
number of visitors that called on him,[36] and he was drunk in Milledgeville,
Georgia, when his troops celebrated the capture of the state capital.[37] And although Kilpatrick was not a cardplayer, he was an inveterate gambler. He built
a race course wherever he made camp[38] and always traveled with his favorite
bangtail, "Lively."[39] Kilpatrick even had a few roosters in his entourage, so if
the track became too muddy for horse racing, he could bet on a cockfight.[40] He
was a poor loser. When one of his best horses was beaten in a race, Kilpatrick
blamed the defeat on the rider and "sent [him] off the ground in disgrace."[41]

Although Kilpatrick was willing to pretend that he did not drink or gamble,
he flaunted his major character defect: womanizing. From the time that he
entered West Point, "Little Kil always had an eye for accommodating women."[42]
Every free weekend that he earned for getting no demerits was not spent with
Alice. Even after his marriage, he "maintained his West Point reputation as . . .
addicted to 'notorious immoralities.'"[43] Kilpatrick often kept a girl in his quarters to perform "sack duty and horizontal drill," according to one account.[44]
And even though many Yankee officers shared his interest in the ladies,
Kilpatrick was almost unique in that he was often in bed when he should have
been in battle. His conquests—white whores, Blacks, and even a Chinese girl—
interfered with his duty.[45]

Stories of his infidelity must have gotten back to Alice, but Kilpatrick
probably cared less. He seemed heartless, one who held no feelings for anyone
but himself. Fellow officers marveled that he was "prodigal of human life,"[46]
that after a battle, where many of his men had been killed, he would be so
cheerful that "one could hardly believe that he had been [engaged] at all."[47]

Although Kilpatrick was indifferent to the sight of men dying in battle, he
took great delight in seeing the pain and suffering that he inflicted upon defenseless Southern women and children. "His pathway in the South was strewn
with devastation," his West Point biographer reported. "[He] authorized acts
which [his fellow] officers . . . shrank from with disgust." The writer continued, "The wanton outrage, the sea of flame, the destruction of . . . treasures . . . is
the excuse of warriors to cover their own want of true courage, humanity and
honesty."[48] Sergent notes that his "obituary in the Alumni Records is the first,

after a decade of stainless knights, to admit that a deceased alumnus might have had a few faults."[49]

To summarize, Kilpatrick was a cocky little man, strong, cheerful, a dandy in his dress, full of boastful talk, set on advancing his own interests. He was also untruthful, one who had questionable morals, a poor tactician who preferred abusing defenseless women and children to confronting his armed enemy in the field.

Despite provable charges of taking bribes, stealing, and then selling horses and tobacco, and impropriety in borrowing money, Kilpatrick was not only freed from jail on 21 January 1863 but also returned to his regiment with a promotion to colonel of the Second New York Cavalry.

7

Joe Hooker

During Kilpatrick's stay in prison, the Civil War continued to develop. General Henry W. Halleck, commanding the Union forces in the West, decided in early June to disperse his men to assume a defensive line along the lower Tennessee border. Buell's army moved east toward Chattanooga; Grant saw his army split in two, with Sherman taking two divisions west to occupy Memphis while General John A. McClernand and the other two divisions headed north to set up camp at Jackson, Tennessee; and General William S. Rosecrans (in charge of Pope's former troops) remained just below the state line at Corinth, Mississippi.[1]

The Confederates soon took advantage of Halleck's foolhardy division of his forces. In late July General Braxton Bragg slipped past the Union's eastern flank and darted into Kentucky to recruit volunteers and gather provisions. Buell came after him, and finally, on 8 October 1862, they met in battle at Perryville. Although Buell won the bloody affair, which saw almost one fourth of the total number engaged fall dead or wounded, Bragg escaped southeast, back to Tennessee.[2]

Because of his failure to bag Bragg, Buell was relieved of command. Rosecrans took up the chase, and he brought the Confederates to battle on 31 December 1862 at Murfreesboro, Tennessee. In the three-day fray of Stones River, one third of the seventy-five thousand men engaged became casualties. The Union prevailed, and Bragg once again retreated southeast.[3]

The Federal success in the West was not matched in the East. When McClellan was slow to pursue Lee after Antietam, he was replaced on 7 November 1862 by General Ambrose Burnside. The Rebels had fallen back into Virginia, taking up a position along the Rappahannock River, but when Burnside decided to slip by their right flank, moving for Richmond, Lee countered by sliding east to occupy the hills behind Fredericksburg. Burnside attacked these heights on 12 December. Six times he massed his men and charged the impregnable Confederates; six times he was thrown back. The Federals left twelve thousand men dead or wounded on the frozen slopes.[4]

In an attempt to atone for this rout, Burnside tried to flank Lee's left by marching west along the Rappahannock. A cold, winter rain slowed his troops, and he finally bogged down in the mud without ever crossing the stream to confront the Rebels. Upon his return to Fredericksburg, just as Kilpatrick was reporting to duty, Burnside was replaced by General Joseph Hooker.[5]

An 1837 graduate of West Point, Hooker had gained fame during the

General Joseph Hooker. Courtesy of the Library of Congress.

Mexican War, where he was given three brevets for gallantry. He then served in California, resigning in 1853 to take up farming. When the Civil War started, he returned to duty as a brigade commander. He led a division into the Seven Days Battles, then headed a corps at Second Manassas, Antietam, and Fredericksburg.[6] Although Hooker performed well in each battle, many had reservations about his ability as a commander. Hooker was renowned for his preference for liquor and loose ladies. "[His] headquarters," according to Charles Francis Adams, "was a place [that] no self-respecting man liked to go and no decent woman could go."[7]

When Hooker took command, morale in the army was at an ebb. "There is a great deal of croaking," Adams wrote, "and desertion is the order of the day."[8] Hooker's moves toward solving the dilemma were brilliant: the army's rations were upgraded to include fresh bread and vegetables; warm clothing was distributed; a rotating system of furloughs was put into operation; the hospitals were improved; the men were given badges to wear that identified their corps, resulting in organizational pride; and frequent drilling and reviews not only kept the troops occupied but also left them with no time to complain.[9] The program succeeded in raising morale and efficiency to a top level, proving that despite the misgivings of his critics, Hooker was a competent commander.

His greatest contribution to an improved army, however, was in reorganizing the cavalry. Hooker combined all units into one corps under General George Stoneman. The troopers now had their own leader, freeing them from the whims of the infantry commanders.

Stoneman had graduated from West Point in 1846 and had served with the dragoons in the West prior to the Civil War. His initial command in 1861 was head of the cavalry reserve, an administrative role. He then became an infantry division leader, fighting in the Seven Days Battles, Second Manassas, Antietam, and Fredericksburg, where he was received a brevet promotion for gallantry.[10]

His cavalry corps (nine thousand troops) was composed of three divisions under Generals Alfred Pleasonton, William Averell, and David McMurtrie Gregg, plus the reserve brigade of John Buford.[11] Each division included two brigades. Kilpatrick, fresh out of prison and only recently elevated to regimental colonel, was again promoted, placed in command of a brigade assigned to Gregg. He was responsible for three regiments: the Second New York, Tenth New York, and First Maine.[12]

Kilpatrick's headquarters were located at Belle Plain, a small village east of Fredericksburg on the Potomac River. His troopers picketed the banks of the Rappahannock between Port Royal and Fredericksburg;[13] Pleasonton and Averell had responsibility for watching the line along the river west of Fredericksburg.

The time passed peacefully. Despite being within easy rifle range of each other across the icy, shallow water, the adversaries "mutually arranged that there

General George Stoneman. Courtesy of
the Library of Congress.

... be no firing on either side."[14] Willard Glazier went on to remember that
"Squads of soldiers from both armies may be observed seated together on
either side of the [stream] earnestly discussing the great questions of the day.
... During these ... interviews, trading was the order of the day. ... There was
... a special demand [by] the Rebels for pocket knives and canteens."

Such interchanges were, of course, forbidden under the rules of warfare,
but Kilpatrick was too busy to bother with enforcing regulations. Perhaps inspired by the example set by Hooker, he had audaciously brought two Black
women in his tent to serve as his "cooks." The camp buzzed with stories about
his sexual exploits with the Negro girls.[15] A jealous rivalry naturally evolved,

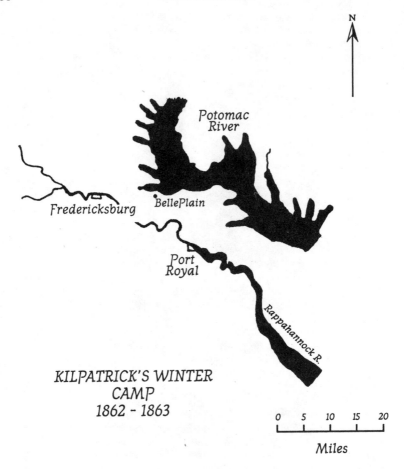

KILPATRICK'S WINTER
CAMP
1862 - 1863

and the two were soon engaged in "a fierce contest in which . . . heads were used as . . . weapons of attack and defense . . . reminding one of the battering-rams of old, used for demolishing the walls of . . . cities."[16] A guard arrested the women, but Kilpatrick quickly ordered their release. He jokingly assumed responsibility for their fights, but only after "they . . . put their heads together more than half a dozen times a day."[17]

When not involved with his girls, Kilpatrick worked at training his men. Hooker insisted on daily drills by all to upgrade the army's fighting skill. Like McClellan he also set up boards to review the officers' abilities, weeding out those judged unfit for command. Kilpatrick was a member of the cavalry board and served as president of a court-martial that disciplined the shirkers.[18]

Always a good trainer, Kilpatrick saw his troopers improve rapidly under his leadership. His men recognized that their growing competence was because of his effort. "There [is] a wonderful unanimity . . . in the brigade," Glazier wrote, "that Kilpatrick [is] the right man in the right place."[19]

On 6 April the cavalry corps displayed the result of their winter's training in a grand review at Falmouth. President Lincoln came down from Washington to see the troopers' parade. "An occasion not to be forgotten," Glazier recalled with awe. "We appeared in our best uniforms and with flying colors. . . . The column was . . . four hours passing in review."[20]

Hooker, too, was impressed with his cavalry, which led him to give them a major role in his strategy for dislodging the Rebels from their entrenched position behind Fredericksburg. "My plans are perfect," he pronounced with glee, "and when I start to carry them out, may God have mercy on Bobby Lee; for I shall have none."[21]

This perfect plan consisted of two phases: the entire cavalry corps would first slip around the Rebels' left flank and into the rear, where they would disrupt the supply line to Lee's army. Hooker hoped this would force a retreat, and he could then move after Lee to bring him to battle on open ground, pinching the Rebels between his oncoming infantrymen and his cavalry, poised in Lee's rear. If the Confederates held to their breastworks below Fredericksburg, Hooker would follow his cavalry's path to flank Lee from his impregnable post, forcing him to turn and fight without entrenchments.[22]

Kilpatrick's brigade moved right on 13 April to join with the rest of Stoneman's command. The cavalry, about ten thousand strong, then rode thirty miles further west to the Orange and Alexander Railroad bridge across the Rappahannock River. The night of 14 April, just as the troopers began preparations to ford the water, thick clouds formed overhead and a heavy rain started to fall. In only a few hours, the stream was flooded, seven feet above normal, and the cavalry found themselves blocked from reaching the far shore. Soon the surrounding ground also filled with water, and as Buford wrote, "The country . . . was like a sea."[23] Stoneman's sodden men stood in place, unable to advance, for nearly two weeks without relief from the storms.

Although he could not be blamed for the rotten weather, Stoneman lost credibility with Hooker because of his failure to cross the Rappahannock. As a result, Hooker decided that he could not depend on his horsemen, and he changed strategy for the upcoming campaign. Instead of using his troopers to attack Lee's rear, he would split his infantry in two, sending a force of foot soldiers behind the Rebels' line to snap the pincer. Stoneman's cavalry would still turn the Confederate flank, but when they reached Southern territory, their efforts would be limited to disrupting Lee's line of supply, doing "a vast amount of mischief [while] bewildering the enemy as to [their] course and intentions."[24]

A second change in Hooker's tactics was a reduction in the size of Stoneman's force. The original plan had assumed that the entire cavalry corps would gallop into Confederate territory; Pleasonton's division, however, was held back to support the Twelfth Corps of infantry, led by General Henry W. Slocum, who would lead the flanking movement against Lee.[25] Just prior to his heading south, Stoneman sent Averell's division west toward Rapidan Station to protect the army's right wing from Rebel cavalry, reported to be lurking in the shadow of the Blue Ridge Mountains.[26] Only about four thousand men, eleven brigades (including Kilpatrick's) under Gregg and Buford, took part in the raid.

Stoneman's troopers crossed the Rappahannock at Kelly's Ford the evening of 28 April. Kilpatrick, bringing up the rear, forded the river the following morning. Upon reaching the Rapidan the afternoon of 30 April, he found the waters at flood stage. "We had an exciting time," Glazier reported later. "Several horses and men were swept down . . . stream and were drowned; none of us escaped the unpleasant [experience of] getting wet."[27] After crossing Raccoon

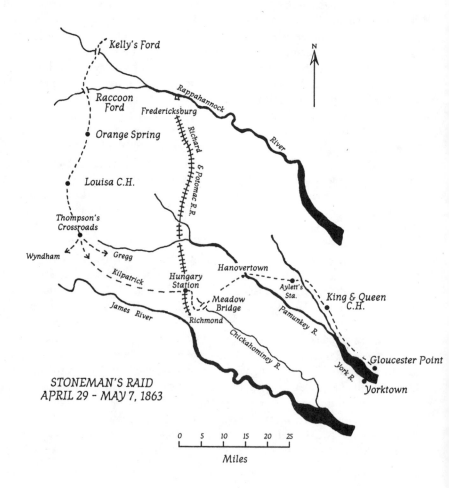

STONEMAN'S RAID
APRIL 29 - MAY 7, 1863

Ford, Kilpatrick found Stoneman waiting for him. The general was afraid of a
Rebel attack on his command, so instead of continuing to advance, he formed
the troopers in a defensive position. They spent that night sitting on their horses.
"[Having] been in the saddle several consecutive days and nights," Glazier
recalled, "many were so exhausted that, dropping to the earth, with bridle and
halter in hand, they fell asleep."[28]

The next morning, a bright, warm sun greeted the weary troopers. Seeing
no sign of the enemy, they galloped south. The command reached Orange Spring
later that morning of 2 May. While Buford's force proceeded systematically to
wreck the railroad station and the buildings close by, Kilpatrick rode on for
Louisa Court House. Sullen civilians watched as his troopers gathered up rations
and forage, then fired the warehouses that had contained these supplies. In the
interim, a band of Rebel cavalry approached the village, but the First Maine
was able to scatter them. Kilpatrick then moved further south to Thompson's
Crossroads, where he waited for Stoneman and the rest of his command.[29]

Stoneman rode up about 11:00 P.M. Under a moonlit sky, he discussed his
plans. "[We have] dropped in [this] region like a shell," he noted, "and I intend
to burst it in every direction."[30] Gregg would divide his force, sending Colonel
Percy Wyndham, commander of the Second Brigade, with two of his regiments to Columbia to demolish the James River Canal, which was used to
supply Richmond with provisions from the Shenandoah Valley. The Twelfth
Illinois, Wyndham's remaining regiment, led by Lieutenant Colonel Hasbrouck
Davis, would hurry east to tear up the railroad track near Ashland, Virginia.
Gregg would also ride east with two regiments, burning bridges on the South
Anna River. Kilpatrick was given the most dangerous mission; commanding
only the Second New York, he would ride southeast to destroy the Virginia
Central Railroad span over the Chickahominy River at Meadow Bridge near
Richmond. Buford and the rest of the troopers would remain with Stoneman at
Thompson's Crossroads, presenting a rallying post for the raiders, should they
be attacked by superior numbers of Rebels. When they had finished with their
destruction, each of the parties would return to Stoneman's camp for the trek
back north. If they found their return to Thompson's Crossroads barred by the
Confederates, the commanders were given the option of seeking refuge further east at the Union depot at Gloucester Point on the York River.[31]

Kilpatrick left camp about 2:00 A.M. on 3 May. When morning came, he
went into hiding in a pine thicket, staying out of sight until nightfall. He crept
forward in the dark within sight of Hungary Station (a main depot on the
Fredericksburg & Richmond Railroad), which he attacked at dawn on 4 May.
No resistance was encountered; the men ripped up the track, torched the station,
and pulled down the telegraph poles and wires. They worked at their leisure.
When the destruction was finally finished, Kilpatrick started the Second New
York down the Brook Turnpike toward Richmond.[32]

"There we were," Glazier recalled, "miles away from any support, with no way to retreat . . . nearer the Confederate capital than ever any Union troops were before."[33] Expecting to be attacked at any moment, Kilpatrick warily rode by the outer line of Richmond's fortifications without meeting opposition. His troopers moved through the second series of breastworks, which were also unoccupied. Suddenly, a Rebel officer, riding a blooded horse, trotted up.

"What regiment?" he demanded.

"The Second New York Cavalry," Kilpatrick barked, "and you, sir, are my prisoner!"[34]

Lieutenant R. W. Brown, aide-de-camp to General John H. Winder, was quickly relieved of his sword and mount (said to be one of Winder's favorites). Indignant over being seized so easily, Brown snorted, "You're mighty daring . . . but you'll be captured [yourself] before sundown!"

"That all may be," Kilpatrick replied with a wide grin, "but we intend to do a mighty deal of mischief first."[35]

After paroling Brown and the eleven men captured along with him, Kilpatrick continued his advance toward Richmond.

When he came within two miles of the Rebel capital, so near that "smoke from workshops and the church steeples were plainly visible,"[36] Kilpatrick spotted an artillery battery, supported by infantry, blocking his path ahead. He had come up to the inner line of defense, which was manned. With no reason to try and enter Richmond, Kilpatrick turned east and headed for Meadow Bridge, his target for destruction.

Kilpatrick's troopers rode to the span without meeting any interference from the Rebels. After crossing over, they burned the bridge, then turned northeast toward Hanovertown. Kilpatrick had decided that it was unsafe to try and retrace his steps back to Stoneman, posted at Thompson's Crossroads, so he headed for Gloucester Point. He used a Black man as a guide, a slave from a nearby plantation who had agreed to betray his master by showing Kilpatrick the way.[37]

When the column moved ahead, a train approached, thundering south to Richmond. Kilpatrick flagged the locomotive to a halt, yanked the startled engineer from his cab, and after setting fire to the cars, started the train under full steam toward the crossing he had just destroyed. "The whole thing . . . disappeared in the deep mud [under] the sluggish stream," Glazier recalled.[38]

Kilpatrick then renewed his flight, galloping eastward all afternoon, into the gathering shadows of evening, and on through the night without a stop. Just before the sun rose on the morning of 5 May, Kilpatrick rode into Hanovertown, where he found a parked train, stuffed with provisions. His sleepless and hungry men filled their haversacks with booty. After they had finished their ransacking, Kilpatrick set the cars afire. He then moved toward the Pamunkey River, where he seized a "one-horse platform ferry-boat [with a] capacity [for] only twenty horses and men."[39] After repeated floats across the water, Kilpatrick burned the ferry to prevent enemy cavalry, now reported on his heels, from following him.[40]

Kilpatrick rode east from Hanovertown without stopping for rest. At 4:00 P.M., a "cold rain storm set in, borne on the flapping wings of a chilly wind,"[41] but he continued to flee, fearful of encountering Confederates. "We filed along the by-ways and neglected paths," Glazier wrote, "frequently immersed in almost impenetrable bushes dripping with rain."[42]

When darkness came, Kilpatrick finally halted to allow his weary men a few hours' sleep. They rose again about 1:00 A.M. on 6 May to resume flight. Seeing their tired faces and the fear in his troopers' eyes, Kilpatrick felt compelled to offer encouragement. "I'll save every man," he yelled as he mounted his horse. "Follow me!"[43]

They arrived at Aylett's Station at dawn. A tiny Rebel force guarded the depot, but they scattered when Kilpatrick's men rode into view. They left behind a wagon train and warehouse filled with corn, wheat, clothing, and other commissary stores. The Federals set fire to the lot, then used a ferry to cross over the Mattapony River, burning the boat once they had reached the far shore.[44]

As they galloped southeast, following the river, they encountered yet another wagon train, laden with ham and eggs and other luxuries, which they "confiscated, appropriated, and destroyed," Glazier remembered fondly.[45]

Kilpatrick was worried about the Rebel cavalry closing on his heels, so he continued to gallop for Gloucester Point without pause. His miserable afternoon's ride, beset by a cold, drenching drizzle, was frequently interrupted by partisan snipers, whose "plan [was] to hide in the thick bushes, and fire upon the rear of our column as we [passed]," Glazier wrote. "It [was] not possible to pursue them [as] time [was] too precious to be wasted."[46]

Night was approaching as the tired troopers rode up to King and Queen Court House. Ahead, in the gathering shadows, they saw their path blocked by a body of cavalry, assembled in battle formation. Kilpatrick was trapped! Unable to retreat because of the Confederates coming up on his rear, he opted to blast his way through the enemy troopers that stood before him. "I at once advanced to the attack," he stated, "only . . . to discover that they were friends, a portion of the Twelfth Illinois."[47] Davis's men had ridden east, too, after finishing their mischief at Ashland Station.

Encouraged by this addition to his numbers, Kilpatrick finally halted to rest his troopers, but he allowed no fires at the bivouac. He would not risk disclosing his presence to the enemy. Early in the morning, he moved for Gloucester Point, arriving on the York River about 10:00 A.M.[48]

Kilpatrick's force was greeted by the Federal garrison as "lions of the day," according to Glazier. "Nothing [was] too good for us. We [had] the freedom of the town, and the subject of our raid [was] the theme of [much] speculation."[49]

In just five days, Kilpatrick had ridden more than two hundred miles, captured and paroled three hundred prisoners, torched a railroad bridge, sunk the ferries along his path, captured two wagon trains, wrecked two locomotives and their cars, burned a depot and several warehouses filled with provisions, tore up miles of iron rails, and severed the telegraph between Hungary Station and Richmond. Rufus King, the general who had been instrumental in getting Kilpatrick released from prison five months ago, was now stationed at Gloucester Point (sent there in disgrace after being found intoxicated during the Second Battle of Bull Run).[50] He wrote a note to the authorities in Washington, praising Kilpatrick's performance during the raid by calling it "one of the finest feats of the war."[51]

Stanton (secretary of war) agreed that Stoneman's raid had been a "brilliant success,"[52] but Hooker scoffed at this high assessment of his cavalry. "Railroad communication between Fredericksburg and Richmond was interrupted but for one day," he complained. "Bridges of importance appeared to have remained untouched. With the exception of Kilpatrick's operations, the raid [did not] amount to much. . . . My instructions [were] entirely disregarded by General Stoneman."[53]

He was right. Wyndham had galloped without opposition to the canal on the James River, but when he began preparing to blow up the structure, he found that he had forgotten to bring explosives. He had no choice but to return in failure to Stoneman's camp. Gregg burned a few insignificant spans to the east, but he became so wary of possible Rebel assault on his troopers that he retired from the field without ever reaching, much less destroying, his key objective, the Aquia Railroad bridge over the North Anna River. Averell's force encountered the Confederate cavalry along the western flank. He attacked their position, but when they withdrew, instead of chasing his adversary, he retired across the Rappahannock River to await further orders. Davis had set fire to a number of small bridges on his route, but the main spans, those over the South Anna River, were left untouched [54]

Not only had the depredation been minimal but also the cavalry had exhausted themselves when they conducted their raid behind Southern lines. Stoneman's force had totaled twelve thousand men at the beginning of the month. On 13 May he reported that "the horses were pretty well used up. . . . A large number need shoeing, and the majority . . . [suffer] mud fever. . . . As to force . . . fit for duty . . . the general can count upon 2,000 . . . provided but little marching is required."[55]

This was devastating news to Hooker. Lee was about to break camp and move north into Union territory. The cavalry was desperately needed to keep track of the Southern troops, but they lay immobilized behind the Rappahannock River.

Lee had the option to maneuver because he had defeated Hooker at Chancellorsville. Three days prior to the cavalry raid, Hooker had opened his campaign against Lee. He moved three full corps of infantry to Kelly's Ford on the Rapidan, crossed the river, and then marched southeast into the area covered with scrub oak and brambles called the "Wilderness." They took up a position along Lee's left flank. At the same time, two other Union corps crossed the Rappahannock at Fredericksburg to feign a frontal assault on Lee, to pin him in position for the charge from the west.

Lee was not fooled. When he learned that the Federals were on his left flank, he, too, divided his troops, sending the bulk of his force west to confront Hooker in the Wilderness. The move so shocked Hooker that he canceled his assault and assumed a defensive position at Chancellorsville, where he awaited a frontal charge from Lee. The Confederate general, however, split his army for a second time, sending Stonewall Jackson on a wide arc to assault Hooker's right flank. The late afternoon blow on 2 May shattered the Union line, and the Yankees fell back along the Rappahannock. Lee sent them reeling over the river the following day.[56]

Embittered by the embarrassing rout, Hooker turned his ire on the cavalry. He first relieved Averell from command, charging him with "culpable indifference and inactivity. . . . It was his duty to do something."[57] Hooker meant to censure Stoneman, too, but before he could do so, the cavalry chief asked for a leave of absence. He was suffering with hemorrhoids, a devastating condition for a horseman.[58] Hooker was quick to accept the request, and on 22 May he named Alfred Pleasonton to head the cavalry.

An 1844 graduate of West Point, Pleasonton saw service in the Mexican War, battled the Seminole Indians in Florida, then moved west with the Second Dragoons. His Civil War experience had all been with the cavalry, where he had built a mediocre record. He was called "The Knight of Romance" for having filed so many unreliable reports on Confederate activities. In the battle of Chancellorsville, however, Pleasonton led a suicidal assault by the Eighth Pennsylvania that saved an artillery battery, used to hold a key position (Hazel Grove) from an attack by Jackson's corps. Hooker rewarded Pleasonton with the cavalry command for this feat.[59]

Pleasonton's division was assigned to Colonel Benjamin F. Davis, Colonel Alfred N. Duffie took charge of Averell's division, and Gregg and Buford both retained their commands.[60]

Kilpatrick remained in charge of Gregg's First Brigade, but he was stranded with the Second New York near Gloucester Point, recuperating from Stoneman's Raid. His other two regiments were at Falmouth. Hooker's solution to the dilemma was a temporary measure: Kilpatrick would remain at Gloucester Point to head a makeshift brigade composed of the Second New York and the

General Alfred Pleasonton. Courtesy of the Library of Congress.

Twelfth Illinois until he was ready to return north;[61] Colonel Calvin S. Douty of the First Maine would lead his regiments, stationed along the Rappahannock, during his absence.

The troops under Kilpatrick at Gloucester Point totaled about eight hundred men. Although most had mounts, only two hundred had animals ready to ride. The others were on foot, waiting for their horses to recover from the strain of their recent raid. Uneasy over being incapacitated and anxious to return to Falmouth, Kilpatrick decided to scour the area for replacement mounts for his cavalry.

The operation was unique in that three branches of the service were involved. Kilpatrick, in overall command, rode with two hundred troopers. He was supported by two hundred infantrymen under Lieutenant Colonel Charles C. Suydam. The soldiers were transported on two gunboats, the *Morris* and the *Winnisimmet*. Lieutenant Commander James S. Gillis, an officer with the U.S. Navy, was in charge of the ships.[62]

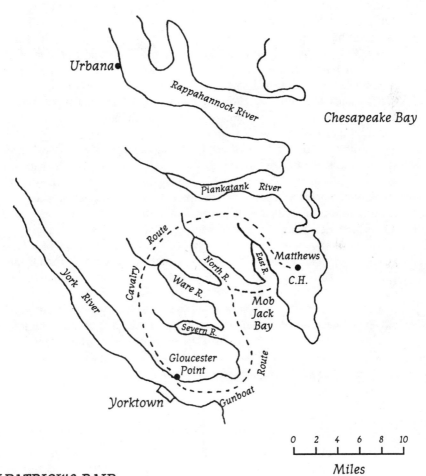

N

Urbana

Rappahannock River

Chesapeake Bay

Piankatank River

Route

Cavalry

North R.

East R.

Matthews
C.H.

Ware R.

York River

Severn R.

Mob
Jack
Bay

Gloucester
Point

Route

Yorktown

Gunboat

0 2 4 6 8 10

Miles

KILPATRICK'S RAID
ON MATTHEW'S C.H.
MAY 19 – 21, 1863

Kilpatrick left his camp at one o'clock the night of 20 May. Galloping first northwest, then northeast, he arrived at the headwaters of the North River about 9:00 A.M. where he met Suydam and Gillis. They had sailed east on the York River during the night, then turned north into Mob Jack Bay, arriving at their anchorage about 5:30 A.M. No enemy was in sight.

With the coast clear, Kilpatrick proceeded east toward Matthews Court House, gathering up all the horses, cows, and sheep in his path. His flotilla sailed back down the North River, then up the East River to stay close by in case of an enemy attack on the cavalry. The only resistance met was a lone "guerrilla," who was killed after he had wounded two of Kilpatrick's men. By the time the troopers reached Matthews Court House, they had accumulated about 300 horses and mules, 150 cattle, and the same number of sheep. Kilpatrick burned five mills filled with grain while in town. After an overnight stay, he began loading animals onto the ships the morning of 21 May. They headed back to Gloucester Point, leaving about 6:00 that night, arriving at Yorktown about midnight. Kilpatrick rode through the evening, reaching home about 8:00 A.M. on the twenty-second.[63]

Although Kilpatrick's raid had been a moderate success, "conducted with spirit," according to a report of the affair by General Erasmus D. Keyes, commander of the area,[64] he had failed to achieve his key objective, that is, gathering enough horses to remount his troopers. He had to stay at Gloucester Point, waiting for his animals to recover their strength.

Robert E. Lee, however, could move at will, and he was planning a most significant move: a march into Pennsylvania to gather provisions for his army. His first step in invading the North was to establish his cavalry's headquarters at Culpeper, where they could screen the infantry's trek north through the Shenandoah Valley.[65] When Hooker heard that Lee had relocated his troopers, he knew that the Rebels were up to something, but with his own cavalry diminished, exhausted because of Stoneman's Raid, he was unable to ascertain just what Lee had in mind. Hooker decided that he needed all his horsemen at hand to scout the Confederate's intentions, and on 28 May he wrote to Kilpatrick, "[P]roceed . . . to Urbana to report to these headquarters . . . Monday morning, June 1."[66]

Kilpatrick's efforts under Hooker (Stoneman) were seen as excellent by his superiors. He was persistent, forcible, and daring. He had succeeded in his missions when all the other cavalry leaders had failed. And although Kilpatrick's horses and men had been exhausted by their hard riding, adding to his reputation as "Kill-Cavalry," he had "spent" his force following orders. Kilpatrick's star was rising at the most critical time of the Civil War.

8

Brandy Station

When Kilpatrick started to head north to Urbana in early June 1863, important movements were also taking place elsewhere. Grant had been stalking Vicksburg, the last primary Southern fortress on the Mississippi River, for months with out success. By mid-April, however, he had finally devised a winning strategy. Instead of a direct charge on the Rebel bastion, he moved his troops south along the opposite shore, looking to cross the river below the city and attack it from the rear. Grant, who began ferrying men over the water on 30 April, darted inland and captured Jackson, Mississippi on 14 May; he then raced west to the back gates of Vicksburg. When he tried to batter through the Confederates' fortifications, however, Grant found them impregnable. Only one option was left: lay siege to the town and starve the Rebels into submission.[1]

In the east, Robert E. Lee was on the move. After his victory over Hooker at Chancellorsville, the Southern leader had decided on a campaign that envisioned the decimation of the Union Army of the Potomac. He would invade Pennsylvania soil, drawing the Federal forces after him. When they closed on him, Lee would suddenly consolidate his troops and pounce on the enemy column. Wave after wave of Confederates would charge into the melee, wiping out the Yankee corps one after another until the Northern army was annihilated.[2]

The key to Lee's strategy was a fast start, to get far enough ahead of his adversary so that Hooker's pursuing columns were strung out, vulnerable to the attack that Lee had conceived. He would mask his march from the Union by moving north through the Shenandoah Valley, using the soaring Blue Ridge Mountains as a shield against prying Yankee eyes. And to make sure that Hooker was kept unaware of his plans, Lee would post his cavalry in the highland gaps where they could challenge any enemy attempt to break through the screen.

Lee opened his campaign by dispatching his troopers to Culpeper between the Rappahannock and Rapidan Rivers.[3] They would hold there as the infantry moved behind them on their way to cross the Blue Ridge, then head north once Lee's army was in the Shenandoah Valley. When Hooker saw that Lee had set

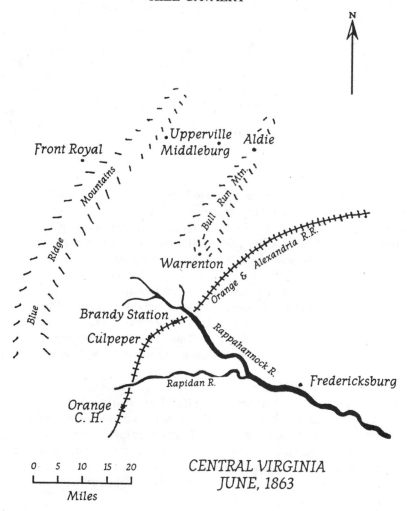

CENTRAL VIRGINIA
JUNE, 1863

up this buffer, he ordered Pleasonton to probe the Rebel front to find out what was going on behind their line. The Northern horsemen would have to be at full strength for this operation, so Kilpatrick was recalled from Gloucester Point. His return through Southern territory was to be conducted as a raid. "Make your march tell!" Hooker advised.[4]

Kilpatrick, leading about eight hundred troops of the Second New York and Twelfth Illinois, headed out of Gloucester Point on 31 May. He rode slowly through Gloucester County, gathering supplies without incident, but upon reaching Saluda, he found that the span over the Dragon River had been burned by the Rebels. "Colonel Kilpatrick was prepared for just such an emergency," an admiring reporter, accompanying the force, stated, "and his pioneers without any unnecessary delay constructed a bridge."[5] Kilpatrick could have continued up stream to the next ford, but he suspected that the enemy was laying in wait for him there, so he crossed at Saluda. When all in his command were on the far shore, he torched the new span, then hurried northeast toward Urbana. He arrived that night.

KILPATRICK'S ROUTE
TO URBANA
MAY 31 - JUNE 2, 1863

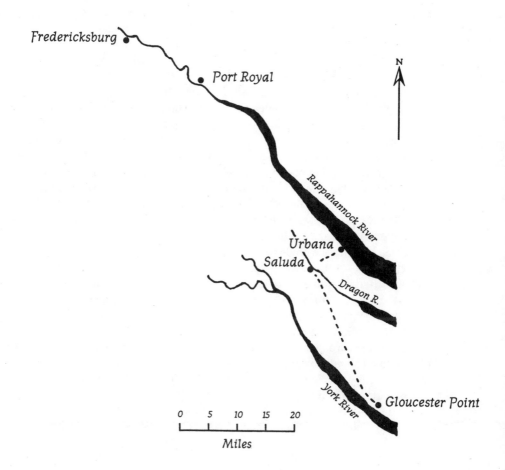

A fleet of ships greeted him: ferries to tote his men over the Rappahannock and gunboats to protect his troops while they crossed. Hooker had even provided an infantry regiment (the Ninety-Fourth New York) to assist in the operation.

Kilpatrick's brigade began boarding the *Long Branch, Star, William W. Frazier,* and *Tallacai* about 9:00 A.M. on 1 June. Twenty-four hours later, all of his men, forty wagons filled with provisions, two hundred extra horses and mules, and about a thousand former slaves had crossed safely to the northern banks of the Rappahannock River. "[It was] one of the most remarkable events of the war," a newsman reported in his article describing Kilpatrick's foray through unoccupied enemy territory.[6]

Kilpatrick started northwest for Falmouth the next day. When he arrived, he resumed command of his old brigade, which was made up of the Second and Tenth New York plus the First Maine regiments.[7] On the night of 7 June, Kilpatrick entertained a number of his officers in his tent. After several hours of recounting the scenes and incidents of their recent raid, he suggested it was time for all to go to bed. "Better turn in early, boys," he said with a grin. "Get as much sleep . . . as possible [because tomorrow] we beard the lion in his den."[8]

Hooker was planning to assault the Confederate cavalry in their camps near Culpeper. He feared that Jeb Stuart was about to raid his line of communications and supply, and he was determined to stop the Rebels in their tracks.[9]

"Disperse and destroy the rebel force assembled in the vicinity of Culpeper," Hooker told Pleasonton. "Destroy its trains and supplies. . . . If you should succeed in routing the enemy . . . follow them vigorously.[10] Pleasonton had sent orders to all his cavalry units to merge at Warrenton. He would launch his assault against the Rebel cavalry from this point, twenty miles above the fords along the Rappahannock that led to Culpeper and Jeb Stuart's camp. All arrived by the morning of 8 June.

Upon reaching the rendezvous, Kilpatrick's men began to hone their swords in preparation for the coming fight. Some were swayed, however, by a story that ran through camp that under the rules of war, any man found with a sharpened saber must be immediately executed. "[A few] susceptible youths," Noble Preston remembered, "proceeded to put an edge on their blades [that was] as dull as their comprehensions."[11]

The Union troopers left Warrenton at 2:00 P.M. on 8 June. Pleasonton's force totaled about eleven thousand men, including Buford's cavalry division (a regular army unit led by Major Charles Whiting plus the volunteer brigades of Colonels Benjamin F. Davis and Thomas Devin); Alfred Duffie's division (two brigades under Colonels Louis P. di Cesnola and J. Irwin Gregg); David Gregg's division (the brigades under Colonels Percy Wyndham and Kilpatrick);

two infantry brigades led by Generals Adelbert Ames and David A. Russell; plus five batteries of artillery.[12]

Pleasonton's plan of attack (actually conceived by Joe Hooker) was to divide his force at the Rappahannock. Gregg, Duffie, and Russell would move across the waters at Kelly's Ford; Buford and Ames would go upstream and utilize Beverly Ford. Once over the river, Gregg's Division (including Kilpatrick) and Russell would head northwest to Brandy Station, where they would unite with Buford to march on Culpeper and assault the Rebels. Duffie's troops would continue west to Stevensburg. When they reached that point, they would wheel right to charge Stuart's flank to catch the Confederates in a pincer.[13]

The marching infantry set the pace south, which was so slow that the command did not reach the area of Kelly's Ford until about 8:30 P.M. The troops knew that the Rebels were in force across the stream because they had seen the dust soaring ahead throughout that afternoon. Stuart's cavalry had been passing in review for Robert E. Lee.[14] The Federal soldiers hid in the forest above the ford that night, taking care to stay out of sight of the Rebel pickets that were patrolling along the stream. No fires were permitted. The men ate their dinner of cold pork and hardtack without coffee.[15] The horses were unsaddled, but they remained bridled, ready to ride at first light.

About 2:00 A.M. the men were wakened with whispers and told to get ready to go. Buford and Ames left first, moving north toward Beverly Ford about 3:00 A.M. They advanced though a heavy fog that clung to the wet, dripping trees. Duffie headed for Kelly's Ford about 3:30 A.M., trailed by Russell, Wyndham, and then Kilpatrick.[16]

Kilpatrick must have sensed that Pleasonton's plan had gone awry, as the ride seemed to take forever. The schedule called for arriving at the river by 4:30 A.M., but over two hours had passed without him seeing any sight of the stream. Duffie had taken the wrong way and become lost. He finally reached the ford about 6:00 A.M.[17] Three hours later, about 9:00 A.M., the last of Kilpatrick's troops splashed through the water and onto the far shore.

If Kilpatrick was upset by this delay, he was probably further agitated by the sounds of battle that boomed from upstream. Buford had crossed the river as ordered about 4:30 A.M. He had expected no resistance, because Stuart was assumed to be encamped at Culpeper, the point where the Union hoped to converge and close their pincer. But when he started his men forward, he immediately encountered the cavalry brigade of Rebel general William E. "Grumble" Jones in his path.[18]

Buford attacked the Confederates by sending the Eighth New York ahead along a narrow road, separated from the woods on each side by deep ditches. Davis, the brigade commander, led the charge. Although he scattered the enemy troopers in his way, Davis lost his life in the skirmish. A lone Rebel horseman, Lieutenant R. O. Allen, rode up, shot him in the head, then turned and galloped away before the Union troops could retaliate.[19]

Jones's encounter with the Union cavalry alerted Stuart to his impending danger, and the Rebel leader quickly set up a defensive line northeast of Brandy Station at the base of Fleetwood Hill. Jones assumed a position centered near St. James Church; General Wade Hampton put his troopers on the right along the Orange and Alexandria railroad tracks; General W. H. F. "Rooney" Lee located his men on Yew Ridge, left and in front of Jones.[20]

When Buford came up to the Rebel line, he saw that the position was too strong to be taken by a frontal attack. He countered by posting Ames's infantrymen in the forest across from the Confederate center, asking them to open a fire that would hold his adversary in place. He then ordered Devin's Brigade south to challenge Hampton while he personally moved the Reserve Brigade north to confront Rooney Lee, entrenched behind a stone wall.[21] Buford began to charge at 8:30 A.M.

The battle was marked by a difference in the arms used by the two adversaries. Most Federals wielded sabers during an attack; most Rebels preferred their pistols. "The only real use [for swords] I ever heard," Mosby wrote, reflecting the Confederate view, "was to hold a piece of meat over the fire for frying."[22] Although it might seem the Rebels held the advantage, their weapons were accurate only for short range—within a saber's slash.

Despite repeated charges by the bluecoats, followed by counterattacks by the Rebels, neither side was able to break the other's line. And after each assault, Buford must have looked left where he expected first Gregg and then Duffie to appear to roll up Stuart's flank. No Federal soldiers came into view.

The Yankee columns at Kelly's Ford had finally crossed the stream. Duffie had marched west toward Stevensburg, but when Gregg (and Kilpatrick) wheeled northwest on the way to join Buford, he found General Beverly Robertson's Rebel brigade standing in his path. Because of the crack of muskets and the roar of cannons to the north, Gregg knew that Buford was engaged and probably needed help. But instead of pushing through Robertson's blockade to get to Buford as quickly as possible, he ordered Russell's infantry to stay and hold the Confederates in place while he turned south, away from the battle, to ride around the Confederate line.[23]

Robertson was as timid as Gregg. He stood fast, allowing the Union cavalry to gallop off unimpeded, and he stayed in position throughout the rest of the day.[24]

Gregg led his columns to the Willis Madden house. The road divided at this point, one lane continuing ahead toward Stevensburg, the other turning north toward Brandy Station. Still following Pleasonton's plan, Duffie continued

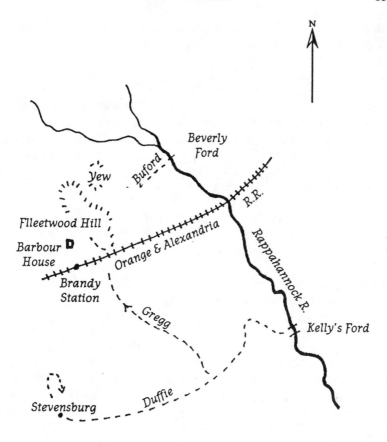

BATTLE AT BRANDY STATION
JUNE 9, 1863

his ride west. Gregg wheeled right and headed for the battle. Wyndham led the way, followed by Kilpatrick.[25]

When Gregg reached Brandy Station about 10:45 A.M., he found the area deserted. The battle was still raging to the right, but the fight was out of view, hidden by a low knoll (Fleetwood Hill) up ahead. Gregg decided to send Wyndham up the heights, to close the pincer on the Rebels. Kilpatrick would hold in reserve, concealing his regiments in the woods south of the railroad tracks.

Wyndham moved forward. Just as he reached the base of Fleetwood Hill, a lone cannon unlimbered on top of the slope and opened a slow fire against the advancing Federals. The threat (only solid shot) was petty, but Wyndham suspected an enemy trap. He thought that the Rebels were trying to lure him up the elevation, where he would be vulnerable to artillery hidden just behind the summit. He stopped, dismounted his troopers, and called his own guns to the front to answer the Confederate "barrage."[26]

The knoll, of course, was barren of both blue and gray troops; all (except those manning the lone gun) were involved in the fray to the north. Wyndham's hesitation gave Stuart just enough time to break off his engagement with Buford and rush both Jones and Hampton back to Fleetwood Hill to front the problem to his rear.[27] Buford could not follow the retiring Rebels because the ground between his line and the slope was still flanked by Lee, who had assumed a new post above Fleetwood Hill.[28]

When the solitary Rebel piece had shot its last shell, the gunners wheeled it off the knoll, out of sight. Wyndham belatedly realized that the Confederates had been bluffing. He could have galloped up the knoll without encountering any opposition. Quickly ordering his men to mount, Wyndham personally led the First New Jersey forward. As they closed on the crest, Jones's Twelfth Virginia approached the peak from the opposite side. They stormed into view, galloping toward the oncoming Northern ranks. The two foes clashed and all semblance of order was lost. The First Pennsylvania and the First Maryland joined the fray, as did the Thirty-Fifth and Sixth Virginia. The slope boiled with battle, every man for himself.[29]

"The dust was so thick," a member of the First Pennsylvania wrote, "we could not tell friend from foe."[30] Another trooper remembered the fight as "indescribable clashing and slashing, banging and yelling."[31]

Where was Kilpatrick? He was still in the glen, south of the railroad track, awaiting orders. When Gregg saw that Wyndham was struggling, he sent a rider to hurry Kilpatrick forward. The courier was slow to deliver his message due to a balky horse. Kilpatrick was then further delayed because, despite knowing that he would soon be called into battle, he had not aligned his brigade. Precious moments were lost as Kilpatrick hurriedly organized his troopers for an attack by echelon, starting on the left with the Tenth New York, next the Second New York in the center, and then the First Maine on the right. But before he could mount his charge, Wyndham had given up the fight and come down off Fleetwood Hill.[32]

The Tenth New York had barely started across the track when they were struck on the right flank by Cobb's Legion of the Confederacy, whose attack scattered the Federals. One of the squadrons was so shaken by the blow that they ran for the rear, rushing by Kilpatrick and continuing "in the greatest disorder" all the way to the Stevensburg Road.[33]

Riding parallel to their comrades, the Second New York galloped forward,

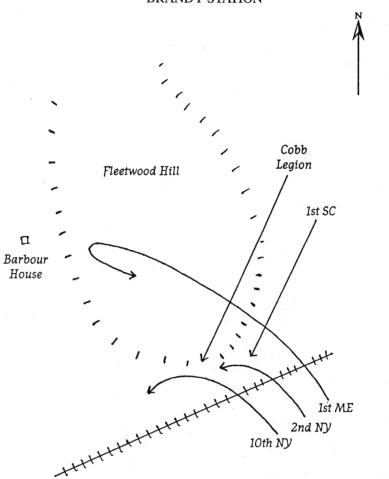

N

KILPATRICK'S CHARGES
BRANDY STATION

only to be hit in their right flank by the Rebel's First South Carolina. They too fled, "floating off like feathers on the wind."[34]

Kilpatrick was distraught at the sight of his troopers being driven so quickly from the field. "[His] excitement," Glazier wrote, "was well-nigh uncontrollable."[35] He turned to his third and last regiment. "Colonel Douty," Kilpatrick exclaimed, "What can you do . . . ?"

"I can drive the Rebels!" Douty shouted.[36]

"Go in and do it!"

Douty led the First Maine forward. Just as he reached the base of Fleetwood Hill, the Rebel cavalry who had routed the Second New York flashed past his front. His charge hit them on the flank, and they scattered, opening a path to the summit. "On [we rode]," Edward P. Tobie wrote, "faster and faster . . . over fences and ditches, driving the enemy. . . .Oh, it was grand!"[37] The First Maine galloped to the crest of the hill and then for a mile along the ridge, all the way to the Barbour House, where Robert E. Lee was watching the battle.[38] Douty halted at this point. The Rebels had closed ranks behind him. He was trapped in the Confederate rear.

Quickly reforming his regiment, Douty headed back the way he had come. The First Maine galloped through the Rebel troopers, fighting as they rode toward the forest where Kilpatrick was assembling the remnants of the Tenth and Second New York.

When Kilpatrick saw the First Maine coming through the Rebel ranks, he wheeled in the saddle and shouted to his two other regiments. "Back, the Harris Light! Back, the Tenth New York!" he cried. "Re-form your squadrons and charge!"[39] They surged up the hill into the melee. "From that moment," Kilpatrick related, "the fight was one series of . . . charging, rallying, and . . . charging until ordered to retire."[40]

Although Kilpatrick had been late to enter the contest, allowing the advantage that Wyndham had gained to slip away, his reputation was again saved by another officer whose performance was so feeble that he made everyone else look good.

As Duffie neared Stevensburg about 10:00 A.M., he found the enemy blocking his path. He charged their meager force and drove them back into and then northward out of the town. The Rebels re-formed above the village on the road to Brandy Station. After easily smashing through that line, manned by Colonel Mathew C. Butler's Second South Carolina, Duffie received desperate orders from Gregg to rush north, "retracing your steps."[41] Instead of following the short route to the fight (which his men had just cleared), Duffie retreated and galloped through Stevensburg and back to the intersection where Wyndham and Kilpatrick had veered toward Brandy Station. He left one of his six regiments in place to deal with Butler's troops. By the time Duffie finally reached the field (about 4:00 P.M.), the battle was over. Pleasonton was retreating.[42]

The Federals had made one last try at defeating Stuart before retiring. Buford, stymied by Rooney Lee's strong position north of Fleetwood Hill, decided to attempt a breakthrough to close the pincer on the Confederates. He assembled Ames's infantry and five regiments of cavalry to assault the Rebels ensconced on higher ground. The attack proved successful. Lee was driven out of his entrenchment. But before Buford could exploit his hard-won advantage, the Ninth Virginia launched a counterassault that pushed the Union back to their starting point. Buford charged again and regained the ground just lost, but was then repelled by an attack by the Second North Carolina and Tenth Virginia.[43]

It was enough. The Federals left the field about 3:00 P.M., trotting slowly rearward, daring the Rebels to follow them. Stuart, however, was content to let them go. He was too exhausted to pursue. Buford's troops crossed the Rappahannock River at Beverly Ford; Gregg (and Kilpatrick) rode over the railroad bridge just downstream.[44]

Pleasonton had sent eleven thousand troops into battle. Almost 9 percent became casualties, 608 being killed or wounded, 363 taken prisoner by the Confederates.[45] Although the losses were much fewer than those usually suffered by infantry in a major contest, they were sufficient to silence Hooker's oft-repeated sneer, "Who ever saw a dead cavalryman?"[46]

Kilpatrick's losses did not support a hero's role. He had only fifty men killed or wounded during the battle, less than half that suffered by each of the three brigades in Buford's command and only about two-thirds of Wyndham's total. And Kilpatrick had over one hundred men captured, more than any other brigade except for Whiting's regulars. Duffie, of course, had minimum casualties, and his numbers helped mask the verity that Kilpatrick had fought neither as hard nor as well as his compatriots.[47]

Pleasonton recognized that Kilpatrick had performed in only an adequate manner. In his official report, he cited a total of thirty-three officers for gallantry. Kilpatrick's name was not included on this list.[48]

To his men, however, Kilpatrick was a hero. They felt that he had done a fine job in leading them, and they showed their appreciation by sending a letter to President Lincoln, signed by seventy-six of the brigade's officers, asking that he be promoted to brigadier general. They based their plea primarily on his role during Stoneman's Raid, declaring that Kilpatrick had carried out the most "daring feat of the war, leading his command within, through, and out of the fortifications of Richmond."[49]

This letter probably influenced the president, because on 14 June 1863 Kilpatrick was raised in rank to brigadier general.[50] He was only twenty-seven years old.

Kilpatrick's lack of tactical skills was most apparent at Brandy Station. He watched the battle raging before his eyes, yet he did not form his troopers to join the fray. Thus when called forward, Kilpatrick was not ready. And when he did finally charge, he fed his force piecemeal into the contest. His feeble efforts possibly cost the Union a victory.

Kilpatrick's aversion to exposing himself to the peril of combat was equally obvious. He remained in the rear during the battle. Although a brigade commander was not expected to lead troops in action, Kilpatrick's counterparts were not restrained. Davis died at the van of his columns; Wyndham was wounded while leading his men in a charge against Fleetwood Hill; and Thomas Devin was cited for gallantry.

Another courageous man was Lieutenant Henry Meyer. He was in the thick of the fight and escaped with his life only because a Rebel's saber thrust caught a two-quart pail hung on his saddle, splitting the pot in two. Meyer had borrowed the bucket that morning from a friend. When he related his good fortune to the owner of the pail, he received a curious response. "How do you suppose," his comrade groused, "I am going to cook my coffee?"[51]

9

Aldie

When the Federal cavalry attacked Jeb Stuart at Brandy Station, they had no idea that two Rebel infantry corps, led by Generals Richard S. Ewell and James Longstreet, were sitting at Culpeper. Both were waiting for orders to move into the Shenandoah Valley, the first leg in their march to Pennsylvania. General A. P. Hill, now head of Lee's third corps, remained at Fredericksburg to confront Hooker's army.[1]

Stuart was surprised by Pleasonton's unexpected attack, but by first holding his ground, then driving the Union from the field, he prevented them from discovering that Lee's infantry was at hand. The secrecy that was essential to Lee's head start toward Pennsylvania was preserved. On 1 June, the day after Brandy Station, Lee started Ewell forward into the Valley.[2] The die was cast that would end at Gettysburg.

Hooker, of course, knew that Lee had pulled troops out of his line across from Fredericksburg and had sent them west, probably on their way to attack Washington. The dust raised by more than forty thousand marching men told the story. And although he could only guess at Lee's plan, Hooker saw that by abandoning their front, the Rebels had left a route to their capital open before him. "Will it not promote the . . . cause," he wrote to Lincoln, "for me to march to Richmond at once?"[3] He felt that an assault on the Southern city would force Lee to give up his campaign and remain in Virginia.

Lincoln disagreed. If Hooker advanced against Richmond, Lee might elect to take Washington. He likened the proposal to a chess gambit, swapping queens. "Lee's army . . . not Richmond, is your objective point," he stated. "Follow on his flank . . . shortening your lines while he lengthens his. Fight him, too, when the opportunity offers. If he stays where he is, fret him and fret him!"[4]

On 13 June Hooker started seven corps toward Manassas, intending to set up a defensive line, facing west, along the Orange and Alexandria railroad track. He soon learned, however, that he had moved too late. Ewell's corps was already down the Valley, and on 14 June they had charged General Robert H. Milroy and driven his garrison out of Winchester.[5]

Desperate to determine Lee's intentions, Hooker sent a letter to Pleasonton

on 17 June, ordering him to "put the main body of your command in the vicinity of Aldie, and push out reconnaissances. . . . [I] rely upon you . . . to give
[me] information [on] the enemy. . . . It is better that we . . . lose men than . . .
be without knowledge of the enemy."[6]

Pleasonton had just completed a reorganization of his corps, consolidating
his force into just two divisions under Buford and David Gregg. The latter's brigades were under J. Irvin Gregg, Kilpatrick, and John B. McIntosh. Kilpatrick's
command included the First Rhode Island, the Sixth Ohio, the Second and
Fourth New York, and the First Massachusetts.[7]

To carry out the order from Hooker, Pleasonton put his cavalry on the road
to Aldie, located on the northern rim of Bull Run Mountain. Kilpatrick led the
advance. He decided that he would split his force so he could approach the
enemy with a pincer. Duffie (demoted from division to regimental command)
would take the First Rhode Island over Thoroughfare Gap to Middleburg, then
turn east toward Aldie. Kilpatrick would push the rest of his brigade on a straight
line to the small village.[8] He left Manassas the morning of 17 June.

The road to Aldie divided at the village; one leg ran west toward Ashby's
Gap in the Blue Ridge, the other branch drifted northwest toward Snicker's
Gap. A low hill rose between the lanes.[9] The rolling country was strewn with
rocks, and the narrow byways were lined with walls of piled stones that rose
and fell in concert with the contours of the land.

Jeb Stuart's Southern cavalry was in force in the area. They were guarding
the flank of Lee's infantry, moving north through the Shenandoah Valley.
Longstreet's corps was waiting between Ashby's Gap and Snicker's Gap as
A. P. Hill's men trudged past them toward the Potomac River.[10] Ewell's corps
was posted at that stream, ready to cross into Maryland.

As Kilpatrick approached Aldie about 1:00 P.M. on 18 June, he studied the
village to look for signs of the enemy. The day was hot, so scorching that
already four soldiers in the Twentieth Maine, moving north to his rear, had
collapsed and died from sunstroke.[11] The tiny homes ahead shimmered in the
heat. Kilpatrick spotted movement. There were Rebel pickets milling in the
town! He whirled in the saddle, and without a second thought ordered a charge.[12]

Lieutenant Colonel Greely S. Curtis hurried the First Massachusetts forward. As the Rebel pickets fled up the road toward Snicker's Gap, the Union
troopers followed, those up front dismounting to perform as skirmishers. The
men to the rear remained on horseback.[13] Just as the regiment came up to a low
ridge crossing the road, the Federals saw that they had been lured into a trap.
Rebels hidden behind the stone wall atop a knoll just left of the lane rose up to
fire into their flank.

The Southern force that Kilpatrick was challenging was General Fitzhugh
Lee's cavalry brigade, led that day by Colonel Thomas Munford. He had five
regiments at hand, posted as follows: the First Virginia, supported by artillery,

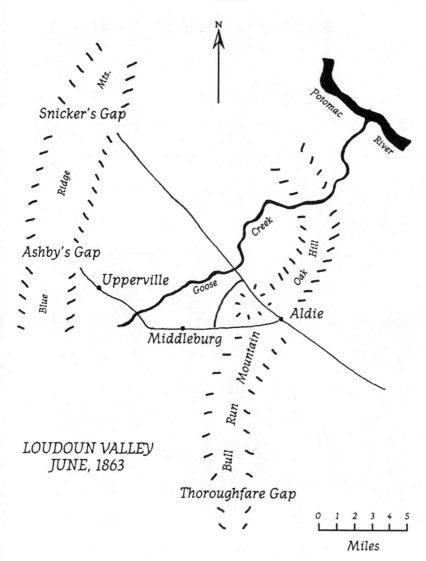

N

Snicker's Gap

Potomac

River

Mts.

Ridge

Ashby's Gap

Blue

Upperville

Creek

Oak Hill

Goose

Aldie

Middleburg

Mountain

LOUDOUN VALLEY
JUNE, 1863

Bull Run

Thoroughfare Gap

0 1 2 3 4 5

Miles

was positioned on the road to Middleburg; the Fourth and Fifth Virginia blocked
the route to Snicker's Gap; the Second and Third Virginia were in reserve, just
nearing the field.[14]

As the First Massachusetts whirled to face the fire of the Southerners on
their right, they opened their left flank to a charge by the Fourth Virginia,
storming from the south. "My poor men were just slaughtered," Charles Adams
recalled. "All we could do was stand still and be shot down."[15]

General James Ewell Brown "Jeb" Stuart. Courtesy of the Library of Congress.

Kilpatrick, seeing the disaster unfold, called for the Fourth New York to rush forward to support the reeling First Massachusetts. They advanced without their leader, Colonel Louis di Cesnola, who had been arrested on a minor charge by Kilpatrick that morning. Di Cesnola came to Kilpatrick and asked to be released from detention so he could join his men in their charge. Kilpatrick reached for his scabbard, withdrew his own sword, and handed it to di Cesnola. "Bring it back bloody!" he growled.[16]

Di Cesnola caught up with his troops and took them up the Snicker's Gap

Road. They soon met remnants of the First Massachusetts, who were fleeing in terror toward the Yankee line. Di Cesnola pushed through the bloodied ranks, but the men trailing him halted, then wheeled to join the First Massachusetts in their rush to the rear. Di Cesnola, with just his color guard, roared up to the Rebel position, turned to wave his force forward, and only then saw that he was alone. Before he could surrender Kilpatrick's sword, di Cesnola was shot, adding injury to his embarrassing capture.[17]

At the same time that di Cesnola began his ill-starred charge, Kilpatrick was mounting an attack on his left, along the road toward Ashby's Gap. He called the Second New York forward, gave them a fiery speech that recalled their rebuff at Brandy Station, declared that now was the time to redeem their lost reputation, and urged them into mounting a fierce assault. They rushed ahead, but soon found, like the First Massachusetts, that Kilpatrick had sent them into an ambush.[18]

When Thomas Rosser moved his cavalry north to face Kilpatrick's initial attack, he left a company of sharpshooters under Captain R. B. Boston behind in a deep ditch, perpendicular to the Middleburg Road. They lay hidden behind a group of haystacks. They remained out of sight until the Yankee troopers galloped in view, then rose to open a savage cross fire that ravaged the Union regiment's ranks.[19]

When the Sixth Ohio, trailing the Second New York, saw their comrades in peril, they wheeled right and flanked the bushwhackers.[20] They captured the whole band, but when they attempted to further their advance, they found the Confederates in strength up ahead, and so they stopped and assumed a defensive position.

Kilpatrick was unnerved by this failure to shatter the Southern line, a disaster of his own making. He had managed the battle badly, feeding regiments piecemeal into the fray, taking unwarranted losses in a futile effort. "His moistened features were covered with dust," Tobie said in his memoirs. "His countenance was dejected and sad, the fire . . . of his eye was gone, and he looked indeed 'a ruined man.'"[21]

Union reinforcements, however, were now at hand. About 4:00 P.M., the first of Irvin Gregg's troopers, who had been following in column, arrived at Aldie.[22]

"What regiment is this?" Kilpatrick asked dully.

"The First Maine!" shouted a dozen throats.

They had saved him at Brandy Station. Kilpatrick knew that they would salvage Aldie, too.

"The response was electric," Tobie stated. "We saw. . . his countenance brighten to a smile, his eyes flash, and his whole frame fill with enthusiasm."

"Forward First Maine!" he shouted. "Follow me!"[23]

Kilpatrick led a charge up the Snicker's Gap Road, his initial exposure to the risk of combat in the Civil War. At the onset of the attack, however, his horse was killed, and he was not at hand when the First Maine drove the Fourth and Fifth Virginia back to their starting line.[24]

Filled with success, Kilpatrick decided to assault the Confederates one more time, and drive Stuart from the field. He assembled the First Maine and the Second New York on the Snicker's Gap Road and gestured toward the Rebels ensconced behind the stone walls up ahead. "There is the opportunity you have asked for," he shouted. "Go! Take that position!"[25]

A series of attacks just before dark forced the Rebels to withdraw to the west. During the final assaults, Colonel Douty, the First Maine commander, was killed.[26] Kilpatrick brought his troops back to Aldie for the night.

"Kilpatrick has done remarkably well," Pleasonton said in his official report on the battle.[27] He was impressed by Kilpatrick's ferocious style, throwing his force heedlessly against the enemy without pause or plan. Hooker had said, "[L]ose men," and "Kill-Cavalry" had complied. His casualties for the day exceeded three hundred men, twice the number he lost at Brandy Station. And two of his five regimental commanders were gone, one dead, the other in enemy hands.[28]

Many were appalled by the inexcusable carnage suffered by Kilpatrick's troops. "I have never seen as many Yankees killed," Munford stated, "in the same space of ground in any fight I have ever seen."[29]

A Union officer challenged Kilpatrick to his face. "I see plenty of your dead," Abner Hard jeered in despair, "but few rebels!"[30]

Pleasonton did not note in his report that nothing had been gained by Kilpatrick from these huge losses. His objective in committing to battle was to break past the Rebel line and determine where Lee had located his infantry. He had failed to do so. In fact he had not even driven the enemy from the field. Munford was guarding Ashby's Gap, not Aldie, and having accomplished that mission, he withdrew instead of continuing to fight for no purpose [31]

And Kilpatrick's losses were not limited to the action at Aldie. He had sent Duffie to Middleburg, where the chief of the First Rhode Island found himself facing superior numbers of Confederates. Rather than prudently withdrawing his regiment, he took up a defensive position, then sent one of his aides to Aldie to request help from Kilpatrick.

Captain Frank Allen left Middleburg about 5:00 P.M. on 17 June. "I found the fields and woods in every direction full of bodies of the enemy," he said, "[but] by exercising the greatest care . . . reached Aldie, and delivered my dispatch to General Kilpatrick at 9:00 P.M."[32]

Kilpatrick had no interest in hurrying to the aid of a comrade whom he had placed in jeopardy. "[My] brigade is so worn out," he replied, "I cannot send any reinforcements to Middleburg."[33] He referred the matter to Gregg, who gave it to Pleasonton, both of whom also refused to send Duffie any help.

He was left on his own to find his way out of danger. The Rebels attacked Duffie about 7:00 P.M. He held on tenaciously, and at 10:00 P.M. he sent another aide to Aldie to beg help from Kilpatrick. None came. By 3:30 A.M., with no assistance in sight, Duffie realized that his only chance to survive was to blast a path through the Rebels. "My command was in a most hazardous position," he wrote, "the enemy being in front, rear, and on both flanks."[34]

Duffie headed for Aldie, fighting for every foot along the way. He finally arrived about 1:30 P.M. the next day, a demoralized leader with only "the gallant debris of my much-loved regiment—4 officers and 27 men."[35] He had started the campaign with 275 troopers.

Had Duffie remained at Middleburg, more men might have been saved because Gregg had taken his troopers to the town that morning. His objective, however, was not to rescue the First Rhode Island, but to learn if the Confederate cavalry still occupied Loudoun Valley. Gregg found Southern pickets in the village. After driving them westward, he retired to establish camp halfway between Middleburg and Aldie, where he waited that night for further orders.[36]

Kilpatrick spent the day at Aldie, where his men rested and recuperated from yesterday's fight. Most sought shelter because it was so warm, "98° Fahrenheit in the shade . . . 122° in the sun," according to Glazier.[37] On 19 June Pleasonton attacked the Confederates with Gregg's brigade. He pushed the Rebels, who had come back to Middleburg, west about a mile to a deep forest that flanked both sides of the road to Ashby's Gap. The Rebels halted at this spot to offer battle. Stuart had three brigades ready to face the Yankees, those assigned to Rooney Lee, Fitz Lee, and Robertson.[38]

Gregg charged the Confederates, crouching behind stone walls. The First Maine carried the line to the left, but on the right, the Sixteenth and Fourth Pennsylvania were unable to dislodge the enemy. The First Maine stood exposed, their flank inviting attack. "I feared for a moment," Gregg said, "we would be repulsed."[39] The Tenth New York, however, rode up on the right, and their furious assault pushed Stuart out of the woods and into the open fields beyond the trees.

The Federals advanced against the Rebel's new position, but their attack was thrown back. Stuart then charged Gregg in the forest, but he, too, was repelled.[40] Both sides had had enough. The battle ended with the Confederates still in control of Ashby's Gap. Pleasonton still did not know if Lee's infantry was moving north.

Kilpatrick was there, but his troopers did no fighting. Only the Sixth Ohio was engaged, and they spent their day in reserve, standing guard for an artillery battery.[41] Despite seeing no action, however, Kilpatrick seems to have told friends that he had performed gallantly in battle. That lie circulated throughout the camps, and as a result, a few were deluded into believing that he was "The Hero of Middleburg."[42]

Late that afternoon a strong wind started to blow, and soon sheets of rain were stinging the men. The fierce storm continued into the night and all through the next day. The troops on both sides welcomed the cool breeze and the chance to rest up for the next battle.[43]

Pleasonton used the respite to write Hooker and report what he had learned from his encounters with the Rebels. He only knew that the enemy had no infantry on his side of the Blue Ridge. He was willing to speculate, however, and Pleasonton offered his opinion that the South had gone into the Valley to draw the Federals away from Richmond so they could safely send troops west to break up Grant's siege along the Mississippi River. The Rebels were not planning an invasion of the North. "The entire movement of Lee's," he professed, "has been with the object of getting off reinforcements from his army to Vicksburg."[44] To prove this assumption, he had to penetrate Stuart's screen, a feat he felt impossible with just his cavalry. "They have all the gaps . . . well guarded," Pleasonton noted. "To face them will require infantry."[45]

Hooker quickly dispatched the foot soldiers, diverting the infantry division under General James Barnes west toward Pleasonton's camp. He also sent advice. "Make your attack in front with a very small force," he said, "and [then] turn the enemy's position with your main body."[46]

Barnes's Division arrived the evening of 20 June. The next morning, about 7:00 A.M., Pleasonton headed west. Just before reaching Middleburg, he divided his command. Buford rode north to try and turn the Rebels' left flank;[47] Gregg, Kilpatrick, and Colonel Strong Vincent's infantry moved down the road toward Upperville and Ashby's Gap. Upon encountering Rebel pickets at Middleburg, Pleasonton attacked with an unusual tactic, a variation of the approach that Hooker had suggested. He ordered three of Vincent's infantry regiments ahead to assault the enemy's line (held by Hampton's and Robertson's troopers) while the fourth circled left to flank the Confederate position. Stuart was forced to withdraw, and when he began his retreat, Kilpatrick's cavalry galloped up the pike to speed the Rebels' backward flight.[48]

"The charges of the cavalry," Vincent wrote "were truly inspiring . . . squadron after squadron hurled the enemy in his flight. . . . [I had] a feeling of regret that we, too, were not mounted and could not join in the chase."[49]

Stuart fell back to Crummer's Run, but a repetition of Pleasonton's strategy soon dislodged the Confederates. They withdrew to Goose Creek, where they took up a new line east of the stream. Pleasonton charged again, using the infantry to flank the Rebels, who were once more routed. They tried to destroy the stone bridge over Goose Creek, but Kilpatrick was too quick for them. He sent the Second New York across the span before the enemy could set their charges.[50]

No real fighting took place throughout the morning and into the afternoon as the Rebels retreated instead of facing up to the ever-pressing Yankees. But upon their arrival at Upperville about 4:00 P.M., the Confederates decided to make a stand. Pleasonton saw that Vincent's infantrymen were exhausted, unable to continue their flanking ploy, so he asked Kilpatrick to drive the enemy out of the small town. Twice Judson sent regiments galloping into the village. They were repulsed both times.[51]

Kilpatrick rode at the head of the Fourth New York during the first charge. He was left behind, a prisoner of the enemy, when his men retired from the town. Fortunately for Kilpatrick, the second Yankee assault was soon underway, and he escaped from his captors and rejoined his troopers as they fled the field.[52]

"If I had the First Maine," Kilpatrick complained when reporting his failure to Pleasonton, "they would go through. [They] would charge straight into hell if . . . ordered to."[53]

Gregg's regiments had spent the day in reserve, but in response to Kilpatrick's plea, Pleasonton summoned the First Maine to the front. They assembled east of Upperville. As they waited for their order to advance, Kilpatrick turned to one of the officers, renowned for his musical ability. "Do you sing any songs now?" he jeered, a heartless comment considering that he was about to send that man into battle and possibly to his death. When he gave the command, "Forward!" Kilpatrick added, "I will go [back to] the remainder of the regiment [where I can] support you."[54] The First Maine rode into Upperville and drove the Rebels out of the village to the hills to the west.

Deciding that the time was ripe to settle affairs, Kilpatrick gathered his troopers for a full-scale attack on the Confederates. The Sixth Ohio, the Fourth Pennsylvania, the Second and Tenth New York, and the First Maine moved forward out of Upperville toward the Rebels. Kilpatrick again rode at the head of his columns, leading his men into yet another trap. The Rebels had hidden sharpshooters in the shrubbery alongside the road. "The two forces swayed to and fro under a galling cross-fire," a reporter wrote. "The officers and men on both sides fought like fiends, and in the excitement, many of the enemy were killed who might have been taken prisoner."[55] Kilpatrick was thrown back, but when the Southern cavalry launched a counterattack, he repulsed their charge. He had prudently hidden his own bushwhackers along the lane.[56]

Buford had returned just before Kilpatrick started his charges. The attempt to turn the Confederate left flank had failed. As fast as Buford maneuvered north, the Rebels had extended their line, and he could not get around them. When he saw that Kilpatrick was engaged, Buford tried to join in that contest, but "ran afoul of . . . ditches and stone fences" that kept him from reaching Kilpatrick's side.[57]

When the sun slipped below the soaring peaks to the west, the fray ebbed and then ended. Stuart retired into Ashby's Gap. "Give me the Tenth New York and the First Maine," Kilpatrick begged, "and I'll charge the gap!"[58] But

Pleasonton turned down his plea. There was no need for any more fighting. He had finally uncovered Lee's plan. Runaway slaves had told him that Ewell's Corps had reached the Potomac River and had started to cross into Maryland. Lee was not dispatching reinforcements toward Vicksburg—he was invading the North![59]

"I . . . return . . . to Aldie," Pleasonton reported to Hooker. "My command has been fighting . . . constantly for four days. . . . [We] must have a day or two to rest."[60]

Kilpatrick's troopers needed the respite more than any others. Despite not seeing any real action until late in the afternoon, "Kill-Cavalry" again had taken inordinate losses. Seventy-three men under his leadership had fallen during the battle. Vincent lost only twenty-one of his infantry in the repeated charging and flanking of the Rebel lines.[61]

While Pleasonton's men rested near Aldie, the Southern force raced north. Lee's whole army (excepting the cavalry) had crossed over the Potomac by 27 June. They spread out like a huge fan into Maryland and southeastern Pennsylvania, confiscating supplies from the farms and villages for their hungry and ragged troops. Citizens of the North were panic-stricken that they would next be victimized by the voracious Rebels.[62]

Hooker followed after the Rebels, but he lagged behind the pace set by Lee by two days. If he was to catch up with the Confederates, Hooker had to know their disposition, and so he sent his cavalry north toward Gettysburg, "to see what they can of the movements of the enemy."[63] Other desperate measures by Hooker included two requests of Washington: the transfer of the thirty-five hundred-man cavalry division under General Julius Stahel, currently assigned to the defense of the capital, to his command; and the release of the ten thousand-man infantry garrison at Harper's Ferry to the Army of the Potomac. "They are but a bait for the Rebels," he said about the latter.[64]

Lincoln agreed to give Hooker the cavalry division led by Stahel, and the troopers moved immediately for Frederick, Maryland.[65] But the president would not give up protecting Harper's Ferry. The garrison must stay in position. Hooker was so upset by this rebuff, he offered to resign. "I am unable to comply with this condition," he said stiffly, "and earnestly request that I may at once be relieved."[66]

Hooker's resignation was quickly accepted, and General George G. Meade was named as the new head of the Army of the Potomac. Meade was born in Cadiz, Spain. His father was a businessman who, because of financial difficulties, sent his family back to the United States when George was yet a baby. He was an 1835 graduate of West Point, began his military career as a civil engineer in charge of designing lighthouses for the Atlantic Coast, earned a brevet promotion during the Mexican War, then returned to his lighthouse career until the start of the Civil War. He had been involved in most of the major battles,

General George C. Meade. Courtesy of the Library of Congress.

had been wounded during the Seven Days, and was in charge of the Fifth Corps at the time he relieved Hooker.[67]

Meade made striking changes in the cavalry immediately after taking command. The most notable was naming Kilpatrick to replace Stahel as head of the Third Division, a position worth two stars signifying a major general. Stahel, while a decent officer, was unfit for leading troopers in the field. Instead of galloping at the van of his force, he rode behind in "a covered spring wagon, drawn by four white mules."[68]

On 27 June 1863 Kilpatrick started his ride north to Frederick to take charge of his division. His promotion was largely due to the fact that Pleasonton thought that he had performed well during the recent campaign. "I especially commend Brigadier General Kilpatrick," he stated in his report, "for [his] gallant zeal and efficiency."[69] He also believed that Kilpatrick fit the ideal mold of a leader. "[An officer] is like an actor on the stage," the cavalry chief said. "With the dramatist's gift, he [retains] the attention of his men, [making] every soldier feel himself [the] hero of the play, [who then] forgets his fears and charges recklessly."[70] It was an exact description of the former West Point thespian, Judson Kilpatrick!

For the first time in the war, during the skirmishes at Aldie and Upperville, Kilpatrick showed personal bravery. He rode at the front of his ranks when they charged a formidable enemy. These assaults were foolhardy, resulting in the unnecessary slaughter of his men, but Kilpatrick shared the peril; he lost his horse in one encounter and was taken prisoner during another charge. He had finally "seen the elephant," as soldiers describe battle.

Kilpatrick would utilize this one-time, brief exposure to the risks of combat for his advantage throughout the war. Although he would never again lead troops in to battle, he made so many references to having done so (once), his compatriots came to accept that he was really intrepid. Kilpatrick was an actor, playing a hero's role, and he successfully created a myth that was greater than the man.

10

Gettysburg

When Kilpatrick arrived at Frederick, Maryland, on 28 June 1863 to assume division command, he was no doubt shocked when he considered the officers just promoted to head his two brigades. Both men were young and relatively inexperienced. Prior to receiving a general's star, each had held the rank of captain. They had accomplished in one day what had taken Kilpatrick almost two years to achieve.

Elon J. Farnsworth, twenty-five years old, was head of the First Brigade, including the First Vermont, Fifth New York, First West Virginia, and Eighteenth Pennsylvania regiments.[1] He was a native of Green Oak, Michigan, had gone to college but never graduated, and had a meager military background. He accompanied Albert Sidney Johnston as a civilian foragemaster on his Mormon expedition in 1858; then when the Civil War started, he joined the Eighth Illinois as an aide to the regimental chief, his uncle, John F. Farnsworth. He had most recently served on Pleasonton's staff, but had done nothing significant to warrant his new rank. "Nature made him a general" was how Pleasonton explained his curious choice of Farnsworth as one of Kilpatrick's brigade leaders.[2]

Although Farnsworth was a relative stranger to Kilpatrick, the officer promoted to head the Second Brigade was a friend from West Point. George Armstrong Custer, also a native of Michigan, was an equally odd selection to don the stars of a general. He had been an abject failure at the U.S. Military Academy. He ranked last in his class, graduating just after Kilpatrick's group, and had been involved in a number of escapades, each of which threatened his expulsion from school. His frolics linked to "loose women" had often included Kilpatrick.[3]

Custer, however, had distinguished himself in the war. While serving as an aide to McClellan and Pleasonton, he had demonstrated bravery and resourcefulness during the battles of the Seven Days, Antietam, and Chancellorsville.[4] He would prove to be a daring, adroit commander for the First, Fifth, Sixth, and Seventh Michigan cavalry regiments.

With Lee's forces advancing rapidly into Pennsylvania, their exact positions

Union general Elon J. Farnsworth, from *Battles and Leaders of the Civil War,*
edited by Clarence C. Buel and Robert U. Johnson. 4 vols. New York: The
Century Company, 1887–88.

unknown, Meade was desperate to obtain intelligence on the Confederates'
operations. He turned to the cavalry for help. "Protect well the front and flanks
of this army," he related to Pleasonton.[5] "It is of utmost importance . . . [I]
receive reliable information of the presence of the enemy, his forces and his
movements."[6]

General George Armstrong Custer. Courtesy of the Library of Congress.

Pleasonton rushed his troopers northward, sending them like a wave toward Pennsylvania. Buford rode along the left flank, Gregg covered the right, and Kilpatrick held the center.[7] Kilpatrick's division rode northeast out of Frederick, Maryland, the morning of 29 June 1863. Custer's Brigade was in the lead; Farnsworth brought up the rear. After an all-day gallop of almost forty miles, the Yankee columns crossed into Pennsylvania. They camped at Littlesville that night. Although the men were exhausted, their faces burned by a torrid sun, their throats choked by dust that had billowed up from the road, they had enjoyed their jaunt. "Getting out of old Virginia was like getting out of a graveyard into Paradise," one remembered. "We were welcomed all the way, the citizens met us with bread, milk, butter, and all kinds of fruit, and bade us Godspeed on our way."[8]

The troops rose early on 30 June and before sunrise were already started on the road toward Hanover. Kilpatrick led the parade, followed by Custer's men, then Farnsworth's regiments. The van rode into Hanover about 8:00 A.M., where Kilpatrick was greeted with sighs of relief by the populace. "Our town is now safe," Reverend William K. Zieber announced loudly.[9] He explained to Kilpatrick, resting awhile at the Jacob Wirt home, that three days ago a Confederate column of cavalry had entered Hanover, confiscated supplies, and then galloped northeast toward York, probably to unite with Rebel general Jubal A. Early's infantry division. This was important news to Kilpatrick, who was headed for York.

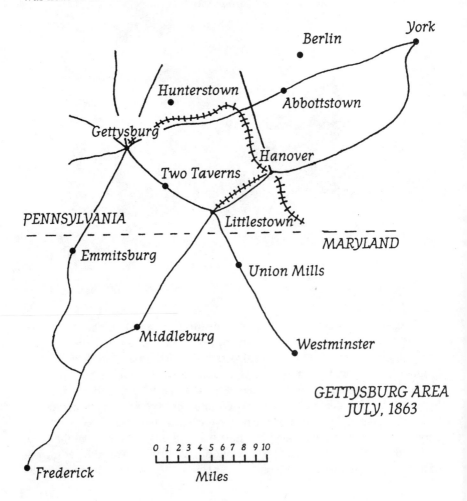

GETTYSBURG AREA
JULY, 1863

0 1 2 3 4 5 6 7 8 9 10

Miles

After a breakfast feast supplied by the ladies of Hanover, Kilpatrick rode out of town and headed northeast toward York. He was serenaded by a choir of pretty girls, singing patriotic songs, as he and his staff moved past the Lutheran Church parsonage.[10]

Custer's Brigade poured into Hanover as Kilpatrick was leaving, and his troopers were welcomed with the same hearty treatment granted Kilpatrick. He left town about 9:00 A.M., and then it was Farnsworth's turn to be feted.

As he rode northeast, Kilpatrick's total attention was on York, where he expected to find Early. He felt safe. He had Buford protecting his left, Gregg on his right—and he had no idea that the enemy might be in his rear.[11] But that was exactly where Jeb Stuart was located, and he was closing on Kilpatrick's column.

Stuart had been ordered by Robert E. Lee to come north into Pennsylvania to provide a screen for Ewell's Corps. He was given a choice of routes: he could cross over the Blue Ridge and then ride along the western edge of the mountains, keeping out of sight of the Yankees and in close touch with the Confederate army; or he could slip through the gaps between the Union corps (camped along a twenty-five mile line from Thoroughfare Gap to Leesburg), turn north to advance between the Northern force and Washington, and then come west past the head of the Federal army to join Ewell. The latter path was more risky, because Stuart's troopers would be isolated from the rest of the Rebels. It was also, however, the more glamorous gambit. Stuart's presence between the Union army and their capital was sure to panic the city. He found that idea so tempting that he could not resist taking the chance. At 1:00 A.M. on 25 June, Stuart moved east with his three best brigades, those led by John R. Chambliss, Hampton, and Fitz Lee.[12]

Stuart slipped past the Federals as planned. But when he turned north, Stuart encountered a problem. He had based his movement on the assumption that Hooker's corps would remain stationary. They had, however, begun to advance toward Pennsylvania, and Stuart found that he could not get around the head of the Union army. He remained to their right, unable to break through to get to Ewell.[13]

The night of 29 June, Stuart's five thousand men had encamped at Union Mills, undetected by Kilpatrick, who spent the evening at Littlesville, just seven miles away. At sunrise Stuart started north, and he arrived at Hanover just as Farnsworth's troops were leaving. Chambliss's troopers were in the lead, and they immediately charged the trailing Union column, the Eighteenth Pennsylvania.[14]

The Thirteenth Virginia attacked the Yankee tail below the town; the Second North Carolina raced through the side streets of Hanover and into the square to batter the flanks of the Eighteenth Pennsylvania. The Federal cavalrymen, who only moments ago had been eating a sumptuous breakfast, saw their ranks split in two. They scattered in every direction to escape the Rebel onslaught.[15] Below the village, Stuart prepared for battle. He unlimbered his artillery on Rice's Hill, near the Keller farm, and opened fire on the Union columns that were riding northeast above Hanover.[16]

Farnsworth's response was just as fast. He turned his troopers around and charged back toward the town. The Fifth New York led the way, followed by the First Vermont and the First West Virginia. The Southern Second North Carolina was overwhelmed and driven southwest, out of the village, where they met the rest of Chambliss's brigade near the Karl Forney farm. They stopped there and made a stand. Dead men and horses, both Union and Rebel, were left strewn up and down the streets of Hanover.[17]

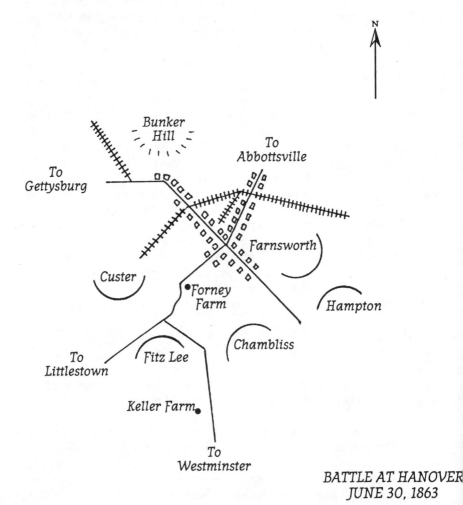

BATTLE AT HANOVER
JUNE 30, 1863

"Please go to [your] homes and into [your] cellars," a Northern horseman cried to the local populace as he galloped back into the square after the Rebels' rout. "In a few minutes there will be [more] fighting in your streets!"[18]

Neither adversary, however, was anxious to take the initiative. Other than the spirited skirmishing near Forney's farm, both foes were setting up their defensive lines. The Confederates entrenched below Hanover, with Fitz Lee's force moving up on the left of Chambliss, and later Hampton's brigade assumed the right. Farnsworth positioned his regiments in a line through Hanover, with the Eighteenth Pennsylvania, Fifth New York, First West Virginia, and First Vermont fixed west to east.[19]

Kilpatrick was riding at the front of his columns when the battle began. When his men whirled about to hurry back to Hanover, he suddenly found himself in the rear, the furthermost post from the fighting. He raced toward the village at a gallop, whipping, spurring, and cursing his mount to move faster. When he finally arrived just about noon, Kilpatrick leaped off his blowing horse and ran into the Central Hotel on the town square, where he would direct affairs. His poor mount collapsed in place, and an hour or so later, lay dead from exhaustion.[20]

In prior battles, Kilpatrick had ordered a charge when he first spotted the enemy. At Hanover, however, he was not there when the fighting began, and as a result, his men had assumed a defensive position. Kilpatrick made a few changes in their posting, such as sending Custer's brigade to the right and below the town to protect the flank, but accepted the stalemate that had evolved. His artillery answered the Southern barrage from below the village. And while his guns bellowed from Bunker Hill above Hanover, Kilpatrick moved quickly to block any Rebel charge into the town. "Store boxes, wagons, hay ladders, fence rails, barrels, bar iron," an observer enumerated, "[were stacked] to prevent the enemy from dashing through the town."[21]

About 2:00 P.M. the artillery duel ebbed, but both the Union and Rebels held to their defensive positions. Perhaps Stuart envisioned a turning movement to his left, but if he had thought of doing so, his men would have quickly objected to an attack. Custer's dismounted troops were armed with a new weapon, the seven-shot Spencer rifle, which gave them an advantage equal to double their force.[22]

The impasse lasted past sunset, and in the dark of the night, about 10:00 P.M., Stuart moved east, circling Hanover to get around Kilpatrick, moving away from Lee's army, which was descending on Gettysburg.[23]

Meade, too, was marching for Gettysburg, and the next morning, the two foes met in violent combat. Toward the end of that historic day, Lee's men pushed the Federals through the village and onto an elevation south of Gettysburg called "Cemetery Hill." Although Lee's victory was resounding, it proved barren, because Stuart's cavalry was not there to mop up. Kilpatrick's stand at Hanover had kept the Rebel horsemen away from the battle.

Kilpatrick, of course, was not aware at that time that blocking Stuart at Hanover would be such an important factor in the Union's ultimate victory at Gettysburg. Later, when he filed his report on the affair, he knew that his role had been critical, and Kilpatrick could not resist embellishing his success. "Ere the shout of the rebel charge had ceased to ring through the quiet street . . . [we] with a rush and blow struck the rebel hosts in full charge," he wrote in flowery prose. "Our troops . . . met the foe in close contact, but [we] were on [our] own free soil; fair hands, regardless of the dangerous strife, waved them [onward] . . . bright, tearful eyes looked pleadingly out from every window. . . . One great effort, and the day was won. [Our] foe . . . had for the first and last time polluted with his presence the loyal town of Hanover."[24]

In the battle, Kilpatrick, even though he had not been there at the start to waste men, suffered greater casualties than Stuart. The Union losses totaled 215; the Rebels saw only 117 fall in the fight.[25]

When the sun rose on 1 July, Kilpatrick headed north, looking to intercept Stuart. He directed the march lying in a wagon, stretched out on his back. The wild gallop of yesterday that had killed his horse had so bruised Kilpatrick's kidneys that he was suffering excruciating pain, unable to mount or ride. He had had the same problem after the battles near Aldie, the first sign of Bright's disease, which would eventually end his life.[26]

The movement was timid. Kilpatrick had given Stuart a ten-hour head start, so he had little chance of catching the Rebels. He could hear the din of battle to the west (where first A. P. Hill and then Ewell attacked the Yankee corps led by Generals John F. Reynolds and Oliver Howard). Kilpatrick's orders gave him the discretion to hurry to the aid of his infantry comrades, but he opted to continue chasing the elusive Rebel cavalry instead of joining the fight. He rode northeast through Berlin, then camped for the night.[27]

On 2 July Kilpatrick received orders to come west to Gettysburg to guard the Federal flank northeast of the town. He rode slowly, and about 4:00 P.M. finally approached his assigned post near Hunterstown. Farnsworth, who was leading the column, reported Rebel pickets up ahead in the village.[28]

Kilpatrick halted a mile short of Hunterstown and prepared to fight. He unlimbered his artillery along the road and sent some skirmishers forward to probe the front. The dismounted troopers spread out, advanced into the town, and drove the Southerners (members of Hampton's brigade) southwest toward Gettysburg. Kilpatrick, upon hearing that the village was now in Yankee hands, rushed into Hunterstown to install a command headquarters in the Grass Hotel.[29] Five roads spread west out of Hunterstown, like the fingers on a hand, and Kilpatrick sent pickets down each to find the enemy. Custer discovered Hampton drawn up on the Brinkerhoff Ridge a mile southeast of the village. "The woods," he reported, "[are] swarming with Rebels."[30]

Kilpatrick decided to attack. His plan of battle had Custer leading a charge down the Gettysburg road toward the enemy's position. The artillery would accompany Custer in his assault. Farnsworth would ride west, to turn Hampton's flank (a path that actually led him away from the fray).[31]

When Custer reached the enemy's front, he prepared to attack with his troops. One squadron of the Sixth Michigan would remain mounted to charge the Rebels' line; the rest of that regiment took up positions on foot, dispersed about the buildings and fields of the Felty Farm. The First and Second Michigan were placed behind the Sixth Michigan, dismounted in a defensive posture. The Fifth Michigan stayed on horseback, in the rear in reserve.[32]

Assuming that he faced at best only a Rebel regiment, Custer foolishly decided to display personal daring by riding with his men in the charge. "I'll lead you this time, boys," he called as he galloped to the front. "Come on!"[33]

The road was narrow, with fence rails lining the lane, limiting Custer's front to only eight men abreast. The band of Federal riders, only eighty in all, were greeted by more than five hundred Rebels, including troops drawn from

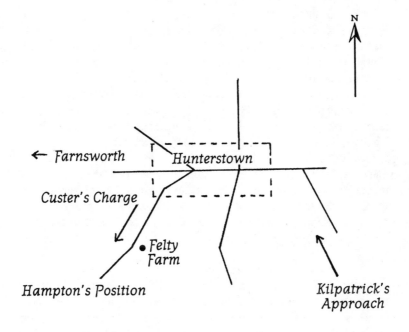

SKIRMISH AT HUNTERSTOWN
JULY 2, 1863

Cobb's Legion, the First South Carolina, and Phillips's Legion. The Northern attackers were easily overwhelmed and sent flying back toward their line. In the brief affair Custer's horse was killed, but he escaped capture or death by clambering aboard Private Norvill Churchill's mount and galloping to the safety of the rear. Over half of the squadron was killed, wounded, or taken prisoner in the rout.[34]

Hampton chased after the fleeing Federal troopers, but when his riders came within range of the men Custer had left dismounted at the Felty Farm, they were greeted by a savage curtain of flame. "Every door and window [of the buildings] were a blaze of fire," H. E. Jackson of Cobb's Legion stated, "and every man who was with me fell."[35] The Rebels' counterattack was smashed by the Michigan cavalry with their seven-shot Spencer rifles, and they left over one hundred men killed or wounded on the field when they retired back to Brinkerhoff Ridge.

After his retreat Hampton opened an artillery barrage on the Union position. The Northern guns replied with their own salvos. Amidst the din of cannons Kilpatrick heard the renewal of the battle, five miles away at Gettysburg. Longstreet was assaulting Meade's troops, ensconced on Cemetery Ridge. The clamorous sounds of his attack in echelon, which peaked in defeat at Little Round Top, echoed throughout the afternoon.[36] Kilpatrick's duel with Hampton continued until dusk.[37]

Hampton (and Stuart, who was nearby) left the field at sunset. Kilpatrick remained in place until 11:00 P.M., when he received orders to rush to Gettysburg to take a position on the Union left. He rode south, but about 3:00 A.M. came to a halt at Two Taverns, where he camped for the night.[38]

At 8:00 A.M. on 3 July Kilpatrick received orders to bring his entire command to Gettysburg to unite with General Wesley Merritt, in charge of the regular cavalry, in attacking Lee's right and rear.[39] Kilpatrick knew that a colossal battle involving over 170,000 soldiers was in progress, and he must have been filled with both trepidation and exhilaration as he formed his troops in column to advance and share in that contest. Farnsworth led the way; Custer brought up the rear.

Kilpatrick arrived on the Federal left about noon. When he started to disperse his force into position to make their assault, Kilpatrick discovered to his horror that over half of his command, Custer's brigade, was missing. In an act of gross insubordination, Custer had turned his men about, and instead of following Kilpatrick south, had hurried northeast to join Gregg's division, posted above Gettysburg.

Gregg had spotted Confederate horsemen approaching him from the north, threatening the Federal rear, and had sent a courier to Kilpatrick to ask him to detach Custer's brigade to him as reinforcements. The rider, racing up on the column from the rear, probably knew that Custer had been mentioned in the message, because he handed the note to him.[40]

Instead of forwarding the appeal to Kilpatrick, Custer decided on his own to go back to Gregg. He not only flouted his orders from Kilpatrick to hurry to Gettysburg, but he also did not even bother to let his superior know that he was deserting the column.[41]

When Kilpatrick learned that Custer had left him to go to Gregg, he must have been infuriated by the show of insubordination. He immediately sent a message to Pleasonton not only to report Custer's disdain for duty but also to demand his immediate return. The Federal chief of cavalry quickly dispatched a courier to Gregg with orders for Custer to head back to Kilpatrick.[42]

While waiting for Custer's return (and probable arrest for disobeying his orders), Kilpatrick planned an assault on Lee's right flank. He contacted Merritt, who had ridden up the Emmitsburg Road and assumed a post on his left, and they agreed to attack in echelon after Kilpatrick's force was reunited. Merritt would initiate the fight by dismounting his troopers for a charge on foot; when the Rebels shifted men from Kilpatrick's front to cope with the assault by Merritt, he would send both Farnsworth and Custer ahead on horseback through the resulting gap.[43]

About 1:00 P.M., just as Kilpatrick was completing his plans, the Rebels suddenly opened an awesome barrage against the Union infantry position along Cemetery Ridge. "The air was filled with projectiles," General Winfield Scott Hancock recalled, "there being scarcely an instant but that several were seen bursting at once."[44] Despite the havoc the shelling raised behind the Federal line, the Yankee gunners held their post and answered the Southern salvos. The sky filled with smoke, exploding bombs, and a deafening roar that made even shouted conversation impossible to hear.

The cannonade ended about 2:00 P.M. All was quiet for a moment, but the stillness did not last. The low rumble of pounding feet arose as almost fifteen thousand Confederates, arrayed in two wide ranks, poured from behind Seminary Ridge to advance toward the Federal line. They marched as if on parade, elbow to elbow, moving with such "a precision and steadiness," according to Hancock, "that [they] extorted the admiration of the witnesses of the scene."[45] General George E. Pickett led the Rebel assault.

"No attempt was made to check the advance," Hancock reported, "until the first line [came] within 700 yards of our position."[46] The Federals then fired with a ruinous effect, blowing gaping holes in the Rebel ranks. Most of those left standing turned and fled back toward their line; a few continued forward to be captured or killed when they clashed with overwhelming numbers of Northern soldiers. Pickett's charge had failed.

Kilpatrick's attack was delayed by the Rebel artillery cannonade, but when the Confederate infantry wave swept past his front on their way to Cemetery Ridge, he saw the chance to lunge behind their advance, to raise havoc in their rear. He could wait no longer on Custer, who had failed to return as ordered. Kilpatrick sent Merritt the order to charge.

Merritt marched up the Emmitsburg Road. When his line of dismounted troopers reached the top of a knoll, where the Ridge Road intersects the main pike, they were greeted with a hail of bullets fired by the Ninth Georgia, positioned at the Currens' farm to the northeast. Their fusillade forced Merritt to wheel left, away from Kilpatrick. He pushed west in an attempt to turn the Rebel flank. Merritt finally got around the end of the Confederate line (defended by only 250 men, a collection of stragglers, disabled soldiers, and few

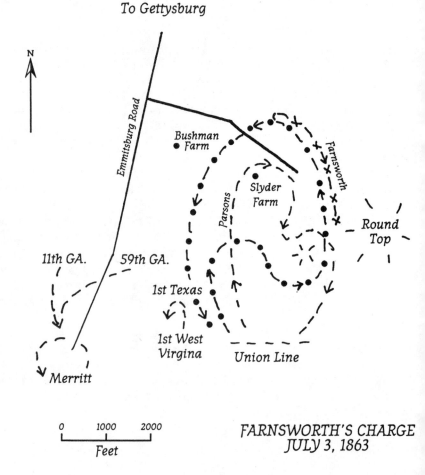

FARNSWORTH'S CHARGE
JULY 3, 1863

Site of Farnsworth's Charge. Courtesy of the author.

unattached cavalry under Colonel John L. Black), but when he tried to come back east toward Kilpatrick to roll up the enemy front, Merritt was hit on his left flank by the Eleventh and Fifty-Ninth Georgia, who had rushed to the scene. They drove Merritt all the way back to his starting point and out of the contest.[47] He failed in both of his objectives: to penetrate the Confederates' position and to force the Rebels to shift men from Kilpatrick's front.

Once Merritt had started his assault to the Union left, Kilpatrick followed in echelon in the center by ordering the First West Virginia ahead on horseback. The landscape that they faced was described by one as "the worst [possible] for a cavalry charge. . . . The whole ground . . . was broken and uneven and covered with rocks . . . [while] under cover of heavy timber and stone fences."[48]

The regiment galloped up to a "rail fence . . . staked and bound with withers," behind which lay the First Texas.[49] When the Union horsemen approached the barrier, they were met by a burst of flame from Rebel muskets. The Federal cavalrymen were staggered by the blast, and they turned about and rode back to their starting line. Fewer than ten fell during the timid charge. Kilpatrick regrouped the First West Virginia and sent them forward a second time, but again the Confederate volleys repelled their assault.[50]

By this time Picket's men were streaming in retreat to the west. Kilpatrick heard of their defeat from an orderly, who dashed up to report the news. "We turned their charge!" he shouted. "Nine acres of prisoners!"[51]

Now was the perfect time to launch an assault. If Kilpatrick smashed into the flank of the panicked Confederates, he could win the battle for Meade and gain eternal glory for himself. Custer was still not there; Farnsworth would have to make the assault on his own.

Kilpatrick rode up to Farnsworth. In a voice quivering with excitement, he ordered him to send the rest of his brigade forward into the fray. "General, do you mean it?" Farnsworth replied. "Shall I throw my handful of men over rough ground, through timber, against a brigade of infantry?" When Kilpatrick gaped with astonishment at Farnsworth's questions, the brigadier added, "These are too good men to kill."[52]

Kilpatrick was no doubt shocked. First Custer had disobeyed orders; now Fansworth was insubordinate. He had lost control of his division! And although the questions asked by Farnsworth were valid, Kilpatrick's mind seemed closed to logic. He responded as if his only concern was to regain command of his force.

"Do you refuse to obey my orders?" Kilpatrick screamed. "If you are afraid to lead this charge, I will lead it!"

Farnsworth rose in his stirrups. "Take that back!" he cried.

"I did not mean it," Kilpatrick mumbled. Like a bully, he backed down when challenged. "Forget it."

After a moment of strained silence, Farnsworth stated, "General, if you order the charge, I will lead it." He then noted, "But you must take the responsibility."

"I take the responsibility."

"I will obey your order."

Two battalions of the First Vermont advanced. Captain H. S. Parson led one, Farnsworth the other. Parsons galloped through the close-growing trees and over the giant boulders into the cleared fields of Slyler's Farm. After passing the house, he wheeled right onto the lane that ran west to east. "The sun was blinding," Parsons wrote. "We were immediately upon the enemy, within thirty paces, [when a] deadly volley . . . was fired."[53]

The salvo scattered the Federal troopers. Parsons and about fifty of his survivors (only a third of the battalion) turned south, rode around a low hill east of Round Top, and then raced through a hail of Confederate bullets back toward the haven of their lines.

Farnsworth led his battalion left of Parsons, then cut east through their wake toward the low hill, where he turned north, riding through timber.[54] The Fifth New York and the Eighteenth Pennsylvania were poised to follow after him, but both were shut off by the Fifteenth Alabama, who closed the gap used by Farnsworth to enter the field.[55]

As the Union troopers moved past Little Round Top, the Fourth Alabama, positioned below the knoll, sent a salvo into Farnsworth's flank. "Saddles were rapidly emptied," one Rebel remembered. "Recoiling from this fire, they turned to their left . . . and [galloped] up the hill toward the [Bushman Farm] occupied by [our] batteries."[56]

Farnsworth escaped this volley, but soon after he rode into the clearing, Confederate cannons to the west "opened a withering fire at close range."[57] His horse was killed. A Union private sprang from his saddle, gave his mount over to Farnsworth, then fled on foot. As most of the command rode south toward their lines and safety, Farnsworth and a few of his troopers turned about to try and retrace the route they had used when entering the field.[58] When he spotted Parsons retreating up ahead, Farnsworth urged his mare to catch up. A small band of Rebel infantry blocked his path. Boldly brandishing his pistol, Farnsworth demanded their surrender, but they instead opened fire and killed him.[59]

The charge had been a fiasco. Kilpatrick had hoped to win glory (at Farnsworth's expense), but instead he gave the enemy "one little spot of 'silver lining' in the cloud that hung so darkly over the field of Gettysburg."[60]

Kilpatrick pulled his regiments back from the front at dusk. The battle was over and the North had won Gettysburg. As he knelt by a sputtering campfire that night, Kilpatrick must have contemplated his performance the afternoon of July 1863. It had been a bad day for him.

Custer still had not returned with his brigade to join the command. And although Kilpatrick was smoldering with anger because Custer had disobeyed orders, he had learned that he could not censure his subordinate. Gregg had fought and defeated Stuart east of Gettysburg that afternoon; Custer had been the deciding factor. His brigade had borne the brunt of the battle, driving the Rebels from the field and keeping the enemy from entering the Yankee rear.[61] Custer deserved arrest for leaving Kilpatrick's column without authorization, but Meade would never allow the reproof of a hero.

And nobody was praising Kilpatrick. Of all the Yankee officers on the field that day, he was the only one to taste failure. His assaults against Lee's right flank had been a farce, the product of a badly flawed battle plan. Merritt's troops had attacked on foot over open ground that was ideal for cavalry. They were no match for the Rebel infantry, who were more experienced in this style of warfare. Farnsworth had led a mounted charge through timberland, laced with rock and undulating hills, a field totally unsuitable for horses. Kilpatrick's strategy had been so poorly conceived that even the lowest of privates could have predicted his defeat.

Worst of all it seemed as if the whole world knew that Kilpatrick had acted stupidly. His argument with Farnsworth had been so loud that even the enemy had heard their shouting and knew that Farnsworth had protested against the charge that had so needlessly cost him his life.[62]

Although Kilpatrick could not erase his performance at Gettysburg, he could try to convince others that he had done better than it seemed. He made the attempt in his official report. He did as much to disparage Custer as he could, noting that his subordinate's leaving the column to go to Gregg had been a "mistake."[63] This was no censure of Custer, but the snide comment at least cast a small shadow on his being present at Gregg's side.

Kilpatrick then made the astonishing claim that he had actually won his part of the battle. He stated that his men had "driven the enemy from one position to another." After the "rebel infantry gathered in great numbers" behind a rock wall, the Northern troopers, "led by the gallant Farnsworth, cleared the fence [and] sabered the rebels in the rear."[64]

Explaining how he had won a victory by retreating from the field was difficult, but Kilpatrick had an answer. "Had the infantry on my right advanced at once . . . the enemy could not have recovered from [their] confusion . . . [the Rebel army] would have been pushed back, one division on another, until, instead of [just] a defeat, a total rout would have ensued."[65] In other words Meade's failure to send the infantry forward to support Kilpatrick's attack was why it looked like he had been beaten. Blaming a superior for your error is a unique if not foolhardy approach to escaping condemnation.

Kilpatrick had one more sin to atone for in his report. He had to quiet the furor over Farnsworth's death. Electing to do so with an eulogy, he said, "Farnsworth, short but most glorious was his career [only four days a general] . . . we can say of him . . . good soldier, faithful friend, great heart, hail and farewell."[66]

He fooled no one. Stephen Z. Starr, a noted authority on the Northern cavalry, documented the probable response to the flowery claims. "Kilpatrick's report," he wrote, "is a shabby, disingenuous fabrication from beginning to end."[67]

Kilpatrick must have sensed the enmity surrounding him. He had lost the confidence of both his men and the superiors who controlled his future. Although a month ago Kilpatrick had been promoted to high rank, his stars were tarnished and his life's plan threatened by the events of Gettysburg. He had to move quickly to restore his falling reputation. Kilpatrick would take risky, desperate steps toward that aim, and his thirst for personal glory would prove his undoing.

11

Back to Virginia

The Rebels remained in position west of Gettysburg all day 4 July. Lee knew the battle was lost and that he must withdraw before Meade launched a counterassault to seal his victory. Lee had to hold, however, for at least twenty-four hours to allow his wagons, carrying the wounded and the provisions gleaned in Pennsylvania, a head start in the race to Williamsport, where the Confederates would ford the Potomac into Virginia. Lee could not risk being attacked in column, encumbered by his trains.[1]

When Meade saw that Lee was not retreating, he thought the Rebels might be planning yet another assault on him. He decided to hold his ground, too. He would rather repel Lee than gamble on losing the already won contest with an attack of his own.[2] The two adversaries spent most of the day eyeing each other from a distance.

Kilpatrick started his morning by giving a pep talk to Farnsworth's men, now under the temporary command of Colonel Nathaniel P. Richmond, who had been leader of the First West Virginia. "Your noble deeds are not passing unnoticed," he noted, "nor will they be unrequited. They are . . . part of grand history." He concluded his speech by saying, "I trust that your future conduct will be a fair copy of the past."[3]

About 1:00 P.M. a soft rain began to fall, and by 3:00 P.M. the shower had intensified into a raging thunderstorm. "The flood gates of heaven . . . opened," Kidd remembered. "It poured and poured. . . . Even [our] heavy gum coats and horsehide boots were hardly proof against it."[4]

Lee started his wagons west about the time the rain began to fall. When Meade heard that the Confederates were on the road back toward Virginia, he prepared to offer pursuit. The cavalry was dispersed to set up a screen between the two armies. Gregg guided his first brigade north to Hunterstown to protect the right flank; his third brigade, led by John McIntosh, rode south toward Emmitsburg to shield the center; Buford's Division plus Merritt's Regulars moved southwest to Frederick to protect the left flank; Kilpatrick, reinforced by Gregg's second brigade under Colonel Pennock Huey, took a direct route after the Rebels to harass their rear.[5]

Kilpatrick's troopers galloped south through sheets of rain to Emmitsburg, where they wheeled right to head up the mountain on their way to intercept the Confederate wagons on the far side of the slope, supposedly coming through Hagerstown. Custer, finally back with the division, led the way.[6]

The Rebel train had planned to cross over the mountain to Chambersburg, where they would turn south to head for the ford at Williamsport. General John D. Imboden, leading the parade, changed his mind as he listened to the pitiful pleas of the wounded, riding in the wagons. "O God! Why can't I die?" one cried. "Stop!" another pleaded. "Take me out and leave me to die on the roadside."[7] Imboden decided he must follow a shorter path to relieve the suffering. He would go along the eastern rim of the range until reaching Fairfield, where he would turn west and use the Monterey Pass to get to Hagerstown. Imboden could not know that this route exposed his rear to Kilpatrick and his

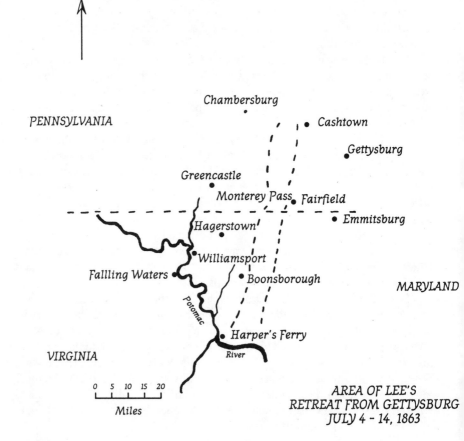

AREA OF LEE'S
RETREAT FROM GETTYSBURG
JULY 4 - 14, 1863

oncoming troopers. Imboden's train, over seventeen miles long, started up the slopes late that afternoon. He moved at a crawl, slowed by a narrow road that was muddy from the still pouring rain. Suddenly, about midnight, just as the tail of his column was passing the summit, consternation rose in the rear. Kilpatrick had arrived and attacked the column!

"On my left was a deep ravine," Kilpatrick recalled in his report on the action. "On my right a steep rugged mountain. . . . [The] road was too narrow to reverse even a gun. It was raining in torrents."[8]

The Union charged with a line of skirmishers, followed by men on horseback. "The darkness was intense," Kidd wrote later. "We plunged into a dense thicket . . . so thick that it was difficult to make headway at all. . . . One had to be guided by sound and not by sight."[9]

Only about fifty Rebels, a squad of the First Maryland under Captain G. M. Emack, stood between the Federals and the wagons.[10] Kilpatrick's force easily pushed this thin front of defenders backward and started to destroy the train and gather up prisoners.

The enemy tried to blunt Kilpatrick's attack. Cavalry led by General "Grumble" Jones galloped back toward the rear of the column. The "narrow and difficult way," Jones wrote, "was so blocked by wagons [that it was] wholly impracticable to push ahead."[11] Emack's tiny band fought on their own for almost two hours. Their feeble effort was enough, however, to allow most of the Confederate wagons to roll safely down the mountain.

Kilpatrick claimed a great victory. "Never under such perilous circumstances did a command behave better," he lied when he reported the brief melee as a fierce battle. "At the top of the mountain . . . the enemy opened on [our] advance with [their] artillery and infantry. . . . At the same time the rear . . . was attacked by Stuart's cavalry. . . . I ordered a charge. . . . No time was to be lost if I wished . . . to save my command."[12]

The booty, according to Kilpatrick, included more than thirteen hundred prisoners, one battle flag, and large numbers of mules and horses. He informed his superiors that the Confederate Second Corps' entire train of about three hundred wagons had been destroyed by his men.[13]

Other sources dispute Kilpatrick's boastful assertions. "The march continued during that day without interruption by the enemy," Lee said to Richmond, "excepting an unimportant demonstration upon our rear near Fairfield, which was easily checked."[14] And although Kilpatrick had captured a meaningful number of prisoners, most were soldiers who had been wounded in the battle at Gettysburg, not those who had defended the train. The Confederates reported only thirty-eight wagons lost during the skirmish.[15]

At sunrise on 5 July, Imboden's largely intact trains headed west to Greencastle, then turned south. They reached Williamsport that evening. Kilpatrick remained in place below Monterey Pass, west of the mountain, all day. He rested his men while sorting the spoils captured during the nighttime contest.[16]

About 5:00 P.M. Stuart's cavalry came in sight, riding down the slope toward the Union camp. Kilpatrick fired his artillery at the enemy but resisted the urge to engage them in hand-to-hand combat. The Rebels, too, had no desire for battle, and they continued westward, past Kilpatrick's front toward Hagerstown. Kilpatrick moved south when it was dark, galloping through Cavetown to Boonsborough, where he rid himself of his prisoners and captured property.[17]

On the morning of 6 July, Kilpatrick gathered his men and moved north to engage the Rebels at Hagerstown. When he reached the town about 11:00 A.M., he met Southern horsemen (Chambliss and Robertson's brigades) in the square. He sent his lead regiment (the Fifth Michigan) forward in a charge. They drove the enemy north, out of Hagerstown, opening a way southwest to Williamsport and the escaped Confederate wagon train. Kilpatrick decided to go after more spoils.[18]

Custer's brigade had barely started on the road toward Williamsport when they heard cannons booming to their front. Buford's Division, advancing below Kilpatrick's course, had reached Williamsport, where he found Imboden's cavalry ready to defend the trains.[19]

Although Kilpatrick wanted to rush to the scene, to throw his troopers into the fray, he suddenly found himself pushed in that direction. An enemy infantry brigade under General Albert Iverson was attacking him from the north, and Stuart had come up to flail his rear. Kilpatrick was advancing to the southwest but facing northeast. If Buford's troops were driven from their field, he would be caught in a pincer.[20]

Kidd caught a glimpse of Kilpatrick as he galloped for the front to ascertain his danger. "He was urging his horse at utmost speed," Kidd said. "His face was pale. His eyes were gazing fixedly to the front . . . he looked neither . . . right nor . . . left. The . . . anxiety on his countenance was apparent."[21]

Stuart's attack was the most serious. He sent General Albert G. Jenkins's riders to the left, where they dismounted to assault Kilpatrick's southern flank. Chambliss's cavalry charged directly down the pike from the east. The Confederate horsemen were repelled, but when Kilpatrick attempted a counterassault, his troopers were thrown back. Kilpatrick's fate was sealed when the Eleventh Virginia followed with another attack from the northeast. They scattered the Yankee horsemen, sending them into a frantic race for Williamsport.[22]

As Kilpatrick's fleeing cavalry approached the village, situated on the Potomac River, they were met by an artillery barrage from Imboden. He had forced Buford to withdraw and was now directing his cannons against Kilpatrick's hard-riding troopers. "[They] had the exact range," Kidd recalled, "and were pouring shell into the position where we were trying to form."[23]

Assailed from front and rear, Kilpatrick had no choice but to bolt south-east, heading back to Boonsborough. He cut across Buford's line of retreat, bringing his compatriot to a halt, subjecting him to further abuse from Imboden's guns. "Kilpatrick's division [was] driven back in confusion," one of Buford's men remembered, "completely blocking the road in to our rear."[24]

When Kilpatrick reached the safety of camp, he found a flinty message from Pleasonton awaiting him. "Why [did you] make application to General French for re-inforcement," his superior demanded, "instead of to [my] head-quarters?" Pleasonton was referring to a note that Kilpatrick had sent the night of 4 July, when he was assaulting Lee's wagon trains in Monterey Pass. Pleasonton was miffed because Kilpatrick had not gone through channels. He offered a rebuke, putting Kilpatrick on a tighter rein, by adding, "You will make frequent telegraphic reports of what is going on."[25]

Kilpatrick saw that his troubles were mounting. Farnsworth's death had started the chain; his late-night assault against Rebels' wagons smacked of success, but he lost that credit when he bypassed channels by sending a note directly to General William H. French; and now he had to admit that he had just been whipped by the Rebels. Kilpatrick tried to escape blame for the rout by shifting the responsibility to Buford. He related that at the onset of the hostilities, he had "placed [his] command at [Buford's] disposal." He went on to mask his drubbing. "I left one brigade to hold the enemy in check, and marched . . . with the two remaining brigades for Williamsport. . . . General Custer moved down the pike, drove in the rebel pickets, and soon became hotly engaged. . . . [He] was about to advance, with every prospect of success, [but] General Buford sent [word] that he was about to retire. . . . [We] slowly [withdrew] the regiments . . . taking up one position after another, repulsing each [enemy] attack till night."[26]

The Northern cavalry remained in camp for the next two days. Because of the heavy rains, the Potomac was flooding. Lee could not cross the stream into Virginia. He was building a defensive line to hold off the Yankees until the water fell, and rather than attack these entrenchments, the Union horsemen waited for Meade and the infantry to arrive to contest the Confederates.[27]

While Kilpatrick's troopers relaxed, they learned that Grant had won an impressive victory at Vicksburg.[28] After a siege of forty-seven days, he had forced Rebel general John C. Pemberton into surrendering his army of almost thirty thousand men on 4 July. Only Port Hudson remained in Southern control, and when that weak bastion (now under attack) succumbed, the Union would command the Mississippi River. The Confederacy would be cut in two, a disheartening blow to their hopes for independence.[29]

On 8 July Stuart attacked the Union cavalry in their camps. Although his main objective was to keep both Buford and Kilpatrick away from the last of the Rebel infantry columns filing along the western slopes of South Mountain toward the fords on the Potomac, Stuart also wanted to maintain a "predominance of pluck over the enemy."[30]

The assault began about 5:00 A.M. Stuart, fighting on foot (the ground, soaked by an overnight rain, was too muddy for horses), drove the Federals back into Boonsborough. When the Rebels' attack slackened with success, Buford personally led a counterassault. His troopers pressed Stuart's force back across Antietam Creek. The conflict finally ended late that afternoon.[31]

"I have had a rough day," Buford confessed in his report of the fray.[32] Kilpatrick failed to file an account of his participation in the action, but others offered telling testimony of his faint heart. "General Kilpatrick, with two squadrons of his command, galloped down the road [to] within a short distance of the enemy," Colonel William Gamble noted later. "[He] halted, looked at [the Rebels], and retired."[33]

Kilpatrick was indeed intent on retreat that afternoon. "Buford is about to withdraw to the mountain," he reported in a hysterical telegram to Pleasonton at the height of the clash. "I shall hold the town as long as possible, and then retire, fighting."[34]

For the next five days, the adversaries eyed each other warily as both prepared for a final battle that would finish the campaign. The Rebels strengthened their entrenchments; the Federals assembled their forces, filing into position as the infantry came down from Gettysburg. Kilpatrick's horsemen skirmished with Stuart's cavalry daily, but these fights had no effect on the situation. All the while the waters of the Potomac River receded from flood stage.

On the night of 13 July, during a driving rainstorm, Kilpatrick received orders to charge at first light the next morning. Meade was planning an all-out attack on the Rebel bastion. Lee, watching the stream rising again to his rear, decided he could not risk a battle with his line of retreat blocked by high water, and he ordered a withdrawal. His men started fording the Potomac at Williamsport; the wagons began crossing over a makeshift bridge at Falling Waters.[35]

When Kilpatrick rode forward about 7:00 A.M., he found the Rebels gone from his front. He proceeded toward Falling Waters. "A wild ride," Kidd wrote. "For the whole distance the horses were spurred to a gallop. Kilpatrick . . . afraid he would not get there in time to overtake the enemy . . . spared neither man nor beast."[36]

Major Peter A. Weber headed two squadrons of the Sixth Michigan (B and F), riding at the van of Kilpatrick's column in the run for the river. Upon reaching the stream, he saw Rebel troops (Henry Heth's division) to his front, reclining behind an earthwork on top of a hill, their arms stacked. Weber stopped to await orders.

When Custer arrived, he told Weber to dismount his men and advance on foot to ascertain the Confederates' strength. He complied, but before Weber had moved forward, Kilpatrick stormed onto the scene. "Remount!" he ordered. "Charge the hill!"[37]

Weber reassembled his troops, placed himself at their head, and gave the call, "Forward!" He led less than one hundred men against ten times their number, "cutting right and left with his saber, cheering on his men." The Confederates reeled from Weber's fierce charge, but "the audacity of the thing dazed them for [only] a minute." The Rebels recovered to make short work of their daring assailants."[38] Weber's body was one of the many Union dead found lying on the field after the enemy left the ground.

Kilpatrick later declared that Weber's charge "was the most gallant ever made."[39] His words, however, did not hide the fact that "Kill-Cavalry" had not only committed another useless sacrifice of men but also had ruined the chances for capturing Heth's entire command. Other Federal troops were already moving to the right to block the Rebels' path to the river. Before they could get into position, however, Heth's men, alerted by Kilpatrick's foolish attack, had crossed the Potomac River, ending the Gettysburg campaign.

"I saw two small squadrons [from] General Kilpatrick's division gallop up the hill," one of Buford's men said, "and as any competent cavalry officer would foretell . . . their two squadrons were instantly scattered and destroyed by the fire of the rebel brigade. . . . Not a single dead enemy [was] found when the ground was examined a few hours afterward. . . . Having alarmed the enemy, he [got across] the ford before we could get round to their rear."[40]

The Rebels, too, reported that Kilpatrick's attack had been for naught. "In the melee," Heth wrote, "Pettigrew's horse reared and fell; as he [Pettigrew] was rising, a Federal sergeant shot him in the groin."[41] The Confederates had only two casualties: a Tennessee private and General James J. Pettigrew.

Despite this evidence from both friend and foe that Lee had escaped across the river into Virginia with little harm, Kilpatrick stated in his report that he had "captured a brigade of infantry, two pieces of artillery, two caissons, and a large number of small arms" while engaged with the Rebels.[42] He further claimed that he had achieved this remarkable success without help. "We routed the enemy at all points," he averred, "and drove him toward the river, within a short distance of the bridge, [when] General Buford's command came up and took the advance."[43]

Kilpatrick sent copies of his report to both Meade and the *New York Times*. When Robert E. Lee read the newspaper's account of the battle, he filed a formal protest with Meade. "This dispatch . . . is incorrect," he fumed. "No arms, cannon, or prisoners were taken by [Kilpatrick] in battle. [He] did not capture any organized body of [my] men . . . only stragglers and such as were left asleep on the road."[44]

Meade, suspecting that Kilpatrick was lying, held back official publication of the report. He wanted further proof of Kilpatrick's claims. This evidence was delayed, however, as the writer had gone on sick leave. Although he was still suffering with kidney pain, that was not the reason why Kilpatrick had hurried to West Point. Alice had given birth to a son. He went to see his new baby, named Judson B. Kilpatrick.[45]

Although Kilpatrick always exaggerated his performance in his reports, few knew that he stretched the truth, because he was usually detailing deeds that took place during raids when there were no witnesses to protest against his trumped-up claims. Most believed that he was an intrepid general of cavalry. At Gettysburg, however, Kilpatrick's peers in the Union army could not help but see that he was not the heroic figure they had supposed and that he stayed safely in the rear when his troopers carried out the suicidal assaults that he so heedlessly ordered. Many were appalled. Kilpatrick then added to his growing, unfavorable reputation by turning in false reports, heralding exploits that even the most gullible knew were not true. The less he achieved, the more he claimed to have done. He even attempted to shift blame for his shortcomings to others.

The key to Kilpatrick's character seemed to be that he could not accept failure, that he had to be perfect in every way. And if his actions did not match this impossible standard, he substituted words for feats, as if saying something made it so. Lies were believable as long as they augmented his image. This continuing effort to portray himself a hero was becoming maniacal, however, a sign that Kilpatrick knew he was headed for a hard fall.

12

The Gunboat Expedition

En route to visit Alice and his newborn son, Kilpatrick decided to delay his arrival for a few days in order to help suppress the riots against the draft that had broken out in New York City. He rode directly to the metropolis, where on 17 July Kilpatrick offered his service to General John E. Wool, head of the armed forces charged with putting down the insurrection.[1]

The strife had begun about 6:00 A.M. on 13 July. Instead of going to work, laborers headed for Central Park for a brief organizational meeting, then marched angrily to the provost marshall's offices at the corner of Third Avenue and Forty-Seventh Street, where the draft lottery was scheduled to start at 10:00 A.M. They gathered to protest against the Conscription Act, passed by Congress four months earlier, calling not only for the draft of men into the army but also the arrest of anyone selected who refused to serve.

Opposition to the draft was based on different reasons: most of the men did not want to risk their lives by going to war; many objected to a provision of the law, allowing one to avoid service by paying a $300 exemption fee, a step only the wealthy could afford; and some saw the Conscription Act as an intrusion by the "Black Republicans" to promote cheap Negro labor. Although they had supported Lincoln's aim to preserve the Union, this latter group (made up of mostly Irish immigrants) did not accept his shifting the goal to the ending of slavery. They were not so much bigoted as they were fearful of losing their low-paying jobs to free Blacks while they were away in the army.

When Federal officials attempted to draw draft numbers, the enraged demonstrators swarmed into the building to smash the lottery apparatus. They then set fire to the structure. The destruction quickly spread to nearby stores, whose doors and windows were shattered as hundreds poured into shops to steal goods. Others, more politically motivated, sought out the homes of known Republicans. They trashed the furniture before burning the houses.

The rioting continued for four more days, during which the city's shops were emptied, its public facilities ruined. Streetcar tracks were ripped up, most telegraph poles were toppled, and the ferries that connected the boroughs to Manhattan Island were sunk. Although the above actions were ugly enough, an even darker side to the chaos also emerged. The hard feelings against Blacks were reflected by the torching of the Colored Orphan Asylum and random lynching of Negroes. Eleven Black men were hung before Wool restored order.[2]

Kilpatrick arrived too late to have a role in quelling the riots in New York City, but if his objective had been to share in the laurels, he achieved that goal. Wool informed his Washington superiors that the "gallant and distinguished General Kilpatrick [offered] himself to me . . . for service for a few days."[3]

When calm returned to the city, Kilpatrick moved on to West Point, where he visited with Alice and his baby son for two weeks. He returned to duty on 5 August.[4]

Meade had established his force above the Rappahannock along an arc extending from Falmouth to Warrenton. Lee took up a position that began above the river east of Fredericksburg, dropped below the water where the Rappahannock met the Rapidan, then paralleled the lower stream west. The ground around Culpeper, a no-man's land lying between the rivers, was patrolled by Stuart's cavalry. Kilpatrick, encamped at Hartwood Church, picketed the Federal line eastward; Buford was bivouacked by the railroad bridge over the Rappahannock, where he watched the fords to the west; Gregg was headquartered at Manassas Junction, protecting Meade's right flank.[5]

Both armies, exhausted by the campaign in Pennsylvania, were content to let the other lie at peace in their camps as they recuperated. Kilpatrick, however, refused to recognize that an informal truce was in effect. He sent patrols ahead on daily reconnaissances, and after each, he claimed that an attack from Lee was imminent. "Everything indicates a movement by the enemy," he wired on 20 August.[6] "A large body of troops have been moving . . . opposite Falmouth," he reported the following day.[7] And on 22 August he confirmed that "a force of infantry and cavalry under General Hood . . . [marched] out . . . the Bowling Green road . . . and thence to Port Conway."[8]

The infantry ignored Kilpatrick's dire warnings. They seemed to think that the Southerners were only responding to his probes, and that if he let the Rebels alone, the front would remain serene. "I have seen General Kilpatrick's dispatch," General Warren vouched, "'[but] I do not much fear an advance of the enemy."[9]

Kilpatrick's predictions that the Rebels were about to cross the river to attack the Union soon came to a stop, not so much because the enemy had settled in their camps but because he was distracted by a new interest that occupied most of his attention. Annie Jones, a teenaged prostitute, had come to his bivouac. She boasted of having slept with many key officers in the Yankee army (including Custer, whom she had met in Warrenton last fall). Kilpatrick was so thrilled with Annie, he "forgot" about his wife and baby son at West Point and invited her to share his tent. She accepted and, when not entertaining

Kilpatrick, spent her time dressed in a major's garb and galloping about the grounds on the mare that he gave her.[10]

On 27 August Kilpatrick learned (probably from enemy pickets) that the Rebels were using their position above the Rappahannock to gather forage for their horses. They toted the hay south, shipping it over the river via skiffs at Port Conway. Gunboats, captured from the Yankees, guarded their crossings. He proposed a cavalry assault against the rebel operation. "I should like to move down the river," he said in a wire to Pleasonton, "capture their forces on this side, and destroy the boats."[11]

Pleasonton ignored the request to mount a raid against the gunboats, choosing instead to chide Kilpatrick for talking with the Rebels. "No communication whatever [should] be held between you and the enemy," he directed. "[I] also understand that there was a rebel mail captured by [you] a few days ago. . . . Anything of that kind . . . [must] be forwarded [to me] at once."[12]

Although Pleasonton was unwilling to approve any assaults, he was overruled by his superiors in Washington. Kilpatrick must have sent a copy of his proposal to Halleck, because he wrote Meade to suggest a campaign in which the Union navy would sail up river from the Atlantic Ocean to join the army (coming east) in a dual effort against the gunboats. "The whole operation will be a delicate one," he advised, "and the most careful officers should be placed in charge."[13] Halleck was implying, of course, that Kilpatrick (who had developed the plan) should command the mission.

Meade was no doubt incensed with Kilpatrick for having approached Halleck directly, and he displayed his umbrage by predicting that the bold venture would fail. "I anticipate that Kilpatrick will find the gunboats above Port Royal," he said to Halleck, "where they cannot be reached by our [ironclads], and in a position where the enemy's artillery . . . will . . . bear on their destruction."[14] Meade, however, agreed to let Kilpatrick try his raid, and gave him as much assistance as possible. Buford was sent east to picket the water below Falmouth; Warren also moved left with five thousand of his infantrymen to await orders to hurry to Kilpatrick's support if necessary.

Kilpatrick led two regiments of cavalry, the Fifth New York and First Michigan, augmented by two batteries of horse artillery, eastward at 2:00 A.M. on 1 September. "We all laughed," one of the troopers related, "at the order sending cavalry after . . . craft."[15] Another dubbed the operation, "a most novel scheme . . . Kilpatrick's Gun-Boat Expedition."[16]

The men rode all that day, through the night, and into the following morning without halting. At 3:00 A.M. on 2 September they charged the enemy encampment at King George Court House and drove the Rebels out of the village. During the skirmish, Kilpatrick captured twelve prisoners, whom he decided to use in carrying out his plans.[17]

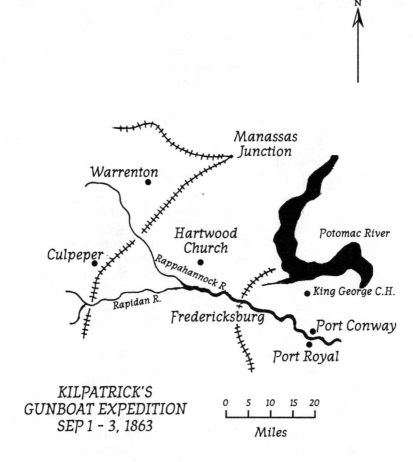

KILPATRICK'S
GUNBOAT EXPEDITION
SEP 1 - 3, 1863

"[We must] fall back," he announced loudly in front of his captives. "The gunboats [will be] alarmed. [Our] expedition [is] a failure."[18]

Kilpatrick then allowed about half of the prisoners to escape, to rush to Port Conway to relate falsely that he was withdrawing from the field. He headed west in the dark for two miles, then whirled to advance to the shores of the Rappahannock. He hid his command in the woods above the river to await the arrival and support of the Union navy.[19]

When the sun rose in the east, with no sign that the Federal warships were coming upstream, Kilpatrick decided that the navy was not coming to his support. And although he could not hope to capture the gunboats, anchored about 650 yards off shore, he could wreck them. Kilpatrick gave the order, and all ten of his cannons were wheeled from under the trees and rushed down to the river, where they unlimbered and began firing at the Southern ships. "[We] gave the Rebels a small cargo of hissing cast-iron," Glazier related in his memoirs, "which waked them up more effectively than their ordinary morning-call."[20]

The Union fire quickly sank one of the gunboats, named the *Satellite,* but before the gunners could concentrate on the second ship, Rebel artillery started blasting away from across the water at the Yankee cannons. The exchange lasted about half an hour, during which time Kilpatrick's batteries put enough shells into the *Reliance* to disable it "beyond hope of being repaired."[21]

Kilpatrick then withdrew, returning safely back to his camp at Hartwood Church. He had done very well, restoring a large part of his reputation, because he had succeeded in an operation that Meade had predicted would fail. But although everyone was impressed by his performance, Kilpatrick could not resist trying to gain even more fame from his exploit by pointing out the navy's shortcoming. "If the iron-clad was here," he groused in his official report, "both boats [would have been] recaptured."[22]

His troopers were amused by the raid. "All hands [ate] breakfast at half-past nine o'clock," Glazier related. "The repast consisted of muddy water, rusty salt pork, and half a hard cracker, termed . . . 'an iron-clad breakfast.'"[23]

Kilpatrick had driven his men, allowing them only nine hours sleep over the three days. He was no doubt in a hurry to return to camp to see Annie Jones. Upon his arrival, he was appalled to find that while he had been away, Annie had left the bivouac to visit the Rebels. Even worse, when she came back, Annie had moved all her belongings into Custer's tent, saying that she preferred his company to Kilpatrick's. Kilpatrick was so angered by Annie's fickleness that he arrested her for being a spy and sent her north to Washington.[24]

Kilpatrick's success in wrecking the Southern gunboats helped to blur the unfavorable image that he had established at Gettysburg. The experience (and subsequent praise) also taught him that he had a knack for raids, rather than combat where he was under the direct eye of his superiors.

The Annie Jones affair, however, would further mar his reputation. In time the whole army would learn of his being thrown over for Custer—embarrassing enough when the rejection was by a good woman, a disaster from a prostitute. This problem did not concern low morals. Pride was at stake, and Kilpatrick was no doubt cut to the quick when the examiner who investigated the incident found the case "amusing."[25]

13

Brandy Station Revisited

As Annie Jones (kicking, screaming, cursing Kilpatrick with every step) was escorted northward toward Washington to a cell in Old Capitol Prison, Longstreet's corps was moving west to reinforce Bragg in Tennessee. Rosecrans had mounted a campaign against the Rebel front, centered on Chattanooga, and President Jefferson Davis had concluded that because Lee's men seemed immune from an assault by Meade, he could safely switch a portion of the Army of Northern Virginia to Bragg's assistance. The infantry divisions of Lafayette McLaws and John B. Hood, plus Edward Porter Alexander's artillery, were sent west on 9 September.[1]

Meade was soon alerted that Lee was withdrawing troops from his front, and he sent his cavalry forward to "find out something."[2] Pleasonton pushed his whole force forward the morning of 13 September.

Stuart was not surprised by Meade's sudden advance. A Confederate physician, Dr. Walter G. Hudgin, whose wife "had recently died of fright . . . [from] the conduct of some of Kilpatrick's men,"[3] saw the Yankee horsemen concentrating above the Rappahannock. On the night of 12 September, he crept through the Federal line, crossed over the stream, and found Stuart to report the imminent attack.

Stuart had no thought of trying to hold his front. He started his wagons toward the Rapidan that evening, carrying the wounded and his provisions to safety.[4]

Kilpatrick crossed the Rappahannock at Kelly's Ford at 6:00 A.M. He sent Henry E. Davies (who now led Farnsworth's Brigade) up front with Custer trailing. When he reached Stevensburg, Kilpatrick turned right to head for Brandy Station. He made the Union's initial contact with the enemy, whose artillery was emplaced on top of Fleetwood Hill. The Second New York (back with Kilpatrick's command at his request) charged the knoll, but a fierce fusillade by the Rebels' cannons forced them to retreat into the woods below the railroad.[5] They held this post until the rest of the Northern cavalry came up on their right.

Pleasonton prepared for battle. He aligned his troops in a line five miles wide, Gregg on the right, Buford in the center, Kilpatrick on the left.[6] They moved ahead, driving the enemy back toward Culpeper.

Kilpatrick was the first Union force to reach the town, where he found the Rebels strongly posted, supported by guns on top of a ridge. Davies moved into position to attack, but he had to wait for Custer, coming up on his left, who was held up by a marsh that blocked his route.

When he finally broke through the mire about 1:00 P.M., Custer saw a Rebel train, loaded with supplies, moving south of town. He looked back and found that only about a hundred men from the First Vermont had managed to follow him through the bog. Rather than pause to allow the rest of his brigade to catch up, he led the few troopers at hand after the enemy cars.[7]

A Confederate battery, posted on a hill between Custer and the railroad track, opened fire on the approaching Union horsemen. Inspired by Custer's audacity, Davies pushed the Second New York forward to support his attack. The Federals galloped "across a deep ravine and a creek, up a steep hill, the road rough and stoney, through a heavy fire of shells . . . up to the muzzles of the guns . . . a charge never surpassed in the records of the cavalry service."[8] They captured two of the Rebels' cannon; Custer's riders grabbed the third piece composing the battery.

To the left a second Confederate battery opened on the Union riders atop the knoll. Davies sent the Fifth New York toward these cannons, but their assault collapsed under the heavy fire of the enemy guns. The Confederates then mounted a counterattack. The Second New York came forward to meet the Rebels, but they, too, were repulsed. Davies, in danger of being routed, threw the First West Virginia, his only remaining regiment, into the fray. They managed to thwart the enemy charge, and the Confederates started to retreat. Kilpatrick's men chased after the retiring Rebels.[9]

The pursuit did not last long. When Kilpatrick saw he could not catch up with the enemy, he called his troops to a halt. Buford took over the field; Kilpatrick moved left to Pony Hill, where he set up his camp for the night.[10]

Custer did not join his compatriots. In his charge up the hill, his horse had been hit by a shell and killed. The ball had struck his boot, tearing the leather and cutting a gash on his foot. He limped toward the rear, where he met Pleasonton.

"I am glad to see you," Pleasonton greeted him. "I was anxious about you."[11]

"How are you?" Custer replied. "Fifteen days leave of absence?" he added, pointing to his bloody foot. "They have spoiled my boots, but they didn't gain much there . . . I stole 'em from a Reb."

Pleasonton not only granted Custer his fifteen days of leave but also added twelve more for good measure, time that the cavalier general would use to return to Michigan to woo Elizabeth "Libby" Clift Bacon, the prettiest girl in Monroe, his hometown.[12]

Although Kilpatrick would not begrudge Custer his good fortune, he must have been infuriated that the furlough was given directly by Pleasonton. He had bypassed the channels of command, encouraging Custer in his insubordinate view of Kilpatrick's leadership, a problem that had begun at Gettysburg. Kilpatrick had been forced to put his displeasure in writing, saying to Custer, "I've noticed in your communications to me a bad attitude. I've only tried to . . . advise—not censure. I hope no ideas erroneous will induce you to forget that it is impossible for me to command the Division without the willing support of my Brigade Commanders."[13]

Cooperation in the Union army was essential now, because of Lee's depleting his force to supply reinforcements to Bragg. Lee was so vulnerable to assault that he had retired from the front, pulling his troops back to the southern bank of the Rapidan River. Meade sensed the opportunity to rout his weakened foe, and he advanced his men up to the water to probe the shore, looking for points where he could cross to bring Lee to battle.[14]

But before Meade could attack, astounding news arrived from the west. Bragg, reinforced by Longstreet's force from the Army of Northern Virginia, had attacked Rosecrans's army at Chickamauga Creek. In the two-day contest, which started on 19 September, the Confederates dealt the Federals a devastating blow, driving them back to Chattanooga, where they were under siege.[15]

Lincoln, dismayed by the defeat, called upon Meade for reinforcements before Rosecrans was starved into submission. On 25 September the Union Eleventh and Twelfth Corps were withdrawn from the Army of the Potomac and started west for Tennessee.[16]

When Lee learned that Meade had decreased his ranks, a role reversal from the situation only two weeks ago, he saw a chance to attack the Union. Keeping Meade occupied would prevent his dispatching further troops to Rosecrans's rescue, and if Lee could maneuver the Federals into falling back to the Potomac River, northern Virginia would be spared a Union occupation during the coming winter season. Lee started to advance on 9 October, going northwest toward Meade's right flank.[17]

Meade realized that Lee held the advantage, so instead of standing firm to offer battle, he began to withdraw. The cavalry was given the task of guarding his rear as he moved northeast toward Washington, D.C.

Although Kilpatrick's performance was good in this second battle of Brandy Station, most of the credit went to Custer. He was the hero, despite (in

Kilpatrick's eyes) his being a poor leader, one who was insubordinate to his superior. The two were competing for glory, and Kilpatrick was determined to win that contest, an unspoken vow that would cause him to shun Custer when he needed him most.

14

The Buckland Races

At daylight, 10 October, Hampton's Division of the Rebel cavalry, led by Jeb Stuart himself, began crossing the Robertson River in pursuit of Meade's retreating men. They advanced in three columns, galloping toward James City where Kilpatrick's division was posted along a ridge east of town. Kilpatrick's mission was to block the enemy's progress, to give the Union infantry room to retire in peace. Davies's brigade was at hand; Custer's troopers were on their way to join the command.[1]

Stuart arrived at the front about noon. "As my object of . . . occupying position at James City had been accomplished," he wrote, "I did not attempt . . . to dislodge the enemy."[2] He instead emplaced his cannons and began lobbing shells toward the Yankee line. Kilpatrick's guns returned the fire.

Thinking that the artillery fusillade was a prelude to a Confederate attack, Kilpatrick held his place. About 4:00 P.M., however, just as Custer's men arrived, Kilpatrick ran out of patience. He ended the vapid exchange by mounting an assault of his own. Davies rode forward against the Rebels. His men galloped in fours toward the enemy front, where they were met by a fierce volley from about 150 sharpshooters hiding behind a stone fence. Stuart recalled the Federal response. "They beat a speedy retreat," he wrote with glee.[3]

During the night Kilpatrick received orders to retreat to Culpeper. He quietly gathered his men and by 7:00 A.M. was en route toward the rear.[4] Stuart, with Hampton's force, followed him.

When Kilpatrick moved northeast, Buford was also heading toward Culpeper. He was rushing up from the southeast, with Fitzhugh Lee's cavalry division closing upon his tail. The Rebels caught up with Buford at Stevensburg, where Fitz sent his men against the rear of the Union columns.[5]

When Stuart, trailing Kilpatrick, heard the chatter of muskets to his right, he saw his chance to catch the Yankees in a pincer. He moved off the road and began riding across the fields for Brandy Station, where he would be between the Union and the Rappahannock River. Kilpatrick, however, discerned Stuart's plan, and he accelerated his pace toward the northeast. "Then began a horse race of converging columns," Kidd related, "Stuart on the left, Buford followed by Lee on the right, with Kilpatrick in the center."[6]

Buford reached Brandy Station first and placed his men atop Fleetwood Hill. A Rebel brigade, led by Thomas Rosser, just promoted to brigadier general,[7] rushed up and formed a line confronting Buford. His force astride the road blocked Kilpatrick's path when he approached the railroad center from the southwest.[8]

Kilpatrick had no idea that Buford was posted ahead. He saw the barrier of Rosser's men to his front, the rest of Fitzhugh Lee's division to his right, and Stuart closing on both his left and rear. He was surrounded!

The situation was thorny but perfect for the dramatics that Kilpatrick relished. He formed his brigades into three lines: Davies was on the right; Kilpatrick assumed charge of the center; Custer took the left. When everyone was set for the attempt to push through Rosser's roadblock up ahead, Kilpatrick told the band to play "Yankee Doodle" as the men raced forward. "The blast of scores of bugles [was added]," Louis N. Boudrye recalled, "ringing forth the charge."[9]

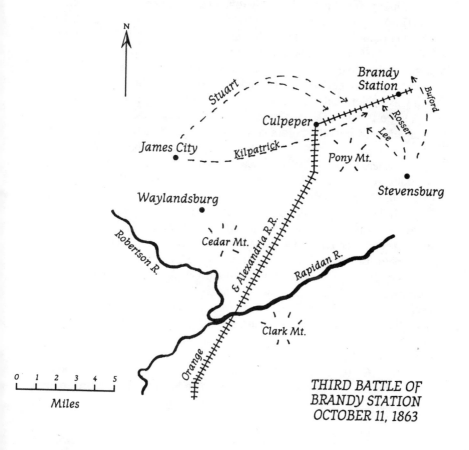

THIRD BATTLE OF
BRANDY STATION
OCTOBER 11, 1863

Kilpatrick's men galloped ahead. "Ambulances, forages and cannon, with pack trains, non-combatants and others, all joined to swell the on-flowing tide," Boudrye wrote.[10]

Rosser, who was facing Buford, was no doubt shocked to find his rear threatened by Kilpatrick's oncoming force. He quickly adapted to the predicament, however, by pulling his troops aside, like a matador toying with an enraged bull, to let Kilpatrick's entourage rush past him. When the Yankees were halfway through the gauntlet, Rosser ordered an assault against Kilpatrick's exposed right flank. At the same time Stuart charged the Federal left. The Union riders, assailed from both sides, fought desperately to disengage themselves, to break free from the Rebels' pincer. "There was a general melee," Kidd wrote, "in which each side performed prodigies of valor."[11] When Kilpatrick's men finally galloped through the enemy onslaught, they found themselves safe at Buford's side.

"All the fighting was done on horseback," Kidd said in his memoirs. "It must have been a pretty picture . . . fluttering . . . battleflags . . . the flash of sabers and puffs of pistol shots—altogether a most brilliant spectacle."[12]

The Yankee cavalry crossed the Rappahannock River that night, assuming a post at the rear of Meade's columns, rushing northeast. The path of retreat followed the Orange and Alexandria railroad toward Bristoe Station, with an ultimate objective of reaching the environs of Washington, D.C.[13]

Stuart's troopers trailed behind and left of the Union columns. He was acting as a shield for Lee's foot soldiers, who were following a wide arc northwest to northeast. Their goal was to reach Manassas ahead of the Federals, to engage Meade in battle before he found safety behind the Washington fortifications. Ewell's corps was taking the longest route, moving toward Little Washington, where they would wheel east to proceed through Warrenton; A. P. Hill's brigades were on a direct route toward Warrenton, where they, too, would turn east to intercept Meade.[14]

Hill, leading Lee's parade, caught up with the Yankees at Bristoe Station. Meade's troops were crossing Broad Run, vulnerable to attack. Without pausing to reconnoiter, Hill ordered an immediate assault. Heth's Division advanced in a line of two brigades, rushing toward the stream filled with men in blue. They never spotted the Federals' Second Corps, hidden behind the railroad embankment to their right. When the Rebels passed directly opposite the concealed Union soldiers, the Yankees rose and poured a savage fire into their open flank. Almost fourteen hundred Confederates were killed, wounded, or captured. The rout halted Lee's pursuit, and Meade proceeded forward without further harassment.[15]

"Well, General," Lee said sadly to Hill as they looked at the bodies scattered across the ground. "Bury [your] men and let us say no more about it."[16]

Lee waited in position for several days, hoping for an attack by Meade.

The Yankees, however, were content to stay above Broad Run, and on 17 October, Lee abandoned his campaign, wheeled about, and began withdrawing south toward the Rappahannock River. Meade dispatched his cavalry to pursue and track the Confederate retreat.[17]

Kilpatrick was bivouacked near Manassas, living in the Shaw House at Sudley Church, when he received Meade's orders to follow the Rebels as they headed south. He was eager to renew clashing with Jeb Stuart, who was guarding the Confederate rear, and showed his pugnacity with a bold comment to his host.

"A fine day," Mr. Shaw noted that morning, greeting Kilpatrick, who was joining him on the porch for breakfast.[18]

"Yes," Kilpatrick growled, "a fine day for a fight!"

Kilpatrick started after Stuart the evening of 18 October, moving southward with Custer leading, Davies following in a separate column to the north. Both encountered Rebels soon after leaving Manassas. Custer became engaged with the enemy near Groveton; Davies met the Southern cavalry close to Haymarket. Neither skirmish lasted long, as a cold autumn rain pelted the adversaries. Kilpatrick's troopers spent a miserable night, huddling around smoldering fires that would not stay lit because of the storm.[19]

The Federal troopers slept late the morning of 19 October, breaking camp about 11:00 A.M. Kilpatrick put his men into one column as he took up the chase of the Confederates. Custer's brigade was in front; Davies's troopers rode in the rear. The skies had cleared, but despite a bright sun shining overhead, the day was crisp and cold.[20]

As Kilpatrick's two thousand-man force approached Buckland, a little town located on the Warrenton Pike at Broad Run, they found the enemy (Hampton's Division of twenty-eight hundred troopers) waiting to greet them. The Confederate cavalry was spread along the west bank, astride the stone bridge crossing the stream. Their position was formidable, as the water was deep, flooded by last evening's rain, and the shore was wooded and steep.[21]

Custer and his staff rode up to the edge of the stream. While he was studying the field beyond the bridge, a Southern cannon opened fire, planting a shell into the midst of Custer's entourage. The officers scattered to safer ground. "They had no desire to be made targets for . . . artillery practice," Kidd recalled. "Fortunately no one was killed."[22]

Knowing that he had to dislodge the enemy if he wanted to get across the river, Custer made his depositions for the task. The Fifth Michigan moved above the bridge, the Sixth Michigan straddled the road, and the Seventh Michigan took a post south of the span. Custer kept both the First Vermont and the First Michigan in reserve.[23]

Custer opened fire on the Rebels as soon as his troops were posted. Armed with repeating Spencer carbines, his men shot quicker than their muzzle-loading adversaries, but the Confederates had more numbers, which offset the Union advantage. Neither foe gained an inch. The Sixth Michigan made one attempt to storm the bridge but was repelled.[24]

In the midst of the impasse, Kilpatrick galloped up on his race horse, Lively. Custer quickly briefed him on the situation, noting that the enemy position was so strong he would need help from Davies to dislodge the Rebels. Kilpatrick refused to provide any reinforcements, suggesting instead that Custer send men up and down the stream to find a ford where he could cross the water, then flank Stuart out of his impregnable post. Custer sullenly agreed to attempt this strategy. Parties were dispersed, and soon the Seventh Michigan reported that they had forded the waters below the span and were headed north to strike the Rebel right.[25]

Kilpatrick (no doubt with a smug smile) ordered Custer to gather his men for an attack against the bridge. When he heard the Seventh Michigan open fire against Stuart's flank, he should charge the span with the rest of his brigade. The two waited for events to unfold.

Stuart, of course, was making his own plan for dealing with Kilpatrick. He had dispatched a messenger to Fitz Lee, whose fifty-two hundred-man division was posted south at Auburn, to tell Lee that the Yankees had reached Buckland. Lee sent back a proposal to lure Kilpatrick into a trap. "Retire before the enemy . . . in the direction of Warrenton," he suggested. "[I] will come in . . . and attack them in flank and rear."[26]

Stuart saw great merit in the scheme. If Lee inserted his troopers between Kilpatrick's smaller force and the span over Broad Run at Buckland, the Union would be trapped between his two Rebel divisions. "I could inflict . . . severe injury," Stuart concluded.[27] He told Lee to come on ahead. When he heard Fitz Lee charge Kilpatrick's rear, Stuart would whirl to attack the Yankee front. Together they would destroy Kilpatrick's command.

By now the Seventh Michigan had reached Stuart's flank and opened fire. Custer mounted his assault. Stuart, while he could have easily repelled the charge, retreated, ceding the bridge to the Federals.

"Well done, Custer!" Kilpatrick yelled when he saw the Rebels retire. "You have driven [Stuart] from a very strong position."[28]

Kilpatrick then proceeded to stroll into Stuart's trap with "his eyes shut."[29] Scouts warned him of spotting enemy cavalry to the south, but he scoffed at their reports. The riders were Union men from Wesley Merritt's division, he insisted, supporting his flank.[30] The Rebels were retreating to the west, and Kilpatrick meant to go after them. Davies's regiments were summoned up front to take the advance. Custer was ordered to reassemble his brigade into column, and when he was finished, to fall in behind Davies.

Custer, no doubt miffed because Kilpatrick had not provided him with the reinforcements he had requested earlier, would not obey the order. It was now

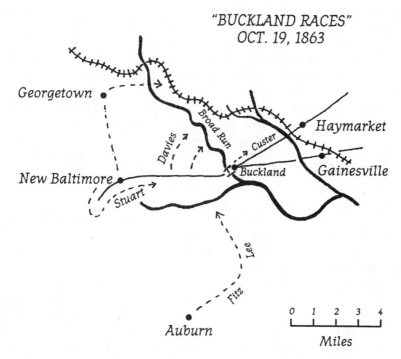

"BUCKLAND RACES"
OCT. 19, 1863

past noon. His men had not yet had their breakfast; he would not move until his troops were fed. Kilpatrick begged, but Custer remained obstinate. The two finally came to a compromise: Custer's wagons would start after Davies; he would follow when ready. The Michigan men dismounted, lit their fires, and began to boil their coffee. Kilpatrick rode off in a huff after Davies.[31]

While Davies moved cautiously down the pike toward Warrenton, the Second New York riding in the lead, followed by the First West Virginia, Eighteenth Pennsylvania, and Fifth New York, Custer's troopers not only ate breakfast but also took a nap. About 3:30 P.M., more than three hours after Kilpatrick had left him, Custer finally mounted his men and headed up the pike. His brigade had advanced only about three hundred yards out of Buckland when one of his men spotted a solitary rider posted on top of the ridge to their left flank.

"That videte is a rebel," he shouted, pointing out the lone soldier. "He's dressed in gray."[32]

"It can't be possible," another scoffed.

"[But] look . . . [he is] riding in a circle . . . a rebel signal; our men don't do that."

The question of identity was answered by a shot as the single sentinel suddenly raised a pistol to fire at the Federal advance. The woods skirting the road then flared with smoke as Fitz Lee's troopers sent a blistering volley toward the Yankee column. Custer's men quickly dismounted, formed a line behind a fence, and answered the enemy with salvos of their own.[33]

The two adversaries both held for the moment; then Lee sent his troops ahead on foot in a line that extended beyond both of Custer's flanks. The Federals fell back to the span over Broad Creek; the Rebels advanced across the road, then turned right, facing Buckland, ready to continue the attack on Custer. They were now interposed between the two Federal brigades. Seeing that he was outnumbered and had no chance of holding the pike open for a Union retreat, Custer decided to mount his men and retire to safety over the stone bridge. Lee sent a part of his force after Custer. The rest he kept in place to await Kilpatrick's anticipated arrival.[34]

When Kilpatrick heard the gunfire to his rear, he must have felt a sinking sensation in his stomach that once more he had blundered into a trap. He sent a messenger ahead to alert Davies (who had just gone through New Baltimore, about five miles from Buckland) to halt the column. Davies, well aware that the sound of battle meant that he was threatened, did more than that. Without waiting for further orders, he turned his brigade about and started to gallop back toward Buckland. His regiments were now riding in reverse order, with the Fifth New York up front, the Second New York in the rear.[35]

Stuart was waiting about two hundred yards away, hidden out of sight, when Davies turned and bolted for the rear. The Confederates gave the "Rebel Yell" as they moved forward after the fleeing Federals. Later Stuart would dub the affair the "Buckland Races" to describe his pursuit of Davies, riding desperately back toward Broad Run.[36]

Kilpatrick, galloping at the van of the retreat, soon met a courier from Custer, who advised him of Lee's presence in force at the span over Broad Run. There was no point in continuing east. Kilpatrick halted and waited for Davies to come up. When the brigade leader arrived, hotly pressed by Stuart's cavalry, Kilpatrick presented his plan to evade the Rebel snare. They must abandon the pike and run for safety through the fields. The Second New York would have to stave off Stuart to give the rest of the brigade time to disperse.[37] When the Yankee troopers began to file off the road, the Rebels led by Stuart smashed through the ranks of the Second New York and bore down on Kilpatrick's command. The Union cavalry offered no resistance, scattering instead in all directions, every man for himself. Kilpatrick was toppled in the fracas, his racehorse, Lively, shot and killed.[38] He grabbed the reins of a loose mare, mounted, and joined with his men in fleeing in disarray from the field. "[A] deploring spectacle," a participant wrote, "[our] cavalry dashing . . . hatless and panic-striken."[39]

Kilpatrick and Davies both rushed north. At dusk they reached the pike, running from Gainesville through Thoroughfare Gap, where they formed the remnants from the Fifth New York and Eighteenth Pennsylvania to fight off the continuing pursuit of Stuart's men. Kilpatrick personally led several charges but was unable to complete his escape until a Union infantry regiment (the 143rd Pennsylvania) finally came forward to force the Rebels to withdraw.[40]

Kilpatrick only lost about 150 men killed, wounded, or captured in the fiasco, but all of his wagons fell into Confederate hands. Included was one of Custer's, containing a pack of personal letters, which was forwarded to Richmond. The Rebels gleefully published them in their newspapers.[41]

Kilpatrick "celebrated" the battle by throwing a party at his headquarters that evening. "There was milk punch and music, both of very good quality," Kidd remembered, "but the punch, palatable as it undeniably was, did not serve to take away the bad taste left by the affair."[42]

In his official report, Kilpatrick (as usual) presented a series of lies to mask his defeat, among them a claim that his force had retired slowly from the field. "[It was] a masterpiece of obfuscation," Starr concluded, "an attitude toward the truth out of the reach of any ordinary man."[43] He was more honest in private. "This is the only cavalry victory," Kilpatrick admitted to friends, "that the enemy can boast over my command."[44]

Stuart said it best. "The rout of the enemy cavalry at Buckland," he wrote, "was the most signal and complete . . . any cavalry . . . suffered during the war."[45]

Although Kilpatrick's defeat at Buckland was embarrassing, the drubbing was unimportant to the war. No ground was lost or won; no strategy changed as a result of the skirmishing between rival horsemen. The event, however, was most damaging to Kilpatrick's career. Both superiors and subordinates lost confidence in his leadership. Custer in particular was upset. "I . . . regret the loss of so many good men," he wrote, "all the more painful that it was not necessary."[46] He felt he could no longer trust Kilpatrick in battle.

Kilpatrick, however, was not particularly concerned by the defeat at Stuart's hands. He had the capacity to ignore adversity, and he remained as cheerful as ever, busily working on new schemes for harassing the enemy. He would eventually propose a plan that promised to make or break his career.

15

A Plan for Glory

After Kilpatrick's "Buckland Races" defeat, Lee's army continued their retreat until they reached the Rappahannock, where they spread out along the southern shore and began to set up their camps for the coming winter. Meade's men, however, following close on their adversaries' heels, were still looking to battle, so when the Yankees arrived at the river, they prepared to confront the Rebels.

When the Federals marched into position above the stream, Kilpatrick took advantage of the brief interim to solve some administrative problems. Most of his men had signed on for three years service, had fulfilled this obligation, and were expecting to be discharged. Kilpatrick gathered his troops to remind them about allegiance to their country, and he convinced all but a few to reenlist for the rest of the war. "[This] patriotic act makes me prouder than ever," he boasted. "The same love of country, the same devotion to the Union and the old Flag . . . burns as bright now as . . . the early days of '61!"[1]

A second problem lay with obtaining supplies. The son of General Meade, Captain George Meade II, acted as quartermaster for the Third Cavalry. Kilpatrick was displeased by young Meade's performance, and with arrogant audacity, he wrote Pleasonton to demand that the aide be relieved from duty because of incompetence.[2] Although the youthful captain may have been inept, Kilpatrick certainly knew that Meade would hear about and take exception to his charges. Inviting the wrath of a powerful superior was an incomprehensible act by a supposedly politically astute man.

General Meade, of course, soon learned of Kilpatrick's impertinent letter, and he was naturally angered by the slur against his son. He threatened to get rid of Kilpatrick by shipping him to a lesser post in the west.[3]

Fortunately for Kilpatrick, his sacking by Meade had a low priority at that time, and the issue faded as the Yankee commander dealt with pressures from Washington to force Lee into battle. Meade proposed a flanking movement toward Fredericksburg. Halleck disapproved this plan, leaving a frontal attack against Lee's position along the Rappahannock as the only viable option.[4]

The Yankees advanced in two lines on 7 November. On the west, General

John Sedgwick led one wing toward the site of the Orange and Alexandria railroad bridge across the Rappahannock; General French hurried a second infantry command toward Kelly's Ford, five miles downstream. The cavalry remained north of the river, guarding the flanks. Skirmishing continued throughout the day with little result. When darkness fell, Lee assumed that the fray had ended, but Sedgwick had other plans. He launched a night attack that drove the enemy out of their *tête du pont* above the river. Over fifteen hundred Rebels were taken prisoner.[5] Sedgwick's troops poured over the water the following morning but found that Lee had left his position, fleeing through the night until he arrived at the shores of the Rapidan River. Meade followed, establishing a new army headquarters at Culpeper; Kilpatrick set up his camp at Stevensburg.

In the lull after the Yankee victory, Kilpatrick's men assumed a lazy routine. "The day is ushered in with the reveille," Boudrye recalled, "the men of each company fall into line . . . drill sends them to the field to learn the tactics of war."[6]

Kilpatrick was readying his troops for yet another try to bring Lee to battle. But just before Meade launched this attack, a telegram arrived from West Point with devastating news. Alice was dead! No details remain to give the reason for her death, but she undoubtedly was a victim of a sudden plague such as influenza, as her demise on 22 November was totally unexpected.[7]

In filing for a leave of absence of ten days to attend the funeral of his spouse and to arrange for the care of his baby son, Kilpatrick asked that his principal aide, Captain Lewellyn G. Estes, be released to accompany him back to West Point. Pleasonton (possibly at the direction of a spiteful Meade) granted Kilpatrick his furlough but refused to allow Estes to leave his post. Kilpatrick was forced to make the sorrowful trip north alone.[8] When he left camp, Meade started forming his army for the move south against Lee.

The Union attack called for a devious turning movement, one in which upon contact with the Southern army, they would swing right, away from Richmond, to flank their enemy. Lee, however, was not fooled. He moved west to block the Federal advance, assuming a position along Mine Run. When Meade saw he was stymied, he retreated back above the Rapidan and went into winter quarters.[9]

About the same time that Meade was mounting his attack against Lee, Grant charged Bragg's lines at Chattanooga. He had assumed command of the besieged Union army back in October, strengthening his force with reinforcements provided by Meade plus the addition of an army under William T. Sherman. While Grant was building up his infantry, Bragg was reducing his numbers. He had dispatched Longstreet's Corps north on 4 November to confront Burnside's army, guarding the mountain gaps by Knoxville.

Grant's advance against the undermanned Bragg began on 23 November. He routed the Rebels off the heights ringing Chattanooga and pressed them

into northwestern Georgia. Longstreet, his rear exposed by the Southern retreat, was forced to abandon his siege of Burnside.

The embarrassing defeat led Bragg to resign as head of the Army of Tennessee, but instead of fading into obscurity, he was "kicked upstairs," becoming military advisor to President Jefferson Davis. William J. Hardee was picked
to take Bragg's position, but he refused the post because of an "inability to
serve." Joe Johnston finally assumed command.[10]

Kilpatrick no doubt learned of Grant's success when he returned to camp
at Stevensburg on 3 December. His troops (settled in their winter quarters,
awaiting the spring when they would renew their fighting) were buzzing about
the Federal victory at Chattanooga. Their attention, however, soon returned to
duty as Kilpatrick introduced a strenuous training schedule. "The winter of
1863–64 was one of hard work," Kidd related. "[Only] at division . . . headquarters . . . was there time for play."[11] Kilpatrick had laid out a track where he
and Custer gambled on horse races almost every day.

In early January, despite his recent difficulties with Meade, Kilpatrick was
among a list of officers nominated for promotion. He would not get his major
general's stars, however, until the Senate approved the advancement. He started
planning a campaign to gain the congressmen's blessing, but before he could
act, Kilpatrick received another woeful wire from West Point. His young son
was dead. Judson B. Kilpatrick died 11 January, possibly from the same disorder that had claimed his mother. Kilpatrick once more asked for ten days leave
of absence to attend the funeral.[12]

On the return trip to Stevensburg, Kilpatrick swung by his family home in
Sussex, where he induced some old friends to circulate a petition in support of
his recent nomination to major general. Fifty-five citizens signed their names
to the affidavit, which was sent directly to President Lincoln.[13]

Kilpatrick also paid a visit to nearby Rutgers College, who crowned the
favorite son with honorary degrees: bachelor and master of arts.[14] These accolades offered further proof that Kilpatrick should be advanced in rank.

When he rode back into Stevensburg on 21 January 1864, "gloomy and
desperate . . . in [a] state to try something wild,"[15] Kilpatrick was told that an
important visitor was waiting to see him. Senator Jacob B. Howard of Michigan had come to talk with Kilpatrick, probably to review his qualifications for
a promotion.[16] Their subsequent discussion no doubt included the maltreat-
ment of Union soldiers held captive in Richmond.

The whole concept of "prisoners of war" had supposedly been eliminated
by a cartel, signed 22 July 1862, providing that "all prisoners . . . [will] be
discharged on parole in ten days after their capture . . . [and] transported to
points . . . for exchange."[17] Two centers for the swapping of captives were
established: Vicksburg, Mississippi, and Aiken's Landing (on the James River,
east of Richmond). The rationale that led to the agreement was supposedly

humanitarian, but the actual impetus was pragmatic. Enlistments in both armies would be enhanced by lessening the threat of possible incarceration.

The plan worked well at first, but problems soon arose that stemmed the exchange of prisoners. When Lincoln issued his "Emancipation Proclamation" on 1 January 1863, the Confederacy was incensed. "[It was] a call for negroes to rise in the most horrible of all warfare," President Davis wrote, "a servile insurrection." In retaliation, he refused to return captured Federal officers.[18] The South also held back all Black soldiers, declaring them to be fugitive slaves.

Another unexpected snag in the scheme was the increase in the number of prisoners. When the men learned that their "penalty" for surrendering was a parole that sent them home, thousands (especially Yankees) decided to get "a little rest from soldiering" by throwing down their arms.[19] Because the South lacked transportation facilities to send captives back through the exchange centers, they usually handed prisoners their papers where they were captured, and the men took a direct route back to their families. The Union authorities attempted to slow this flow by insisting that prisoners must be processed at Aiken's Landing or Vicksburg. When the latter site fell to Grant in July 1863, the tide of Northern prisoners swung east to Richmond, where they were held pending their moving on to Aiken's Landing. The Rebel capital was soon inundated with Federals the South could not adequately feed or house.[20]

Information regarding the plight of the prisoners came from a number of sources, one of whom was a Federal spy who lived in Richmond. Elizabeth Van Lew was a member of a prominent Southern family, dwelling in an old, elegant mansion in the Church Hill section of the city. She hid her nefarious activities by acting demented, causing her neighbors to call her "Crazy Bet."[21]

Mrs. Van Lew not only provided the Federals details as to the number and location of Union captives (one thousand officers at Libby Warehouse, sixty-three hundred enlisted men on Belle Isle in the James River, and about forty-three hundred others scattered about the city in smaller buildings)[22] but also included a plan for a raid that could free the prisoners. She identified the strengths and locations of the Rebel detachments guarding the capital and noted that a force attacking from the west would find no opposition to entering Richmond. To make sure that the Southern force would not contest a charge, Mrs. Van Lew suggested that some diversionary actions be implemented: land some troops east at White House on the Pamunkey River; feint an assault south at Petersburg; and have Meade to the north act as if he meant to confront Lee along the Rappahannock.[23]

She sent her plans to Ben Butler, now in charge of the Army of the James, headquartered at Fortress Monroe. He was intrigued with Mrs. Van Lew's idea, and started to initiate action by contacting Meade to request his cooperation.

Kilpatrick no doubt first heard about this opportunity because of Butler's inquiry, and he saw at once that leading the raid would bring the fame he so badly wanted. Thinking of a means to wrest control of the operation from Butler and knowing that if he proposed a plan to Pleasonton his superior was likely to give the assignment to another, Kilpatrick came up with an ingenious ploy. He would bypass the chain of command by going directly to President Lincoln and induce him to dictate that Kilpatrick lead the charge on Richmond! And he apparently convinced Senator Howard to take this note to the chief executive.

Before Howard could convince Lincoln to order the raid by Kilpatrick, Butler launched his assault on Richmond. His plan, however, did not follow the tactics suggested by Mrs. Van Lew. Instead of marching his troops against the capital from the west, Butler decided to hurry up the Peninsula and mount a frontal assault from the east. He did, however, ask that Meade fake an attack from the Rapidan to occupy Lee's attention while he was advancing on the city.

Sedgwick, temporarily commanding Meade's army, did not like Butler's plan, "looking on it as childish,"[24] but Washington insisted that he cooperate. On the morning of 6 February, the Sixth Corps started wading the Rapidan River at Morton's Ford. The cavalry advanced along both flanks, Kilpatrick to the right, Wesley Merritt's troopers on the left.[25] After a brief but furious skirmish with the enemy, the Union retired to await word of Butler's raid.

General Isaac J. Wistar led the attack, which included four thousand infantry and two thousand cavalry. They broke camp at 9:00 A.M. on 6 February. Wistar's troopers moved ahead to take Bottom's Bridge across the Chickahominy River, twelve miles east of Richmond, to open a path into the city for the trailing foot soldiers. When these troopers reached their objective about 3:00 A.M. the following morning, they were surprised to see the span defended by a host of Rebels. The Confederates had been alerted to the oncoming Union by a deserter, William Boyle, a Yankee soldier whose sentence to death for killing an officer had been set aside by Lincoln. Wistar mounted a feeble charge against the bridge at daylight, failed to dislodge the enemy, and then withdrew in ignominy back to Fortress Monroe.[26]

On 11 February, after learning of Kilpatrick's plans to free the Yankee prisoners held in Richmond (probably from Senator Howard), Lincoln sent a wire to Pleasonton. "Order General Kilpatrick to proceed to Washington," he wrote, "and report to the President . . . it is not expected that [he] will be absent more than two or three days."[27]

Pleasonton had no idea why Lincoln was calling for Kilpatrick, but he followed the president's orders and released his subordinate from duty for the visit.

Upon reaching the White House on 12 February, Kilpatrick saw that Lincoln held more interest in him as a courier than a soldier. The president had published an amnesty proclamation back in December, offering a pardon to Southerners who took an oath of allegiance to the Union. Few Confederates had responded to the overture. Rather than admit his idea was perhaps naïve, Lincoln thought people were not coming forward because they had not heard about his new policy. If Kilpatrick rode to Richmond, could he distribute leaflets on the amnesty proclamation along his way? Kilpatrick (with no doubt false enthusiasm) informed the chief executive that this was not only possible but also a superb plan. Lincoln was so pleased with this answer that he immediately approved the raid and sent Kilpatrick next door to the War Department to provide Stanton with details.[28]

Kilpatrick submitted a formal proposal for the raid on 16 February. He would start by crossing the Rapidan River at Ely's Ford with four thousand troopers and six guns and head for Spotsylvania Court House. Two groups would disperse at this point to tear up the railroad tracks behind him, preventing Lee from sending infantry south to disrupt the raid. Both would scatter Lincoln's amnesty proclamation along the path to their destinations. One band would rejoin the main column at Carmel Church near the North Anna River; the second raiding party would move independently below the James River to wreak havoc with the railroads and a canal in that area. Kilpatrick would then lead his men through Hanover Junction, down the Brook Pike, and on into Richmond, where he would release the prisoners. He suggested that Butler might help in this endeavor by bringing a force east from Fortress Monroe. The retreat would be either north through Fredericksburg or east to West Point on the York River.[29]

Stanton sent Kilpatrick's plan on to Meade, asking for his opinion as to its viability; Meade gave a copy to Pleasonton for his review. The latter, furious with Kilpatrick for having bypassed the chain of command, protested against the scheme. "[It] is not feasible," he pronounced. "Before Kilpatrick could do much damage, their [the enemy's] vulnerable points would be secured. I cannot recommend it."[30]

Although Meade no doubt concurred with Pleasonton, he saw Kilpatrick's scheme in a different light. Lincoln obviously favored a raid, and good politics suggested that he should support the president. And this was his opportunity to get rid of Kilpatrick. By agreeing with the cavalryman that a dash to Richmond was "practicable," Meade could induce Kilpatrick to risk the impossible. His resulting failure would be the perfect excuse for Meade to relieve an obnoxious subordinate from command. Meade was probably baiting this trap when he said that the raid could be "the greatest feat of the war."[31]

Kilpatrick, blinded by the brilliant rays of potential glory, never considered the consequences of failure. He was so eager to proceed with the raid that he proposed a bet to Pleasonton: "$5,000 that I enter Richmond."[32] His superior accepted the wager.

On 18 February, although he had received no official authorization to proceed, Kilpatrick knew that his raid was approved. He received instructions to dispatch an officer to Washington to handpick horses, "the very best, well shod able to take the strain of . . . hard, merciless riding."[33]

Although he had much to accomplish before embarking on the raid, Kilpatrick devoted a great deal of his time during the following days to getting ready for a party. The Union Second Corps was hosting a Washington's Birthday Ball on 22 February. Many important people would attend, and he meant to impress them and gain their support for his promotion.

Guests began to arrive in Culpeper on Friday, 19 February, the day after Kilpatrick's orders about horses. First to show up were three hundred young women, partners for the soldiers, who came south from Washington by rail. They were followed by a host of dignitaries, including Senators Morton S. Wilkerson and Zachariah Chandler; Vice President Hannibal Hamlin; Senator William Sprague and his new wife, the former Kate Chase (daughter of Salmon P. Chase, Lincoln's secretary of the Treasury); a group from the British Embassy; various socialites from New York City; and even a few of the Supreme Court judges. Kilpatrick made sure that congressmen stayed in the ornate mansion in Stevensburg that he had confiscated for his headquarters.[34] They were trapped there, forced to hear him plead his case for promotion.

On 20 February (Saturday night), the celebrities met in Culpeper for patriotic addresses. Kilpatrick took a turn at the podium, and "his speech was the gem of the evening," according to Kidd. "[He] stirred up no end of enthusiasm."[35]

The ball was held Monday evening in a building erected just for this occasion. The infantrymen had cut down scores of trees in the area, sawed them into planks, and assembled the boards into a structure that stood one hundred feet long and fifty feet wide [36] Music and dancing continued through the night, and everyone had a grand time. Even the taciturn Meade stayed up past 3:00 A.M.

On Tuesday, 23 February, the activities ended with a review by the Second Corps. Kilpatrick's cavalry opened the parade, riding in "their usual combination of Gypsy and Don Cossack." The artillery and infantry followed. Late in the day, the troopers reappeared to make a mock charge. "[It] was entertaining enough," Lyman stated, "but rather mobby in style."[37]

Although most of the guests started north on Tuesday, one man remained behind to visit with Kilpatrick. Colonel Ulric Dahlgren, son of the eminent admiral, John A. Dahlgren, was "tall, fair, handsome, and polished," the perfect picture of a soldier.[38] He had lost a leg while pursuing Lee's troops after Gettysburg and was just now returning to active duty. Lincoln had told him that Kilpatrick was planning a raid on Richmond, and Dahlgren wanted to join the entourage.

**Union colonel Ulric Dahlgren, from *The Photographic History of the Civil
War,* edited by Francis Trevelyan Miller. 10 vols. New York: The Review of
Reviews Company, 1911.**

Kilpatrick was delighted to have Dahlgren in his force. The young colonel, only twenty-two years of age, brought not only the prestige of his family's
name but also a record of unwavering courage. And he believed in the enterprise. "If successful," Dahlgren had related, "it will be the grandest thing on
record."[39]

To accommodate Dahlgren, Kilpatrick introduced a major change to his plan. His new associate would lead the separate detachment to the James River, but instead of destroying the railroad tracks and canal below the capital, Dahlgren's troops would charge into Richmond from the south at the same time that Kilpatrick moved against the city from above. He would be responsible for liberating all of the captives from Belle Isle and Libby prisons.[40]

Meade, too, altered the plan that Kilpatrick had first written for Stanton. "To distract the enemy's attention and prevent the detachment of any force toward Richmond," Meade ordered a simultaneous advance by infantry (Sedgwick's Sixth Corps) toward Madison Court House, and cavalry (assigned to Custer) against Charlottesville.[41] The latter was available because Kilpatrick refused to allow him to take part in the raid, no doubt a punishment for past insubordination. Meade also denied Kilpatrick the aid he had requested from Butler. A force would come out of Fortress Monroe, but the men would halt at New Kent Court House. Their mission was to protect the retreat from Richmond, not to join in the assault on the Southern capital.[42]

On 24 February Kilpatrick received his orders, which were deliberately vague, designed to give him a free hand in directing the raid. "Proceed by such routes and make dispositions as from time to time you . . . find necessary . . . you will not be confined to any specific instructions," the dispatch read.[43]

He immediately began gathering his troops, but instead of choosing specific regiments from the divisions, Kilpatrick summoned just "the flower of [each outfit] . . . mounted on its best horses."[44] The mission was kept secret. Upon arriving at Stevensburg, the men were only told to "go into camp and make [themselves] comfortable."[45] Few of them, however, had any doubts as to their future. "This looked extremely raidish," Major W. H. Spira observed, and like most, he looked forward to a gallop behind the enemy line. "It is easier to get . . a hundred for a raid," he noted, "than . . . one to groom an extra horse."[46]

On 27 February Meade gave Kilpatrick final approval to ride on Richmond. In doing so, he laid the trap he would later spring against Kilpatrick. "No detailed instructions are given," Meade said, "since the plan of your operation has been proposed by yourself. . . . [I] consider success possible with secrecy, good management, and the utmost expedition [on your part]."[47] In other words this scheme was all Kilpatrick's idea, and if he failed, it would be his fault.

On the eve of his ride for Richmond, Kilpatrick should have been concerned over placing himself in a "no-win" situation. If he failed to free the

Union men held prisoner in the Southern capital, Meade would sack him for not achieving this objective. And if he succeeded in his daring mission, his fame would probably be temporary. Meade and Pleasonton, incensed because Kilpatrick had bypassed them to induce the president to assign him command of the raid, were determined to destroy his reputation, and they would soon find some excuse to remove him from duty.

Kilpatrick, however, seemed oblivious to the danger he faced. Flushed by the plaudits of the politicians attending the Washington's Birthday Ball, he gloried in the present's glow without any thought to either problems from the past or perils of the future. This was typical for Kilpatrick. He lived only for the moment, for which he always found reasons to regard as pleasant. He was no doubt grinning with anticipation when he broke camp at dusk on 28 February 1864.

16

The Richmond Raid

Dahlgren, leading 460 troopers, moved southeast toward Ely's Ford on the Rapidan River at 6:00 P.M. on 28 February 1864. His initial mission was to wade the stream and round up the Rebel pickets below the water before they could alert their superiors to the Union presence.[1]

The Federal advance reached the ford about 11:00 P.M. and captured sixteen Confederates along the shore. Dahlgren then headed toward Spotsylvania Court House. "It was a complete surprise," Kilpatrick gloated in a 1:00 A.M. note to Pleasonton. "No alarm was given."[2] But he was wrong.

As Dahlgren rode toward the ford, two Federal troopers, straggling at the rear of the column, were captured by Rebel scouts on foot. The Confederates forced their prisoners into the forest, mounted their horses, and then caught up with Dahlgren's parade. They stayed with the tail of the line as it crossed the river, then peeled off to hurry to Wade Hampton's headquarters to warn the Southern cavalry leader that the enemy had moved below the Rapidan.[3] The secrecy, so essential to Kilpatrick's success, was breached. Within hours after the start of his raid, the Rebels were already preparing their pursuit.

Kilpatrick left his camp about 7:00 P.M., only an hour after Dahlgren's departure. His force was composed of about thirty-six hundred mounted men, supported by six cannons, six ambulances, eight caissons, and three wagons.[4]

Captain Joseph Glosloski described the scene as Kilpatrick's troopers crossed the river. "The first night of our march was beautiful," he wrote. "Myriads of stars twinkled in heaven . . . [as] the moon threw its silvery light upon [the] Rapidan."[5] The men rode their horses at a steady walk with no stops to rest.

When the main column reached Spotsylvania at 8:00 A.M. on 29 February, they encountered an old woman with a flock of geese. The Yankee troopers charged the gaggle, whacking at their heads with sabers. "Quite a few were decapitated," Spira admitted.[6]

The distraught female tried to defend her poultry, but her only weapon, a broom, was no match against the Federals' swords. "You'ns all ought to be

ashamed of you'ns selves," she sobbed, "to come heyer and destroy we'ns
things. You'ns are nothing but nasty dirty Yankees."[7]

Kilpatrick and his troopers found her despair amusing, and they had a
good laugh before continuing their ride south toward Mount Pleasant. They
stopped at the Po River, above the small village, for lunch. While the trek was
supposedly made in haste, the men had taken time to forage along their way.
"A chicken, a goose, a ham, or a side dangled from almost every saddle,"
Spira stated, "but [we had] scarcely . . . time . . . to cook a cup of coffee."[8]

While the men were eating their lunch, Kilpatrick sent a cocky message
back to Pleasonton. "Twenty miles closer to Richmond, and all right," he wrote.
"Will double my bet that I enter Richmond."[9]

Kilpatrick led his column by the towns of Mt. Pleasant, New Market, and
Chilesburg to the North Anna River, where he crossed via Anderson's Ferry.
The riders continued to push forward, reaching Beaver Dam Station on the
Virginia Central Railroad about 5:00 P.M.[10]

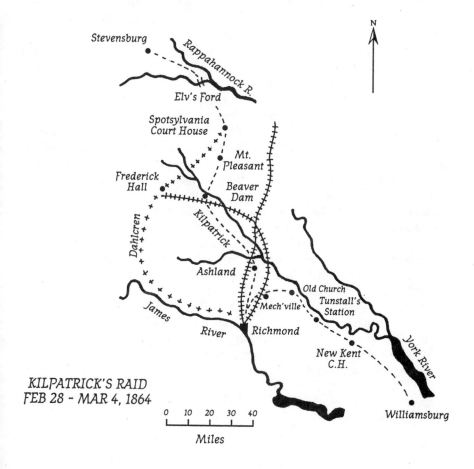

KILPATRICK'S RAID
FEB 28 – MAR 4, 1864

0   10   20   30   40

Miles

After halting in town, Kilpatrick attempted to contact Dahlgren, who had diverged right at Spotsylvania Court House and was now at Frederick Hall, ten miles west of Beaver Dam Station. He was following a parallel route to Kilpatrick's, moving faster so he could reach the James River, cross, and then gallop into Richmond from the south at the same time as Kilpatrick's assault from the north. Gloskoski, the signal officer, found a high point to unfurl his flags, but the effort to reach Dahlgren proved futile. The view was blocked by trees, plus the weather had suddenly turned foul. Ominous dark clouds boiled overhead and a cold wet wind had started to blow. Rain, mixed with snow, began to fall.[11]

Amidst the gloom, Kilpatrick dispersed his troopers to destroy the town. "Twenty wooden buildings were at once set on fire," Gloskoski wrote, "forming one sheet of flame, rising high above the surrounding woods, and the black forms of our soldiers jumping around [the burning structures] seemed from a distance like demons on some hellish sport."[12]

While the buildings blazed, a train chugged toward the depot from the south. The engine stopped short of the burning town, and about twenty-five Rebels leaped to the ground and advanced toward Kilpatrick's men. They fired a volley, then scattered to escape the Federal counterattack that followed. The train left the Confederate band stranded as it hurriedly backed up, returning to Richmond.[13]

Kilpatrick knew that the retreating engine would alert the Confederate capital to his approach and that he had to move quickly before the enemy could prepare their defense, so he called his troops to saddle and headed south again. "Now it stormed in earnest," Gloskoski remembered. "Sharp wind and sleet forced men to close their eyes. The night was so dark . . . even the river in front could not be seen. . . . So complete a darkness I never saw."[14]

The weather was bad enough, but now the Rebels were beginning to harass the column. Bullets flew out from the sides of the way as bushwhackers shot and then fled before the Federal riders could answer the volleys. "The flashes from the enemies firing as we [rode past] seemed like fireflies of a summer's night," one related.[15] The road was blocked at a number of spots by fences and felled trees. Kilpatrick had no choice but endure this hounding, since he could not afford to slow his progress.

About 8:00 P.M., Kilpatrick halted to allow the column to close (his troopers were strung out for miles behind him) and to give his force a chance to eat. "The men were weary, wet, cold, and hungry," Kidd recited, "but there was no complaining."[16] The trek had been difficult, but everyone was still looking forward to their mission in Richmond.

Kilpatrick started out again at 1:00 A.M. on 1 March. He had intended to cross over the South Anna River at Ground Squirrel Bridge, but his guide (a Negro who supposedly knew the area) was confused by the impenetrable darkness and led the force toward Ashland instead.[17] When the day dawned, the weather improved. The sky was cloudy, and it was still very cold, but the sleet that had coated the men with ice during the night had abated, replaced by a penetrating drizzle.

While the Federals trotted southeast in the growing light, they encountered and captured some enemy pickets, fronting a Rebel detachment guarding the railroad bridge above Ashland. The prisoners said (falsely) that the strength of the nearby force totaled two thousand troops. These Confederates were in perfect position either to strike the flank of the Union column or to follow Kilpatrick into the Southern capital and attack his rear, catching him in a pincer. "Something of some sort had to be done," Spira recorded, "[or] a trip to Richmond for us, not under Kilpatrick's command, was a probability."[18]

Kilpatrick quickly devised a clever strategy. He sent Major William P. Hall with 450 troopers to fake an attack on the Confederates, who would assume that Kilpatrick's target was the bridge. While they held their place, protecting the span, he would rush south with his main force. Other enemy soldiers in the area, hearing the engagement, would hurry to that point, taking them away from his path into the capital.[19]

While Hall rode north, Kilpatrick crossed the South Anna River. He halted briefly to rip up the railroad track, then proceeded down the Brook Turnpike. By 10:00 A.M., he stood at the outer defensive line of the Rebel capital, exactly on schedule. "[We could] look into the streets," Kidd related, "and count the spires on the churches."[20] Dahlgren's troops should have been charging into the city at that very moment.

Kilpatrick listened, but the only sound of battle came from the north, where Hall was engaged with the Confederates guarding the bridge. Kilpatrick advanced slowly. His Union riders passed through the vacant outer bastion, five miles from the city, and continued down the Brook Turnpike. They met only token resistance, which was easily brushed aside.[21]

At 1:00 P.M., when he arrived at the intermediate line defending Richmond, about a mile from the city, Kilpatrick's van was suddenly subjected to cannon fire. The salvos came from artillery posted above and below the pike, two hundred yards in front of the breastworks. Kilpatrick was about one thousand yards from the bastion.[22]

Peering anxiously through the cold, murky mist, he saw that except for a few houses scattered along the left of the pike, there was no cover for his troops. And the only path available to horses was the road. The fields alongside were soft and muddy, intersected by wide, deep ditches.[23]

Davies, riding with Kilpatrick, offered a strategy for broaching the barricade. He would dismount five hundred men and send them ahead through the fields on the left. Using the homes as a shield, he would flank the Rebel guns and force them to retire. This would allow Kilpatrick to bring his artillery forward

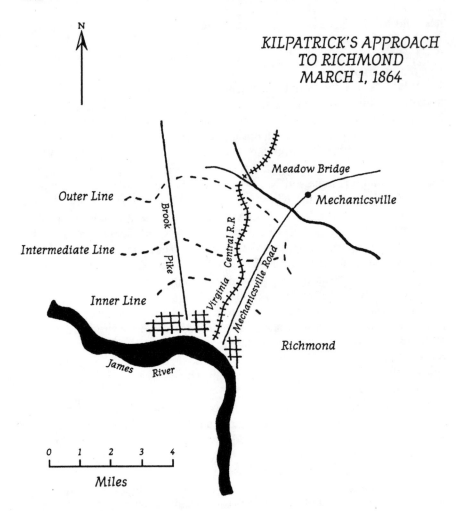

N

KILPATRICK'S APPROACH
TO RICHMOND
MARCH 1, 1864

Meadow Bridge

Outer Line

Mechanicsville

Intermediate Line

Brook Pike

Virginia Central R.R.

Mechanicsville Road

Inner Line

Richmond

James River

0   1   2   3   4

Miles

to open against the bulwark. When the pieces began firing (as if to support the assault on the left), the enemy would be distracted, clearing the way for a charge by the bulk of the command directly down the pike to smash through the barrier blocking their way.[24] Kilpatrick approved the plan.

The scheme worked to perfection. When Davies's men got within range of the Rebel cannons, they opened fire, and the Confederates withdrew their pieces behind their breastworks.[25] Kilpatrick's cannons were rushed forward, and they started a barrage against the fort. The enemy, which "did not appear to be formidable in numbers," answered with musketry. Their aim was poor, as they kept missing the most conspicuous target, Captain Estes, Kilpatrick's adjutant, who "was exposing himself in most audacious fashion . . . his cape lined with red thrown back on one shoulder."[26]

Those watching from the rear were filled with anticipation. "The goal was in sight," Kidd recalled. "An order to [form] into a line of squadron columns was . . . expected. That a dash into the city or at least an attempt . . . be made nobody doubted."[27]

Kilpatrick, however, hesitated. The time was 3:00 P.M. Dahlgren's band had still not made their appearance. Had he and his men been taken prisoner? Kilpatrick could hear the whistle of a locomotive to the north. Were the Rebels about to attack his rear? He saw movement behind the Confederate breastworks. Was the garrison being reinforced? The sky up above was darkening. Was the storm about to renew its fury? Kilpatrick would later admit to having such concerns.[28] But he must have been worried about other factors, too.

Perhaps for the first time Kilpatrick saw the futility in his plan to free the Federal captives. Even if he passed through the barricade up ahead into the capital to open the doorways to Libby and Belle Isle, what could he do then? He had made no provisions for feeding and arming the prisoners, or transporting them to safety. Kilpatrick could only assemble the men into a herd and drive them north like a drove of cattle, while the Rebels circled and sniped like wild Indians at his slow-going column. The most likely result would be his own capture and imprisonment.

Kilpatrick cared about his personal safety. He was not brave. In previous battle situations, he had usually pushed his force forward while he cowered in the rear. In this instance, however, if he stayed behind, Kilpatrick risked even greater danger, with hordes of Rebels charging from above in pursuit of his advance. His "safest" option, should he attack, was to ride straight ahead with his men toward the enemy lying in wait to shoot him.

For whatever reason, at the crucial moment in the raid, Kilpatrick found that he lacked the courage to continue. He recalled Davies and his men and ordered a retreat northeast toward the haven of Butler's camp.[29]

When the Federal horsemen retired, disappearing into the fog like exorcised ghosts, the Rebels behind the breastworks no doubt gave a collective sigh of relief. Only five hundred in all, heavy artillerymen from four Virginia battalions who had had no prior experience as infantry,[30] their best hope had been to hold off Kilpatrick's superior numbers, not to drive them away. They were content to see the Union riders leave and offered no pursuit.

About 5:00 P.M. Kilpatrick's van reached Meadow Bridge, where Major Hall and his 450 troops rejoined the column. He had left his confrontation up north when he heard the fight break out below along the Brook Turnpike. Kilpatrick guided his force over the Chickahominy River, set fire to the span behind him, and then moved back toward Mechanicsville, where he planned to spend the night. The weather had turned nasty. "A raw, rainy night," Kidd remembered, "and snow was falling. . . . It was very dark."[31]

Kilpatrick went into camp about two miles southwest of Mechanicsville, along the pike running back toward Richmond. As foraging parties spread out to gather up provisions, the troopers prepared for the long, cold night facing them. "We were without shelter," Spira recalled, "not a tent . . . in the command. Everything was wet, so that it was almost impossible to build a fire, which meant no coffee."[32]

While the men huddled in "magnificent discomfiture," Kilpatrick was busily planning his next move. His foragers had brought back word that the Southerners had concentrated all of their available forces along the Brook Turnpike and that the Mechanicsville Road into Richmond lay undefended. At 10:00 P.M., Kilpatrick suddenly decided that he would try to enter Richmond after all. He would mount a night attack with two detachments, each composed of five hundred men. One was assigned the task of freeing the Union officers held in Libby Prison; the second would make an attempt to kidnap President Davis.[33] Kilpatrick would remain in position with the rest of his troops (about twenty-five hundred men) "to cover their retreat with the prisoners."[34]

Men were roused, horses were saddled, and columns were formed by midnight. But just as the attacking force was set to depart toward their objective, consternation exploded in the rear. The enemy was attacking Kilpatrick camp!

Wade Hampton, who heard about Kilpatrick's Raid within a few hours of its start, had left his headquarters at 10:30 P.M. on 29 February. He rode south with about three hundred troops, determined to collar Kilpatrick. After twenty-five hours of hard riding, Hampton had finally reached his prey. He made his plan carefully. One hundred men would dismount and move forward as skirmishers; two field guns would accompany the pickets and the rest of the Rebel force would follow on horseback. When those in the lead reached the edge of the Union camp, the cannons would fire, the signal to charge.[35]

The assault was a complete shock to the Yankees. "The only order was to retreat,"Kidd stated.[36] "Stand to horse! Mount! Form ranks! By fours, march!," Spira recalled everybody yelling. "[And] Kilpatrick's voice was heard above all others."[37]

"I was forced to recall my [two detachments] to resist this attack," Kilpatrick confessed. "Considerable confusion ensued."[38] He led his force west on the road to Old Church, stopped to offer a brief stand, then at 1:00 A.M. continued to retire. "It was impossible to distinguish roads," Spira wrote. "Splash! Splash! through the thin mud, following the splash ahead of us . . . following someone who . . . knew the road."[39]

At 8:00 A.M. on 2 March, Kilpatrick arrived at an intersection just below Old Church, stopped for breakfast, and then headed east again. The enemy, who had been nipping at his heels all through the cold and rainy night, continued to

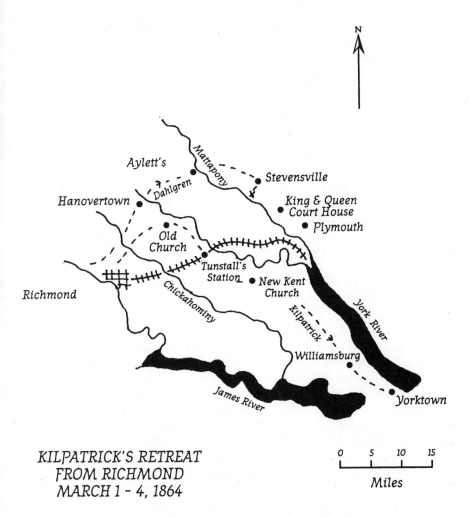

KILPATRICK'S RETREAT
FROM RICHMOND
MARCH 1 - 4, 1864

torment the ranks, and Kilpatrick finally lost his patience. He halted, formed battle lines, and charged the band who had been hounding his column. "This was the last we saw of the enemy," Spira wrote. "They gave us no further trouble."[40]

Kilpatrick held in place for five hours, hoping to see Dahlgren and his party come into view, but the compatriots did not show. At 1:00 P.M. he renewed the retreat. The troops rode through Putney's Ferry and White House Landing, in hope of discovering a way across the Pamunkey River, but they could not find the boats needed for the crossing. When they reached Tunstall's Station, Kilpatrick devised a scheme to fool the enemy into thinking he led a sizable host. He had the men dismount and prepare for the evening. "No sooner were fires well ablaze," Spira related, "than we were ordered . . . 'Saddle up [and] move camp.' This was kept up until the whole country was lit up . . . to create the impression [of] a large force."[41]

At 5:30 P.M., soon after Kilpatrick had finally halted for good, Captain John F. B. Mitchell with 250 survivors from Dahlgren's band straggled into the camp. Dahlgren had been leading them east, trying to find Kilpatrick, but during the previous night, the young colonel with about one hundred of his troopers had gotten separated from the column. His fate was unknown.[42]

Mitchell brought Kilpatrick up-to-date. After tearing up the railroad track and distributing leaflets on Lincoln's Amnesty Proclamation at Frederick's Hall, Dahlgren's party had hurried south to the James River. There, the morning of 1 March, Dahlgren divided his force in two. Mitchell led one hundred men east toward Richmond, destroying canal locks and burning mills along the way; Dahlgren, with the rest of the riders, looked for a spot where they could ford the water to approach the capital from the south.[43]

Dahlgren's guide, Martin Robinson, an ex-slave who was familiar with the area, led the party to Jude's Ferry, where a ford was located. The river, however, was at flood stage, and it was impossible to wade across. Dahlgren, thinking he had been duped, hanged the Negro for his supposed treachery.[44]

Pressing east above the James, Dahlgren halted to rest at Short Pump, about eight miles west of Richmond. Mitchell and his band caught up with him there. They had just begun their final drive toward the city when they heard Kilpatrick skirmishing with the Rebels on the Brook Turnpike.[45]

About five miles outside of Richmond, Dahlgren started to confront bush-whackers. He continued to push forward, but by the time he reached the out-skirts of the capital, the opposition to his advance was overwhelming. The young colonel was forced to retreat westward, intending to wheel north as soon as possible to unite with Kilpatrick. In the darkness, beset by the cold, driving rain and snow, Dahlgren with 100 of his men lost contact with the rest of his column. Mitchell led the 250 troopers with him in a wide arc, riding nonstop all night 1 March and all day 2 March until he reached Kilpatrick at Tunstall's Station.[46]

On Thursday morning, 3 March, Kilpatrick formed into column and moved east toward Butler's line on the Peninsula. His entourage was increased not only by Mitchell's band but also by the addition of hundreds of slaves who had come to his bivouac from the surrounding plantations in a flight for freedom. "[They] trudged, often weary and footsore, keeping up with the columns," Spira recorded, "from the gray-haired [men] bent over with age, to the little pickaninny scarcely large enough to toddle, all anxious to be free."[47]

That forenoon, Kilpatrick was met by Colonel Samuel P. Spear with the Eleventh Pennsylvania Cavalry, sent by Butler to usher the raiders to his lines.

He guided Kilpatrick to New Kent Court House, where an all-Black brigade of infantry was waiting. The combined command continued on to Burnt Ordinary, where they stopped for the night.[48]

During the afternoon Kilpatrick had left the ranks to check on his flanks. He soon encountered some bushwhackers. A number of the troopers escorting Kilpatrick were captured or killed while he was scampering back to the safety of the column.[49]

Kilpatrick woke his force early on 4 March to resume the trek east. They passed through Williamsburg about 10:00 A.M. and finally rode into Yorktown, Butler's headquarters, about 4:00 P.M. The raid was over.[50]

The slaves left the column at this point, heading into "Slabtown," the village that Butler had constructed to house the contraband. "Such a shouting, hallooing, 'glory, glory, hallelujah,' singing, hugging, kissing . . . I have never seen," Spira said. "Many a trooper . . . drew his coat sleeve over his eyes, as something welled in his throat.[51]

The troopers bivouacked southeast of Yorktown, next to where the colored regiments were stationed. The Negroes had fine facilities: large "A" tents for sleeping, clean straw for beds, even a sutler's store offering delicacies.[52] This camp was located on high, dry ground. Kilpatrick's men, in their wet, muddy, uniforms, eyed the scene with jealous eyes as they looked up from the boggy turf assigned to them.

That night, for the first time since leaving the banks of the Rapidan River, Kilpatrick's troopers finally took the offense. They charged the Blacks' quarters about midnight, rousted the Negroes out of their straw beds, and drove them from their tents, which Kilpatrick's men took back to their own bivouac. "All's fair in love and war," Spira explained lamely.[53]

While his men were improving their lot, Kilpatrick was attempting to do the same for himself. He wrote his initial report of the raid. "I have failed to accomplish the great objective of the expedition," Kilpatrick had to confess. He then tried to gloss over his lack of success with the usual series of lies. "I . . . lost less than 150 men," he purported, despite knowing that not only were over two hundred missing from his detachment but also that Dahlgren with another hundred troopers were probable casualties. Kilpatrick went on to proclaim, "The entire command is in good order, and needs but a few days' rest."[54] In truth the men might recuperate quickly, but the horses were so spent they would be useless for weeks to come.

Pleasonton was not willing to give Kilpatrick the time he needed to rejuvenate his force. "His command is composed of picked troops from all divisions," he observed, "and the organization and effectiveness of the remaining divisions is seriously hampered by the absence of [this] large number."[55] He made arrangements for Kilpatrick's men to return to duty via ships.

Members of the Third Brigade set sail from Yorktown on 5 March. The

First Brigade left on 9 March. The Second Brigade was held in camp because Kilpatrick needed them for yet another raid.[56] He had learned that Dahlgren's band had been ambushed on 5 March. Most had been captured. The young colonel had been killed and his body "horribly mutilated."[57] Kilpatrick set out to gain revenge.

The plan for the raid had been prepared by Wistar, the infantry commander who had led the ill-fated attempt to free the Yankee prisoners in Richmond back in February. Colonel Noble Preston, with seven hundred of Butler's cavaliers plus four hundred of his own, would leave Yorktown about 3:00 A.M. on 9 March, make contact with the enemy below King and Queen Court House, and start driving the Rebels north. Wistar would take twenty-seven hundred infantry by boat up the York River later that afternoon. Upon disembarking at Sheppard's Landing, he would slip into position behind the enemy and pounce on them as they moved past his post.[58]

Preston moved too quickly. He pushed the Confederates so hard that they passed the point of ambush before Wistar's men took up position. The enemy had raced on to King and Queen Court House. Kilpatrick, who had come upstream with Wistar, took command of the cavalrymen and started after the Rebels. As he advanced, gray clouds formed overhead, and rain began to fall. The storm took the heart out of Kilpatrick's usual ardor. He halted his men at Plymouth, sending Butler's seven hundred, led by Colonel Benjamin F. Onderdonk, to contest the Confederates at King and Queen Court House.[59]

Wistar was dismayed, "disappointed in every way," when he discovered that Kilpatrick had lost interest in the raid.[60] To revive the cavalry leader's spirits, Wistar suggested another target: Saluda, a small town to the east. Kilpatrick grudgingly headed in that direction, halting on the western banks of the Dragon River that night. He had agreed to move across the stream and occupy the village but found that impossible. The waters were flooding and the bridge was out.

The next morning, despite Onderdonk's return after his successful rout of the Rebels at King and Queen Court House, Kilpatrick was still unwilling to resume the raid. He made a cursory study of the rising river, concluded that he could not get across, and advised Wistar that he was awaiting further instructions.[61] He remained in position throughout the rest of the day.

All efforts to rouse Kilpatrick failed. On 12 March Wistar finally gave up. He ordered Kilpatrick to go back to Yorktown. The Northern cavalry returned to their base camp, boarded a ship, and had set sail for Washington, D.C., before Wistar and the infantry reached home.[62]

When Kilpatrick arrived at Washington, he sent his men into bivouac at Alexandria; he rented a comfortable room at Willard's Hotel.[63] He needed to be located in the heart of the capital, close to politicians who could protect him from a major change in the army's structure. Grant had been promoted to lieu-

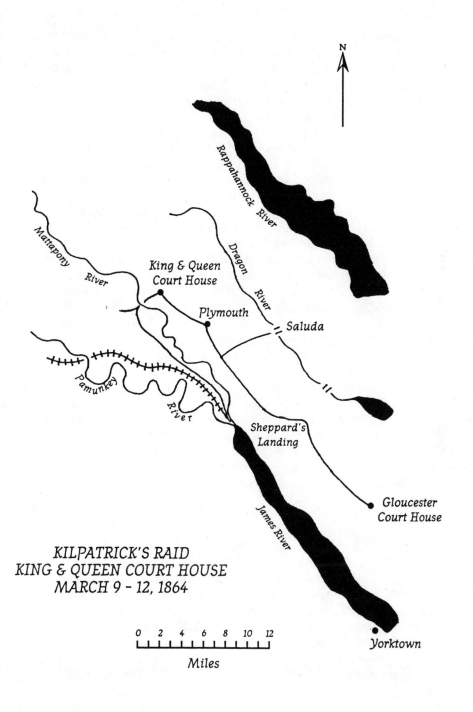

N

Rappahannock River

Mattapony River

Dragon River

King & Queen Court House

Plymouth

Saluda

Pamunkey River

Sheppard's Landing

James River

Gloucester Court House

KILPATRICK'S RAID
KING & QUEEN COURT HOUSE
MARCH 9 – 12, 1864

0 2 4 6 8 10 12
Miles

Yorktown

tenant general in charge of all Union forces.[64] His headquarters would be with
the Army of the Potomac, and Grant was sure to bring some favorite officers
east to serve under him. Kilpatrick had to be certain that his role as a division
commander of cavalry was not taken from him (a real possibility, given the
failure of his raid) and handed over to one of Grant's pets.

The same night of his arrival, however, Kilpatrick was ordered to gather
his men and start at once for Stevensburg. One of his troopers had come into
town, and when challenged by a Negro sentry had killed the Black soldier with
a swipe of his saber. General Auger (whom Kilpatrick had alienated earlier in
the war) decided that Washington could do without cavalry ruffians, and had
issued the instructions that sent the division packing.[65]

Kilpatrick reached Stevensburg on 15 March, where he began his report
on the raid. He presented his itinerary in great detail, listing the properties
destroyed, the numbers of Rebels killed or captured, and the disposition of
amnesty proclamations. When Kilpatrick came to his moment of truth, his
retreat instead of charging into Richmond, he wrote that "the enemy was rapidly receiving reinforcements . . . [and] any attempt to enter the city at that
point would [have brought] bloody failure."[66] He concluded by attributing his
lack of success to Dahlgren and Butler. "If Dahlgren had not failed in crossing
the river . . . or had the enemy at Bottom's Bridge been forced to remain at that
point by a [threat of assault] from the direction of Yorktown, I should have
entered [Richmond] and released our prisoners."[67]

No one believed Kilpatrick's ridiculous claims. Meade, who earlier had
declared that the venture was "practicable," dismissed the report with a single
comment. "Kilpatrick's raid," he wrote, "was an utter failure."[68] He then added
to Kilpatrick's disgrace by comparing his exploits to Custer's. "[The diver-
sionary] expedition to . . . Charlottesville," Meade stated, "was perfectly successful."[69]

Theodore Lyman, one of Meade's aides, offered the best assessment. "I
fancy," he chortled, "[that] Kill has rather dished himself."[70]

One can picture Kilpatrick as he trotted down the road to Richmond. Talk,
talk, talk! He must have expounded with expertise on every subject under the
sun, citing his own expertise (most of which was drawn from a fertile imagination) for authority. And while he spoke with eloquence, using the flowery phrases
of a politician, his incessant verbiage was laced with profanity, linking him to
the common soldier. It is no wonder that while his superiors and peers often
found him a boor, those who served under Kilpatrick both liked and respected
him. He oozed confidence and it was contagious.

When he reached the Rebel capital, Kilpatrick was face to face with the golden opportunity that he had sought since the commencement of the Civil War. As George King so aptly wrote, he was "only one mile from Richmond, perhaps one mile from being Governor of New Jersey . . . one mile from [becoming] President of the United States."[71] His failure to take rein and charge condemned him to "[history's] special purgatory—the footnote."[72]

Some of the men (e.g., Kidd) castigated Kilpatrick as a coward; others (e.g., Tobie) made excuses for him. But none would ever again accept him in the same light he enjoyed before the Richmond Raid.

17

The Dahlgren Papers

Just prior to leaving on his raid, Kilpatrick met with Dahlgren to review last minute details. One of the subjects discussed was an address intended to inspire the men. "You have been selected from [assorted] brigades and regiments as a picked command," the speech said, "to attempt a desperate undertaking—an undertaking which, if successful, will write your names on the hearts of your countrymen in letters that can never be erased."[1] Dahlgren had supposedly written this piece, but the words had a ring that reminded one more of Kilpatrick. This treatise, one of the "Dahlgren papers," would become the key to ending Kilpatrick's career with the Army of the Potomac.

After blessing the speech, writing "Approved" and then his signature in red ink, Kilpatrick ordered Dahlgren to begin the raid.[2] He led his men across the Rapidan, rode all night, and about eleven o'clock on the morning of 29 February he arrived at Frederick's Hall, where he halted to tear up the railroad tracks. He then continued south. Once again he galloped through the dark of evening, beset by a driving rainstorm, until he reached the James River at dawn on 1 March. Dahlgren expected to cross over the stream and attack Richmond from below, but the rushing waters were above flood stage with neither a ford or bridge in sight. "[Our] guide had known it," one of the men recalled, "and in his indignation, the colonel hung him."[3]

Dahlgren then trotted east above the James, looking to assault the city from the west. Along the way, his troopers halted from time to time to destroy property. One of their stops was at the home of James M. Morson. Attempts to torch his fine mansion were stymied by loyal slaves, who quenched the flames as fast as fires were set. The Yankees did, however, confiscate wine from the cellar, which was drunk from stolen silver goblets as they resumed their trek.[4]

The Federal horsemen came within five miles of the Confederate capital that afternoon without encountering serious opposition. At that point they were finally met by citizen soldiers (a miscellany of factory workers, old men and boys, and government clerks), who had come out of Richmond to contest the Union's advance.[5] They hid in the brush along the sides of the road and fired out of the growing darkness as the Yankees rode past their concealed positions. Dahlgren withstood these salvos until he arrived at the very outskirts of the city, where he found the enemy in strength. He sent his troopers ahead in a charge, but the Rebels refused to yield. Dahlgren had no choice but to withdrew his force.[6]

Heading west, then northeast in an attempt to catch up with Kilpatrick, Dahlgren rode all night "as fast as the men and horses could stand it."[7] He moved so quickly that most of his force failed to keep up with him. Less than one hundred troopers remained with Dahlgren to greet the cold, gray dawn of 2 March.

Dahlgren knew that the Rebels were looking for him and expecting the Federals to hurry east for the haven of Butler's lines. He was going in that general direction, but to avoid the probable roadblocks ahead, Dahlgren decided to follow a wide arc to ride around these traps. He led his small force through Hanovertown, crossed over the Pamunkey River (using a boat) and continued northeast to Aylett's. After swimming the Mattapony River, he finally turned east. At 4:00 P.M., as he approached Bruington Church, Dahlgren was assaulted in the rear by Rebels. His plan to elude pursuit had failed.[8]

After beating off the enemy's attack, Dahlgren started southeast for Stevensville. He arrived at the small village at dusk and decided to stop and rest awhile. The oncoming darkness would allow him to escape the enemy. He planned to turn west, ride back to the Mattapony, and then follow that steam southeast to Gloucester Point and safety.[9]

About 11:30 P.M. Dahlgren started the last leg of his journey. He had just begun when the van ahead halted. Some unknown people were lurking in the shadows up front. Thinking he could bluff his way past the ambush, Dahlgren spurred his mount to the head of the column. "Surrender," he cried, "or I will shoot!"[10] The answer was a flurry of rifle shots that toppled Dahlgren from his horse. He fell into a ditch, dead, struck by five bullets. His troopers scattered, every man for himself.

The bushwhackers who shot Dahlgren had been gathered together by Lieutenant James Pollard, head of H Company, Ninth Virginia Cavalry, who was by chance home on leave. His command included twenty-five of his troopers and the home guard unit led by Edward W. Halbach, a schoolteacher, whose "men" were his students.[11]

William Littlepage, a thirteen-year-old boy, was among those who fired at Dahlgren. He saw the Union officer fall and decided to creep forward and search the body, hoping to steal a watch. In the darkness Littlepage rummaged through the dead man's pockets. He missed finding the watch (which was in Dahlgren's overcoat), but he did discover some papers, a notebook, and a cigar case. He took his booty to Halbach.[12]

The schoolteacher waited until sunrise before looking at the material that Littlepage had brought him. When he read the papers, Halbach gasped with horror. One was an address to the Northern troopers, telling them their names would be written on the hearts of their countrymen. The oration went on to exhort the raiders, "[D]estroy and burn the hateful city [Richmond]; and do not allow the rebel leader and his traitorous crew to escape."[13] Another paper defined the objective in greater detail. "The city must be destroyed and Jeff. Davis and cabinet killed."[14] The notebook had yet a third reference to this objective for the mission: "Jeff Davis and Cabinet must be killed on the spot."[15] Kilpatrick evidently had not been satisfied with his assignment to tear up railroad tracks, distribute the amnesty proclamation, and free the Union prisoners. He had come south to assassinate President Davis, too!

The papers were rushed into Richmond and presented to President Davis, who found the Yankee threat amusing. "This means you, Mr. Benjamin," he said with a smile to his secretary of state.[16]

Others, however, were enraged by the thought of Yankee assassins invading Richmond. Braxton Bragg, Davis's military advisor, demanded that the men who had accompanied Dahlgren (most of whom had been easily captured that morning) be executed and the papers published, "calling the attention of . . . the civilized world to the fiendish and atrocious conduct of our enemies."[17] Robert E. Lee stepped forward to quash any thought of killing the Northern captives. "Acts in addition to intentions," he pointed out, "are necessary to constitute crime."[18] But the obnoxious orders were given to the press, who ran lead articles in their 5 March editions.

When the Federal leaders read "The Dahlgren Papers" in the Southern newspapers, most assumed the Rebels had made up the stories about assassinations just to arouse Confederate passions. Meade, however, thought the orders were true, and he must have suspected that Kilpatrick was their author, because on 14 March he contacted the cavalry leader, asking "whether any . . . directions of the character . . . printed in the public journals were given to his command."[19]

Kilpatrick realized that he was being accused of hatching a plot, unacceptable in "civilized warfare." His career was at stake. He responded with caution. He asserted that after careful examination of those who had accompanied Dahlgren, "all testify that he published no address whatever to his command, nor did he give any instructions . . . of the character alleged in the rebel journals."[20] He did not disavow that such orders had been given to Dahlgren. And while Kilpatrick did claim that the portion of the speech calling for the murder of Davis and his associates was false, "published only as an excuse for the barbarous treatment of the remains of a brave soldier" (someone had chopped off the little finger on Dahlgren's left hand to steal his diamond ring),[21] he offered no comment on the other two documents that mentioned a plot to assassinate the Rebel leaders.

Meade was not satisfied by Kilpatrick's devious letter, and he proceeded to interrogate other members of the raiding party. He soon learned that one of the two bands assembled by Kilpatrick at Mechanicsville had been instructed to enter Richmond and capture President Davis. Captain John McEntee offered the most damaging testimony, revealing that Dahlgren had told him about the plan to kill the Southern government figures.[22]

While these facts did not prove that Kilpatrick had decided on his own to include assassination of the Confederate leaders as an objective for his raid, it seemed probable he was guilty of doing so. "Kilpatrick's reputation and collateral evidence in my possession," Meade wrote, "[support] this theory."[23]

Kilpatrick had to go, and Grant furnished the means to send him packing. On 4 April, he relieved Pleasonton from duty and named a western associate, Philip H. Sheridan, as his replacement.[24] Sheridan then requested that his friend, James H. Wilson, be transferred to assume control of one of the three cavalry divisions.[25] Meade no doubt jumped at the chance to recommend Kilpatrick as the man who must lose his command. He was demoted to brigade level and assigned to serve under Gregg, which was the worst of all conceivable punishments.[26] Kilpatrick would suffer daily contact with all who knew well of his disgrace.

In an attempt to avoid the purgatory that Meade had devised for him, Kilpatrick requested to be transferred to the western theater. He based his appeal on the grounds that he outranked Wilson and that he should not be forced to serve under a junior officer.[27] Sheridan, no doubt wary of the likely problems with Kilpatrick's continuing presence, endorsed the request, and on 15 April Kilpatrick was ordered to report at once to William Sherman, commanding the Military Division of the Mississippi.[28]

"The Dahlgren Papers" underwent one more step prior to Kilpatrick's departure for his new post out west. Robert E. Lee sent Meade a letter about the plot to burn Richmond and assassinate President Davis and his cabinet. "[Did] the design . . . as set forth in these papers [photos enclosed] . . . have the sanction and approval of your authorities?" he asked.[29]

Meade contacted Kilpatrick, and on 16 April he once more denied having given any instructions alluded to in "The Dahlgren Papers." His statement was sent by Meade to Lee as evidence that "neither the United States Government, myself, nor General Kilpatrick authorized, sanctioned or approved . . . any act not . . . in accordance with the usages of War."[30]

After writing this final denial, Kilpatrick bid good-bye to his men and headed west. He did not wait around to greet Wilson, who took command of the division on 17 April.

"The Dahlgren Papers" added to Kilpatrick's reputation as an adherent of total war, one who considered the enemy to include the entire Southern population. He would fight the Rebels in the field and in their homes. This trait no doubt influenced Sherman to accept Kilpatrick into his army.

The plot to kill President Davis, however, went beyond just a wild scheme that was quickly disavowed by most of the responsible men in the North. The concept of assassination had been introduced. Kilpatrick had failed, but in time another more daring would succeed. Perhaps John Wilkes Booth was inspired by "The Dahlgren Papers" and the Richmond Raid.

18

Atlanta

Grant's plan for winning the Civil War was to confront the Confederates on all fronts at the same time.[1] This type of coordination had been lacking in the past, and the South had taken advantage of having idle men by rushing them along interior lines to another theater where reinforcements were needed. They had defeated Rosecrans at Chickamauga by using this tactic, and Grant was determined that the Rebels would be denied this option. "He would go after Lee," Sherman recalled, "and I was to go for Joe Johnston."[2]

Sherman was lucky to still be involved in the war. In1862, when he declared that the conflict would be bloody and long, and that millions of men would be required to conquer the South, he was thought insane and relieved of duty. The setback was symptomatic of a troubled life. Born in Lancaster, Ohio, in 1820, he was orphaned at an early age and raised by U.S. Senator Thomas Ewing. Sherman attended West Point, had a quiet thirteen-year career, then left the army to try his hand at business. He failed at both banking and law, and in 1860 he had just embarked on his fourth profession as superintendent of the Louisiana State Seminary of Learning and Military Academy when the Civil War beckoned.[3]

Grant had brought Sherman back from oblivion, and they shared in the Yankee success at Shiloh, Vicksburg, and Chattanooga. Sherman was then named to replace Grant after his friend was called east to command all the Union armies.

Sherman had three forces at hand: the Army of the Cumberland (61,561) commanded by George H. Thomas, supported by two divisions of cavalry, 4,662 riders under Kenner Garrard and 2,342 troopers led by Edward M. McCook, plus one brigade of horsemen assigned to Kilpatrick; the Army of the Tennessee (22,308) under James B. McPherson, who had no cavalry at hand; and the Army of the Ohio (9,262) led by John M. Schofield, bolstered by one cavalry division, the 2,951 troopers under George Stoneman.[4] Sherman's numbers totaled more than twice those available to his foe, Joe Johnston.

Kilpatrick's first assignment was to bring his command to division strength. He assembled three brigades. One was led by Lieutenant Colonel Robert Klein,

General William T. Sherman. Courtesy of the Library of Congress.

in charge of two regiments, the Third Indiana and Fifth Iowa; Colonel Charles C. Smith headed the Second Kentucky, the Eighth Indiana, and the Tenth Ohio; and Colonel Eli H. Murray's force included the Ninety-Second Illinois and the Third and Fifth Kentucky. Kilpatrick's troops totaled 1,750 men.[5]

Sherman's force was gathered at Chattanooga. Johnston had assumed a defensive position at Dalton, Georgia, twenty-five miles to the southeast. The

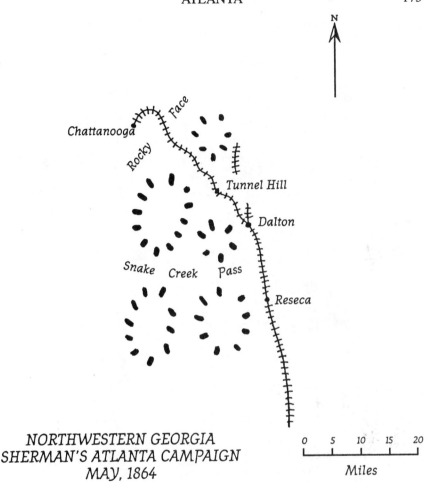

NORTHWESTERN GEORGIA
SHERMAN'S ATLANTA CAMPAIGN
MAY, 1864

campaign began on 6 May. Grant had already forded the Rapidan in Virginia to confront Lee when Sherman started forward to meet Johnston.

The topography favored Johnston. A range of mountains, known as "Rocky Face," lay between the two adversaries, with only one gap, "Buzzard Roost," offering a direct route into Dalton. To hold Sherman at bay, Johnston had not only lined the "gravely" hills with cannons but also dammed Mill Creek, which flowed through the pass. The gap was flooded [6]

Seeing that he could not push his way through the pass, Sherman decided on a flanking movement. He posted Thomas at Buzzard Roost, placed Schofield to the north, and then sent McPherson in an arc to the south. He was to advance through Snake Creek Pass and Sugar Valley into Johnston's rear near Resaca. After tearing up the railroad tracks, the Confederates' supply line from

Confederate general Joseph Wheeler, from *The Photographic History of the Civil War,* edited by Francis Trevelyan Miller. 10 vols. New York: The Review of Reviews Company, 1911.

Atlanta, McPherson would put his men in a defensive stance, blocking any Rebel retreat. Johnston would be neatly trapped, and Sherman could destroy his army at leisure.[7]

McPherson started on 8 May with Kilpatrick's cavalry screening his advance.

Before departing for the front, Kilpatrick sent a sarcastic note across the lines to his Rebel counterpart and former West Point classmate, Joseph Wheeler. "As soon as the weather permits," he wrote, "I will pay you a visit."

"Come ahead when you are ready," Wheeler answered. "We will give you the warmest reception you ever had."[8]

While the exchange suggested animosity between the two, Kilpatrick and Wheeler were actually good friends. They had been among the shortest cadets at the Academy, and this lack of stature seemed to have created a bond between them.

Kilpatrick arrived at Snake Creek Pass on 9 May. He found the defile undefended and hurried through the gap for Resaca. McPherson and the infantry rushed after him. Sherman, when he learned that his troops were about to enter the enemy's rear, was elated. "I've got Joe Johnston dead!" he yelled as he pounded his supper table with glee. "Now we'll ride [to] tell [Thomas]."[9] His joy, however, proved short-lived.

When Kilpatrick rode up to Resaca, he saw that the small village was filled with Confederates. He decided not to try to rout a superior force but moved instead around the town to take up a position to the north along the railroad, where he awaited the infantry's attack.[10] McPherson, however, proved to be timid. He withdrew his army back to Snake Creek Pass, calling Kilpatrick after him. "We should have captured half of [Johnston's] army," Sherman groaned later.[11]

Seeing that he was outflanked, Johnston started to retire from Dalton on 10 May. His entire army was soon ensconced at Resaca. At the same time, Sherman was moving his troops along the same track taken by McPherson, and by 13 May he had his force in place, ready to open the first battle.[12]

Kilpatrick's cavalry rode at the front as the Federals advanced on Resaca. When they approached the town, the Yankee troopers were greeted with a volley from Rebel pickets, who then fell back in retreat. Kilpatrick urged his mount ahead after the fleeing enemy. He never realized that once again he was rushing into an ambush. He galloped up a knoll, then came to a stop in a grove to study the distant ground. Polk Prince, a Confederate skirmisher hiding in the same forest, took aim and fired.[13] His bullet toppled Kilpatrick from the saddle. Friends carried the pale and bleeding officer to the rear.

The doctors found that the ball had "entered the inner side of the left thigh . . . behind the femoral artery and femur and passing out on the opposite side a little back but very close to the sciatic nerve . . . the muscles of the posterior . . . thigh [were lacerated] very severely."[14] The wound was not life-threatening, but Kilpatrick would need a lengthy period for recuperation. He rode north in a carriage for his home at West Point;[15] Murray took charge of the division.

As he lay in bed in his home at West Point, recovering from his wound,

Kilpatrick had the chance to keep up-to-date on the progress of Grant's strategy to attack the Rebels on all fronts. He saw repeated failure.

In the Far West, Nathaniel Banks had been assigned the task of defeating the enemy in Texas. He had started up the Red River in early March, leading forty-five thousand men plus an armada of twenty-two ships toward Shreveport, Louisiana. Banks had hoped to launch his invasion from this point. But on 8 April, as he was approaching Mansfield (only forty miles below his target), Banks was attacked by nine thousand Rebels under General Richard Taylor. He was routed, losing 20 cannons and 175 wagons filled with supplies. His gunboats were left exposed in the now falling water of the Red River. Throughout the following weeks, the Confederates made strenuous efforts to destroy the Federal fleet. Five of the vessels were captured or sunk, but the rest escaped via the clever expedient of building dams that brought the river back up to navigable levels. On 13 May the last of the Union ships passed into the deep waters at Alexandria, and Banks retreated eastward unimpeded. His campaign was over, its mission miscarried.[16]

Success was just as elusive for the Yankees below Richmond. Benjamin Butler started up the James River on 5 May with thirty thousand men, intending to attack the Rebel capital from the south. He landed his army at Bermuda Hundred (a plantation eighteen miles from Richmond) and headed west between the James and Appomattox Rivers. After advancing only a few miles, Butler stopped to build entrenchments along the neck of the peninsula, where the unfordable streams to his flanks were four miles apart. He failed to realize that while the bulwarks protected his force from assault by the enemy, they also provided the Rebels with an impregnable defensive line. The South, led by General P. G. T. Beauregard, quickly brought their troops forward, and by 17 May Butler found himself trapped behind a fortress of his own making. "The enemy had corked the bottle," Grant groaned with disgust, "and with a small force could hold the cork in place."[17]

Grant had hoped to assault Richmond from the west, too, but his generals failed him in the Shenandoah Valley. Franz Sigel mounted the first attempt. When he led his army up the valley, the Rebels under John C. Breckenridge moved to block his path at New Market. The Confederates were so desperate for troops (outnumbered two-to-one), they had been forced to call students from the Virginia Military Institute into service. The boys proved decisive as they helped rout Sigel on 15 May.[18]

David Hunter replaced Sigel. He marched south through the Valley all the way to Lynchburg, Virginia, before finding opposition. Jubal Early with Lee's Second Corps had rushed from Richmond to confront the Federals. On 18 June Early moved against Hunter, who fled at the sight of the Confederates. He ran west into the Appalachian Mountains, opening a path for Early to advance unimpeded down the Shenandoah Valley, across the Potomac into Maryland,

and then east up to the outskirts of Washington, D.C. Grant was asked to deplete his army to rescue the capital, and Horatio G. Wright's Sixth Corps came north 11 July, just in time to thwart Early's threat.[19]

Grant himself had had limited success. He had crossed the Rapidan on 5 May, fought Lee to a standstill in the thorny brush of the Wilderness, then attempted to flank the Confederates by moving in an arc southeast. Lee, however, blocked his path at Spotsylvania Court House. They fought a series of battles over the next two weeks, during which the Federal cavalry under Philip Sheridan rode into Lee's rear. Stuart parried this thrust, but in the 11 May encounter at Yellow Tavern, he received a mortal wound.[20]

Unable to break through Lee's position at Spotsylvania, Grant made another try at maneuvering. He reached the banks of the North Anna River on 23 May, only to find the enemy again standing in his path. Lee's line was so strong that Grant elected not to risk battle. He moved southeast, headed for Cold Harbor twelve miles east of Richmond. Lee countered by taking up the defense above the Chickahominy River, between the Union army and the Southern capital. On 3 June Grant mounted a massive attack. His charge lasted only eight minutes, during which time he suffered over seven thousand casualties.[21] The North's losses since crossing the Rapidan River had reached sixty-five thousand, as many soldiers as Lee had in his force.[22]

After resting his battered army for over a week, Grant moved south again, this time crossing the James to take up a position below Butler. His hopes of capturing the Southern capital that spring were gone. The only option left was the mounting of a long and tedious siege of the Richmond/Petersburg environs. "[I] propose to fight it out on this line," Grant had written earlier, "if it takes all summer."[23] Wags in the North were now asking, "Which summer?"

On the other major front, Sherman had charged Johnston at Reseca on 15 May, two days after Kilpatrick was wounded. His attack was meant to pin the Confederates in place while Kenner Garrard's cavalry and an infantry division under General Thomas W. Sweeney arced right around the battlefield to sever the Western and Atlantic Railroad in the Confederates' rear. When Johnston discovered that the Federals were about to cut off his source of supply, he hurriedly retired south along the tracks.[24]

This railroad linked both armies to depots in the rear where each had stored provisions (Johnston at Atlanta, Sherman at Nashville). It provided the key to Johnston's strategy. By retreating, following the tracks southeast, he came closer to his source of supply while drawing Sherman further away from his deposits. His adversary would be forced into depleting his army, dropping off men as he advanced to guard the ever-lengthening lifeline to his rear from raids by the Southern cavalry. Sherman's advantage in numbers would fade away, and when the odds grew relatively even, Johnston could whirl and fight a decisive battle to win the campaign.[25]

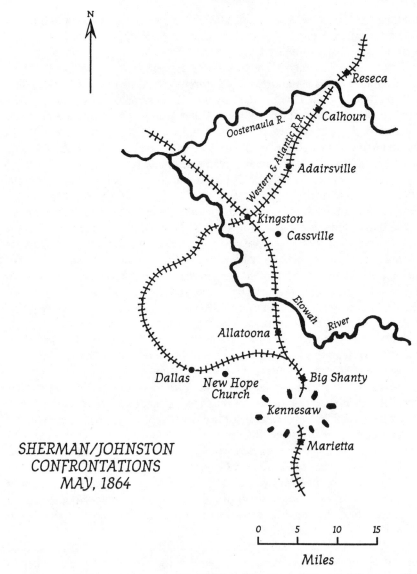

N

SHERMAN/JOHNSTON
CONFRONTATIONS
MAY, 1864

0   5   10   15

Miles

Johnston stopped to entrench at Adairsville, Cassville, and Allatoona Pass as if to offer battle. Each time the Yankees moved to flank his position, he abandoned his works and withdrew southeast. Johnston finally accepted battle on 25 May at New Hope Church. Four days of fighting saw the Federals suffer over three thousand casualties from repeated charges against the Rebels' strong emplacement.[26]

Unable to dislodge Johnston, Sherman moved east to Big Shanty, hoping to slip around the Confederates' right flank. Johnston retired to above Marietta, assuming an impregnable post atop Brush, Pine, and Lost Mountains, then moving a few days later to entrenchments on the slopes of Kennesaw Mountain.[27] Sherman was so frustrated by this last ploy, he ran out of patience, and on 27 June he ordered his troops to make a frontal assault against the Rebels' line. The result was a disaster. Over twenty-five hundred Northern soldiers fell in their attempt to drive the enemy from the rocky elevation.[28]

Following his repulse at Kennesaw, Sherman returned to his strategy of maneuver, using his superior numbers to confront the Confederates while at the same moment flanking their position. Johnston was forced to abandon his mountain stronghold on 2 July. He moved into a new position below Marietta. Sherman soon threatened his left with McPherson's army, and on 4 July the Rebels retreated to the northern banks of the Chattahoochee River. Their backs were now only about five miles above Atlanta.[29]

Although the river posed a formidable barrier, Sherman was not daunted. He spread his troops out in a wide line to find a way around Johnston's position, and on 8 July the Union (Schofield's troops) crossed the river at the mouth of Soap Creek on the Rebel right. Johnston had no alternative but to fall back into Atlanta and man the extensive bulwarks that circled the city. Sherman (like Grant at Richmond) began preparations for a siege. He approached from above with McPherson's force on the left, Schofield in the center, and Thomas on the right, due north of Atlanta.[30]

When news of Sherman's investment reached the North, the citizens groaned aloud at the ineptitude of the Federal military efforts. Banks, Butler, and Hunter had all failed in their campaigns; Grant's driving Lee back into Richmond had been too costly in terms of casualties for anyone to accept his exploits as a success; and now Sherman was entangled in a siege of Atlanta. The end of the war seemed out of sight, and many would accept disbanding the Union if it would bring peace.

Lincoln noted the growing resentment toward the war in general and himself in particular. He had been nominated by his party for a second term at the Republican convention in Baltimore on 8 June, but because of the failure of Grant's multiple campaigns, many of his cohorts were unhappy at having favored his candidacy. "It seems exceedingly probable," Lincoln wrote in a personal memo, "that this administration will not be re-elected."[31]

In this darkest hour, President Jefferson Davis of the Southern Confederacy came to the Union's rescue. He fancied himself a military expert, and he disagreed with Johnston's strategy of continued retreat. Davis wanted his generals to fight the enemy. When Johnston refused to commit to a plan of attack, Davis relieved him from duty on 17 July and named John B. Hood as his replacement.[32] Sherman no longer faced the grind of breaching Atlanta's fortifications; Hood, who was a heroic soldier but a poor tactician, would charge from behind his bulwarks to assault Sherman. "They would become the aggressors," Grant crowed, "the very thing [I] wanted."[33]

Kilpatrick no doubt sensed that victory at Atlanta was at hand. Although not fully recuperated from his wounds, he headed south from West Point in late July to resume his command and share the glory from Sherman's triumph.[34] Too weak to mount a horse, he rode in a carriage. His fourteen-year-old nephew, William J. Kilpatrick, sat beside him. He would serve as an aide to his uncle during the day, then read his school lessons at night. The latter schedule was suspect, as the lad was "not particularly ambitious in his studies."[35]

Upon reaching the front on 23 July, Kilpatrick found that although the fight for Atlanta had already started, his command would not take part in the action. He was assigned to protect the railroad track to Sherman's rear, all the way from the Etowah River back to Tunnel Hill.[36]

Hood had attacked Sherman's right on 20 July, losing over five thousand men in a futile charge on Thomas's position to the north (Battle of Peachtree Creek).[37] He then tried to turn the Yankees' left at Bald Hill, east of the city, on 22 July (Battle of Atlanta).[38] McPherson, the Union defender, lost his life during this fray, but his troops repelled the enemy attack. The Confederates lost eight thousand more irreplaceable men. Hood had taken more casualties during his few days as leader of the Southern force than Johnston had suffered in his two months of directing the campaign.[39]

While Hood paused to catch his breath, Sherman turned his artillery on Atlanta, and the Federal gunners started an unending bombardment of the city.[40]

Although the cannonade made life unpleasant for the Rebel occupants of Atlanta, Sherman knew that they could withstand the barrage as long as supplies continued to reach the city via the railroads to the south. He had to cut that lifeline if he was to rout Hood out of his bastion. Sherman planned a two-prong operation: General Oliver Howard (who had taken over McPherson's command) would move west behind Thomas and Schofield, then march south to rip up the railroad track below Atlanta; the cavalry would carry out a pincer movement (McCook on the west, Stoneman and Garrard to the east). The horsemen would ride in parallel, then unite at Jonesborough, a depot twenty miles south of Atlanta, where they would destroy the Macon and Western Railroad. After this mission was completed, McCook and Garrard would return north; Stoneman and his men would head south to free the Union captives held in the Macon and Andersonville prisons.[41] The infantry and cavalry both moved out on 27 July.

Howard was the first to make contact with the Confederates. On 28 May, west of Atlanta on his way south, he was attacked by Rebels under Stephen D. Lee. The enemy mounted wave after wave of charges in a desperate attempt to prevent the Union from reaching the railroad below the city (Battle of Ezra

Church). Howard fought off the determined assaults, inflicting five thousand more casualties on the South, but was kept from reaching the vital tracks supplying Atlanta.[42]

"Oh Johnny," a Union soldier called out during a break in the action. "How many of you are left?"[43]

"About enough for another killing," was the grim reply.

Howard's infantry had failed in their attempt to reach and wreck the railroad south of Atlanta. Sherman soon heard that his cavalry, too, had not fulfilled their mission. On the east, Stoneman and his twenty-one hundred troopers ignored their part in attacking Jonesborough. They were so set on freeing the Federal prisoners held at Macon and Andersonville, they rode straight south, leaving Garrard and his four thousand men to handle the enemy defenders, horsemen led by Joe Wheeler.

The Rebels hurried out of Atlanta, intercepted Garrard at Flat Rock, and contested his advance. The Union troopers skirmished for awhile, then retired back north.[44]

With Garrard gone, Wheeler turned his attention to the remaining Union forces. Alfred Iverson's three cavalry brigades were sent after Stoneman; Wheeler went west with his troopers to join William H. Jackson's regiments in confronting McCook.[45]

Stoneman had advanced to Macon without opposition, but when he reached the outskirts of the town, he found his path blocked by local militia. Stoneman panicked when he saw enemy soldiers ahead and turned around, intending to run back toward Atlanta. He then collided with Iverson's force, who had caught up with the Federals. The Rebels were entrenched across the road. Stoneman tried to push past the barricade, but the Southern cavalry held their position. Anticipating that the militia from Macon would attack his rear at any moment, Stoneman made a curious decision. He would surrender himself and a portion of his command, using the diversion to give the rest of his men "as much start as possible" in making an escape.[46] The unique ploy failed. Most of those who scattered were quickly captured, joining the prisoners they had come to free.

To the west, McCook's thirty-two hundred-man force crossed the Chattahoochee, then rode back over the stream to Palmetto, where they tore up tracks of the Atlantic and West Point Railroad. After destroying two miles of the line, McCook galloped east again. He halted awhile to attack and burn a wagon train of supplies headed for Atlanta, then moved for Lovejoy Station, where he proceeded to uproot several miles of track of the Macon and Western Railroad. Probably nervous because neither Stoneman nor Garrard had appeared as scheduled, McCook decided to retire, and he returned west toward Newnan, south of Palmetto, into a trap of his own making.[47]

A trainload of six hundred Confederate infantry under Philip D. Roddey

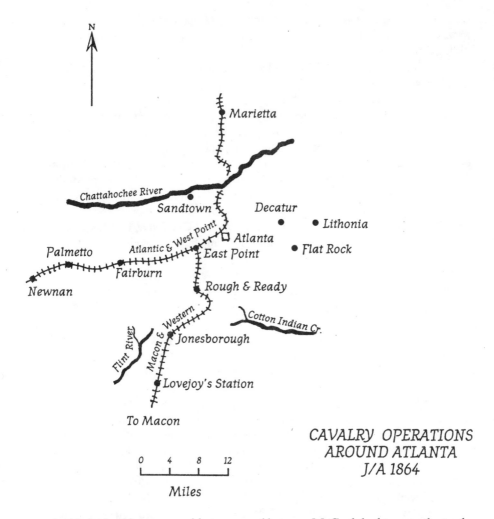

N

CAVALRY OPERATIONS
AROUND ATLANTA
J/A 1864

0   4   8   12

Miles

had halted at Newnan, unable to proceed because McCook had torn up the track. When Roddey learned that the Yankee cavalry was coming back his way, he formed his troops and headed east to confront the enemy.[48]

When McCook noted that he was riding into a battle, he whirled about to escape the snare, only to encounter Wheeler closing on his rear. "I was completely surrounded," McCook stated, "and compelled to abandon everything."[49] His men ran west into Alabama. Only six hundred of the troopers (including McCook) evaded capture, and they did not return to Sherman's camp until 4 August.

Sherman was disgusted with his cavalry's efforts. The Union horsemen had not only failed in their mission but also lost more than two thousand of their men. To replenish the ranks, he called Kilpatrick and his command to the front.[50]

"I [was] now . . . satisfied that cavalry could not . . . make a sufficient lodgment on the railroad below Atlanta," he recalled, "and that nothing would suffice but for us to reach it with the main army."[51]

Leaving Thomas above Atlanta, Sherman called Schofield south to join with Howard for an attack on the railroad that supplied the city. But before he could launch his infantry against the track, Hood made an incautious move that put the assault on hold. He opted to send his cavalry north to destroy the line from Nashville that brought provisions to the Yankees. When Wheeler departed on 14 August, taking four thousand of his troops with him, he left Hood both weaker in numbers and without the "eyes and ears" that kept him alert to the enemy's activities.[52]

When Sherman was told that Wheeler's cavalry had moved north, he asked his horsemen to reconnoiter the ground below Atlanta to confirm this report. On 15 August Kilpatrick hurried south, east of the railroad; Garrard rode along the western flank.[53]

Garrard soon encountered enemy resistance, but instead of pushing through their barrier, he quickly returned to his base above Atlanta. Kilpatrick, however, advanced past the Rebel outposts, galloping to Fairburn, where he tore up some track and burned the depot. He then moved on to East Point, the final stop on the Macon and Western line before entering Atlanta. Kilpatrick met little opposition during his probe of the field. "The enemy's cavalry has certainly been with drawn from this [area]," he reported, "[and] both railroads [are] exposed to raids."[54]

Sherman was pleased by Kilpatrick's efforts. "[He] is first rate," he declared. "He acts in earnest."[55] Garrard, however, was censured for his timidity. "[He is] as useless as so many sticks," Sherman snorted. "I am . . . convinced that if he can see a horseman . . . [in his] spy glass, he will turn back."[56]

While Garrard remained in camp nursing a pride wounded by Sherman's scathing comments, Kilpatrick was called to the commanding general's headquarters. He was asked if his men could break up the railroad below Atlanta.

"It [is] not only possible," Kilpatrick answered, "but comparatively easy."[57]

"Kilpatrick displayed so much zeal and activity," Sherman related, "I was attracted to him at once."[58] He decided to hold off on his infantry movement against the line below Atlanta. He would give the cavalry one more chance, sending Kilpatrick's division (augmented by two brigades taken from Garrard) on a mission to ravage the railroad. "Break up the Macon road all to pieces," Sherman urged in one of a number of orders sent to Kilpatrick.[59] "[Your] real task is not to fight but to work," he said in another.[60]

Kilpatrick's force assembled about his headquarters at Sandtown the evening of 18 August. Before starting on the raid, he called all forty-five hundred men into a hollow square and gave them a pep talk, exhorting each to give him his hearty cooperation, obedience to orders, and at all times prompt and energetic action.[61] The troopers then mounted up and began to ride south.

The Federal advance at first was uneventful, but about 10:00 P.M., pickets from the Sixth Texas rose from the brush to try and impede Kilpatrick's path. He easily pushed them aside. These Rebels sent word back to Lawrence S. Ross that a large number of Union troopers were riding south, and the Confederate cavalry leader rushed his eleven hundred-man force out of East Point to intercept the enemy column. Ross charged Kilpatrick's left flank about 12:30 A.M., forcing him to turn a brigade out of line to fight off the assault while the rest of the command continued south. Kilpatrick reached Fairburn at 3:30 A.M. on 19 August and started to rip up the Atlantic and West Point Railroad track.[62]

Although Ross had been unable to stop Kilpatrick's column, he did not give up trying to harass the Yankees. He divided his small force, sending half of his troops south to get in front of Kilpatrick while he took the rest of his men toward the Northern rear.[63] Ross arrived at Fairburn at dawn, and he immediately ordered a charge. Kilpatrick managed to fend off the attack. As the Rebels retired, he reassembled his troops and headed east toward his main object, the Macon and Western Railroad at Jonesborough.[64]

The Federals moved down the Fayetteville Road, many on foot because the area was "thickly wooded . . . a very bad place for cavalry."[65] At one point, however, the forest gave way to cornfields along both sides of the path. Suddenly, shots rang out. The other half of Ross's men lay hidden amid the stalks in ambush. Kilpatrick could not wheel and charge his tormentors, due to rail fences that lined the lane. He was forced to run the gauntlet. About two hundred of his force fell before he finally emerged from the trap.[66]

When Kilpatrick came to the Flint River, he found that the bridge had been torched by the Rebels and that the water was too deep to ford. The enemy stood on the opposite bank, ready to oppose his passage. Kilpatrick brought his cannons forward, unlimbered, and sent a salvo into the Confederates' ranks. They scattered. After securing the far shore with a small force who swam the stream, Kilpatrick fixed the span, and then continued his trek to Jonesborough. He reached the town about 2:00 P.M., only to find the rail center defended. Three hours passed before he finally pressed the Rebels into a retreat.[67]

Kilpatrick posted pickets to the north and south, then began to destroy the tracks. "It was a wild night," one man recalled; "the sky lit up with burning timbers . . . the continuous bang of carbines, the galloping of staff officers . . . up and down the streets . . . the terrified citizens peering out of their windows . . . Kilpatrick's . . . band [playing] national airs, with the shouts of men—all [created] a weird scene never to be forgotten."[68]

About 11:00 P.M., the Confederates attacked with their infantry from the south. The assault was repelled, but Kilpatrick knew that the Rebels would soon renew their charges. He could not remain in Jonesborough. He decided on a daring move. Kilpatrick would start east as if he was withdrawing, but instead of turning north, once he was out of sight of the enemy he would circle south to resume destroying the track at Lovejoy's Station.[69]

Hurrying cross-country in the darkness, riding through the woods and brambles, Kilpatrick reached Lovejoy's Station by midmorning. He was shocked to find that the Rebels had not been fooled by his ploy. They were positioned along the rails standing guard. The Federals immediately charged the Confederates, but their assault was repulsed. As Kilpatrick pondered his next move, he saw that the enemy's cavalry was blocking his rear. "In twenty minutes," he related, "I . . . was completely enveloped."[70]

In past such crises, Stoneman had surrendered; McCook had disbanded his command, with every man for himself. Kilpatrick, however, was more audacious. He called his entire force together and ordered Colonel Robert G. H. Minty to lead the men in a charge through the Rebel cavalry, who were dismounted along a defensive line to the east. He would follow later with the stragglers.

The plan worked! Minty's assault scattered the Confederate horsemen, opening a path for those on foot, ambulances filled with the wounded, ammunition wagons, pack mules, and the artillery. The Negroes from nearby plantations, who had joined the raiders to gain their freedom, rode the mules in the wild dash. "With kettles and pans rattling, and darkies flying for dear life," one observer recalled, "the scene [was] ludicrous as well as grand."[71]

"It was the most perfect rout," Kilpatrick wrote later, "any cavalry has sustained during the war. We captured four guns . . . three battle-flags . . . ambulances, wagons, [and an] ordnance train."[72]

Once freed from the encircling Rebels, Kilpatrick came to a halt and turned about to face his adversary. He fought for one hour and forty minutes, allowing his trains time to start north, east of the railroad, without opposition. When a torrential rain exploded on the scene, Kilpatrick saw his chance to break off the action, and he, too, withdrew, heading north. The enemy followed through the stormy darkness.[73]

At daylight on 21 August, when Kilpatrick arrived at Cotton Indian Creek, he found the river "swollen to an enormous height" from the rain.[74] With no bridge available, and the Rebels harassing his rear, Kilpatrick had no choice but to swim for safety. He lost fifty horses and almost all of his mules to the swift current but did manage to land both his men and artillery on the opposite shore.[75]

As he continued to trudge north, Kilpatrick noted that the enemy had given up their pursuit. He halted at Lithonia for the night (the first rest for his troops in three days) and arrived at Decatur the morning of 22 August.[76] He had circled the enemy's position (as the South's Jeb Stuart had done in 1862), losing only three hundred men.

"[I] destroyed 3 miles of the road about Jonesborough," Kilpatrick boasted in a report to Sherman, "and broke pieces for about 10 miles more, enough to disable the road for ten days."[77] While the commanding general was pleased with Kilpatrick's efforts, he could not help but note that while he was reading this dispatch, he could hear the shrill whistles of locomotives as they moved in and out of Atlanta.[78]

"This raid was more brilliant than successful," one of Kilpatrick's raiders admitted. "The railroad [we] succeeded in destroying [was] repaired in one day."[79]

Kilpatrick was oblivious to having failed to carry out his mission. "Two days after [his] return," Howard wrote in his memoirs, "one would hardly [know] that [Kilpatrick] had been defeated at all."[80] As the trains continued their runs from the south, he ignored their presence, boasting instead about the battle flags he had captured.

Finally accepting that the "cavalry could not or would not work hard enough to disable a railroad," Sherman decided to revert to his original plan.[81] He would take his troops south, rip up the tracks, and stop the flow of supplies into Atlanta. Hood, deprived of his provisions, would be forced to abandon the city.

Sherman moved on 25 August. Pulling his army out of their trenches, he sent the Twentieth Corps north to protect the railroad bridge across the Chattahoochee while the rest of the infantry marched south, parallel to the river, toward their objective. Kilpatrick rode on the right flank, guarding the column from improbable attack from the west.[82] Even the Yankee artillery was withdrawn from the front, ending a barrage that had been continuing for over thirty days.

Hood assumed that the enemy was retiring, that Wheeler had severed their railroad supply line to the north. "Sherman has been starved out," he declared. "We have won!"[83]

He soon learned the truth. And when Sherman aligned his men for their attack on the railroad, Hood had no choice but to resort to desperate measures. He divided his army, shipping two corps under Hardee south to Jonesborough, while his third corps remained to man the city's defenses.[84]

Sherman attacked on 31 August. Schofield, unopposed, rushed into Rough and Ready and started to tear up the track below Atlanta. About ten miles further south, Howard's men (including Kilpatrick, posted on the right at the end of the Union line) were attacked by Hardee before they could mount their own charge. "At first [the enemy] entirely ignored my command," Kilpatrick wrote in his official report. "This I determined he should not do."[85] He opened fire on the Rebel flank, drawing attention to the cavalry. Hardee turned and attacked Kilpatrick, driving him along with Howard's infantry back across the Flint River.[86]

Accessing the situation, Hood concluded that the enemy had little interest in dislodging Hardee, that Sherman's objective was to hustle Schofield and Howard north to assault Atlanta. He recalled Lee's corps from Jonesborough to shore up his defenses.[87] Hood guessed wrong.

Schofield headed south on 1 September to unite with Howard in attacking Hardee's lines at Jonesborough. Despite the loss of the corps returning to Atlanta, Hardee held his ground that afternoon, but when darkness fell, he retired to Lovejoy's Station.[88]

When Hood learned that Hardee had been attacked to the south, he recognized that Atlanta was lost, that his line of supply was irretrievably cut, that he would have to abandon the city. He sent word to Lee to turn around and head south to rejoin Hardee; Hood himself gathered the troops in the city, and at dusk began to move after the rest of the army; and when he was gone, a few Rebels left behind proceeded to blow up the artillery shells that the Confederates could not take with them. Eighty-one railroad cars of ordnance were destroyed the night of 1 September.[89]

Sherman heard the explosions, and feared that Hood had attacked the men he had left guarding the railroad bridge on the Chattahoochee. But on the morning of 2 September he learned that Hood had instead abandoned the city. His plans had worked; the campaign was over. "Atlanta is ours," Sherman wired Washington, "and fairly won."[90]

The victory electrified the North. For the first time since the War began, it seemed likely that the Yankees would win the conflict. On a more personal note, Lincoln saw his reelection assured. "Success to our arms . . . was . . . a political necessity," Sherman noted, "[and] the brilliant success at Atlanta filled that requirement."[91]

While Sherman could have continued the fray by chasing after Hood, he chose instead to retire into Atlanta to enjoy the fruits of his victory. Kilpatrick remained south until 5 September, when he returned north to assume his bivouac at Sandtown.[92]

While serving under Sherman, Kilpatrick found the same luck that he had enjoyed in the East. His efforts, although vigorous, were not too successful. His peers, however, performed so poorly that Kilpatrick seemed heroic when compared to McCook, Stoneman, and Garrard.

More important to Kilpatrick's career was the personal relationship he built with Sherman. His superior liked him. Kilpatrick in turn was both impressed with Sherman and most appreciative of his allowing him a second chance for glory.

Kilpatrick repaid Sherman, giving him an allegiance he had never showed another superior, and between the two, they would wreak a devastation on the South that to this day has never been forgotten or forgiven.

19

The March to the Sea

Sherman hoped to spend the whole month of September in Atlanta recuperating his force. "Since May 5th we have been in one constant battle or skirmish," he wrote Halleck, "and we need rest."[1]

To be sure that his troops were not disturbed, Sherman ordered all civilians out of the city. They could go either north or south, he did not care, but Atlanta would become a pure military garrison. "If the people raise a howl against my barbarity and cruelty," he declared, "I will answer that war is war . . . not popularity-seeking."[2] Kilpatrick could not have expressed his own sentiments better.

Hood, however, was not about to sit idle and allow his adversary to relax in peace. Borrowing his tactics from the Union, he decided to take his army north and cut the tracks carrying supplies into Atlanta from Nashville.[3] Sherman had starved him out of the city; he would do the same thing to the Federals. And when the enemy came north to reopen their lifeline, he would whirl about and fight a battle at a site of his choosing.

On 21 September Hood moved his force from Lovejoy's Station to Palmetto. He then forded the Chattahoochee River on the twenty-eighth and moved north along the Western and Atlantic tracks. The Rebel army, reduced by casualties and desertion to only about thirty-three thousand troops, captured Big Shanty on 4 October, severing the railroad into Atlanta.[4]

Although Sherman had no wish to turn around and in effect retreat along the same route he had taken to Atlanta, Hood's lopping off the Union's supply line gave him no choice. He left the Twentieth Corps behind to guard the city and began marching north after Hood on 4 October. Sherman led five corps—sixty thousand men—in his pursuit of the Confederates. Kilpatrick's cavalry was up front, keeping Sherman informed of the enemy's location ahead.[5]

The Yankees caught up with Hood near Reseca on 14 October. The scene was set for a major battle, but at the last minute, Hood saw that it would be futile to assault Sherman. He was outnumbered and had little chance for victory.

Hood left the railroad and took his army seventy miles west to Gadsden, Alabama, where he opted on a different plan for dealing with Sherman. Instead of ripping up the tracks that supplied the Federal army, then fighting to prevent the enemy from repairing the break, he would rush north to Nashville, the Union's main depot, and destroy the provisions at their source. Sherman, deprived of his food and ammunition, could no longer stay in Georgia, and Hood would have avoided a battle.[6]

Sherman, however, thwarted the Rebels' new strategy by abandoning his chase of Hood. "He can turn and twist like a fox," the Union commander explained, "and wear out any army in pursuit."[7] He would let the Confederates march unimpeded to Nashville. But when they finally reached the depot, the enemy would find the Federals waiting to greet them. Thomas was sent north to assemble a defending army, drawn from the garrisons scattered throughout Tennessee.[8]

While Hood hurried north, Sherman would take his force back to Atlanta, then "push into Georgia [to] break up . . . its railroads and depots, capture its horses and negroes, [and] destroy the factories at Macon, Milledgeville, and Augusta."[9] He would feed his men with provisions appropriated from the surrounding plantations. When he reached Savannah, Sherman would set up a new base, drawing his supplies from the warehouses on Hilton Head Island that supported the Union fleet blockading the eastern seaboard. "I can make the march," he assured Grant, "and make Georgia howl."[10]

Before heading for the sea, however, Sherman looked to make a key change in the leadership of his cavalry. Rosters showed that eighty thousand troopers were assigned to his department, but only about ten thousand were present for duty, scattered along a four hundred-mile line that extended from Atlanta back to Memphis.[11] With Hood advancing on Nashville, Sherman had to bring some semblance of order to this sad situation, to confront the Confederate horsemen led by Nathan Bedford Forrest and Wheeler. But since his three armies each had their own head of cavalry, Sherman had no one man he could charge with resolving the problem.

Sherman decided to consolidate all the cavalry under a single chief, and he sent a request to Grant to recommend an officer from his army for the position. He noted that none of his generals were qualified for the post, using Kilpatrick as an example. "[He] is well enough for small raids," Sherman wrote, "but I . . . want a man of sense and courage."[12]

Grant suggested the man who had replaced Kilpatrick as division cavalry commander in the Army of the Potomac, James H. Wilson. Sherman accepted Grant's choice.[13] When Wilson arrived at Reseca on 22 October, he took charge of all the troopers by relieving the three army chiefs from duty.

Although Kilpatrick must have been chagrined at having to report to his one-time successor, he hid his rankling with a self-effacing note to Wilson. "You may safely expect everything from me," he wrote, "that energy, zeal, and a cheerful compliance with all orders can bring."[14]

Kilpatrick could afford to be patronizing, because he had learned that instead of serving with Wilson, he would be reporting directly to Sherman, accompanying the force marching to the sea. Wilson and the rest of the cavalry would be posted at Nashville, supporting Thomas in his confrontation with Hood.

In discussing this plan with Sherman, Wilson must have questioned whether Kilpatrick was qualified for such an important role, because the general was firm in defending his preference. "I know [that] Kilpatrick is a hell of a damned fool," Sherman averred, "but I want just that sort of a man to command my cavalry on this expedition." He explained the slur by adding another. "If I used such language," he said later, "it [was] because . . . that was what a good many of [my] officers were in the habit of calling [him]."[15]

Kilpatrick was sent to Marietta to gather the troopers he would guide through Georgia to the sea. While he was there, he learned that Sheridan (who had assumed command of the Yankee forces in the Shenandoah Valley) had won a decisive victory over Early on 19 October at Cedar Creek. This was their third battle in four weeks, each a Union success, bringing an end to the Confederates' dominance in the Shenandoah.[16] While he would have wanted to celebrate Sheridan's triumph over Early with a salute of cannons, Kilpatrick must have followed Sherman's example. "We cannot afford to burn gunpowder," the general wrote Washington, "but our men can make up in yelling, which is just as good."[17]

The cavalrymen who cheered for Sheridan had been organized by Kilpatrick into two brigades. Colonel Eli H. Murray commanded the twenty-eight hundred men in the First Brigade, which was composed of the Ninth Pennsylvania, the Eighth Indiana, and the Second, Third, and Fifth Kentucky. His outfit was supported by the Tenth Wisconsin Light Artillery. Murray, a native of Kentucky, had served in the West since the start of the war. He was at Shiloh, fought at Murfreesboro, took a part in the pursuit of John Hunt Morgan during his raid into Indiana and Ohio, then joined Sherman for the Savannah campaign. He was first a journalist after the war, then served as territorial governor of Utah, a post he was holding at his death.[18]

The Second Brigade totaled twenty-seven hundred troopers, assigned to five regiments: the Fifth, Ninth, and Tenth Ohio, the Ninth Michigan, and the Ninety-Second Illinois. Smith D. Atkins, a native New Yorker, who had been a lawyer in Illinois prior to the war, was the brigade leader. He had fought at Forts Henry and Donelson, then at Shiloh under Grant. He resigned in the spring of 1862 to form a new regiment, which he brought to the field in 1863 at Chickamauga. When the war was over, he returned to Illinois to be a postmaster, then became the editor of the *Freeport Daily Journal*.[19]

Sherman had hoped to lead six infantry corps southward into Georgia, but Thomas insisted that he needed additional men to defend Nashville against the oncoming Hood. Sherman reluctantly agreed to this request, and in late October he dispatched the Fourth Corps to Thomas. A few days later, he sent more troops north, the Twenty-Third Corps (Schofield's Army of the Ohio).[20]

The four corps remaining for the march to the sea were organized into two commands: Oliver Howard headed the right wing, composed of the Fifteenth and Seventeenth Corps; the left wing, including the Fourteenth and Twentieth Corps, was led by Henry Slocum.[21] Sherman's orders called for the two elements to advance in parallel columns. They would set out each day at 7:00 A.M. and march for fifteen miles. Special details would gather food from the farms along the way. The foragers were cautioned to leave each Southern family enough provisions so that their survival was not endangered; entry of private residences was forbidden; and although Sherman's objective was to destroy all property that could support the Confederates' war effort, decisions on what to burn was left to just the four corps commanders.[22]

Sherman did offer one exception in his order governing the conduct of the soldiers on the march. The cavalry might "appropriate freely and without limit," allowing Kilpatrick, once imprisoned for thievery, a license to steal.[23] Sherman must have expected Kilpatrick to abuse his authority, which perhaps explains his comment, "I can . . . make Georgia howl."

Everyone was ready to move by 15 November, and early that morning Kilpatrick led Sherman's sixty thousand-man army south out of Atlanta. Riding west of the Flint River, Kilpatrick screened the infantry led by Howard to his right. That wing was advancing toward Macon; Slocum's men were heading east toward Augusta. The real target of both wings, however, was in the center: Milledgeville, the capital of Georgia.[24]

The weather was perfect, a warm sun in a cloudless sky, when Kilpatrick's riders crossed over the Flint and moved into Jonesborough. No Rebels had opposed their advance that day. As the men prepared to bivouac for the night, they could see thick smoke rising to the north. Sherman had put the torch to Atlanta.

"The heaven is one expanse of lurid fire," an observer described the conflagration. "The air is filled with flying . . . cinders; [the] buildings covering two hundred acres are in ruins or flames; every instant there is the sharp detonation . . . of exploding shells. . . . The city . . . exists no more."[25]

When he arose on 16 November, Kilpatrick was given a report from his scouts. The Rebel cavalry was positioned to the south near Lovejoy's Station. When Hood had discovered that Sherman had given up chasing him, he had sent Wheeler's thirty-five hundred men back to Georgia to confront the Yankees. "Little Joe" had reached the Atlanta area on 12 November, where he joined with about three thousand of the state militia under Gustavus W. Smith. This force blocked Kilpatrick's path to Macon.[26]

Kilpatrick moved quickly to meet the Rebels. Upon his arrival at Lovejoy's

Station, he ordered an attack by Murray and the First Brigade against Wheeler's troopers, ensconced behind earthenworks. The charge scattered the Confederates, and they retreated south "in great confusion" to Bear Creek Station, where they made a second stand. Atkins pressed the Second Brigade forward. They, too, routed the enemy, pushing Wheeler and the militia further backward to Griffin.[27]

Rather than continuing his pursuit of the Confederates, Kilpatrick turned east and started toward Jackson. He moved slowly, waiting for the return of troopers dispatched right and left to gather food and forage; their appearance was delayed by the heavy rain pelting from the west. Howard's infantry filed in parallel north of the cavalry, keeping the horsemen between them and the enemy. The Rebels, however, had no interest in the column. Wheeler was convinced that Kilpatrick was headed for Macon, and he was galloping for that town to prepare a defense.[28]

On 18 November, when Howard reached the banks of the Ocumlee River, he found the stream above flood level because of the continuing storm. He had pontoons for a bridge, but the fast-flowing current made the laying difficult. His men worked for hours building the span. Kilpatrick crossed the water at

3:00 A.M. on 19 November, then galloped south for Clinton. He meant to fake an assault on Macon, to hold the enemy in place while Howard's infantry completed its passage over the river.[29]

When Kilpatrick stood in place on 20 November, his men pillaged the nearby plantations. "They drove off every cow, sheep, hog," one mistress remembered, "took every bushel of corn and fodder, oats and wheat—every bee gum, burnt the gin house, screw, blacksmith house, cotton, etc."[30]

The rain, which had been falling for three days, turned to sleet on 21 November. Kilpatrick's cavalry shivered in the saddle as the temperature dropped, and Howard's soldiers trudged by their rear, headed for Gordon on the Georgia Central Railroad. When the infantry was safely past the point guarded by the cavalry, Kilpatrick took his command south to Griswoldville, a small industrial village west of Howard's objective. Upon arriving, he sent the Second Brigade toward Macon to front the enemy while the First Brigade devastated the depot. "The station was destroyed," Kilpatrick boasted, "pistol, soap and candle factories burned."[31]

Thinking that Kilpatrick intended to attack their town, the Rebels in Macon decided not to wait for the assault. On the morning of 22 November, they started east to confront the Federals. Shortly after dawn, Wheeler's cavalry charged Kilpatrick's rear as he moved up the road for Milledgeville. The Union troopers repelled the sally, then stepped aside as Charles C. Walcutt's infantry brigade came west from Gordon to assume the defense at Griswoldville.[32]

A light snow powdered the road as Pleasant J. Phillips led his inexperienced militia toward Walcutt's line, located amidst the Duncan farm, east of Griswoldville. Their initial charge was a disaster: units fired at each other instead of the enemy, and others lost their way in the woods and ravines along the Yankee front, while the few who actually assaulted the Federal position were devastated by cannon and musketry. The Rebels had no chance of driving Walcutt's men from their strong position, yet they advanced six more times before returning in defeat to Macon. "It was awful," a Union soldier moaned, "the way we slaughtered those men."[33] "I was never so affected [by] the sight of dead and wounded before," said another. "Old gray-haired . . . men and little boys not over 15 years old . . . lay dead or writhing in pain."[34]

Kilpatrick, after watching the disaster from the flank, took his cavalry east to Gordon that evening. The men spent the next day resting, but Kilpatrick rode ahead to Milledgeville to report to Sherman. The commanding general had been traveling with Slocum, whose force had followed the Georgia Railroad out of Atlanta. They tore up the track, burned the grain storage buildings along the line, and killed the livestock they could not use, leaving nothing in their wake that might serve the enemy. When they reached Madison, Slocum's infantry turned south, passing through Eatonton on their way to the Georgia capital. They marched into Milledgeville on 22 November.[35]

Sherman assigned Kilpatrick a new objective. When his troopers arrived in Milledgeville on 24 November, Thanksgiving Day, he was to lead them east for Millen to free the Yankee captives held in the prison there.[36] The cavalry rode into the state capital on schedule, but before he started the men toward Millen, Kilpatrick participated in a mock legislative session in the Senate chamber.

The room was swarming with blue-clad soldiers, most of them intoxicated from liquor they had found in the cellar of the capitol. Kilpatrick, who had had his share and more of the whiskey, staggered to the podium to address the assembly.

"I am a very modest man that never blows his own horn," he shouted, "[but] I must honestly tell you that I am Old Harry on raids."[37]

"Mr. Speaker," came a cry from the crowd, "I believe it is always the custom to treat the speaker."

"Yes," Kilpatrick replied, waving a large flask at the interrupter. "I beg to inform this honorable body that I am going to treat the speaker." When he tilted his head back to take a long swig, the soldiers roared their approval.

At this point, a group dubbed "The Committee on Federal Relations" took over the dais from Kilpatrick. Some of the men sang, "We Won't Go Home Till Morning"; the rest started to debate a resolution they had drawn for returning Georgia into the Union (all yelling at the same time, each trying to be heard above the other's voice). Kilpatrick decided that it was time to leave the proceedings. He reeled through the mass of revelry, tottered outdoors, and started to assemble his men for the ride to Millen.

While Kilpatrick was heading east, Wheeler and his men were galloping north, passing the Yankee front. He now knew that Sherman held no intention of attacking Macon. Wheeler assumed that Augusta must be the Union target, and he was on his way to that city to add his troops to a force of ten thousand soldiers, led south out of North Carolina by Braxton Bragg.[38]

The night of 24 November, the Federal cavalry camped at a plantation about ten miles east of Milledgeville. When they arrived there that afternoon, Kilpatrick had sent them into the surrounding countryside to collect remounts. Over five hundred horses had been confiscated, far more than the number needed to replenish the cavalry's worn animals. When Kilpatrick arose the next morning to view the horde, he saw the surplus and decided that if he could not use the beasts, neither would the Confederates. He ordered his men to kill most of the lot by throwing a blanket over their heads, then bashing them between the ears with an ax.

The plantation owner watched with horror as a mountain of dead horses grew on his front lawn, their corpses already beginning to stink. "My God!" he muttered, knowing that he had no means of burying so many animals. "I'll have to move away!"[39]

Once the slaughter was completed, Kilpatrick began his move to Millen. He rode thirty miles that day, camping that night on the banks of the Ogeechee River. The next morning, 26 November, when Kilpatrick continued eastward, he received word that his objective to free the Yankees incarcerated at Millen had been foiled. The enemy had abandoned the prison, taking their captives south beyond his reach.[40] Kilpatrick sent this news back to Sherman. He replied with new orders: burn the railroad bridge across Brier Creek north of Waynesborough.[41]

This mission gave Kilpatrick pause. He was now on the left of the army, between Slocum's Wing and the Confederates at Augusta. He was exposed to probable attack. Taking his troops above Waynesborough would increase his vulnerability, Kilpatrick decided on trickery. He would guide the bulk of his force below Waynesborough, where they would start to rip up the railroad track; a picked unit of two hundred men under his adjutant, Major Estes, would slip out of the column and steal northeast to carry out the dangerous task of burning the trestle.[42] To further confuse the enemy, that night in the house at Sylvan Grove where he was headquartered, Kilpatrick discussed "in private" his plans to assault Augusta, making certain that his hostess (a loyal Southern woman) could overhear his whispered conversation.[43]

The ruse failed. When Kilpatrick failed to show up in front of Augusta, Wheeler came after him, hurrying southeast with his troopers. He drove Estes's band away from the railroad bridge before they could complete its destruction, then followed the retreating Yankees to Kilpatrick's main camp below Waynesborough.[44] The enemy charged at 1:00 A.M. on 28 November.

The Rebels made repeated attacks throughout that night, their forays hidden by a dense fog that made them impossible to see until they were almost on top of the Yankee troopers. Kilpatrick was so scared he sent an officer racing westward for relief from Sherman's infantry. "Wheeler's cavalry [is] all around [us] with a vastly superior force," the messenger yelled upon reaching the rear. "[We] are out of ammunition, [and] men and horses [are] utterly worn out. [Hurry] to our support or . . . all [will] be lost!"[45]

When dawn arrived, Kilpatrick started to ride westward toward his oncoming saviors, the brigade of soldiers led by General Absalom Baird. Kilpatrick would later downplay his rout, claiming that after fighting off Wheeler's attacks, "I deemed it prudent to retire to our infantry."[46]

The withdrawal was conducted in echelon. One brigade would stand firm as the other slipped past them; the second force would then take up a defensive position, allowing the first to make its retreat. Despite Wheeler's men nipping at their heels, the Union cavalry made good progress in moving west.

Toward evening on 28 November, the process unraveled. Instead of stopping as scheduled, Atkins continued moving to the rear, trailed by Murray, leaving Kilpatrick with only a few troopers to protect him and his aides to the rear.[47] He failed to catch the misstep because he was focused on a personal matter. While he was at Waynesborough, Kilpatrick had met a Black prostitute. He had asked the girl to accompany him on the retreat and was looking ahead to a "night of folly."

The Rebels approached his camp near Rock Springs about dawn. After capturing the picket guards without a shot, the enemy riders galloped into the clearing and up to the cabin where Kilpatrick was asleep with his paramour. His troopers opened fire in defense of their debauching commander. When he heard the rattle of muskets, Kilpatrick jumped out of bed and raced outside into the middle of the melee. "Clad in a skullcap, drawers, undershirt, and slippers," he leaped onto the bare back of a sorrel horse and started a desperate run for his life.[48] With a flurry of bullets whizzing past his ears, Kilpatrick escaped, leaving behind his uniform, a gold-mounted sword, two ivory-handled six-shooters, his best horse (a spotted stallion), and the Black mistress.[49]

Kilpatrick, of course, did not report this incident in his account of the retreat. Instead, he declared that after "fighting . . . through the rebel lines," he stopped and turned to "give [Wheeler] a severe repulse." Kilpatrick claimed he was exposed to "one of the most desperate cavalry charges [he had] ever witnessed," which "was most handsomely repulsed at all points."[50] Had this been true, he might have added that he directed the engagement dressed in only his underwear.

Wheeler, writing about the same skirmish, said his men "hurled themselves upon the enemy," who became so "terrified . . . as to flee in uncontrollable fashion."[51]

Neither commander disputed that Kilpatrick and his men arrived at Louisville the night of 29 November, where they joined with Slocum's Wing. The cavalry rested the next few days, staying close to the protection of the infantry.[52]

While he was at Louisville, Kilpatrick took up with another Black whore, "a good looking mulatto." He entertained her one evening by imposing on a nearby plantation mistress to serve them an elegant dinner. The neighbors were shocked by the affair, not so much because the girl was a Negro but because she was a prostitute, the most unwelcome of visitors to a Southern home.[53]

Sherman's infantry moved east on 1 December with Kilpatrick's troopers riding along their left flank. Wheeler's cavalry came down from the north to harass the columns, but the Yankee horsemen parried all of their thrusts. The Union troops camped that evening near Buck Head Creek. The next day the Federals continued their trek. They advanced fifteen miles before stopping for the night at Gisholm's Plantation. They reached Thomas Station, eight miles below Waynesborough, on 3 December. Kilpatrick's men stood guard as the foot soldiers ripped up the tracks of the Augusta and Savannah Railroad.[54]

On 4 December Kilpatrick and his cavalry, supported by the infantry division under Baird, moved north in a feint on Augusta. About five miles south of

Waynesborough, their joint force found Wheeler's men, dismounted behind a hastily built barricade. Kilpatrick brought Atkins's Brigade to the front and ordered them to mount a charge on the Confederate position. The Federal horsemen galloped ahead but were unable to break through the Southern line of defense.[55]

Kilpatrick re-formed his men, putting mounted troopers on each flank. He then ordered his artillery, posted in the center, to open fire on the Rebels. After a fierce barrage by the guns, the cavalry mounted their second advance. "The whole line moved forward in splendid order," Kilpatrick proclaimed proudly, "and [my men] never halted one moment until the barricades were gained and the enemy routed."[56]

Wheeler explained his retirement differently. When he saw the Union infantry forming in Kilpatrick's rear, he knew that his position could not be held. He fell back into the village, made another short stand, then withdrew to a strong post just outside of Waynesborough.[57]

The Federal troopers followed close on Wheeler's heels. When Kilpatrick reached the Rebels' new front, he decided to offer a personal challenge. "Come out, you set of cowardly skunks," he called. "You claim that you can whip Kilpatrick every time! . . . Try it; and I'll not leave enough of you to thrash a corporal's guard. I am Kil himself!"[58]

Wheeler, however, had decided not to continue the fray. Convinced that Kilpatrick was leading Sherman's army against Augusta, he retreated to the northwest, where Bragg's troops could offer him support. Kilpatrick chased Wheeler to Brier Creek, halted there to torch the railroad trestle that Estes had failed to destroy, then turned about to head after Sherman, now well on his way toward Savannah. He halted for the night at Alexandria.[59]

While en route south that afternoon, Kilpatrick stopped at a plantation called "Ivanhoe." Drawing the Black butler, Jacob Walker, aside, he asked the servant "where the family silver could be found," obviously meaning to steal the treasures for himself. The faithful slave said that everything had been shipped to Augusta. As he replied, Kilpatrick took notice of the "gleam and glitter [of gold studs] that shone from the negro's brawny breast." He began to liberate Jacob of his jewelry. The Black defended his buttons by claiming that they were only brass. Kilpatrick allowed Jacob to keep the studs, offering the lofty explanation, "I don't wish to go off the gold standard."[60]

Kilpatrick claimed he had won a great victory over the Rebels at Waynesborough, and he issued congratulatory orders to his men. "I take great pleasure in tendering the thanks of the general-in-chief . . . to the gallant officers and men of my command for [their] brilliant cavalry action and victory at Waynesborough," he said. "You have won the admiration of the united Army. . . . Soldiers! I am proud to command you."[61]

With Wheeler's cavalry to the north and out of the way, Kilpatrick rode southeast to rejoin Sherman's columns. The men under Howard and Slocum were moving along the peninsula between the Savannah and Ogeechee Rivers. Since both infantry flanks were protected by the streams, Kilpatrick assumed a defensive post to the rear. He camped the night of 5 December at Jacksonborough; split his command the following morning, sending Atkins toward Springfield while Murray rode for Hudson's Ferry; trailed Sherman's men to Sisters Ferry on 7 December; then reunited his command about ten miles south of Springfield on 8 December.[62]

All the time they were moving southeast, the Union men ravaged the Georgia countryside. They burned farm buildings along their route; killed the cows, pigs, and chickens that they could not use; and destroyed the bridges after crossing the waters that they spanned. While the infantry generally avoided pinching personal possessions from the people, whose livelihoods were being ravaged, Kilpatrick's horsemen stole at will. Ladies' clothes and jewelry were a special favorite of the cavalry. "The dirty, grimy, sweaty, heavily bearded troopers thought it great fun to [don] this finery," John M. Gibson observed, "and pirouette like burlesque queens on a . . . runway."[63] Photographers accompanying the army took pictures of these perversions, which were published in Northern newspapers (e.g., *Harper's*). "They . . . disgrace themselves in the eyes of . . . decent people," a Georgia girl stated, "displaying the . . . jewels they have stolen from our homes."[64]

Kilpatrick had no interest in men wearing dresses. He remained devoted to real women, especially the Black harlots who had attached themselves to his command. One evening he took three prostitutes with him to a plantation house, where he demanded that the hostess cook dinner for his party. If this was not bad enough, the refined lady was also subjected to listening to a "most familiar and indecent conversation" between Kilpatrick and his whores.[65]

Wheeler, of course, heard of the abusive activities of Kilpatrick and his men, and felt compelled to write a letter of protest. "The history of no war, however barbarous, can tell of atrocities equal to those daily and hourly committed by your command," he wrote.[66]

Kilpatrick was quick to reply. After accusing Wheeler of committing the same depredations, stealing from the local populace, he went on to justify his men's actions. "War is terrible," he stated, "and the people of Georgia are now being made to feel this in all its force."[67]

Although this exchange of letters suggested that a bitter animosity had grown between the two former West Point classmates, they actually remained the best of friends. Wheeler, for example, returned a handwritten journal that Kilpatrick had "left by accident at a house where you spent the night"—a chide about Kilpatrick's narrow escape in his underwear.[68]

On 9 December Kilpatrick's troopers followed the infantry to a point eleven miles northwest of Savannah. While Sherman prepared to lay siege to the port city (defended by a small Confederate force led by General Hardee), Kilpatrick began to sidle south below the town. By 11 December his cavalry was ten miles southwest of Savannah, bivouacked near McAllister's Plantation on the banks of the Ogeechee River.[69]

Kilpatrick proposed to Sherman that his cavalry attack Fort McAllister, which guarded against entry to the Ogeechee from the sea. "I promise to take the fort," he stated, "and let in the fleet."[70]

Sherman granted the request, but Howard protested this decision. No doubt wanting the glory for himself, he stated that Kilpatrick was too impetuous; he

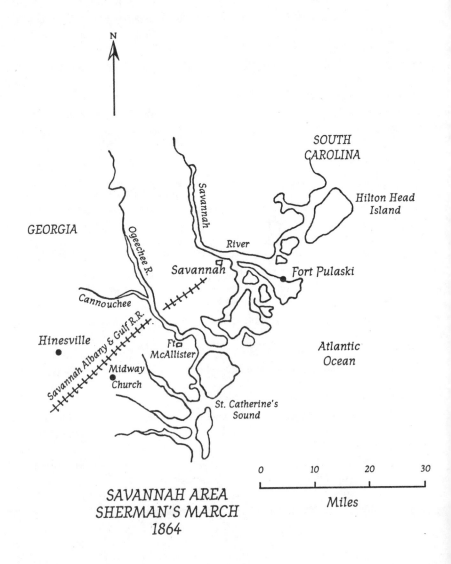

SAVANNAH AREA
SHERMAN'S MARCH
1864

would mount a "sudden dash" that was certain to be repelled.[71] This argument convinced Sherman to change his mind. The infantry would make the assault; Kilpatrick was ordered to advance to the ocean and make contact with the Union navy.

Kilpatrick took his troopers south on 13 December to St. Catherine's Sound, where he spotted the Federal gunboat, *Octorara,* anchored offshore. He sent Estes in a rowboat to the ship and established the first communication between the North and Sherman's army since the general left Atlanta.[72]

That same day William B. Hazen's division stormed and captured Fort McAllister.[73] His exploit opened the Ogeechee River for the navy to steam upstream to deliver supplies to Sherman's troops, relieving them of their need to forage for food. Ample provisions were on hand, and there were twenty tons of accumulated mail for the soldiers.[74]

While Sherman prepared his siege of Savannah, the cavalry went into bivouac to rest and recuperate. The troopers were not required in the investment of the port. Kilpatrick set up his headquarters at Midway Church, thirty miles southwest of Savannah. Murray's First Brigade camped with Kilpatrick; Atkins's Second Brigade was posted to the north, on the banks of the Cannouchee River.[75]

While at Midway, Kilpatrick no doubt heard the details of Thomas's victory over Hood in Tennessee. When the Confederates moved north toward Nashville, Thomas dispatched twenty-two thousand men under Schofield to Pulaski, Tennessee, to delay the enemy until he had completed his defenses. Hood, however, dashed past Schofield's position, and on 29 November he stood at Spring Hill between the two Union forces. As Hood slept in success that night, Schofield slipped past him and took up a strong post at Franklin. Hood was so angry over losing his advantage that he ordered a direct charge against the entrenched Federals. The result was disaster. More than six thousand troops and six general officers were lost by the Rebels in the five-hour, futile battle of 30 November.[76]

The remnants of Hood's army staggered northward to the gates of Nashville, where they assumed a defensive position. Thomas came out of the city on 15 December and dealt Hood the most decisive defeat of the Civil War. Less than 18,000 of the 33,500 who had started the campaign survived the desperate retreat to Alabama, and many of these men deserted as soon as they reached safe soil. When the army was returned to Joe Johnston in early 1865, only five thousand reported for duty.[77]

Although Sherman would soon have to battle with this hard core of Confederates still willing to fight, he found those defending Savannah no problem. They abandoned the port the night of 20 December 20. The Union troops occupied the city, which Sherman dubbed "a Christmas-Gift" in a letter sent to Lincoln on 22 December.[78]

The campaign was over, and there was glory for everyone, including Kilpatrick, who received a note of congratulations from the commanding general. "The operations of the cavalry have been skilful and eminently successful," Sherman said in his letter. "You may have it on my signature that you acted wisely and well . . . whipped a superior cavalry force, and took from Wheeler all chance of boasting over you."[79]

Kilpatrick was overwhelmed. "I would not exchange the happiness [your note] has given me for all the wealth in Savannah," he replied to Sherman. "I will do more, dare more than ever to have [you] say at the close of the campaign . . . I am satisfied with my cavalry."[80]

When Sherman marched through Georgia, the Rebels assumed that he intended to assault their cities. Consequently, they concentrated their meager forces first at Macon and then at Augusta, which allowed the Federals to advance without opposition. The infantry destroyed military targets—railroads, bridges, factories—along their way; Kilpatrick's troopers and Sherman's "bummers" (infantry stragglers) vandalized and burned the defenseless homes. The atrocities still remembered by Georgians today can mostly be attributed to Kilpatrick.

Sherman could have censured Kilpatrick for his outrageous behavior, especially for his numerous affairs with Black women, but he chose to say nothing. This served further to seal the bond that Kilpatrick felt for his superior and this allegiance would endure beyond his own demise.

When Sherman passed away in 1891 (ten years after Kilpatrick's death), his funeral was held in New York City. While people passed reverently by his casket, a woman stood guard, arranging the flowers that smothered the bier. Kilpatrick's widow was standing in his stead, continuing his devotion to Sherman.[81]

20

South Carolina

Sherman had decided that Savannah should be spared the devastation dealt the Georgia countryside during the Federal March to the Sea, and his generals made sure that his order was obeyed. Kilpatrick, for example, sent one battalion per day into the city to "enjoy themselves generally," but they were instructed to "conduct themselves as to reflect no discredit upon [his] command."[1] He refused, however to extend this decency to the citizens of Liberty County, thirty miles south of Savannah, where he had bivouacked his cavalry.

Kilpatrick set up his headquarters at Midway Church, a Congregationalist chapel founded in 1754. He chose the site primarily because of a walled

Midway (Georgia) Church. Courtesy of the author.

Walled Graveyard. Courtesy of the author.

graveyard next door, which he planned to utilize as a corral to hold the livestock, stolen from surrounding homes. This small facility was the social center
for the families who lived in the area. Most of them were highly cultured,
residing in large plantation mansions, built with profits gleaned from rice fields
that were farmed by their slaves. Two of the area's settlers, Button Gwinnett
and Lyman Hall, had signed the Declaration of Independence [2]

The troopers camped in tents next to the church, which became their slaugh-
terhouse. Kilpatrick ordered his men to move the elegant organ downstairs
from the gallery circling the sanctuary and used it for a butcher's block. Livestock were driven into the tiny chapel, killed, and dressed. The bloody car-
casses were then slung on hooks that hung from the balcony. When it was time
to cook the meat, the fires were stoked with wooden grave markers from the
cemetery. Because the burial records were also burned by Kilpatrick's cavalry,
more than seven hundred of those interred in the church grounds cannot be
identified today.[3]

Foraging was conducted daily by teams composed of from twenty to forty
riders, who scattered in all directions away from Midway Church. They visited the same plantations over and over, mounting atrocity upon atrocity.

"Every separate gang ransacked the house afresh, entering every room and
taking whatever they desired," remembered Joseph LeConte. "Broken trunks,

View from Balcony. Courtesy of the author.

smashed bureaus, overturned wardrobes—everything [was] topsy-turvy. . . .
[There was] no use to put things in order to again be disturbed."[4]

"It is impossible to imagine the . . . uproar and stamping through the house
. . . yelling, cursing, quarreling and running from one room to another in wild
confusion," Mary Jones Mallard recalled about a raid on her mansion. "These
men belonged to Kilpatrick's cavalry . . . their conduct . . . a horrible night-
mare, too terrible to be true."[5]

"They came in swarms," John Stevens wrote, "and having stripped me of
everything, attempted to pass to a neighbor's plantation, but had not proceeded
far before I saw them skedaddling back. . . . They had heard a Confederate
gun."[6]

"Give me your watch!" one demanded of Stevens.

"I have no watch for you."

"You're a damned liar! A negro boy said you had one."

"Go to the boy for it."

"I'll shoot you!" Kilpatrick's man threatened.

"Fire away," Stevens replied, opening his coat to show a target. "You cannot deprive me of many years."

The Yankee trooper backed away. "This ended the first day's scene,"
Stevens remarked.

Several days later, having robbed the "whites of all of their possessions,

Kilpatrick's troopers turned to the Black population. "An old colored preacher . . . who for a long time had been bedridden . . . [lost] everything, even his blankets."[7]

Within a few weeks, the once wealthy people of Liberty County were destitute. They were forced to beg Kilpatrick's officers for permission to sweep rice off the floors of the nearby mills in order to have something to eat.[8]

While Kilpatrick may have shared in the plundering of the plantations, he probably spent more time in his tent. He had a new mate for his bunk. Molly, a young Chinese girl, had joined his entourage as a laundress. Shortly thereafter, Kilpatrick enticed her into sleeping with him.[9]

He was probably in a hurry to seduce his China doll because Kilpatrick knew that the army's stay in Savannah would be short. Sherman had been called north to join with Grant against Lee at Richmond. His advance into the Carolinas was delayed, however, because Secretary of War Stanton had come to Savannah to visit. He attended a cavalry review on 11 January. The parade was held to celebrate Kilpatrick's promotion to the brevet rank of major general. He had been given this honor as a reward for his good performance during the march through Georgia.[10] Kilpatrick wore a gaudy new uniform that day, "a dark-blue coat of rakish cut . . . sky-blue trousers . . . golden gauntlets and sash, all . . . corded with gilt lace."[11]

Soon after Stanton returned to Washington, Sherman led his force north. His plan was the same as the march through Georgia, moving in two wings, each faking an assault on the towns to the flank, then converging to the center. Howard's pseudotarget would be Charleston; Slocum would head toward Augusta; the true point of concentration would be Columbia, the capital of South Carolina. Sherman would then drive for North Carolina, leaving only desolation in his wake.[12]

The Federals would advance without any lines of supply, gathering food and forage from the farms along the way until they reached a new base, Goldsboro, North Carolina, located about fifty miles inland from Wilmington. Although the port was still in Southern hands, its bastion on the ocean guarding the city, Fort Fisher, had just been captured by a Union force.[13] When Sherman came north, they would push west, first taking Wilmington, then opening the railroad into Goldsboro. Sherman planned a short stop to rest and resupply his troops there before resuming his drive to join Grant against Lee.

The march through Georgia had been somewhat restrained, the destruction (excepting Kilpatrick's activities) directed only against properties of military importance to the enemy. South Carolina, however, would be treated differently. This state would suffer for being the first to abandon the Union. "We will let her know," one soldier swore, "that it isn't so sweet to secede."[14]

He took his cue from Sherman. "[My march will be] one of the most horrible things in the history of the world," he vowed. "Even the Devil himself couldn't restrain my men."[15]

Sherman gave Kilpatrick firm evidence of his intention to ravage South Carolina. "How shall I let you know where I am?" Kilpatrick had asked while discussing his mission with the Federal commander. "Oh, just burn a barn or something," Sherman had replied. "Make a smoke like the Indians do."[16]

Kilpatrick, of course, was quick to copy Sherman's temper toward the Confederacy. "In after years, when travelers passing through South Carolina . . . see chimney stacks without houses," he announced at a dinner with his officers prior to their leaving Savannah, "[they] will ask, 'Who did this?' Some Yankee will answer, 'Kilpatrick's cavalry.'"[17] Another quote that reflected his intentions was directed toward the soldiers of Slocum and Howard. "There'll be damn little for you infantrymen to destroy," he growled, "after I've passed through that hellhole of secession."[18]

Howard's wing traveled by boat to Beaufort, South Carolina, on the Atlantic Coast, then started west as if swinging around the swampy seashore toward Charleston. Slocum moved northwest, a corps on each side of the Savannah River, as if advancing against Augusta. Kilpatrick's troopers rode with Slocum south of the water.[19]

When the cavalry left their encampment on 28 January, a woeful Chinese girl rode in a wagon toward the rear of the column. Kilpatrick had ordered Molly away from his command, but she had found that she was pregnant. "He has done me so and is trying to go back on me," she complained bitterly to her companions, "[but] I will stick to him and make him take care of the baby for it is his."[20]

The ground along the Savannah River was all marsh, and a continuing rain during the march added to the mire, making travel almost impossible. The men corduroyed the road with hewed logs, but still their progress was slow. They reached Sister's Ferry on 30 January. Slocum spent the next four days laying pontoons across the waters, and on 3 February he united his command by bringing the corps below the stream over the river. Kilpatrick's riders led the infantry north toward Barnwell to carry out the feint on Augusta.[21]

After three days of plodding through mud and muck, Kilpatrick's force reached the Salkehatchie River just south of Barnwell. He found a small band of the enemy posted on the opposite shore. The bridge spanning the stream had been set on fire. Using the billowing smoke as a screen, Kilpatrick forded the water above and below the Rebels' position, moved inward on the flanks of the Confederates, and pushed his adversary aside.[22] The cavalry rode into Barnwell, "as pretty a little village as the eye could wish to look upon," about 4:00 P.M.[23]

Kilpatrick's troopers immediately began their wreckage. "They . . . fired Wm. deTreville's office, the Ivestman's store, [and] the Ferguson's barn," Mrs.

N

NORTH
CAROLINA

Charlotte

Monroe

Lancaster

Chester

Winnsborough

Broad R.

Monticello

Alston

Catawba R.

SOUTH
CAROLINA

Saluda R.

Lexington

Columbia

North Fork

Aiken

Augusta

South Fork

Orangeburg

Santee R.

Blackville

Branchville

Barnwell

Edisto R.

Salkehatchie R.

Charleston

Sister's
Ferry

Beaufort

Savannah

SHERMAN'S MARCH
THROUGH SOUTH CAROLINA
1865

0   5 10 15 20

Miles

Randolph Sams related in a letter to her husband. "Mrs. Oakman screamed," she went on, "when the Yankees rode up the street."[24]

When he spotted the frightened lady, Kilpatrick became gallant and escorted Mrs. Oakman back to her home. He found to his delight that she had a beautiful daughter. He spent the evening with the Oakmans—evidently a memorable night, since the next morning Kilpatrick proposed marriage to the young girl. She, however, refused his offer.[25]

Kilpatrick stabled his horses that night in the Church of the Holy Apostles. "To show the inhabitants how little he thought of them," a townsman recalled, "the Baptistry . . . was used [as] a watering trough."[26]

On the morning of 7 February, while Kilpatrick spent his time torching the courthouse in the town square, his men continued their ravaging of people's houses. "They behaved more like enraged tigers than human beings," Mrs. Sams said in her letter, "running all over the town, kicking down fences, [and] breaking in doors and smashing glasses."[27]

Kilpatrick held a Nero ball that night at Banksia Hall, an elegant home north of town. "Regarding [their invitations] as orders," Smith Atkins wrote, "[the women] like sad ghosts went through the whirling mazes of the dance, while their . . . dwellings were in flames. It was the bitterest satire . . . [I] ever witnessed," he added, "and justly stained the reputation of Kilpatrick."[28]

Twenty-nine buildings were set aflame that evening, including ten dwellings,

Banksia Hall/Barnwell, South Carolina. Courtesy of the author.

five stores, Walker's Hotel, the Male Academy, eight offices, the Masonic Hall, Pechman's carriage shop, Sadler's stables, and the *Barnwell Sentinel,* the local newspaper.[29] The latter was burned by "a dirty little Pennsylvanian villain," according to one observer.[30] "The night was dark but starlight," another said. "The flames from the burning buildings lit up the heavens for miles."[31]

In reporting this success to Sherman, Kilpatrick made a joke of his setting the village aflame. "I changed the name [Barnwell] to Burnwell," he boasted.[32]

Sherman laughed at the jest and repeated the story to other officers. At the same time, however, he realized that his cavalry head had gone beyond the bounds of decency, and he wrote Kilpatrick to remind him of his orders not to treat civilians harshly. "Spare dwellings that are occupied," he said, "and teach your men to be courteous to women."[33]

On 8 February Kilpatrick headed north to Blackville, a depot on the South Carolina Railroad, to join a detachment he had sent there the day before. They had met and routed a small force under Wheeler, who had come east out of Augusta. Slocum's foot soldiers had also reached the station 7 February, and they were busy tearing up the track when Kilpatrick rode up with rest of his troopers.[34]

To give the foot soldiers time to finish their task of ripping up the rails, Kilpatrick led his cavalry west to set up a screen between the infantry and the Rebels, who had retreated into Aiken, South Carolina. He established his camp

Railway Depot/Blackville, South Carolina. Courtesy of the author.

at Johnson's Station on 9 February. When he learned from some captives that "Wheeler's command [was] scattered," Kilpatrick saw the chance to loot Aiken. He wrote Sherman, asking him to supply infantry support for the raid. "I will render Wheeler powerless to . . . annoy your flank or wagons again during the campaign," he promised.[35]

Sherman doubted the wisdom of a charge on Wheeler. "I don't care about Aiken," he replied, "unless you can take it by a dash." And he refused to provide Kilpatrick with foot soldiers. "It won't pay . . . to detach infantry for . . . a single occasion," he noted.[36]

Kilpatrick was so determined to pillage Aiken, however, that he ignored Sherman's presage, and on the morning of 11 February he led Atkin's Brigade toward the town. They stopped at a farm along the way, where Kilpatrick was given a second warning that Aiken might not be just a walkover. The housewife revealed that Wheeler and Frank Cheatham, the new chief of the Army of Tennessee, had been at her home earlier that day.[37] Kilpatrick would not believe that the Rebels were in force with both cavalry and infantry at hand.

When the cavalry approached Aiken, they spotted an enemy detachment ahead. The Rebels quickly retreated; Kilpatrick led the Ninety-Second Illinois after the Confederates. In a repeat of so many past errors, he galloped into an ambush.[38]

Wheeler had formed his force into a hollow square, the men hidden along the back streets of Aiken. One side of the setup had been left open for Kilpatrick to enter. Once all the Yankees were inside the box, Wheeler would snap the trap by sending a column across the Federal rear, blocking their withdrawal, exposing them to fire from four directions.[39]

Fortunately for Kilpatrick he had spacing between his column of four regiments. The Ninety-Second Illinois was in Aiken and the Ninth Michigan had not yet come up when Wheeler attacked. "There was a clash of horses, flashing of sabres, a few minutes of blind confusion," a Yankee rider described the contest, "and then those who had not been knocked out of their saddles by their neighbor's knees or had not [sliced] off their horse's head instead of the enemy's [were] running away or being run from."[40]

Kilpatrick led the desperate retreat. He claimed that his men "handsomely repulsed" the Rebels, but in truth, even as he approached his camp at Johnson's Station, three enemy riders were galloping close enough to Kilpatrick to be grabbing at him, trying to wrest him from the saddle.[41] He was so frightened that as soon as he was safely behind his line, he instantly "ordered tents struck, men to boot and saddle, wagons limbered . . . everything readied for hasty and immediate retreat."[42] Kilpatrick soon learned, however, that the Confederates chasing him totaled only about fifty men. Quickly recovering his composure, he ordered a charge into the handful of Rebels, which sent them reeling back to Aiken.

"[We were] most furiously attacked by Wheeler's entire command,"
Kilpatrick wrote in his official report, "[and] . . . fell back, fighting gallantly,
disputing every foot . . . to my position at Johnson's Station."[43] He later lied in
a letter to Sherman about his defeat. "It was not a general fight," he claimed,
"but simply a reconnaissance."[44]

The infantry on the scene knew better and teased Kilpatrick about his rout.
Probably fearful that Sherman would learn the truth, he complained in his note
about the insults from Slocum's force. "Wheeler as usual reported a victory,"
he moaned, "which a portion of our army seems only too willing to believe."
He then attempted to demean his tormentors by inferring that they, too, had
suffered a prior defeat at the hands of the Rebel troopers. "Unfortunately for
me," he wrote with sarcasm, "Wheeler did not . . . have the good fortune to . . .
rout, as at Waynesborough, one of our infantry corps."[45] Kilpatrick no doubt
hoped that Sherman would not recall that he, not the infantry, had been scattered in that skirmish.

Kilpatrick's outburst was childish, and Sherman wisely ignored the complaint.

On 12 February the cavalry rode north, guarding the left flank of Slocum's
force, which was now advancing toward Columbia. Kilpatrick forded the southern branch of the Edisto River that day and camped that evening four miles
beyond the stream. The next morning, Slocum's columns turned left, starting a
feint on Charlotte, putting Kilpatrick's cavalry between and in front of the two
infantry wings. He splashed over the north fork of the Edisto on 14 February,
and the next day he came within nine miles of Lexington, a town twenty miles
west of Columbia.[46] His force entered the village on 16 February and immediately began their usual sacking.

"The Chivalry have been stripped of most of their valuables," Thomas L.
Myer (a Union lieutenant) wrote in a letter to his wife. "Fine gold watches,
silver pitchers, cups, spoons and forks . . . are as common in camp as blackberries
. . . I have about a quart . . . of rings, earrings, breastpins . . . for you and the
girls."[47]

Myer then described how the booty was usually meted to the men in
Sherman's army. "Each company [exhibits] the result of their [daily looting],"
he reported. "One-fifth . . . [the] finest choice, falls to the share of the commander . . . and [his] staff, one-fifth to field officers of the regiment and three-
fifths to the company."[48] The latter was allotted among the troops via nightly
auctions, where soldiers bid on those items they wanted to buy. The sale was
generally conducted by the regimental leader, which explains why today an
auctioneer carries the honorary title of "Colonel."[49]

The Union army's take from the towns of South Carolina was tremendous.
"Gen. Sherman has silver and gold enough to start a bank," Myer claimed. "His
share of gold watches alone at Columbia was two hundred and seventy-five."[50]

Howard's men had moved warily into the state capital on 17 February. Such caution was unnecessary, as Columbia was weakly defended. Only Wade Hampton, who had come south from Virginia with fifteen hundred troopers, and Carter L. Stevenson's contingent of two thousand men from the Army of Tennessee stood in the way.[51] The rest of the Rebels in the region were scattered. Bragg had taken his ten thousand troops out of Augusta and back to North Carolina, where he found reinforcements from Virginia under Robert H. Hoke ready to help face the Yankee threat to Wilmington from the sea;[52] the Georgia militia (under General D. H. Hill) remained in Augusta and refused to leave the state.[53] Hardee's nine thousand-man Savannah garrison had departed Charleston but was heading north, to the right of Sherman's advance, looking to gain the Federal front;[54] and two thousand of the ragged remnants of the Army of Tennessee led by Cheatham were marching above and left of Sherman's columns, also trying to reach the head of the Union movement.[55]

Sherman burned Columbia on 17 February. On that day, Kilpatrick was riding north, leaving Lexington aflame behind him. "A blackened ruin only remained in its place," Joseph LeConte related.[56] Devastation such as this was kindled all through the piedmont of South Carolina by the marauding Federal army. "The middle of the day looked black and gloomy," David P. Conyngham remembered, "for a dense smoke arose on all sides, clouding the very heavens."[57]

Kilpatrick led his troopers across the Saluda River on 17 February, rode to Alston on the Broad River the following day, rested his men by the stream for twenty-four hours, and then moved into Monticello on 20 February.[58] He found (to his glee) that the town housed a "female institution," a school for young women. Kilpatrick decided at once that he would host a dance that evening, and to assure that he would not be disturbed, he hurried back to the infantry trailing him to inform them that the ladies were under his protection and that the soldiers need not enter the village.

Alerted to the prospects of a night of fun and frolic, Captain Dexter Horton and Colonel George Este filled a wagon with delectable food and drove into Monticello to crash Kilpatrick's soiree. He was infuriated to see the two infantry officers ride up, but the girls were delighted. They asked the Federals to join the party. While Kilpatrick scowled in the background, Horton and Este danced the night away.[59]

On 21 February Slocum's men wheeled east, which put Kilpatrick again on the infantry's left flank. He continued north, obeying his orders received that day from Sherman to "move . . . so as to seem to be the advance of the whole army in the direction of . . . Charlotte."[60]

Upon his arrival within five miles of Chester on 22 February, Kilpatrick learned that eighteen of his cavalrymen who had left the column to "forage" had been captured, then killed by Wheeler's troopers. "Some had their throats cut," he exclaimed in his report to Sherman. "I have sent Wheeler word that I intend to hang eighteen of his men."[61]

"It leaves no alternative," Sherman agreed in his reply to Kilpatrick's note. "You must retaliate."[62]

Before Kilpatrick could carry out his threat to avenge the killing of his men, he received an answer to his note to Wheeler. The Southern horsemen denied that his cavalry was involved in any murder of Yankee soldiers. "I will have the matter promptly investigated," he vowed, "and see that full justice is done."[63]

Wheeler's response placated Kilpatrick. "I feel satisfied that you will . . . investigate the circumstances attending the murder of my men," he wrote, "[and] that the guilty parties will be [caught] and punished. . . . I shall take no action at this time."[64]

When this storm had blown over, Kilpatrick soon found himself embroiled in a controversy with the Yankee infantry, who were appalled by the degeneracy of his cavalry. On 29 February troops led by Alpheus S. Williams caught five of Kilpatrick's men ransacking a house. They pinned cards saying "Housebreakers" to their breasts, tied the culprits to a tree, and then marched the corps by the trussed troopers.[65]

Instead of accepting the obvious guilt of his horsemen, Kilpatrick accused the infantry of the same crimes accounted to his men. "Stragglers from the Twentieth Corps were here yesterday," he whined in a note to Sherman, "committing acts most disgraceful." He then added his intent to gain revenge for the affront to his command. "No foraging parties [will] pass through or out of my lines," he said, "and I shall dismount and seize all horses ridden by infantrymen."[66]

General Williams took clever advantage of Kilpatrick's uncooperative bluster. While admitting that he had punished the troopers for "throwing the furniture of an old woman into the streets and threatening to burn her house," he stated that such discipline was only for "the good of the service." He then belittled Kilpatrick. "I have the most kind and respectful feelings toward [him]," he wrote (facetiously), "and I regret exceedingly to find that the . . . tone of his communication does not indicate a reciprocity . . . on his part."[67]

Sherman, of course, saw through Kilpatrick's presuming position, and he sent him a tart note. "There is no need of rejoinder," he advised coldly. "Accept [Williams's] disclaimer without discussion or question."[68]

While this exchange was taking place, Kilpatrick's men had moved east, entering Lancaster on 25 February. During his stay in this village, Kilpatrick asked Wheeler to visit his camp to discuss swapping prisoners. The threats by both to execute captives in retaliation for atrocities committed in the field had made each anxious for the safety of friends held by the other. Wheeler rode into Lancaster on 27 February. "The interview was very pleasant," an observer wrote, "considering the circumstances."[69] Twenty Rebels and twenty Union men returned to their commands.

Kilpatrick was probably in a mellow mood because Marie Boozer had joined his entourage. She was, according to John S. Preston, "the most beautiful piece of flesh and blood [I] had ever beheld."[70] The daughter of a Northern sympathizer, she and her mother had fled Columbia when Sherman burned the city; they were headed north when they found refuge with Kilpatrick.

Although he was no doubt sleeping with the handsome Marie, Kilpatrick showed a decorum unusual for him. Each had their own bedroom (separated by a hallway) on the second floor of Daniel W. Brown's home in Lancaster. He

Marie Boozer. Courtesy of the South Carolina Library, University of South Carolina.

went outside during the afternoons to listen to serenades by his band, then at night sat in the parlor, where he and his staff discussed the events of the day. Marie stayed in her room. The two, however, shared meals together. When they left Lancaster, she rode under white blankets piled to her shoulders in the fine carriage that Kilpatrick had appropriated from the Browns.[71]

Kilpatrick's old wound was bothering him. His surgeon offered to take a look at the problem, but he refused treatment. "Never mind," he replied, "I will be all right after [a] little [while]."[72]

The pain, of course, was far too severe for Kilpatrick to ride a horse, so he traveled in Marie's elegant carriage, laying with his head in her lap "for greater consolation in troublous times."[73] This was his position when he rode into North Carolina on 3 March 1865.

The South Carolina campaign presents a microcosm of Kilpatrick's military career. In his only actual battle, he walked into an ambush at Aiken and was routed. He pillaged the defenseless countryside, burning people's houses, stealing their possessions, and even desecrating the churches in Liberty County and Barnwell. And in his reports to Sherman, Kilpatrick was less than truthful. His personal conduct was outrageous. He was involved in several affairs with ladies; wrote angry letters to the Rebels, but never carried out any of his threats; and he became involved in incriminations with the Union infantry. With the North close to finally winning the war, however, interest in impeachment had waned, and so Kilpatrick escaped censure for either his performance or his behavior.

21

North Carolina

By March of 1865 the end of the Civil War was in view. Although Grant had yet to dislodge the Confederates from the trenches south of Richmond at Petersburg, he had pushed his lines north and west to the point where the Rebels under Lee no longer had sufficient troops to defend their front. The Southern capital was due to fall at any moment.[1]

Further south, Sherman was on schedule toward reaching his goal of Goldsboro, where he planned to rest and resupply his troops before making the final push north to join Grant. Slocum's wing was moving through Chesterfield; Howard's men were marching further east through Cheraw. When they entered North Carolina, each would wheel right to continue the advance to Goldsboro. Kilpatrick, who had already crossed the state line, was positioned above the infantry, ready to protect their flank.[2]

The Rebels that Kilpatrick was screening offered a reasonable threat to Sherman's army. Joe Johnston, restored to command, was consolidating the scattered groups of Southern infantry to defend North Carolina. Some of the men were now in Charlotte; the rest were rapidly nearing the city. The two small bands of cavalry had been recently combined into a formidable unit under Wade Hampton.[3] Johnston knew that he had to attack Sherman now, before he was reinforced by Union troops advancing from the sea. Schofield had come east with his infantry and had occupied Wilmington on 22 February. He left part of his twenty-three thousand men there; the rest were sent to New Bern. And he was about to head west from both points to Goldsboro to join with Sherman.[4]

Kilpatrick led his men over the Pee Dee River on 6 March and reached Rockingham on 7 March. He found Southern cavalry occupying the town, but managed to drive them north out of his way. Kilpatrick continued his push east on 8 March, but after fording the Lumber River, he was forced to halt. "I struck the rear of Hardee's column," Kilpatrick explained later, "moving for Fayetteville."[5] Johnston had finally discovered that Sherman was headed for Goldsboro, and he had started his army after the Federals.

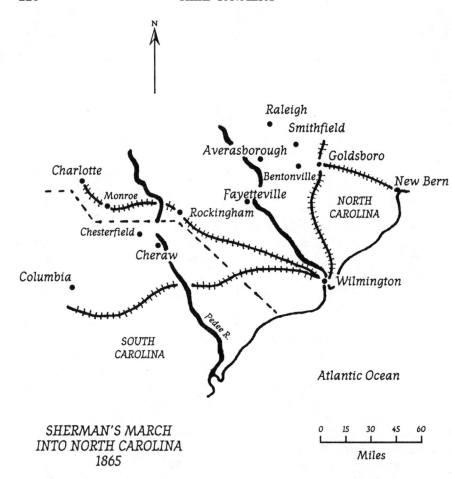

SHERMAN'S MARCH
INTO NORTH CAROLINA
1865

Miles

During this pause, Kilpatrick also learned that he had inadvertently driven a wedge into the Southern columns. The Confederate infantry was up front; Hampton's horsemen were in his rear. He saw the chance to ambush the Rebels as they had so often bushwhacked him. Kilpatrick set out to lay his trap. He positioned his First Brigade (now led by Thomas J. Jordan, who had taken Murray's place at the beginning of the Carolinas campaign) across the southernmost road and Atkins's men above him to await the enemy.[6]

On the morning of 9 March, Kilpatrick learned that a third road north of Atkins was available to the Rebel horsemen. Suspecting that the Confederates might use that route, he sent three regiments under George E. Spencer to block the path.[7] Kilpatrick waited in place all day but saw no sign of the enemy.

Toward evening, as the sky darkened and a pouring rain started to fall, Kilpatrick concluded that the Rebel cavalry had slipped past him. He decided to head to Spencer's post and shift him eastward, toward Fayetteville, to set up a new roadblock. Kilpatrick assembled his headquarters entourage (including Marie Boozer) to accompany him north.[8]

Kilpatrick's tiny column moved slowly, winding through the soaring pines that dripped with rain. Suddenly a burst of brilliant lightning revealed that the detachment was surrounded by enemy horsemen. Kilpatrick had stumbled into one of Hampton's units, also moving east. "My escort . . . was captured," Kilpatrick admitted when reporting the confusing incident, "but I escaped with my staff."[9]

Upon reaching Spencer, Kilpatrick ordered a shift to the east to Monroe's Cross Roads. The Union cavalry arrived about nine o'clock that night.[10] Kilpatrick and Marie went to bed in a tiny cabin in the center of a clearing. The horsemen slept on the wet ground, facing the front where Hardee's infantry was thought to pose the greatest threat. The storm passed on, and all was quiet.

Kilpatrick never considered the fact that his captured escort would reveal his destination to the enemy. They did, of course, and Hampton immediately made plans to attack the Yankee camp at Monroe's Cross Roads. He brought his cavalry forward and soon found that Kilpatrick had left his rear undefended. The few pickets in place were easily removed from the scene without a shot being fired. Since both flanks to the north and south were impenetrable swamps, only the Union front offered a means of retreat. And Hampton thought that he could slip some troopers between the camp and the Federal infantry, posted to the east, which would guarantee his capture of the Kilpatrick's headquarters. Wheeler was assigned the task of blocking the Yankee front; General M. C. Butler would lead the charge from the west.[11]

At first light, with the "air so obscured by mist that one could hardly realize the night had ended," Butler's men galloped into Kilpatrick's camp.[12] They achieved total surprise. "We could not surround them," a Rebel gloated as he pointed to his own dozen or more captives.[13]

When Kilpatrick heard the enemy charging into his camp, he leaped from his bed and rushed outside. A "sorry looking figure in his [undershirt] and drawers," he gasped with dismay at the melee that was unfolding about him.[14] Kilpatrick was frozen in place when a Rebel raced up to demand that he identify which of the frightened Federals was their leader.

"There he goes," Kilpatrick cried as he pointed toward a fleeing Yankee, "[the one] on that black horse."[15]

As the Rebel trooper galloped after the misidentified rider, Kilpatrick frantically mounted a horse tethered nearby and once more raced in his underwear for his life.

Marie was still in the cabin. After hurriedly putting on her clothes (hiding under her full skirt Kilpatrick's battle flag, the one that Alice had sewn in the early days of the war), she came outside and started for her carriage "as if with the vague idea in her dazed head that it was high time to be leaving."[16] She soon realized, however, that it would not move without horses.

Seeing that she was in imminent peril from the bullets that were whizzing throughout the area, a gallant Rebel dismounted to lead the "forlorn, forsaken damsel" into a drainage ditch where she would be safe. Despite the best efforts of her champion, Marie "[kept] lifting her head from time to time [to peer] above the ditch to see what was going on."[17]

Having rounded up all the Yankees that had not escaped his "Morning Call on Kilpatrick," Hampton should have pushed east to complete the rout. The Rebel cavalry, however, was so enticed with the booty lying about that they stopped to fill their haversacks with loot. And because Wheeler had failed to interpose his men between the camp and the regiments to the front, the way was open for the Federals to return in force. As Kilpatrick was no doubt looking for clothes to wear, his troops, despite being "deprived of the animating presence of their general," drove Hampton away.[18] The enemy took their prisoners with them, but left Marie behind.

Hampton was not ready to give up. But when he brought his men back to the camp to continue the battle, he saw that the Union infantry (a brigade from the Twentieth Corps) had reached the scene. Hampton prudently withdrew.[19] Because the Yankee foot soldiers had not engaged the Rebels, Kilpatrick claimed he had recaptured his headquarters without any help. His assertion, however, failed to quiet the laughing taunts that followed his rout. Throughout the army, the affair be came known as "Kilpatrick's Shirt-tail Skedaddle."[20]

Kilpatrick's losses were severe: 19 killed, 68 wounded, and 103 missing. The enemy took his "hat, coat, pants, sword, and pistols," plus "three of Kilpatrick's private mounts, [a] black . . . a piebald, and a bay."[21] But his own personal battle flag, thanks to Marie's full skirt, had been saved.[22]

The rout was extremely embarrassing to Kilpatrick, and for once, he had the courage to admit it. "I had been working hard for promotion to a major generalship," he noted in a later discussion with Hampton, "but when I heard the Rebel yell . . . in my camp, I said, 'Well, after all these years, all is lost.'"[23]

As soon as he could get organized, Kilpatrick began to advance toward Fayetteville (and the protection of Sherman's infantry). His line of march wound through vast pine woods (as opposed to the farmland of South Carolina). His riders, under strict orders from Sherman, spared the few, ramshackle houses they saw along the way, but the urge to burn was too strong to be suppressed. They set the forest on fire. "The smoke could hardly escape through the green canopy above," a trooper wrote, "and being like a pall, it created a feeling of awe as though one were within the precincts of a grand . . . cathedral."[24]

Kilpatrick spent the next four days in Fayetteville as he rested his force and waited while the infantry closed up. Located on the Cape Fear River, the squalid town had direct access to the sea, and on 12 March, the *Davidson* steamed up to the docks from Wilmington. "The effect was electric," Sherman recalled.[25] He quickly prepared some dispatches for Washington, which were sent back to the coast via the sloop. A few refugees, including Marie, also made the journey. She was anxious to leave the area, having seen enough of Kilpatrick and his dangerous camp.[26]

When Marie reached Wilmington, she quickly wed a Union officer as a ticket to take her north to New York City. She left her new husband soon after her arrival and sailed for Europe, where she then married a French count. She had many affairs over the years, and legend says that her final days were tragic. Marie supposedly became the concubine of a warlord in China, who cut the tendons in her ankles to prevent her from running away, then stuffed her with food because he liked his females fat. She weighed more than three hundred pounds at her death.[27]

Sherman spent his time in Fayetteville destroying much of the property that could be useful to the Rebels. His men burned the arsenal, all the railroad buildings, many of the shops, some factories, a tannery, and all three of the newspaper offices.[28]

Taking their cue from Sherman, Kilpatrick's cavalry resumed their plundering of people's homes. The mansion owned by Duncan Murchinson was particularly devastated. Horsemen ran their sabers through the beautiful oil portraits hung on the walls, smashed the furniture, and poured thick molasses into the piano. "Go ahead, boys," their officer called. "Do all the mischief you can."[29]

At another home, one of Kilpatrick's troopers took the family's large Bible outside, opened its pages, and tied the book to a mule's back. He meant to use it as a saddle.[30]

Even the Black slaves were made to suffer. "They took all the corn outen the crib," one moaned. And when a sudden shot rang out, she knew, "[They] wuz killing our turkey."[31]

Sherman left Fayetteville on 15 March. On that same day he ordered Schofield at New Bern and Alfred H. Terry at Wilmington to start their troops west. The plan was to converge with the men moving east at Goldsboro on 29 March.[32]

Kilpatrick led the Federal advance out of Fayetteville. While he galloped north, followed by four infantry divisions from Slocum's wing, feigning a move against Raleigh to hold the Confederates in place, the rest of Sherman's army took a more direct path toward Goldsboro.[33]

Johnston, who was unsure of Sherman's destination, was concentrating his men at Smithfield, halfway between Raleigh and Goldsboro, in position to move quickly to either of the two cities. He planned to assault the Federals before their reinforcements arrived from the sea. Hardee was on his way to Smithfield when he received word that Sherman's force was on his flank. He stopped just below Averasborough to await the enemy.[34]

While Kilpatrick was approaching the village, his men captured Colonel Albert Rhett, an enemy officer who had become lost in the woods. He had galloped up to a Union squad, who Rhett thought belonged to Hampton's force. When told he was a prisoner, Rhett replied with a threat to report the troops to their superior as having used "disrespectful language" in addressing him. "He was soon undeceived," Sherman chuckled, "and . . . conducted to Kilpatrick."[35]

"I was taken by my own fool mistake," Rhett admitted in his interview with Kilpatrick, "but you damned Yankees won't have it your way for long. We've got 50,000 fresh men waiting for you."

"Yes," Kilpatrick snarled back, "and we'll have to hunt every swamp to find the damned cowards."[36]

His words were combative, but Kilpatrick acted with restraint. He dismounted his horsemen, dug entrenchments, and sent a courier back to the rear to ask the infantry to rush forward to help meet the enemy. He waited in vain for their arrival, which was delayed by the hard rain that poured all through the night.[37]

Early in the predawn of 16 March, Hardee started to probe Kilpatrick's line to determine its strength, to see if he faced all of Sherman's army or just a diversionary force. Slocum's men had not yet arrived on the field, so Kilpatrick had to defend the charges on his right all alone. "We held them in check four hours," a trooper recalled, "and then the infantry relieved us."[38] He failed to add that the cavalry was low on ammunition and that their situation was perilous when the foot soldiers finally moved into position.[39]

The Union infantry immediately charged the Rebels and forced them to retreat to their main line. Further attacks, however, failed to dislodge Hardee from behind his entrenchments. That afternoon, Kilpatrick massed his whole division on the right to assault the Rebel flank. "He got a brigade on the road," Sherman related, "and though it fought well and hard, [the cavalry] drew back."[40] Dusk was approaching before a final surge by the infantry pushed the Confederates from their strong position, opening a direct route to Goldsboro to the right.[41]

After another "miserable stormy night," Slocum led his detached divisions eastward the morning of 17 March. Kilpatrick's cavalry rode to his left, defending the flanks of the columns. Howard's infantry, south and ahead of the left wing because of the latter being delayed by the skirmish at Averasborough, was also "wallowing along the miry roads" toward Goldsboro.[42] Slocum crossed over the Black River that day, then slowed his pace on the eighteenth so that his straggling ranks could close up. By evening he was within five miles of Bentonville.[43]

The Confederates at Smithfield were closely monitoring the Yankee advance. "There was an interval of a day's march between [Sherman's] wings," Joe Johnston related. "I determined . . . to attack [his] left wing."[44] The Rebels had 18,000 men on hand: 7,500 under Hardee, 4,000 led by Alexander P. Stewart, and 6,500 reporting to Bragg. Johnston placed this force across the road to Goldsboro, just below Bentonville.[45]

On the morning of 19 March, Slocum's van encountered the Confederates blocking their forward progress. Jefferson C. Davis, commanding the Fourteenth Corps, deployed his men, sending one brigade north, another astride the road, and two below the path. When Slocum came up, he decided to assault the Southern entrenchments, and he brought Alpheus Williams's Twentieth Corps forward for an attack on the right. Before these troops had reached their position, however, the Rebels under Hardee charged the Federals' left flank in an attempt to roll up the Yankee line. Davis's force above the pike was driven southward in frantic retreat.[46]

Slocum quickly prepared a new defensive line below the road, facing north. While he was directing troops into this position, Kilpatrick galloped up from the left and reported that the cavalry was "on the field ready and willing to participate in the battle."[47] Slocum sent the horsemen back to the rear, where they would be out of the infantry's way.

Seeing that the Federals were safely ensconcing themselves behind their hastily built entrenchments, Johnston withdrew his men to the northwest, still blocking the route into Bentonville. He remained in this position on 20 March, skirmishing when necessary to retain his post, but when Union reinforcements began arriving to bolster Slocum's wing, first the Fifteenth Corps, then troops from Howard's force, Johnston decided to abandon the field. He headed for Smithfield on the twenty-first.[48]

His route to Goldsboro reopened by Johnston's retreat, Sherman resumed his march on 22 March. He arrived in that city the next day, where he was greeted by Schofield's army. The campaign was over.[49]

Kilpatrick camped his troopers at Mt. Olive, a village about fourteen miles southeast of Goldsboro along the tracks to Wilmington, where he received praise from Sherman. "The cavalry on this march was handled with spirit and skill," he said. "General Kilpatrick was always willing to attack, but I restrained him . . . it was important to retain our cavalry . . . to cover the flanks of our long wagon trains."[50] The latter comment was obviously made to refute Kilpatrick's critics in the infantry.

"This day I met our great chief on the field of battle, amid the dead and dying of our enemy, who has again fled before our proud, advancing banners," Kilpatrick reported in a letter to his troops, "and my ears were made to tingle with [his] grateful words of praise. . . . Soldiers, be proud! Of all the brave men in this army, you have the right to be . . . General Sherman is satisfied with his cavalry."[51]

Although Sherman openly praised Kilpatrick for his performance in North Carolina, there were signs that he was not really happy with his chief of cavalry. He did not publicly censure him for the embarrassing "Morning Call" by Hampton's troopers, but in private Sherman no doubt warned Kilpatrick to clean up his act, particularly his involvement with girls such as Marie Boozer. Kilpatrick, who usually was immune to all criticism, paid attention. He would continue his womanizing, but in the future he would make attempts to hide his "affairs of the heart."

Sherman also offered excuses for Kilpatrick's timidity, saying that his refusal to fight was because of orders. The fact that he recognized this trait does not speak well for a subordinate. And Sherman must have seen the infantry's contempt for Kilpatrick. His being sent to the rear during the action at Bentonville was a snub that no commander could ignore.

Fortunately for Kilpatrick, time was on his side. The war would come to an end before deteriorating relations with Sherman could cause him harm.

22

The End of the War

Sherman had hoped to supply his troops with fresh food and new uniforms upon his arrival at Goldsboro, but he found that this was impossible. The tracks to Wilmington were so dilapidated, no trains could come inland. Several days were needed before the rail could be repaired. He would have to continue foraging in order to feed his army.[1]

"Gather all the food and forage of the country you can," he wrote Kilpatrick. "[I] care not how close you pinch the inhabitants."[2]

While his army rested at Goldsboro, Sherman went north to City Point outside of Richmond to confer with Grant. The two generals developed their strategy for the next phase of the war. Grant would continue besieging Lee; Sherman would feign an attack on Raleigh, then slip by Johnston to assume a position at Burkeville, Virginia, forty-five miles west of Petersburg, between the two Confederate armies. This would not only prevent their junction but also block Lee's path of retreat when Grant finally drove him from the Southern capital.[3]

When Sherman returned to Goldsboro, he reorganized his force for the final campaign of the war. His two wings were dissolved in favor of these commands: the Army of the Ohio (Schofield); the Army of Georgia (Slocum); and the Army of the Tennessee (Howard). Kilpatrick's cavalry would continue to be independent, reporting directly to Sherman.[4] The Federals would start north on 12 April.

On 6 April, however, Sherman discovered that he must change his plans. Grant had smashed through Lee's front below Richmond and entered the city. The Rebels were fleeing westward, looking to turn the Union line and then head south to join with Johnston in North Carolina.[5]

Sherman's new strategy called for him to confront Johnston and drive him away from Lee's probable path south. His starting date for heading north was pulled up to 10 April. "You may act boldly and even rashly now," Sherman advised in his orders to Kilpatrick. "This is the time to strike quick and strong. We must get possession of Raleigh."[6]

Sherman left Goldsboro on 10 April with his infantry in the lead, the cavalry riding on his left flank and toward the rear. Johnston contested the Yankee advance as he fell back toward Raleigh. The Union occupied Smithfield on 11 April.[7]

The next morning, the governor of North Carolina, Zebulon B. Vance, decided to negotiate a separate peace with the Union. He sent two commissioners, David L. Swain, the president of the university at Chapel Hill, and W. A. Graham, one of the state's former governors, eastward on a train to meet with the oncoming Federals.[8] Their engine was stopped outside of the capital by Wade Hampton, whose men were fighting with Kilpatrick, now leading the Union advance. When he was told about their mission, Hampton allowed the peace party to pass through his line toward Sherman, but he soon changed his mind and recalled the dignitaries. As Swain and Graham rode back toward Raleigh, Kilpatrick's troopers (who had slipped between Hampton's cavalry and the capital) captured the commissioners. The Yankee horsemen stole their valuables, then escorted the Rebel spokesmen to Kilpatrick.[9]

Glowering at his prisoners dressed in civilian clothes, long-tailed coats and beaver hats, Kilpatrick chastised them for their entering a skirmish area. "As . . . you had started to see General Sherman," he then announced, "see him . . . [you shall]."[10] He sent them to a nearby farmhouse to await his clearing a path to the rear.

The two Confederate dignitaries reboarded their train that afternoon and began their ride toward Sherman. When they passed through the Federal army, they saw the soldiers celebrating. The Union men had learned that Lee had surrendered to Grant at Appomattox Court House, Virginia.[11]

"Our army went wild with excitement," George W. Nichols stated. "Our troops gave cheer after cheer to express their joy. . . . Then the bands burst forth in swelling strains of patriotic melody."[12]

The music was not really all that grand. "They played once or twice, drank some, played some more, then drank some more," another related. "The band finally got so they were trying to play two or three tunes at once."[13]

Sherman greeted the commissioners warmly and accepted their bid for "an amicable and generous arrangement with the State government."[14] Because it was now late in the day, he insisted that Swain and Graham spend the night with him. They could return to Vance in Raleigh in the morning.

On 13 April the Southern commissioners started back toward Raleigh. They soon came upon Kilpatrick, who stopped their train to learn the results of their meeting with Sherman. When told that the Yankee commander had accepted their plea for peace, he responded with a warning. "We will give you hell," Kilpatrick glowered, "if I meet any resistance in Raleigh."[15]

When Swain and Graham reached the city, they found the capital deserted. Vance had expected them to return yesterday, but because they did not show as scheduled, he assumed that their mission had failed. He and the rest of the state officials had fled west. William H. Harrison, the mayor of Raleigh, had started east with a delegation to surrender the town to Kilpatrick.[16]

Rain was falling in torrents when the city's officials intercepted the oncoming Federal cavalry. "General Kilpatrick, I presume," a spokesman greeted the van.[17]

"That is my name," Kilpatrick growled in reply. "Whom do I address?"

"My name is Rayner . . . and I have been selected to formally surrender the city of Raleigh."

Kilpatrick accepted this submission by issuing another threat. Although promising to protect both property and people who gave him no problems in the city, he would pursue "with relentless fury" any "traitors in armed opposition."[18]

The Yankee cavalry followed the mayor's entourage into Raleigh. As they rode into the Capitol Square, a lone Rebel faced the Union horsemen. "God damn 'em," he shouted as he raised his revolver. "Hurrah for the Southern Confederacy!" He fired five wild shots, then whirled to flee from the Federals. His mount stumbled, however, and he was thrown from the saddle. Union troopers pounced on the Southern soldier, a Texas lieutenant named Walsh, and took him to Kilpatrick.[19]

"Don't you know," Kilpatrick rasped, "what the penalty is for [armed] resistance after terms of surrender have been agreed upon?"

"I know nothing about a surrender."

"Orderly," Kilpatrick responded, turning to an aide by his side, "take this man out where no ladies can see him and hang him."

Walsh turned white. He begged for some time to write a final letter to his wife, but Kilpatrick refused his plea. The Confederate officer was taken to a tree near the governor's mansion, where he was summarily executed.[20]

The Federal cavalry paused in Raleigh only long enough to chop down the flagpole in front of the capitol and raise the Union stripes atop the dome. They then rode west after the retreating Rebels. Kilpatrick halted at Morrisville for the night.

The following morning, 14 April, a rider galloped up under a white flag to Kilpatrick's bivouac. Captain Rawlins Lowndes brought a message from Johnston to Sherman, requesting a truce. The Confederate military was not preparing for surrender. They were seeking a halt to the hostilities to "permit the civil authorities to [make] the needful arrangements to terminate the existing war."[21]

Kilpatrick sent the letter on to Sherman, then invited Lowndes to remain at his camp while awaiting an answer. Although the offer was genially made, the two adversaries were soon at each other's throats. Kilpatrick started the fracas by stating that the Rebel's early morning attack on him outside of Fayetteville had been "unfair." He would never have been routed and forced to flee in his underwear had the Confederates had the courage to contest him face to face.

"I will make you [a] proposition," Lowndes said. "You . . . take fifteen hundred men, and General Hampton . . . will meet you with a thousand . . . all to be armed with [only] the saber. The two parties will [mount] in regimental formations, opposite to each other, and at a signal . . . will charge."[22]

Kilpatrick refused to accept the challenge.

Sherman's reply to Johnston's proposal was returned to Kilpatrick's quarters that afternoon. "I am fully empowered to arrange with you any terms for the suspension of further hostilities," he stated, "and will be willing to confer with you to that end." Sherman, however, had failed to spot the subtlety in Johnson's message, suggesting a negotiated peace where the Confederacy would survive. He thought the Rebels were ready to surrender and had included his conditions for capitulation, "the same . . . as made by Generals Grant and Lee at Appomattox."[23]

Accompanying Sherman's message to Johnston was a letter to Kilpatrick. "[It] is the beginning of the end," the commander wrote. "Send my answer [to Johnston] at once."[24]

Kilpatrick, however, was no longer at his camp. After arguing with Lowndes, he had moved on to Durham Station, and he evidently did not receive the two letters until the next day. This lag in forwarding Sherman's reply to Johnston delayed their meeting for twenty-four hours.[25]

The hurried advance to Durham Station had little to do with the war. Kilpatrick was involved in yet another tryst, which took place in the elegant mansion of Dr. R. Blacknall. The physician's family occupied the west end of their house; Kilpatrick slept with his new mistress in the east wing.[26]

Kilpatrick's lover had first joined his entourage back in Georgia. She was a beautiful woman with black hair, dark eyes, and an olive complexion. Once the wife of a Southern gentleman, she had left her husband when the Federals passed by her home. She started north when the cavalry arrived at Savannah, stopped at New Bern, then came inland to Goldsboro to rejoin Kilpatrick in North Carolina.[27]

Mindful of Sherman's probable admonition to behave himself, Kilpatrick tried to hide this indiscretion by dressing his paramour in a soldier's uniform, calling her "Charley." Estes, his adjutant, had also taken a mistress (a blue-eyed, fair-haired girl) who wore men's clothing, too. She named herself "Frank."[28]

"[They] were vulgar, rude, and indecent women," Blacknall fumed later when he reported the incident, "but fitting companions for a man of General Kilpatrick's character."[29] There was a third female who stayed at Dr. Blacknall's house with Kilpatrick. Poor Molly, heavy with child, looked after the other ladies. She justified her staying close to Kilpatrick by making herself useful as she washed and ironed the other women's clothing.[30]

On 15 April, after forwarding Sherman's letter on to Johnston, Kilpatrick wrote his commander to protest the plan to meet with the enemy to discuss their surrender. He felt that the proposed conference was a ruse to gain time for the Confederates to elude their adversary. "I don't think Johnston can be trusted," he pronounced. "I believe his army is marching on . . . if he can escape he will do so."[31]

"Johnston can be trusted," Sherman replied, "for he knows well the cause is hopeless."[32]

Although Sherman assured Kilpatrick that the enemy was ready to surrender, the commanding general was worried. The Confederates' rear was not blocked, and they had a railroad at hand to speed their escape. If the Rebels fled, he could not catch them. Johnston could disband his army into small bands, scatter throughout the South, and fight on for months or even years. Sherman could not let that happen. When he met with Johnston, he would offer terms that were so attractive that the Rebel commander would give up his partisan option and end the war.[33]

Johnston quickly accepted Sherman's tender to talk. A meeting was scheduled for noon, 17 April, at a point halfway between Raleigh and Hillsboro.[34]

Sherman boarded a train early that morning and rode to Durham Station, where he was met by Kilpatrick. The cavalry escorted the commanding general and his staff northwest.[35]

Johnston's party, accompanied by Hampton's men, headed southeast out of Hillsboro. They met Sherman's band in open country. As Federal and Rebel troopers glared suspiciously at each other, the two leaders shook hands, then retired in to a nearby cottage (owned by James Bennett) to begin their discussions.[36]

The cavalries started to mingle outside the small farmhouse. Although most of the men were amiable, Hampton was aloof and cold, his expression "bold beyond arrogance."[37] He was upset when he saw some of his troopers displaying friendship toward the Federals. "Fall in!" he ordered, intending that they stand aside in formation.

"The war is over," Kilpatrick protested. "Let the men fraternize."[38]

"I do not intend to surrender!" Hampton shot back. He turned again to his cavalry, and repeated, "Fall in!"

"General Hampton," Kilpatrick interceded. "You compel me to remind you that you have no authority here."

"Permit me, sir," Hampton sneered, "to remind you that Napoleon said that [any] general who would permit himself to be surprised is a very poor soldier, and I surprised you at Solomon's Corner."

"Yes, but what did Napoleon say of one general who after having surprised another, allowed himself to be whipped by his opposite in his [under]shirt and drawers?"

The confrontation between the cavalry chiefs grew more bitter with every word. Hampton was glowering at Kilpatrick with a look "savage enough to eat little Kil" when Johnston and Sherman, hearing the shouts, came running outside. They quickly stopped the encounter. Once calm was restored, the two generals returned into the Bennett House to resume their discussions.[39]

Much to Sherman's surprise, Johnston had not come just to surrender his force. "Instead of a partial suspension of hostilities," he proposed, "we might . . . arrange the terms of a permanent peace."[40] Johnston wanted to parley not only the capitulation of all the Rebel armies still in the field but also the conditions under which the Confederate states might reenter the Union. He assured Sherman he could obtain the support of President Davis for such an agreement.

Sherman, of course, had no authority to negotiate such a pact, but these were "objects of ambition," and he eagerly proceeded with the discussions.[41] Late that afternoon, all terms excepting amnesty for Davis and members of his cabinet had been settled. The two parted, planning to finalize the agreement the next day.

When Sherman arrived back in Raleigh, he published the news that he had received earlier that morning, that Lincoln had been assassinated the evening of 14 April while watching a play at Ford's Theater in Washington. Sherman related that Lincoln's murder had not been sanctioned by the Confederates, a statement meant to prevent vengeance by his troops against the local citizens. "I watched the effect closely," he wrote later, "and was gratified that there was no single act of retaliation."[42]

Johnston and Sherman met again at the Bennett House on 18 April. To avoid a repeat of yesterday's acrid confrontation between Kilpatrick and Hampton, Johnston stopped his escort short of the cabin and came ahead alone. John Breckenridge, Davis's secretary of war, soon joined them. Sherman wrote out the agreement, which called for disbanding all of the Confederate armies, recognition of the state governments from the South upon their representatives taking an oath of allegiance to the Union, reestablishment of federal courts, the guarantee of political rights to Southern citizens, and a declaration of general amnesty. Sherman and Johnston then signed the pact and rode back to their headquarters. Their truce would remain in effect while they waited for confirmation from Washington.[43]

Both President Andrew Johnson and Stanton were shocked by Sherman's signing a political agreement granting terms to the South that they could not support. Grant was sent down to North Carolina to relieve Sherman from command and accept the surrender of Johnston's army. Grant made the trip, but he refused to cashier his friend. Sherman was instructed to meet again with Johnston and inform him that Washington had disapproved their pact. If his adversary did not submit now under the same conditions that Grant had given to Lee at Appomattox Court House, he would resume the war in forty-eight hours.[44]

Sherman and Johnston met at the Bennett House on 26 April. While they were conferring inside the dwelling, their cavalry chiefs were renewing their confrontation outside of the cottage. Kilpatrick challenged Hampton to a fence-jumping contest. Although the Southern horseman was in no mood for sportive competition, Hampton could not resist the opportunity to best his cocky counterpart. He nodded for Kilpatrick to go first.

Kilpatrick charged the barrier. His horse rose in the air, but "came down awkwardly . . . its belly thumping the wood, then struggled clumsily across" the rail. Hampton no doubt was laughing as he "twitched his bridle, galloped forward in his turn, and leaped . . . [easily] over the fence."[45]

This contest between Kilpatrick and Hampton marked the end of conflict in North Carolina. Johnston surrendered his army to Sherman and the war was essentially over. Within a few weeks, the rest of the Rebels had also capitulated.

On 28 April, Sherman called all of his commanders to Raleigh to receive new orders. Schofield's Army of the Ohio and Kilpatrick's horsemen would remain in North Carolina as garrison troops; Howard's and Slocum's soldiers would march north for Richmond on their way out of the service and back to their homes.[46]

Kilpatrick moved his headquarters to Greensboro, where he took up residence in Alexander Eckle's home. He took his new mistress, Charley, still dressed in a soldier's uniform, with him. This attempt to disguise his paramour failed.

"[She] came in a closed carriage and drove to the back door," one observer related, "where [she] was met by General Kilpatrick, who kissed her affectionately when she alighted. That first excited [my] suspicion as to [her] sex."[47]

"I . . . saw General Kilpatrick in bed with Charley hugged up close together," another recalled. "I know Charley was a woman for I have seen her naked."[48]

"I know [she] were a woman," a third witness said, "for I have seen [her] making water. . . . [She] always let down [her] pantaloons and squatted."[49]

"General Kilpatrick was very fond of Charley," a fourth observer noted, "and [he] used to lie pretty close to her in bed."[50]

Molly, too, went to Greensboro, where she did the washing and ironing for Kilpatrick and Charley. The poor Chinese girl remained determined that he take responsibility for her coming child.

While living in Greensboro, Kilpatrick encountered one of his former class-mates from West Point, who had served the Confederacy. The Rebel officer was now destitute. After a long conversation, Kilpatrick pressed two $100 bills into his friend's hand.

"I may never be able to repay you," the Southerner protested.

"If you can pay it, I know you will," Kilpatrick said. "And if you don't it is all the same. You would have helped me in a like position."[51] The end of the fighting appeared to have mellowed Kilpatrick's hatred for the South.

The enemy showed that they, too, could be generous. A few days after the war's end, a Confederate rider trotted up to Kilpatrick's headquarters bearing a present from Wheeler. He was returning Kilpatrick's mount, "Spot," cap-tured during the 29 November raid on his camp at Rock Springs, Georgia. Delighted to see his favorite mare again, Kilpatrick shipped the animal back to his farm in New Jersey.[52]

In late May, Washington celebrated the North's victory in the war with two huge parades. Grant's armies, including the cavalry, marched on the twenty-third; Sherman's force, without his troopers, filed past the dignitaries on the next day.[53]

While Kilpatrick no doubt regretted his missing out on the festivities, he did bask in the promotions that followed the parades. He was named a captain of artillery in the regular army on 31 May. And one week later, he received the permanent rank of major general of volunteers. "During the march of General Sherman's army through Georgia and the Carolinas," Schofield stated in his behalf, "General Kilpatrick had to contend with a superior force of the enemy's cavalry, and yet accomplished [his] task . . . with remarkable success."[54]

Shortly after this promotion, Kilpatrick applied for a leave of absence to visit West Point. His superiors granted the furlough, and on 13 June 1865, he left Greensboro (and escaped Molly).[55] But Kilpatrick did not head north for New York. He went to New Jersey to begin the second phase of a life's plan: to run for governor of his home state.

In starting a political career, Kilpatrick carried the rank of major general into that arena. He believed that his performance as a Federal officer would sway voters to elect him to public office. His opponents would cull his military record to find facts that would discredit Kilpatrick; they would learn that this task was easily accomplished.

He entered the war as an infantry captain. Kilpatrick was an early hero, the first Yankee officer to be wounded in combat, but he could not explain how he was hit in the rump at Big Bethel while supposedly facing the enemy.

Upon joining the cavalry, Kilpatrick gained renown for his intrepid raids into the heartland of Virginia. He was a daring marauder (especially when compared to his more timid compatriots), but the results of his audacious exploits were barren. The damage done was always temporary at best. And in the process, Kilpatrick exhausted his horses and men. He was seldom at hand during the crucial times when service by the cavalry might have made a difference in battle. Pope at Second Manassas and Hooker at Chancellorsville both lost in part because Kilpatrick was too tired to fill their needs.

Spending the several months between these main battles in prison, accused of stealing horses and taking bribes, did little to advance Kilpatrick's military reputation.

In the Gettysburg Campaign, Kilpatrick risked face-to-face combat for the first and only time during the war. His regiments fought poorly at Brandy Station, but he won glory because of the total Union effort. The battles at Aldie and Uppervile saw Kilpatrick leading a cavalry charge, and this brief show of courage earned him a general's star. Those in command were kind enough to overlook that he had repeatedly been lured into ambushes by his adversary.

Kilpatrick's sorry performance in Pennsylvania was the turning point of his military career. Although he defeated the Rebels under Jeb Stuart at Hanover (the battle had ended by the time Kilpatrick finally reached the field), he blundered at Gettysburg by ordering Farnsworth to make a fatal charge. And the obvious lies in his official reports of the campaign revealed to his peers that Kilpatrick's reputation had been built on words, not deeds.

During the fall of 1863, Kilpatrick's command did well during the Second Battle of Brandy Station, but George Custer was the real and recognized hero. The crushing defeat that followed at Buckland proved that Kilpatrick was incapable of combat command.

Desperate to save his rapidly deteriorating reputation, Kilpatrick bypassed his superiors when he appealed directly to Lincoln for approval to mount a raid on Richmond. While he gained the assignment, his personal cowardice caused the mission to fail. Kilpatrick's disgrace was compounded when orders calling for the assassination of Jefferson Davis were found on the body of Dahlgren, his second-in-command. This barbarity (probably concocted by Kilpatrick) was so shameful to the North that he was relieved from duty.

Kilpatrick was reprieved by Sherman, who offered him a post in his western army. His only role in the Atlanta campaign was an unsuccessful raid to sever the railroad tracks below the city. Kilpatrick's effort, however, was much more strenuous than that mounted by the other cavalry heads. He won Sherman's confidence and was included in the force that started for the sea.

During the march through first Georgia, then South Carolina, the cavalry was responsible for protecting the flanks of the infantry from enemy assault. The Confederates never once threatened the Union ranks, and Sherman gave

Kilpatrick credit for this feat. He did not recognize that the Rebels had no intentions of attacking Kilpatrick. They were intent on defending Macon and Augusta while the Union was in Georgia, then Augusta and Charleston during the Northern trek through South Carolina. Kilpatrick faced opposition only twice, at Waynesborough and Aiken, and in each instance was routed by the enemy.

The conduct of Kilpatrick and his cavalry as they rode through the Deep South was despicable. Sherman intended to forage and destroy only military targets, but Kilpatrick's men spent most of their time robbing the civilians of their valuables, then burning their houses. Kilpatrick was too busy bedding women of ill repute to attempt any control of his outrageous troopers.

Kilpatrick's lust for harlots almost cost him his life while in North Carolina, when the Rebels charged his camp in a "morning call." He escaped wearing only his underclothes, the second such instance during the campaign. He managed to avoid any further embarrassments to the end of the war.

Two factors favored Kilpatrick's claim to being a military knight: he had been involved (but not instrumental) in many of the key conflicts of the war; and his side emerged victorious. Neither offered sufficient grounds to press his cause for election to office. And there were too many loose women, too many stolen valuables, too many burned homes in his background. Kilpatrick had built his base on shifting sand. His character would become the main issue in every political race, and his opponents would successfully exploit this conspicuous weakness.

23

Ambassador to Chile

New Jersey usually supported the Democratic Party, but after their success in the War, the Republicans thought they had an excellent chance of capturing the governor's seat in 1865. Their strategy was to "wave the bloody shirt," to run a campaign on issues relating to the recent hostilities.

Meeting in Trenton on 20 July, the delegates adopted a platform that congratulated themselves for winning the War of Rebellion. They deplored the death of Lincoln, endorsed President Johnson's administration, and chided the Democrats for their Southern sympathies, e.g., discouraging volunteers, which forced state officials to offer high bounties in order to fill assigned quotas, opposing the raising of Negro regiments, and failing to provide soldiers with their vote while away in the field. As "Union-Republicans" they promised to run an efficient government, to reward each honorably discharged veteran with a bonus, and to sustain the Monroe Doctrine in Mexico. They also supported the Thirteenth Amendment, which abolished slavery. New Jersey was the only state above the Mason-Dixon Line that had not yet ratified that amendment.[1]

Three candidates were in the running for the Republican gubernatorial nomination. Marcus L. Ward, backed by William H. Seward (secretary of state), Stanton, and other radicals, was chairman of his party's national executive committee and was expected to win the convention's nod. His main opponent was Alexander C. Cattell, the president of the Corn Exchange Bank in Philadelphia. Kilpatrick, having had little time to prepare for the campaign because he had been out of the state, serving in the military, was considered a dark horse.[2]

Ward won the nomination as the Republican candidate on the fourth ballot. Most competitors would have accepted the party's decision and agreed to support Ward in the fall campaign, but Cattell refused to assume that role. He declared that because Ward could not possibly defeat the Democratic entry, he would dedicate his efforts (and money) to electing a Republican legislature. Cattell anticipated that a grateful state congress would send him to Washington as a senator.[3]

On 3 August the Democrats named Theodore Runyon as their candidate for governor. The party platform blamed the extremists in the North and South for causing the Civil War, opposed Negro suffrage, and criticized the radicals' program for military occupation of the Confederate states. They advocated the use of the Monroe Doctrine in Mexico and pledged a veterans' bonus.[4]

The Republican leaders in Washington realized that the party could not win the gubernatorial campaign in New Jersey without making a fervent effort. Stanton and Seward turned to Kilpatrick. If he would spend the coming months speaking throughout the state in support of Ward and bring about his election, they would reward him with an ambassadorship.[5]

On 10 August Kilpatrick asked the army to extend his leave of absence to 24 September. Military officials gave him the additional days, and he began to campaign.[6] "I am not willing to see the rebels of the South, whose hands are yet red with the blood of our fallen braves, restored to all their old rights and privileges," he repeated over and over. "I will not stand tamely by and see the triumph of that band of pitiable traitors in my native State who, while professing loyalty to the Union . . . have ever gloried in the progress of treason—men who now call themselves Democrats."[7]

Kilpatrick's effort was decisive. Ward received 2,789 more votes than his opponent and was elected governor of the state. "[His] majority would have been larger," Kilpatrick blustered, "[except] for the same old trouble with [my] back and kidneys, which prevented me from filling all of [my] engagements."[8] He claimed credit for having "saved New Jersey to the Republican Party"[9] and turned to Washington for the overseas post promised by Stanton and Seward. They kept their bargain. On 15 November 1865 Kilpatrick was named "Envoy Extraordinary Minister Plenipotentiary" to Chile at a salary of $10,000 per year, plus an additional $500 for embassy expenses.[10]

Early in 1866, Kilpatrick boarded the *Henry Chaunery* in New York and set sail for Chile. His party included Mrs. E. S. Shailer, his first wife's mother, who had agreed to act as his official hostess at the embassy; his secretary, Colonel Cooke; and two aides, General Vickers (his brother-in law) and Captain Northrup.[11]

While at sea, Mrs. Shailer met Mrs. Williams, a pretty young woman who was headed for Panama to meet her husband, an officer on the U.S. Navy sloop-of-war, *Cyarce*. She introduced her new friend to Kilpatrick, who immediately took her under his wing as "one of our party."[12] The ship docked on the east coast of Panama, where Kilpatrick and his group disembarked to take a train across the isthmus to the Pacific shore. They would board a new vessel there for the final leg to Chile.

Upon reaching the west coast of Panama, Kilpatrick met Mrs. Williams's husband, who asked a favor. His ship was going to San Francisco but would make frequent stops at ports along the way. They would not return to the United States until March. His wife could not remain in Panama, and because he had no friends in California where she might stay to wait his coming, could she accompany Kilpatrick to Chile and then set sail to the north?[13]

Kilpatrick gallantly agreed to attend to Mrs. Williams, but he soon discovered that his "duties" were not limited to being a chaperon. On his third night in Panama, just before starting for Chile, Kilpatrick "began to entertain doubts of her virtue."[14] He evidently not only took the young lady to Chile (enjoying her "comforts" during the passage) but also kept her there with him for almost a month.

Kilpatrick arrived in Chile on 15 February, where he found the nation at war with Spain and the president "out of town" and unable to accept his credentials. He lived in a private estate in Valparaiso with his lover (whom he introduced as his wife) while awaiting accreditation, and they were entertained often over the following weeks by Americans living in the coastal city.[15] When he finally moved to Santiago on 12 March, Kilpatrick ended his liaison with Mrs. Williams. He had assumed that she would head for San Francisco and her husband, but to his horror she took to the streets and began openly selling her favors. Despite his boasts of having seduced the young lady, Kilpatrick was forced to claim that he was astonished to learn that she was a woman of abandoned morals, and he sent letters of profuse apology to those who had opened their doors to him and his supposed wife.[16]

While he was putting out that fire, Kilpatrick was busy starting another: an intervention into the war between Chile and Spain. The issue at hand was whether the Spanish fleet, anchored in the harbor of Valparaiso, would bombard the port because of Chilean insults to their queen. Although the adversaries were ready to forgive and forget with a twenty-one gun salute to each other, neither was willing to accept the ignominy of firing the first shot. Kilpatrick scurried back and forth between Covarrubias, Chile's foreign minister, and Admiral Mendez, the Spanish commodore, trying to resolve the impasse.[17]

His efforts failed, and on 27 March Mendez issued a manifesto that he would "open his batteries upon the city of Valparaiso on Saturday morning [March] 31st . . . at 8 o'clock, thus giving four days to non-combatants for their removal."[18] The Chileans' reply was that they would not resist with even "a single shot" so that "the barbarity of the act [would] be patent to the world."[19]

While the Chileans would not act in their defense, Kilpatrick was eager to do so. He called a parley of diplomats from England, France, Russia, and Italy to formulate a plan of thwarting the Spanish squadron. Meeting in Valparaiso at 2:00 P.M. on the twenty-seventh, the ambassadors listened in shock as Kilpatrick suggested they form an armada from their ships at hand, attack Mendez, and drive his galleons from the harbor. He was proposing that they commit their countries to a war with Spain. The dignitaries were too polite to repudiate Kilpatrick's wild scheme directly. Instead, they asked for time to consider the idea and agreed to reconvene that evening. Late that afternoon the

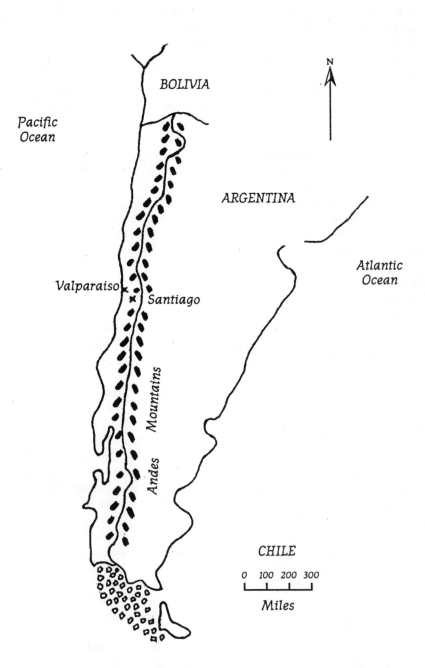

N

BOLIVIA

Pacific
Ocean

ARGENTINA

Atlantic
Ocean

Valparaiso

Santiago

Andes Mountains

CHILE

0   100 200 300

Miles

English minister requested a second delay until ten o'clock the following morning.[20]

That night, as Kilpatrick was feverishly preparing his plans for war, he learned that the English and French ambassadors had no intention of continuing the discussions and that both had gone back to Santiago via the evening train. "They departed," Kilpatrick complained in a memo to Seward, "without giving any reason for [their being] so abrupt and discourteous."[21] He did meet the next day with the rest of the foreign representatives, but they refused to act without the support of England and France.

Having only two U.S. ships at Valparaiso, Kilpatrick decided against mounting the assault on his own. "I could not risk the certainty of war with Spain," he reported to Seward, "when we have just emerged bleeding and exhausted from the mightiest struggle the world has ever seen."[22] Seward was no doubt pleased that his ambassador to an insignificant country such as Chile had elected within a month of assuming his post not to commit his nation to a major war.

Mendez opened his batteries against Valparaiso at 9:00 A.M. on 31 March. The bombardment lasted for three hours, during which over two thousand shells were sent flying into the port. The governor's palace, the railroad station, four public warehouses and their contents, the customhouse, and twenty-five private dwellings were battered. Kilpatrick estimated the loss at $15 to $20 million.[23]

Following his attack against Valparaiso, Mendez sailed north for Callao. Peru was an ally of Chile, and he planned to shell their port city, too. Kilpatrick countered by dispatching the U.S. gunboat *Vanderbilt* after the Spaniards. When he reached Callao, Stringham (the ship's captain) found the Peruvians ready to defend their city. They had cannons in place, but their gunners were inexperienced. He sent his artillerists ashore, and when Mendez opened his bombardment, the Americans, manning the pieces, returned fire. One Spanish galleon was sunk, and Mendez was mortally wounded, which ended the fighting in the Southern hemisphere.[24]

With peace restored, Kilpatrick began to enjoy the comforts of diplomatic life in a foreign city. Santiago was an elegant capital with many beautiful homes and gardens. The Chilean elite had grown rich from their farms and mines, and "they enjoyed their wealth . . . [spending] money freely on luxuries and pleasures."[25] The marbled halls of their palatial mansions were lined with paintings from the national school, and native music and literature were both in vogue. As the U.S. ambassador, Kilpatrick was frequently included as a guest of honor at the parties held in such houses, and he proved to be a most engaging representative for his country, a man who was both liked and respected.

Kilpatrick's new world, however, was soon menaced by a letter from Seward. A report of his indiscretions with Mrs. Williams had reached the United States. While the newspapers made no mention of a specific name or place (saying that "one of our South American Ministers . . . has veiled with his . . . diplomatic cloak the scarlet robes of a publicly abandoned woman"), the secretary of state immediately associated the articles with Kilpatrick. "It is supposed that the one . . . to whom the paragraph refers may be yourself," Seward stated. "The President deems . . . you should . . . deny the charge."[26]

Faced with a probable recall, Kilpatrick took his time to offer a careful defense. His letter of 31 July 1866 was rambling, however, and bordered on the hysterical. "This mail [was] astonishing to me," he wrote Seward, "[in] that I have received no word . . . of any charges against me."[27] Because the State Department had not indicted him, Kilpatrick was saying that he should not have to offer any explanations. He then proceeded to account for his situation.

"My enemies," he stated, "have been most anxious to see me disgraced." Kilpatrick accused Thomas H. Nelson, his predecessor as ambassador, and Mr. Cash, a reporter, of making up lies about his conduct. Their motive was revenge for his having offended them by replacing Nelson and by failing to offer Cash a job with the legation.[28]

Kilpatrick insisted that he brought only Mrs. Shailer, his mother-in-law, with him to Chile. He enclosed testimony from prominent Chileans to support his claim.[29] Seward had read the newspaper accounts, however, which related that the minister in question had flaunted his mistress only to Americans, and he would have dismissed these letters from locals as proof that Kilpatrick was innocent of the charges against him.

Although he admitted that had met Mrs. Williams during the voyage south and that he had later come to "suspect" her morals, Kilpatrick claimed that he had left the "abandoned" female in Panama.[30] If he had, it would have been the first known instance where Kilpatrick had failed to exploit a sexual opportunity. And Seward must have been aware of Kilpatrick's war reports, which were notorious for their lies. He could not seriously accept Kilpatrick's word as confirmation of his virtue.

Kilpatrick concluded his defense with a demand that an investigation be conducted into his behavior (no doubt knowing that both the distance between Washington and Chile and the embarrassment to Seward if the allegations were found to be true made this probe improbable). "At least," he begged, "let me know who my defamers are."[31]

When the newspapers dropped the issue, Seward followed suit, and Kilpatrick was allowed to remain in Chile. He was greatly relieved and attended to his duties with a renewed vigor. Claims from American businessmen who suffered losses in the bombardment of Valparaiso were sent to Spain through his office.[32] In September, Kilpatrick went to an inaugural ball honoring President Perez. "It was a brilliant affair," he related to Seward, "and a pretty good indication that [I] stand well in the estimation of . . . people [here].

. . . None but the friends of the Government . . . were invited."[33] And about a month later, during one of his quarterly inspections, Kilpatrick uncovered a scandal at the U.S. Navy hospital at the port city of Talcahuano. Trumbull, the American consul, was stealing money by filing claims for the treatment of sailors who had long since been released as patients and returned to their ships. Trumbull was fired and a new man named to his post.[34]

Despite his hectic schedule, Kilpatrick found time for the ladies, one in particular. Louisa Valdivieso was a very pretty, very petite woman. She was only five feet tall, and her dark hair was so long that when not braided around her head it tumbled to the floor.[35] Her family was most prominent in Chile. An uncle, Ramosa Valintine Valdivieso, was the archbishop of the Catholic Church, and a cousin, Erasires Valdivieso, was an important politician, who in a few years would be elected president of Chile.[36] Kilpatrick and Louisa were betrothed, then married in the cathedral in Santiago by her famous uncle on 3 November 1866.[37]

The year of 1867 was probably the best of Kilpatrick's life. His role as ambassador was largely ceremonial, and he was not stressed by his daily duties. "I have the honor to report," he wrote more than once to Seward, "that nothing of political importance has transpired at this capital since my last dispatch."[38]

In mid-October, the U.S. Army sent Kilpatrick a letter, reminding him that the furlough granted during the spring of 1865 so he could enter the political campaign in New Jersey had been revoked in December of that year. Because he had never reported for duty, he had been AWOL for more than two years. The army, however, was not looking to arrest Kilpatrick; he was on their lists as an artillery captain and was blocking the promotions of those below him. They asked for his resignation. Kilpatrick immediately gave up his commission, effective 1 December 1865.[39]

He and Louisa were kept busy attending the many social functions that involved the diplomatic corps. As the ambassador for a major country and now a member of one of Chile's leading families, Kilpatrick enjoyed a prestige that was second to none. That fall, however, their activity slackened. Louisa was pregnant. She gave birth on 3 November 1867 to a baby girl. Kilpatrick called his daughter Julia Mercedes Luisa; her first name was in honor of his mother.[40]

In the spring of 1868, with Louisa busy with the baby, Kilpatrick decided to take some time off for a trip into the Andes Mountains. He left Santiago on 3 February. Riding a mule, Kilpatrick reached the base of the mountains on the first day, climbed the slopes as high as the tree line on the second day, and attained the first peak on 5 February. Traveling along a "zigzag path by which the higher chain is crossed," he marveled at the "great heaps of sulpheric rock, lava, and ashes." He continued to press forward, despite a "rarified atmosphere affecting man and beast," and on 8 February arrived at the summit. "The view was indescribably grand," he wrote to Seward. "There is barely standing room for two or three persons . . . we found it necessary to lie down to avoid being swept off by the wind."[41]

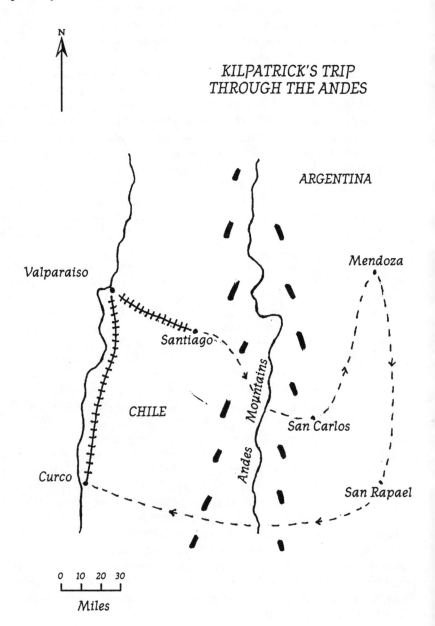

KILPATRICK'S TRIP
THROUGH THE ANDES

Descending the heights into Argentina, Kilpatrick made a stop at San Carlos, then rode in a coach north to Mendoza, a city recently devastated by an earthquake. "The ruins still lie as they fell," he stated, "[but] on the border, a new town . . . has already sprung up. The buildings are good, the streets wide, well paved, and adorned with shade trees."

Kilpatrick then headed south to San Rafael, a military outpost set up to guard against attacks from hostile Indians living below the fort. He participated in a "grand ostrich hunt," then began his trek back across the Andes to Curco on the Chilean coast. He returned to Santiago via train.

"I regard my experience," he remembered, "as belonging to the most valuable of my life." Kilpatrick anticipated an enormous potential for the Argentine pampas, which could be "a garden of fertility" when irrigated, and offered to "ever be zealous to aid any undertaking [toward] the . . . opening of these treasures to the world."

Perhaps inspired by his visit to the Andes, Kilpatrick took up painting as a hobby. He produced a number of fairly good renditions of the local landscape, which he framed and hung on the walls of the embassy.[42]

Kilpatrick no doubt envisioned a future for himself in Chile, where as the U.S. ambassador he could closely attend to investments he might make in Argentina. He soon learned, however, that his idyllic life was threatened. A new president would be elected in America in 1868, and friends must have informed him that Grant, the likely winner, had stated that he would not retain Kilpatrick in his post. The affair with Mrs. Williams would cause his recall.

To prevent this from happening, Kilpatrick decided to use the same tactics that resulted in his being named the ambassador to Chile in 1865. He would return to the United States, campaign for Grant, and thereby earn both his gratitude and a reprieve from recall. To do so required a leave of absence, and therein lay the problem. Seward would never grant him a furlough for political purposes. Kilpatrick's dilemma was solved by a sad note from New Jersey. His sister, Charity, had died. "This leaves my old mother entirely alone," he wrote Seward. "I had been so occupied in public affairs before departing for Chile as to . . . prevent me from attending to the . . . interests . . . of my family. My return to the United States . . . is now an imperative duty."[43]

Seward was no fool. Suspecting that Kilpatrick was up to no good, he pointedly asked him if his reasons for coming home included taking part in the coming fall campaign. "Absolutely not," Kilpatrick replied. "I guarantee that I will not."[44] On the basis of that pledge, Seward granted Kilpatrick a leave of three months.

Kilpatrick and Louisa left Chile on 15 August. When they reached New York City one month later, instead of going to the bedside of his aged mother in New Jersey, the couple checked into the Metropolitan Hotel. The following evening, Kilpatrick spoke to "The Boys in Blue" (a group of veterans) assembled at the Cooper Institute. "You waded through seas of blood to save the Union," he began, "and your votes in the present contest will stem the tide of rebel victory and roll it foaming back upon the foe." He lauded his party for freeing the slaves and lambasted the Democrats, denouncing them as "the embodiment of all traitorous designs."[45]

Seward, of course, was incensed and called Kilpatrick to Washington on 19 September to explain why he had broken his promise. But after meeting with the secretary of state, who no doubt insisted that he cease and desist his campaigning, Kilpatrick went to the White House to induce President Johnson to overrule Seward. "He [does] not disapprove of my conduct," Kilpatrick crowed triumphantly in a letter to Seward. "I have entered the present political contest . . . [because] I consider it my duty. . . . With your permission, [I will] remain in this country until the end."[46]

Kilpatrick's note was "as supercilious as egotistical," Gideon Welles wrote, "flippantly snapping his fingers at the Secretary of State and defying him."[47]

During the following weeks, Kilpatrick traveled widely, "making a fool of himself," Welles stated, "running all over the country [giving] partisan speeches."[48] He spoke mostly about the Civil War and particularly about the Rebel cavalry leader, General Nathan Bedford Forrest. Kilpatrick accused the former slave trader of committing atrocities against the Blacks during the war. While the Confederate trooper might have been guilty of a few these charges, most were just figments of Kilpatrick's vivid imagination. "[Forrest] nailed negroes to . . . fences," he claimed, "set fire to the fences, and burned the negroes to death."[49]

Forrest was incensed over Kilpatrick's falsehoods, and on 28 October he wrote a note, published in the *New Haven Register,* challenging Kilpatrick to a duel. "I am ready to meet him in any way he may choose," Forrest bristled. To add emphasis to his dare, he called Kilpatrick a "blackguard, a liar, a scoundral, and poltroon."[50]

Forrest's letter must have frightened Kilpatrick. The Rebel officer, a strapping figure, six feet two inches tall, had killed at least thirty Federals in personal combat during the war.[51] Facing Forrest could only result in certain death. Kilpatrick dodged the duel by replying that he could not agree to Forrest's challenge because he did not "regard him as a gentleman."[52]

And besides, Kilpatrick had a new target to vituperate against. Party managers had come to Kilpatrick to ask his help with a problem. Ben Butler, the Republican nominee for a Massachusetts seat in the House of Representatives, was speaking out against their man for president. Butler was still indignant toward Grant for relieving him of duty during the final days of the Civil War. The party had decided to oppose Butler by supporting Richard H. Dana, an independent candidate. Would Kilpatrick head north to campaign for Dana? They would pay him $200 a day.[53]

He immediately accepted the offer and rushed to Massachusetts to begin denouncing Butler. Kilpatrick also padded his pockets by accepting speaking fees from the local party officials, who were unaware that he was also being compensated by the national committee for his efforts.[54]

William E. Chandler, one of those in charge of Grant's campaign, was unaware of Kilpatrick's assignment, and he was upset by the attacks against Butler. He sent a telegram to Kilpatrick, asking that he stop railing against a fellow Republican. "I will answer to General Grant for my conduct," Kilpatrick sneered back. "If you are a friend of Butler, you cannot be the friend of Grant . . . I shall [see that] . . . he is acquainted with your conduct toward one who fought with him . . . while you [were] at home . . . resting your legs beneath your office desk in Washington."[55]

Butler, a wily politician, needed no help in combating Kilpatrick. He responded to the attacks by releasing to the newspapers the details of Kilpatrick's involvement with Mrs. Williams in Chile.[56] Media across the country repeated this tale, the first time that the names and place of the sordid affair had been revealed. Kilpatrick was so enraged that he challenged his accuser to a duel on Salem Green, but Butler (no doubt with a chuckle) refused the dare. A friend, Henry J. Raymond, wrote a long letter defending Kilpatrick, which was published by the *New York Times,* but it proved to be too late. The damage was done. Butler's revelation had ruined Kilpatrick's reputation.

Grant was elected president in November 1868, and a few weeks after taking office he recalled Kilpatrick as the ambassador to Chile, naming his brother-in-law, Judge Louis Dent, to the position. The Senate, however, was horrified by such a blatant display of nepotism, and they refused to confirm Grant's choice.[57] Kilpatrick had gained a reprieve.

Knowing that his days as ambassador were numbered, Kilpatrick began making plans for a new career. He contacted a booking agent, the National Lecture Bureau in New York City, and arranged a speaking tour that would start in the fall of 1870.[58] After finally attending to his private matters, he and Louisa started back to Chile on 1 June 1869.

Although he no longer had any heart for his post—e.g., he refused to file his quarterly reports because he had run out of the proper government form[59]— Kilpatrick could not leave Chile. Louisa was pregnant. She gave birth to another girl (Laura) on 24 December 1869.[60]

Through the early weeks of 1870, despite a probable promise to Grant that he would soon relinquish his position and return to America, Kilpatrick stayed in Chile. His new baby was sick and too weak to travel.

On 17 March an impatient Hamilton Fish, the new secretary of state, sent Kilpatrick a pointed note, saying, "We will accept your resignation."[61] Kilpatrick, however, could not leave his post as now he, too, was ill. "He is confined to bed," an aide related, "has quite lost his voice, and his neck is double its normal size."[62]

Kilpatrick's condition did not improve, and finally on 9 May 1870, knowing that he could get proper treatment only in the United States, he submitted his resignation. He set an August date for his departure and asked that Grant delay until September the end of his official duties. "You . . . can find in me," he facetiously wrote the president, "a true and fearless friend."[63]

When Louisa and Kilpatrick sailed from Chile, they had to leave without their new baby. Laura was far too frail to travel. Kilpatrick asked her grandparents, who would watch over the girl, to mail him her photograph every three months so he could see her progress.[64] Rosa, Louisa's sister, came north with the couple to be her companion through the coming years.

Kilpatrick reached New York City in late September and immediately went to a hospital, where physicians operated on his neck.[65] Their surgery was successful. His resignation was accepted, and for the first time in his adult life, Kilpatrick became a private citizen.

Of all his talents, Kilpatrick's ability as a forceful speaker was his best, which he proved in the 1865 New Jersey elections. He earned his post as ambassador to Chile. Of all his defects, Kilpatrick's lecherousness was his worst, which he proved with his affair with Mrs. Williams on ship and in Chile. To tryst was foolhardy, and he suffered dearly for his brief fling.

Although Kilpatrick stated that he had left Mrs. Williams in Panama, too many people disputed his claim. The most interesting of these was Mrs. Shailer, his mother-in-law, who could only have been repulsed by his blatant indecency. She never testified to his innocence and displayed her disgust in a most unusual manner. In 1895, years after Kilpatrick's death, she petitioned and received permission to remove her daughter's body and headstone from next to Judson's grave at West Point to be sent back to New York City for reinterment.[66]

Kilpatrick's initial efforts as an ambassador upon his arrival in Chile threatened to create war between the United States and Spain. But once his amateurish intervention had passed, he proved a fine representative for his country. He had natural social grace, and with the contacts established through his marriage, he became liked and respected by those he was supposed to influence.

When he discovered that he was probably going to be recalled, Kilpatrick returned to the United States and hurried into the political arena with the same abandon shown during the war. And just as the Rebels had so easily lured him into their snares, Benjamin Butler neatly bushwhacked the one who had come to efface him. Others might have saved Kilpatrick from disgrace, but after his snubs of both Chandler and Seward, few Republicans would come to his rescue.

But just as he had weathered his errors during the war, Kilpatrick succeeded in civilian life. None had more talent and experience for lecturing than he, and Kilpatrick would find outstanding repute in this new field.

24

Farmer/Lecturer

Upon his return to the United States, Kilpatrick moved into rooms at the Metropolitan Hotel in New York City, where he completed writing his first lecture, "Sherman's March to the Sea." He traveled to Boston on 31 October 1870 to address a paying audience at Music Hall. His presentation was "a pronounced success," according to the *Sussex Independent,* and offers for Kilpatrick to talk elsewhere poured into the office of the National Lecture Bureau.[1] He spent the winter delivering this same speech "in all the principal cities of the Union," and in each he received high accolades.[2]

Kilpatrick left the lecture circuit in May 1871 and came home to his family's farm near Deckertown. He intended both to supervise the spring planting and to mount a second try to be governor of New Jersey. He opened his campaign by presiding over the county's Fourth of July festivity. "The day [was] ushered in by the ringing of bells, displaying the . . . colors, and firing a national salute at sunrise," one observer recalled.[3] This was followed at 10:00 A.M. by a long parade (led by Kilpatrick), which included a band, a company of mounted ex-cavalrymen, and then civic groups, such as the "Temperance Organization in regalia."[4] Speeches filled the afternoon. When darkness fell, a dazzling fireworks display ended the ceremonies.

The main rival to Kilpatrick for the Republican nomination was a prominent Methodist, Cornelius Walsh. Just prior to the convention, Kilpatrick attempted to dismiss Walsh by circulating reports that his opponent had withdrawn from the campaign. The move backfired. Walsh protested loudly over the dirty trick, and Kilpatrick was forced to write a public letter of apology for his "mistake."[5]

The Republicans met in Trenton on 7 September. With Kilpatrick already in disgrace because of his foolish claims regarding Walsh's withdrawal, his character became the major issue of the campaign. His affair with Mrs. Williams was probably introduced to the delegates. A friend, General Hoxsey from Passaic, tried to refute these charges, but when his address was repeatedly interrupted by hoots from the crowd, he lost his temper. "The fiery manner of

. . . his speech was doubtless well intended," the *Sussex Independent* related, "but it seriously damaged General Kilpatrick's chances."[6]

Another supporter, Dr. Welling, tried to introduce the resolutions of former soldiers that Kilpatrick had earned an outstanding military record. "He had only read a portion . . . when [he] was abruptly ruled out of order."[7]

On the first ballot, Kilpatrick trailed two candidates, Walsh and John Davidson, receiving only 179 votes out of the 876 cast. Walsh won the nomination on the second poll.[8]

Although disgusted by his defeat, Kilpatrick agreed to support the Republican Party. "He has swallowed the pill at the risk of choking. . . . Considerable greasing was necessary," the local newspaper wrote. "[He] opened the campaign with a speech at Jersey City on Friday evening last."[9] His effort, however, proved ineffectual. The Democratic candidate, Joel Parker, won the election by five thousand votes.[10]

Kilpatrick returned to the lecture circuit that winter. In addition to his still popular speech, "Sherman's March to the Sea," he prepared a second address for that season. "Incidents and Battle Scenes of the Rebellion" (a report on the Battle of Gettysburg) was also acclaimed by audiences, leading to an extensive tour of the West in early 1872, followed by a March trip to California, where he received $3,000 plus expenses for only twelve appearances.[11]

While Kilpatrick was lecturing across the country, the Republican Party was engrossed in a rebellion by some of its members. They were dissatisfied with Grant, especially his policies regarding reconstruction of the South, his abuse of the civil service system, his opposition to specie payments, his support of high tariffs, his attempt to annex the island of Santo Domingo, and his refusal to consider effective control of corporations.[12] In the spring of 1871, they started a third political party, calling themselves "The Liberal Republicans." Carl Schurz, a senator from Missouri and former Yankee general, was the leader of the dissidents. They met in Cincinnati in May 1872 to nominate a candidate to oppose Grant in the coming presidential election.

Schurz and his friends had planned to nominate Charles Francis Adams to carry their banner, but they soon found that the convention had been wrested from their hands. Political opportunists "had descended, like vultures, in quest of prey."[13] They took charge, naming Horace Greeley, the fiery editor of the *New York Tribune,* to run against Grant. This choice was ludicrous, as Greeley was opposed to the party's platform. When the Democrats met in Baltimore on 9 July, they recognized that their only chance of winning the election was to select Greeley, a longtime Republican, as their candidate, too.[14]

Kilpatrick, who had returned to his farm for the summer, took stock of the situation and saw the opportunity to gain revenge against Grant for recalling him from his post as ambassador to Chile. Two years ago he had told the president, "You . . . can find in me a true and fearless friend"; in 1872, he announced that he was "out and out for Greeley."[15]

The Democrats, of course, were delighted to have an orator such as Kilpatrick amenable to campaign for Greeley, and they asked him to come to New York City to plan his speaking schedule for that fall. On 27 July, as he and Louisa were relaxing in their suite at the Astor Hotel, a friend brought him that day's edition of the *New York Times*. The newspaper listed the supporters of Greeley under various headings, including "Disturbers of Public Peace, Traitors, Gamblers, Men of Notorious Bad Character, Under Current Indictment," etc. Kilpatrick had been given his own paragraph, which described him as "a former Minister to Chile, [who] tried to force an abandoned woman into Chilean society, and was recalled . . . [he has] long been a reproach to the Republican Party . . . now happily gone over to the Democrats."[16] Enraged by the article, Kilpatrick rushed to the Tombs Police Court to swear an affidavit that he had been libeled by Louis Jennings Jenkins, editor of the *New York Times*.[17]

"[He] makes it look as though . . . Chilean ladies had been obliged to associate with a prostitute," he complained. "I am charged with disgracing a high calling, [which is] an insult . . . thro' me to the republic . . . I will see if the law will give me no redress, and if the penalty is Blackwell's Island [Prison], I . . . insist on Jennings going there."[18]

"We are always ready to correct an injustice," Jennings responded, "but . . . in this case, we elect to go to trial in a Court of Law. . . . The charge reproduced in these columns has been published at one time or another in pretty nearly every paper in the country, and has never been disproved."[19]

While lawyers on both sides prepared for the suit, Kilpatrick began to campaign against Grant. "He used to peddle cord-wood," he accused, "and it is still an open question . . . [if] he [brought] back the proceeds of his sales to his wife and family, or spent it all in drinking."[20]

Grant's managers were infuriated by this attack on the president's reputation, and they looked for additional means of discrediting Kilpatrick. They found the answer in North Carolina, where a number of people came forward to tell what they knew about his secretive affair with "Charley."[21] The depositions must have been shown to Kilpatrick, along with a threat to publish them, because he suddenly cut back on his speaking engagements. He stopped assaulting Grant's character, and his suit against the *Times* never came to trial.

Grant was reelected president by a huge majority that November, leaving Kilpatrick (now a pariah to the Republican Party) with no option but to return to his lecturing career. This was not a barren choice. He had earned over $12,000 in his appearances the prior year.[22] On Christmas Eve, when he would have much rather been with his family, Kilpatrick gave "Sherman's March to the Sea" to an appreciative audience at Montgomery, New York.[23]

Kilpatrick spoke widely in 1873. In addition to "Sherman's March to the

Sea," which by now he had delivered about four hundred times (thirteen instances in the city of Boston alone) and his speech on Gettysburg, Kilpatrick had expanded his repertoire with a third presentation, which he entitled "The Stump." He gave the history of political speaking, including "many amusing anecdotes of the orators of the past," as well as "laughable descriptions of grand mass meetings."[24] His audiences loved him. Typical of their response was the report of a visit to Romeo, Michigan, in February 1873. "We gave the General a sleigh-ride about town," a correspondent wrote, "with horses richly plumed with the colors [that] he so nobly defended. The hall . . . was densely packed . . . it was a grand success."[25]

That spring Kilpatrick returned to his farm, which he managed during the summer months. Here, too, he found great renown. "He has the best grain in the state," one observer reported. "His blooded hogs are of the best breeds, and his poultry is unequaled."[26] He even displayed entrepreneurial skill. Kilpatrick installed new equipment for pressing hay, which he bought from his neighbors and sold in New York City at a tidy profit.[27]

Kilpatrick's genius for farming led to his being asked during October 1873 to initiate a chapter of The Order of Patrons of Husbandry (more commonly called the "Grange") in northwestern New Jersey.[28] Although he faced this venture with his accustomed vigor, Kilpatrick's participation in a local group was most unusual. Up to this time he had never joined any of the community clubs, such as the Temperance League or the Wantage Vigilantes, a circle of about one hundred citizens whose primary mission was to capture (and perhaps hang) any horse thieves who dared to operate in Sussex County.[29]

With fall approaching, Kilpatrick also began work on a new speech for the coming lecture season: an attack on Grant and the corruption of his administration. "We are given to day to drink of the cup of moral horrors, a huge goblet . . . of infamies in which Credit Mobilerism . . . Walworth parricides . . . Fisk-Stokes compound of debaucheries . . . [are] all mixed up in hell-broth as our daily potion," he wrote in an impassioned letter to his agents in New York City. He proposed a return to the examples of past heroes, e.g., George Washington, in a speech entitled "Old Landmarks." "Their moral teaching must be held sacred," he exclaimed, "and the banner of noble sentiment be lifted high again."[30]

Kilpatrick left home in October 1873 on a three-month tour of the country. Upon his return in January, he stopped at Willard's Hotel in Washington, D.C., where he encountered some former Union soldiers at the bar. They started trading war stories.

"The woods swarmed with rebels," Kilpatrick remembered about Chancellorsville, a battle in which he actually had no part. "I had two horses shot out under me."

"What did you do then, Kil?" an enraptured listener inquired.

"Why, I jumped on a Government mule; a ball knocked me off, but the mule charged right ahead into the rebel ranks."

"I saw that mule," a voice called from outside the host gathered around Kilpatrick. "He came right into our lines."

All eyes turned to the speaker, Colonel Mosby, the famous Confederate partisan. "Well," Kilpatrick replied with a smug nod of his head toward his onlookers. "I'm glad to see my words confirmed. You really saw him?"

"Yes, sure."

"Head shot off?"

"No, died from mortification."[31]

Kilpatrick was a good sport and he no doubt joined his companions in chuckling at Mosby's barb. He got a semblance of revenge the following winter by cowriting with a friend, James Moore, a play entitled *Allatoona*.[32] The heroes were all Yankees and the villains were all Confederates. "It is a romantic mish-mash of northern boy meets southern girl," a reviewer commented, "starting in the cadet barracks at West Point and ending in a trench in Georgia, with the impression the [pair] will live happily ever after if no one throws an untimely shell their way."[33] Kilpatrick's mawkish, five-act drama was never produced on the legitimate stage during his lifetime.

In the spring of 1875, Kilpatrick returned home to tend to his farm. And in the fall, he once more set forth on the lecture circuit. His new oration this year was called "The Irish Soldier," a testimony to the immigrants who had fought for the Union. He discovered after a few performances, however, that people from the Old Sod were not popular with the general population, and he was forced to revert to past presentations in order to fill his speaking schedule.[34]

The year 1876 had a presidential election. Kilpatrick was still an outcast with the Republicans and had no interest in supporting the Democrats, so he was left with no choice but to stay out of politics. While others campaigned for either Rutherford B. Hayes or Samuel J. Tilden, Kilpatrick lectured on the Civil War. In August, while traveling from Rochester to Albany via train, Kilpatrick was robbed as he slept of a $500 opal and diamond ring.[35] He could afford the loss. An article appearing a few months later in the local newspaper revealed that he had become so wealthy he "sent [his] shirts to the laundry" and had recently "taken a Russian bath."[36]

Kilpatrick was home that winter because his mother was desperately ill. Mrs. Julia Kilpatrick died on 30 December 1876. She had planned her own funeral (selecting the hymns, the pallbearers, and even how she wanted to be displayed in the casket), and Kilpatrick tenderly followed each of these wishes.[37] After burying his mother next to the grave of his father in the Clove cemetery, Kilpatrick moved his wife and daughter to New York City for the rest of the winter.[38] The farm was too sad a place for him to stay for now.

Although he continued pursuing his dual careers as farmer and lecturer throughout 1877, Kilpatrick found that his life had become too dull. He looked for something more exciting to do and conceived the idea of hosting a grand reunion for Civil War veterans from New Jersey at his farm. The affair was scheduled for August 1878.

Because Sussex County was the most remote of sites, odds of attracting a huge gathering to this event were small, but Kilpatrick solved this problem in typical fashion. He lied by advertising that President Hayes, the current governor of New Jersey, ex-general George McClellan, and Generals Sheridan and Sherman had all agreed to attend the reunion.[39] The lure of these famous names brought thousands of letters from former soldiers throughout the state, each saying they would be eager to make the difficult trek to his farm.

Their arrival would pose a huge dilemma for the people of Deckertown. The six hundred inhabitants were about to be deluged by over five thousand veterans and fifteen thousand sight-seers, each of whom would need food and shelter. They would come by train (e.g.,five a day from Jersey City, four hundred passengers per trip) and by wagon. And a few of these visitors were not coming to watch the reunion. "Our streets will be filled with pick pockets and gamblers," the local newspaper warned; "places of resort will be thronged with base women."[40]

Kilpatrick, aided by a committee of local citizens, prepared for the onslaught. He removed fences on his farm, cut down his yet-to-ripen crops, and piped water from a faraway spring to the front of his home. A twenty-acre field facing his house was leveled, and a tented grandstand for two thousand people was erected in the center of the meadow. The outer sides of the plot were defined by eighty wooden stalls, which Kilpatrick had rented to Overton, a caterer from New York City.[41]

The day the festivities opened, the village itself had a circus atmosphere. The houses were decorated with banners and signs welcoming the visitors. Booths lined the streets, some selling food, others offering games of chance including wheels of fortune, three-card monte, and a shooting gallery. "Vagabonds of every description" drank beer and munched peanuts as they watched tightrope performers. And "strolling musicians made the air merry with . . . sounds of violin, banjo, bones, hand-organ and accordian."[42]

The reunion began at 3:00 P.M. on Tuesday, 27 August, with a parade filing from the town to Kilpatrick's farm. He rode his old spotted horse (the one Wheeler had returned at the end of the war) at the front of the procession. Dressed in a new blue uniform (cut to fit his now rather rotund figure), his bald head hidden by a cap, Kilpatrick looked grand as he led the way out of the village. The various regiments fell in behind him. Streams of eager onlookers brought up the rear. Upon reaching his home, Kilpatrick dismounted and climbed the dais, where the key dignitaries—ex-generals Daniel E. Sickles and John C. Robinson—were already ensconced. President Hays, Sherman, and Sheridan and Governor McClellan were conspicuous by their absence. The troops passed in review, then headed into the fields north of the grandstand to encamp.[43]

A reception was held under the giant tent that evening. After an opening prayer at nine o'clock, a short business meeting was conducted. Kilpatrick then delivered a rousing address.[44]

All day Wednesday was consumed in practice for the mock battle that was to take place the following afternoon. That night, a professional troupe of actors, led by actress Laura Lane, offered Kilpatrick's play *Allatoona* to an audience of about fifteen hundred seated in the grandstand. "The presentation was a wonderful success," an observer said, "considering the nature of the place, the absence of . . . theatrical [props] and the brief time available for rehearsal."[45]

Over forty thousand persons showed up for the mock battle that Thursday afternoon. "Everywhere moving crowds and dust," an onlooker recalled.[46] Kilpatrick mounted Spot at noon and proceeded to guide the elements into position. An artillery battery was located atop a low hill beyond the parade field. When the guns opened fire, about one thousand men dressed as militia charged up the right slope and captured the cannons. An equal number of Union-clad veterans then assembled on the left, bounded up the elevation, and, after "a long, rattling fire of musketry," drove the militia off the peak.[47]

The crowd cheered, but the "battle" had not yet ended. More militia advanced from the right; a throng of veterans charged from the left; they met in the center at the base of the knoll. "In the excitement," an observer wrote, "the opposing men joined in a hand to hand contest."[48] When he saw the fighting start, Kilpatrick grabbed a white flag and galloped into the melee. After restoring calm, he rose in the stirrups, delivered a stirring speech, and then led the men up to his house, where they passed in review, saluting Louisa as she stood on her portico.[49]

Late that afternoon, a repeat performance of his play *Allatoona* was presented in the tented arena. A farewell ball that night ended the encampment.[50]

Kilpatrick paid a dear price for hosting the reunion. "The farm looks as though a fire had swept over it," the newspaper noted. "About 70 acres have been turned from sod to dust."[51] But Kilpatrick's share of the profits from the sale of food and beverages more than offset this loss.[52]

That fall, while Kilpatrick resumed his lecturing with a tour of the West, Louisa went to New York City to keep her eye on Julia. She was attending boarding school at the Convent of the Sacred Heart in Manhattanville.[53]

In early 1879 Kilpatrick continued his lectures. His hectic schedule included visits to New Jersey, Pennsylvania, upstate New York, Michigan, Canada, and New England. Fame followed wherever he went. "As to prices, number of engagements, and grand success," an observer stated, "no lecturer stands above General Kilpatrick."[54] But the trek was taking a toll. He was drained. "I cannot feel the inspiration of the battles . . . as I formerly could," he admitted to a friend. "My lectures are losing their attention."[55]

In May, on the verge of collapse, Kilpatrick felt that he had to end the tour. "I return home tired out," he wrote to J. S. Bliss, the agent who had planned his schedule, "having lectured 167 times so far this year."[56]

While resting at his farm, Kilpatrick heard that Grant, after spending over two years on a world tour, had come home to try for a third term as president.[57] Kilpatrick would not allow it! Kilpatrick reentered politics, seeking a role as a New Jersey delegate to the 1880 Republican Convention, where he could oppose Grant's candidacy. He won the seat, and in June of that year he set out for Chicago.[58]

In addition to Grant, the nominees were William Windom, John Sherman, James A. Garfield, George F. Edmunds, Elihu B. Washburne, and James G. Blaine. New Jersey (and Kilpatrick) supported Blaine, a former newspaper editor *(Kennebec Journal)* from Maine. He had been elected to the state legislature in 1858, entered Congress in 1862, and in 1869 rose to Speaker of the House of Representatives. Although he seemed an ideal candidate, "a commanding figure, a born leader who exuded a magnetism that drew men to him," Blaine was under the cloud of corruption. He was known to have accepted $125,000 from the Little Rock and Fort Smith Railroad for saving them from a revocation of their land grant.[59] Although many were appalled by such malfeasance, Kilpatrick evidently found nothing wrong with Blaine's using his seat for personal gain.

The balloting began on 7 June. Grant received about 300 votes, Blaine 284, and Sherman 93. The other candidates split the remaining 74. This pattern held through the next thirty-five shows of hands. On 8 June, on the thirty-sixth try, Sherman's supporters switched to Garfield. The others opposed to Grant followed suit, and the former Union general (now a congressman from Ohio) won the nomination.[60]

Late that day Kilpatrick mounted the podium. He gave a stirring address praising Garfield, then turned to support Chester A. Arthur from New York for vice president. "He seconded [the] nomination with all his heart," a correspondent for the *New York Times* said.[61] Later at a victory celebration at the New Jersey headquarters, Kilpatrick gloated over Garfield's success. "Grant men should be satisfied," he remarked, "for [while] they had not obtained one soldier, they forced the nomination of another."[62]

The Democrats met in Cincinnati in July and nominated Winfield Scott Hancock as their candidate. Kilpatrick began a whirlwind tour to support Garfield but soon found his efforts unnecessary. Hancock refused to campaign. He kept at work in the army, thinking it unseemly to actively seek the presidency.[63]

Upon his return to New Jersey in September, Kilpatrick found that his local friends had nominated him as their candidate for the House of Representatives. "My voice is worn, and I myself am very tired," he said in accepting a place on the fall ticket, "but I thank you for the great honor . . . you have this day done me." He then announced the position that he would take in the coming campaign. He would run against the South. "Not one dollar of the people's money . . . to reimburse you for property lost prosecuting the war against the Union!" he thundered. "Not one dollar for your emancipated slaves; not one dollar to pension a rebel soldier."[64]

Kilpatrick campaigned diligently through the following months. "It was a battle, the dustiest . . . ever fought in politics," a reporter wrote. "It was one grand cavalry charge all along the line." But in reality Kilpatrick had no chance to be elected. His district (the four counties of Sussex, Somerset, Hunterdon, and Warren) was mostly Democratic, and his opponent, Henry S. Harris, won the seat in November. Kilpatrick, however, lost by only twenty-five hundred votes, which was the closest that the Republicans had come in many years. "I hold the friendship of [my supporters] above all earthly treasures," Kilpatrick stated in his concession speech. "In comparison, Congressional honors are . . . feathers in the wind, bubbles on the water."[65]

He could afford to be philosophical. Garfield had won the presidency and had appointed Blaine his secretary of state. Both were indebted to Kilpatrick for his assistance in keeping Grant from the nomination and then helping Garfield win the election. Kilpatrick meant to collect his due. He wanted to return to Chile as U.S. ambassador.

Kilpatrick and Louisa moved to Washington that winter, where he pressed his case. He advanced every reason that he could muster: he had served the Republican Party for years; Louisa was a Chilean, a natural asset to the post; they had not seen their daughter, Laura, living with grandparents in Chile, since 1870; having been an ambassador before, he was uniquely qualified for the position; his health was failing (because of efforts to help both Blaine and Garfield), and a change in climate was essential to his recovery.[66]

Despite Kilpatrick's persistence, Garfield remained reluctant to name him the ambassador to Chile. In April, Kilpatrick returned to New Jersey and resumed his lectures, but Louisa stayed in Washington to keep up the pressure.[67] Garfield finally relented. On 1 June 1881, he recalled Thomas A. Osborn and named Kilpatrick to the coveted post.[68]

In his role as a lecturer and farmer, Kilpatrick found the fame he had sought for his life. He stood at the top of his class in both endeavors, earning both the adulation and approval of the masses, his peers, and those he served. But it was not enough. His career plan had called for military, then political, glory, and he seemed unable to substitute his success from other fields for his failures as a soldier and office-seeker. And so he abandoned the arenas where he been a champion for one last fling at civic renown, choosing the dubious path as a diplomat for his road to the presidency.

25

The End

Kilpatrick, Louisa, her sister Rosa, and Julie boarded a boat for Chile on 21 June 1881. A friend seeing them off asked if the wound he suffered at Reseca still troubled him. "Yes," Kilpatrick groaned, "I'll never get rid of that until it kills me."[1] Prophetic words!

They arrived at Santiago on 20 July and Kilpatrick had a happy reunion with Laura, the daughter he had left behind more than ten years ago. He offered his credentials to the president of Chile on 25 July.[2]

Conditions in Chile were very similar to those that he had faced back in 1866. Kilpatrick's salary was $10,000 per year, the same rate he was paid during his first term as ambassador;[3] the local elite enjoyed a cultural opulence made possible by affluence; and the country was at war. The adversaries were the nations to the north, Peru and Bolivia.

The War of the Pacific had evolved from a dispute over the guano deposits on the west coast of South America (lower Peru, the arm of Bolivia extending to the sea, and northern Chile). The latter had developed these interests. In 1878 Bolivia levied a tax on the nitrate shipments made from her territory. Chile (because her capital and labor had created the commerce) demanded a portion of the payments. Bolivia, however, refused to share these revenues.[4]

While this impasse might have been resolved through negotiation, Chile saw no need to make concessions. She was a strong nation, inhabited by Spanish (Basque) descendants who spoke a common tongue. Her army and navy were both equipped with modern weapons, and she enjoyed an excellent transportation system, a railroad running along the entire length of her twenty-five hundred-mile coast. Bolivia was less evolved. She had no army or navy of consequence, and her people (Aymara Indians) had difficulty communicating because each tribe had its own unique dialect. Her ally, Peru, suffered similar problems.[5]

Chile headed north on 14 February 1879 and impounded the Bolivian nitrate fields. When Peru stepped in to try to negotiate a peace, Chile declared war on her, too. She captured the Peruvian deposits, then advanced on the Lima. The capital fell on 16 February 1881.[6]

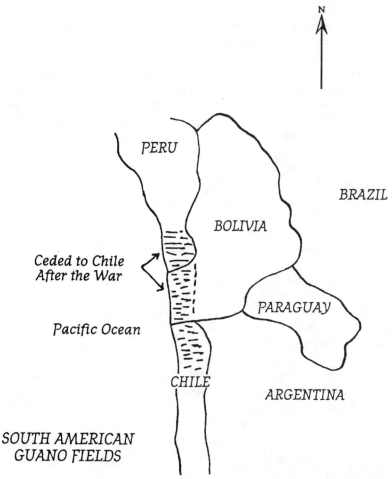

N

PERU

BRAZIL

BOLIVIA

Ceded to Chile
After the War

PARAGUAY

Pacific Ocean

CHILE   ARGENTINA

SOUTH AMERICAN
GUANO FIELDS

The United States, in an attempt to bring peace to the area, proposed a return to past territorial boundaries and a payment of reparations by Bolivia and Peru to Chile for her costs of the war. Chile, however, insisted on retaining all of the land she had conquered. Kilpatrick was asked to convince Santiago to accept the U.S. position.[7]

While Kilpatrick was discussing the situation with the Chilean officials, Stephen A. Hurlbut assumed the position of ambassador to Peru. A native of Illinois and one of Lincoln's cronies, Hurlbut had been a political general during the Civil War, one who had "exercised every opportunity to line his own pockets."[8] He was elected the first commander in chief of the Grand Army of the Republic. Charges of corruption and drunkenness marred his reign, but he survived because of his support of Grant in the 1868 campaign. Hurlbut was appointed ambassador to Colombia in 1869. He served in the House of Representatives from 1872 through 1876.

Hurlbut's first act was to assure Peru that the United States would "under no circumstances permit the annexation of territory by Chile."[9] He had completely misrepresented the American position, but Santiago did not know this. They saw a coming U.S. intervention on behalf of Peru and turned to Kilpatrick for support. The situation was made to order for him to charge impetuously into the arena, to mount a podium and make an impassioned speech, to seize and hold the center stage. He did nothing. He was sick in bed.

Kilpatrick's health had been declining almost from his arrival in Chile. He was suffering from Bright's disease, a failure of the kidneys. The trouble stemmed from his years on horseback during the Civil War. His wife wrote Blaine on 30 August, "[M]y husband is . . . confined to his room with . . . a problem with his stomach and lungs."[10]

On 13 September Kilpatrick informed Blaine that his legs were so swollen that he could not leave his room. "I spend most of the time [in] my bed," he said, "[but am] doing the best I can . . . to fulfill the duties of my mission."[11]

Garfield died on 19 September from the gunshot wound he suffered on 2 July while awaiting a train in a Washington railway station. His assassin was Charles J. Guiteau, a disgruntled office seeker. Blaine wrote Kilpatrick to inform him of the president's death; in acknowledging the letter, Kilpatrick noted, "My health is but a little better."[12]

That October, Kilpatrick gave up all pretense of carrying out his mission as ambassador and went to a farm outside of Santiago, where he hoped the country air would aid his recovery.[13] He wrote no correspondence to Washington over the next two months.

In late November, when his spasms and pains started to subside, Kilpatrick thought he was getting better. "I would be well now," he declared, "if it was not for these swollen limbs."[14]

On 2 December Kilpatrick felt well enough to sit in his parlor, where he could look out the window and enjoy the view. He even composed a note to Blaine. "For four months I have been very ill," he wrote, "and in the last two months at the point of death, unable . . . to [sign] my own name. I'm now just able to sit up." He then reviewed the situation in Chile. Kilpatrick ended the letter, "I should like to give you details, but am unable [due to] extreme weakness to dictate another sentence."[15] Louisa penned his words on paper, and he signed his name with a pitiful scribble.

After a lunch of chicken, toast, asparagus, and strawberries, Kilpatrick returned to bed. He had only a glass of cold milk for dinner. When someone suggested he take candy, Kilpatrick laughed. Suddenly, at 9:45 P.M, his head sagged and he died.[16] He was forty-five years old.

Kilpatrick's body lay in state at the farm. The walls of the room were draped in black velvet, and flowers covered the casket. Louisa arranged his army uniform atop the bier. Two days later the corpse was taken to Santiago and placed in the capitol. Thousands of people, "from school children to the highest dignitaries," passed by to pay their respects to Kilpatrick.[17] He was buried in the Valdivieso vaults in the parochial church of Sagrario in Santiago.[18] The Chilean government paid all the expenses for his funeral.

About a year later, Kilpatrick's body was brought back to the United States and reinterred in the cemetery at West Point. Classmates and the troopers who served under him in the Civil War donated money to pay for the imposing monument that today marks his grave.[19]

Epilogue

Congress granted Louisa Kilpatrick a Civil War widow's pension of $100 per month, which she used to raise her girls in America. After Julia and Laura were grown and gone, she returned to Santiago to be with her parents. Louisa died on 30 April 1926.[1]

Laura provided Kilpatrick with offspring, who like him, lived on life's center stage. She married Harry Hays Morgan (the son of a Louisiana Supreme Court justice) in 1894, and, through her father's former friends in the Republican Party, obtained a position for him from President William McKinley as American consul to Bern, Switzerland.[2] This office paid only $2,000 per year, but it opened the channels into world society, which Laura exploited shamelessly.

The couple had four children. Harry Judson Kilpatrick Morgan was born in 1898. When he was nineteen years old, he joined the U.S. Army and fought with the American forces in the Argonne campaign. After World War I, Harry moved to Paris, where he fell in love with a local actress. When she spurned his proposals, he attempted suicide by shooting himself.[3] He soon recovered, met a gay divorcée (Ivor O'Conner Trezvant), and married. Ivor was a fun companion who could drink most men under the table, but she was also addicted to drugs. Their union ended several years later.

Just like his grandfather, Harry was not handsome. He had "a weak face, an underslung jaw, with a dull look in his eyes." The balding young man must have been a bon vivant, because he soon met and married another pretty divorcée, the wealthy heiress Edith Arnold. Her money bought him a villa in Cannes, a ski chalet in St. Moritz, and a racing car. He spent the rest of his life indulging himself.[4]

Consuelo Morgan was born in 1902. She lived in Europe until she was fourteen, when Laura made arrangements for her to stay in America with a casual friend, Edith Gould, a former actress who had married well. Edith would "prepare" her for society. Four years later, Consuelo returned to Europe for an arranged marriage to Jean Marie Emmanuel de Maupas du Juglart, a wealthy French count whose title went back to the eleventh century.[5] Their wedding was widely acknowledged as "the event of the Parisian summer social season."

In two years they were divorced. "I have the profoundest contempt for you," he wrote. "You disgust me," Consuelo answered.[6] She soon met and married Benjamin Thaw, a first secretary of the American Embassy in Brussels and an heir to a great Pittsburgh fortune of shipping, railroads, and coal. His uncle, Harry Kendall Thaw, was infamous for shooting the famed architect, Stanford White, because of his affair with Thaw's wife, the ex-show girl, Evelyn Nesbit.[7] Theirs was a happy marriage, and Consuelo and Benny dominated the social scene until his death in 1937. She then wed another wealthy man, Alons B. Landa.

Laura's last two children were identical twins, Thelma and Gloria, born in 1904. During World War I, they attended the Convent of the Sacred Heart in Manhattanville, the same boarding school that their mother and Aunt Julia had gone to when they were young girls. At age sixteen, the twins left the academy to live in an apartment of their own in New York City. Their father sent them $200 a month for expenses.[8]

Using their mother's contacts, the girls made an entry into society. They went to parties, frequented nightclubs, and joined in charitable functions. "They are alike as two magnolias," one observer stated, "and with their marble complexions, raven tresses and flowing dresses, [and] . . . foreign accent, they defuse an Ouida atmosphere of hothouse elegance and lacy femininity."[9] "Cholly Knickerbocker," the renowned society columnist, dubbed them "The Magical Morgans."

In the fall of 1922, Thelma married James Vail Converse, grandson of Thomas N. Vail, founder of Bell Telephone Company. Although he seemed a fine catch, Thelma soon learned that "Junior" was a boor, a mean drunk who had spent his inheritance and now begged his relatives for money. He abused and cursed her, and within a year, she had left him, fleeing to Brussels to seek a divorce.[10]

Belgium insisted that she must file for divorce in the United States, so Thelma moved to California, where she began a movie career. She supposedly had an affair with comedian Charlie Chaplin, then became engaged to stage star Richard Bennett.[11] But in the winter of 1925, while visiting in Paris, she met Lord Marmaduke Furness, an immensely wealthy, hard-swearing, high-living English peer. They were wed in June 1926.[12]

Thelma was only one of many romantic conquests by Lord Furness, and despite bearing him a son, she found herself at home alone most of the time. She was ripe for an affair of her own. During the summer of 1929, she met a new paramour, the Prince of Wales and future king of England, Edward Albert Christian George Andrew Patrick David Windsor.[13]

He called her "Toodles." They lived together surreptitiously for almost five

Gloria and Thelma Morgan, twin granddaughters of General Kilpatrick. Photo by Cecil Beaton. Reproduced by permission of Sotheby's of London.

years. Thelma was so confident over her future with David that she divorced her husband in 1932. By 1934, however, she had become tired of "the little man" and had a brief affair with Prince Aly Khan. The king-to-be, of course, heard of their tryst, and he responded by turning to one of her friends for his new paramour. Later, when Thelma was asked, "If you could live your life over, what would you have done differently?" she replied, "I would never have introduced Wallis Simpson to the Prince of Wales."[14]

Gloria, her twin sister, met her future husband at the party following Thelma's 1922 marriage to "Junior" Converse. Reginald Claypoole Vanderbilt, great grandson of the fabled "Commodore," was thirty-nine years old, divorced, a prodigal who had already squandered his $25 million inheritance. He "subsisted" on the $250,000 annual proceeds he received from a $5 million trust, laid aside when he was a boy for his future children. Reggie had no job. He listed his occupation as "gentleman."[15]

When Reggie proposed to Gloria in 1923, he admitted he was a poor catch. His health was precarious (he was suffering from cirrhosis of the liver), and he had no estate. If he passed on, their children would only share the $5 million trust with his daughter from a previous marriage. She could expect to inherit nothing. "It's you I love," she answered, "not your name or the Vanderbilt money."[16] They were wed on 23 March 1923.

Eleven months after the marriage, Gloria gave birth to a daughter, who would later become famous as "Little Gloria" Vanderbilt. Although she and Reggie were thrilled with the baby, their happiness was short-lived. He died ("drank him self to death") in September 1925.[17]

The Vanderbilt lawyers arranged an annual allowance of $48,000 for Gloria, paid from her child's share of the trust receipts. She used this money to live in Europe, where she resumed her role in society, being at the right place at the right time with the right people. While she played, Little Gloria was tended by a nanny.[18]

In 1927 Gloria fell in love with Gottfried Hohenlohe Langburg, a penniless Bavarian prince, nephew of Queen Marie of Rumania, granddaughter of both Queen Victoria of England and Empress Marie of Russia. They planned to marry, but the Vanderbilt lawyers intervened. Little Gloria's money could not be used to finance their romance. If she wed, the funds from the trust would be cut off. Because "Friedel" could not support her, Gloria sadly broke off their engagement.[19]

The lawyers' action was in part provoked by her mother, Laura, Kilpatrick's daughter, who lived with Gloria and was helping to rear the child. Obsessed by her own relationship to the famed Vanderbilts and terrified that Gloria might do something foolish toward breaking this link, she commenced a curious campaign that attacked Gloria's fitness as a mother. Laura wanted custody of the little girl assigned to Reggie's sister, Gertrude Vanderbilt Whitney. She must have thought that the Vanderbilts would reward her with a great amount of money for having saved Little Gloria from neglect.[20]

Laura's efforts culminated in July 1934, when she and the Vanderbilts contested Gloria's guardianship in a lawsuit in New York City. Thelma rushed to America to help her sister.

"Mothers don't do to their children," she protested to Laura, "what you are doing . . . blacken their characters before the world."

"You be careful, Thelma," Laura snapped, "that I don't take your child away."[21]

The trial dominated the newspapers for months. In November, the court took Little Gloria from her mother and made her a ward of the state.[22]

Kilpatrick would have reveled over the notoriety of his grandchildren. He would have followed them throughout their travels in Europe, hobnobbing with the royal, the rich, the renowned, regaling them with stories of his valiant- ness during the war. And if he had lived to see the custody battle over Little Gloria, Kilpatrick probably would have been in court to speak on his grand- daughter's behalf. One can almost hear the opening words to his address. "I waded through seas of blood to save the Union."

Notes

PROLOGUE

1. James H. Kidd, *Personal Recollections of a Cavalryman with Custer's Michigan Cavalry Brigade in the Civil War* (Iona, Mich.: Sentinel Printing Company, 1908), 243.
2. Ibid., 244.
3. Ibid., 246.
4. Ibid., 247.
5. Ibid., 248.
6. Ibid., 248–49.

CHAPTER 1. ANTEBELLUM

1. Therese A. Erskine, Sussex Country Library, Newton, New Jersey, letter to author, 13 August 1992.
2. *Sussex Independent,* 9 August 1878.
3. Pamela Daniels and Kathy Weingarten, *Sooner or Later* (New York: Rinehart & Company, 1982), 269–71.
4. George W. King, "The Civil War Career of Hugh Judson Kilpatrick" (Ph.D. diss. University of South Carolina, 1969), 3.
5. Ibid., 4.
6. James Moore, *Kilpatrick and Our Cavalry: Comprising a Sketch of the Life of General Kilpatrick with an Account of the Cavalry Raids, Engagements, and Operations under His Command, from the Beginning of the Rebellion to the Surrender of Johnston* (New York: Hurst & Company, 1865), 27.
7. Mary Elizabeth Sergent, *"They Lie Forgotten": The United States Military Academy 1856–1861 Together with a Class Album for the Class of May, 1861* (Middletown, N.Y.: The Prior King, 1986), 150.
8. King, "Civil War Career," 4.
9. Comte de Paris, *History of the Civil War in America* (Philadelphia: Porter & Coates, 1875), 1:17–18.
10. Sergent, *They Lie Forgotten,* 150.
11. *Thirteenth Annual Reunion of the Association of the Graduates of the United States Military Academy at West Point, June 12, 1882* (Philadelphia: Times Printing House, 1882), 45.

12. Alfred Davenport, *Camp and Field: Life of the Fifth New York Volunteer Infantry* (New York: Dick & Fitzgerald, 1879), 458.

13. *Official Register of the Officers and Cadets of the U.S. Military Academy* (West Point, N.Y., June 1857), 13.

14. Sergent, *They Lie Forgotten*, 150.

15. King, "Civil War Career," 8.

16. Sergent, *They Lie Forgotten*, 150.

17. James H. Wilson, *Under the Old Flag* (New York: D. Appleton & Company, 1912), 1:369.

18. *Official Register of the Officers and Cadets*, 11.

19. Sergent, *They Lie Forgotten*, 150.

20. David M. Potter, *The Impending Crisis, 1848–1861* (New York: Harper & Row, 1976), 276.

21. Ibid., 306.

22. Ibid., 340.

23. Morris Schaff, *The Spirit of Old West Point: 1858–1862* (Boston: Houghton Mifflin, 1907), 150–51.

24. Wilson, *Under the Old Flag*, 1:369.

25. Sergent, *They Lie Forgotten*, 150.

26. *Official Register of the Officers and Cadets*, 10.

27. Susan Walker, United States Military Academy Archives, West Point, New York, letter to author, 15 June 1992.

28. Sergent, *They Lie Forgotten*, 150.

29. *Official Register of the Officers and Cadets*, 9.

30. Moore, *Kilpatrick and Our Cavalry*, 33.

31. Robert Selph Henry, *The Story of the Confederacy* (Indianapolis, Ind.: Bobbs-Merrill, 1931), 20–21.

32. Clifford Dowdey, *Experiment in Rebellion* (Garden City, N.Y.: Doubleday, 1946), 22.

33. Jay Monaghan, *Custer: The Life of General George Armstrong Custer* (Boston: Little, Brown, 1959), 38.

34. *Thirteenth Annual Reunion*, 46.

35. *Official Register of the Officers and Cadets*, 9.

36. Moore, *Kilpatrick and Our Cavalry*, 30.

37. Ibid., 34.

38. Sergent, *They Lie Forgotten*, 102.

CHAPTER 2. BIG BETHEL

1. Sergent, *They Lie Forgotten*, 102.

2. Philip Haythornthwaite, *Uniforms of the Civil War* (New York: Sterling Publishing Company, 1990), 24.

3. James P. Snell, *The History of Sussex and Warren Counties, New Jersey* (Philadelphia: Everts & Peck, 1881), 81.

4. Emerson G. Taylor, *Governeur Kemble Warren: The Life and Letters of an American Soldier, 1830–1883* (Boston: Houghton Mifflin, 1932), 47–49.

5. Judson Kilpatrick Personal File, RG 94, National Archives, Washington, D.C.

6. Stewart Sifakis, *Who Was Who in the Union: A Comprehensive, Illustrated Biographical Reference to More Than 1,500 of the Principal Union Participants in the Civil War* (New York: Facts On File, 1988), 121.

7. Davenport, *Camp and Field,* 11.

8. Ibid., 30–31.

9. Ibid., 34.

10. Joseph B. Carr, "Operations of 1861 About Fort Monroe," in Clarence C. Buel and Robert U. Johnson, eds., *Battles and Leaders of the Civil War* (New York: Thomas Yoseloff, 1956), 2:145.

11. Davenport, *Camp and Field,* 39.

12. *New York Times,* 4 June 1961, 1.

13. Davenport, *Camp and Field,* 50.

14. U.S. War Department, *The War of the Rebellion: A Compilation of the Official Records of the Union and Confederate Armies* (Washington, D.C., 1880–1891), ser. 1, vol. 2, 78.

15. Carr, "Operations of 1861 About Fort Monroe," 148.

16. Ibid.

17. Official Records, ser. 1, vol. 51, pt. 1, 3.

18. Official Records, ser. 1, vol. 2, 84.

19. Davenport, *Camp and Field,* 51.

20. Ibid., 55

21. Official Records, ser. 1, vol. 2, 97.

22. Davenport, *Camp and Field,* 56.

23. Ibid., 57.

24. Ibid., 58.

25. Ibid.

26. Official Records, ser. 1, vol. 51, pt. 1, 4.

27. Carr, "Operations of 1861 About Fort Monroe," 150.

28. Davenport, *Camp and Field,* 65.

29. Benjamin F. Butler, *Butler's Book* (Boston: A. M. Thayer & Company, 1892), 269.

30. Benson J. Lossing, *Pictorial History of the Civil War* (Philadelphia: Douglas McKay, 1866), 1:510.

31. *New York Times,* 12 June 1861.

32. Sergent, *They Lie Forgotten,* 150.

33. Major J. Owen Moore, "General Kilpatrick: A Brief Biography," *Sussex Independent,* 23 December 1881.

34. King, " Civil War Career," 28.

35. Official Records, ser. 1, vol. 2, 89–90.

36. Moore, "General Kilpatrick," *Sussex Independent,* 23 December 1881.

37. *New York Times,* 14 June 1861, 8.

38. Ibid., 1.

39. *New York Times,* 19 July 1861, 8.

40. William C. Davis, *Battle at Bull Run* (Garden City, N.Y.: Doubleday, 1977).

41. *New York Times,* 3 August 1861, 5.

42. Judson Kilpatrick Personal File.

43. Ibid.

CHAPTER 3. DRILLS AND MISDEEDS

1. Willard Glazier, *Three Years in the Federal Cavalry* (New York: R. H. Ferguson & Company, 1874), 23.

2. Frederick Phisterer, *New York in the War of the Rebellion, 1861–1865* (Albany: J. B. Lyon Co., 1912), 1:751.

3. *New York Herald,* 10 September 1861, 1.

4. Ibid.

5. King, "Civil War Career," 36.

6. *New York Times,* 11 September 1861, 4.

7. Stephen W. Sears, *George B. McClellan: The Young Napoleon* (New York: Ticknor & Fields, 1988).

8. George B. McClellan, *McClellan's Own Story* (New York: Charles L. Webster & Company, 1886), 66.

9. James M. McPherson, *Battle Cry of Freedom: The Civil War Era* (New York: Oxford University Press, 1988), 349.

10. Stephen Z. Starr, *The Union Cavalry in the Civil War* (Baton Rouge: Louisiana State University Press, 1979), 2:67.

11. Bruce Catton, *The Army of the Potomac* (Garden City, N.Y.: Doubleday, 1952), 2:75.

12. Louis N. Boudrye, *Historic Records of the Fifth New York Cavalry, First Ira Harris Guard: It's Operations, Marches, Raids, Scouts, Engagements and General Services during the Rebellion of 1861–1865* (Albany, N.Y.: J. Munsell, 1868), 18.

13. Glazier, *Three Years in the Federal Cavalry,* 136.

14. King, "Civil War Career," 154.

15. Theodore Lyman, *Meade's Headquarters, 1863–65: The Letters of Colonel Theodore Lyman,* ed. George R. Agassiz (Boston: Atlantic Monthly Press, 1922), 17.

16. William Woods Averell, *Ten Years in the Saddle: The Memoirs of William Woods Averell, 1851–1862,* ed. Edward K. Eckert and Nicholas J. Amato (San Rafael, Calif: Presidio Press, 1978), 334.

17. Official Records, ser. 1, vol 5, 16.

18. Ezra J. Warner, *Generals in Blue: Lives of the Union Commanders* (Baton Rouge: Louisiana State University Press, 1964), 298.

19. Starr, *Union Cavalry,* 1:237.

20. Ibid., 235.

21. Ibid.

22. Sergent, *They Lie Forgotten,* 150.

23. Judson Kilpatrick Deposition File, RG 94, National Archives, Washington, D.C.

24. King, "Civil War Career," 40.

25. Judson Kilpatrick Personal File.

26. Ibid.

27. William Howard Russell, *My Diary North and South* (Boston: T .O. H. P. Burnham, 1863), 2:414–15.

28. Official Records, ser. 1, vol. 8, 830.

29. *New York Times,* 8 January 1862, 1.

30. Carl Sandberg, *Abraham Lincoln: The War Years* (New York: Harcourt, Brace & World, 1936), 1:225.

31. Sifakis, *Who Was Who in the Union,* 230.

32. Official Records, ser. 1, vol. 8, 830.

33. *New York Times,* 21 January 1862, 1.

34. Official Records, ser. 1, vol. 8, 551.

35. James Hamilton, *The Battle of Fort Donelson* (New York: Thomas Yoseloff, 1968).

36. Joseph E. Johnston, *Narrative of Military Operations, Directed during the Late War Between the States* (New York: D. Appleton & Company, 1874), 102.

37. Judson Kilpatrick Deposition File.

38. E. B. Long, and Barbara Long, *The Civil War Day By Day: An Almanac, 1861–1865* (Garden City, N.Y.: Doubleday & Company, 1971), 164.

39. George B. McClellan, *Report on the Organization and Campaigns of the Army of the Potomac: To Which Is Added an Account of the Campaign in Western Virginia, with Plans of Battle-Fields* (New York: Sheldon & Company, 1864), 132.

40. William C. Davis, *Duel Between the First Ironclads* (Garden City, N.Y.: Doubleday, 1975).

41. Alexander S. Webb, *The Peninsula: McClellan's Campaign of 1862* (New York: Charles Scribner's Sons, 1881), 85.

42. Glazier, *Three Years in the Federal Cavalry,* 59.

43. Judson Kilpatrick Deposition File.

44. Ibid.

45. Ibid.

46. Official Records, ser. 1, vol. 12, pt. 1, 432.

Chapter 4. McClellan

1. Wiley Sword, *Shiloh: Bloody April* (New York: William Morrow, 1974).

2. Charles Dufour, *The Night the War was Lost* (Garden City, N.Y.: Doubleday, 1960).

3. Official Records, ser. 1, vol. 12, pt. 1, 429.

4. Ibid., 438.

5. Ibid., 430.

6. Glazier, *Three Years in the Federal Cavalry,* 63.

7. Official Records, ser. 1, vol. 12, pt. 1, 431.

8. King, "Civil War Career," 47.

9. Official Records, ser. 1, vol. 12, pt. 1, 432.

10. Warner, *Generals in Blue,* 12.

11. Clifford Dowdey, *The Seven Days: The Emergence of Lee* (Boston: Little, Brown, 1964), 50.

12. Long, *Civil War Day By Day,* 207.

13. Webb, *Peninsula,* 86.

14. Robert G. Tanner, *Stonewall in the Valley: Thomas J. "Stonewall" Jackson's Shenandoah Valley Campaign, Spring 1862* (New York: Doubleday, 1976).

15. Official Records, ser. 1, vol. 12, pt. 3, 267.

16. Judson Kilpatrick Deposition File.

17. Official Records, ser. 1, vol. 12, pt. 1, 31.

18. Douglas Southall Freeman, *R. E. Lee: A Biography* (New York: Charles Scribner's Sons, 1934), 2:74.

19. Official Records, ser. 1, vol. 12, pt. 1, 713–15.

20. Joseph Cullen, *The Peninsula Campaign, 1862* (Harrisburg, Pa.: Stackpole, 1973).

CHAPTER 5. JOHN POPE

1. Edward J. Stackpole, *From Cedar Mountain to Antietam: August–September 1862* (Harrisburg, Pa.: Stackpole, 1959), 13.

2. Sifakis, *Who Was Who in the Union*, 315.

3. Official Records, ser. 1, vol. 7, pt. 3, 474.

4. Official Records, ser. 1, vol. 12, pt. 2, 21.

5. Warner, *Generals in Blue*, 269.

6. Ibid., 23.

7. John S. Mosby, *The Memoirs of Colonel John S. Mosby* (Bloomington: Indiana University Press, 1959), 128.

8. Jeffry D. Wert, *Mosby's Rangers* (New York: Simon & Schuster, 1990), 30.

9. Official Records, ser. 1, vol. 11, pt. 3, 330.

10. Glazier, *Three Years in the Federal Cavalry*, 74.

11. Ibid., 75.

12. Official Records, ser. 1, vol. 12, pt. 3, 330.

13. Ibid., 484.

14. Mosby, *Memoirs*, 129.

15. Official Records, ser. 1, vol. 12, pt. 2, 102.

16. Ibid., 103.

17. Ibid.

18. Official Records, ser. 1, vol. 12, pt. 3, 502.

19. W. W. Blackford, *War Years with Jeb Stuart* (New York: Charles Scribner's Sons, 1945), 88.

20. Official Records, ser. 1, vol. 12, pt. 3, 502.

21. Ibid.

22. Ibid., 490.

23. Ibid., 412.

24. Ibid., 582–85.

25. Ibid., 525.

26. Sifakis, *Who Was Who in the Union*, 25.

27. Official Records, ser. 1, vol. 12, pt. 2, 124.

28. Ibid.

29. Ibid., 125.

30. Henry C. Meyer, *Civil War Experiences under Bayard, Gregg, Kilpatrick, and Custer* (New York: Raulston & Newberry, 1911), 7.

31. Official Records, ser. 1, vol. 11, pt. 1, 82.

32. Martin Schenck, *Up Came Hill: The Story of the Light Division and Its Leaders* (Harrisburg, Pa.: Stackpole, 1958), 154.

33. Official Records, ser. 1, vol. 12, pt. 2, 89.

34. Ibid., 90.

35. Henry R. Pyne, *The History of the First New Jersey Cavalry* (Trenton, N.J.: J. A. Beecher, Publisher, 1871), 95.

36. Ibid., 96.

37. Colonel Francis C. Kajencki, *Star on Many a Battlefield: Brevet Brigadier General Joseph Karge in the American Civil War* (Rutherford, N.J.: Fairleigh Dickinson University Press, 1980), 79.

38. Pyne, *History of the First New Jersey Cavalry*, 97.

39. Official Records, ser. 1, vol. 12, pt. 2, 90.

40. Ibid., 91.

41. Lenoir Chambers, *Stonewall Jackson* (New York: William Morrow, 1959), 2:145.

42. Official Records, ser. 1, vol. 12, pt. 2, 91.

43. Alan T. Nolan, *The Iron Brigade: A Military History* (New York: Macmillan, 1961), 80–98.

44. Stackpole, *From Cedar Mountain to Antietam,* 45.

45. Otto Eisenschiml, *The Celebrated Case of Fitz John Porter: An American Dreyfus Affair* (Indianapolis, Ind.: Bobbs-Merrill, 1950), 64.

46. King, "Civil War Career," 57.

47. Meyer, *Civil War Experiences,* 13.

48. Ibid.

49. Official Records, ser. 1, vol. 12, pt. 2, 370.

50. Meyer, *Civil War Experiences,* 14.

51. Official Records, ser. 1, vol. 12, pt. 2, 256.

52. Glazier, *Three Years in the Federal Cavalry,* 103.

53. Official Records, ser. 1, vol. 19, pt. 1, 1091.

54. Noble D. Preston, *History of the Tenth Regiment of Cavalry, New York State Volunteers* (New York: D. Appleton Company, 1892), 43.

55. Ibid.

56. Official Records, ser. 1, vol. 19, pt. 1, 1092.

57. James V. Murfin, *The Gleam of Bayonets: The Battle of Antietam and Robert E. Lee's Maryland Campaign, 1862* (New York: Thomas Yoseloff, 1965).

58. Preston, *History of the Tenth Regiment,* 45.

59. Ibid.

60. Ibid., 46.

61. Ibid.

62. Ibid., 44.

63. Judson Kilpatrick Deposition File.

64. Ibid.

65. Ibid.

66. Ibid.

67. Ibid.

68. Ibid.

69. Ibid.

70. Judson Kilpatrick Personal File.

CHAPTER 6. DESCRIPTIONS

1. J. H. Foster, "They Selected Out Home for General Kilpatrick's Headquarters," in Katharine M. Jones, ed., *When Sherman Came: Southern Women and the "Great March"* (Indianapolis, Ind.: Bobbs-Merrill, 1964), 234.

2. Frank Crawford, "Your Charlie," *Civil War Times Illustrated* 31, no. 6 (January/February 1993): 66.

3. Lloyd Lewis, *Sherman: Fighting Prophet* (New York: Harcourt, Brace, 1932), 404.

4. Burke Davis, *Sherman's March* (New York: Random House, 1980), 134.

5. Glazier, *Three Years in the Federal Cavalry,* 136.

6. Meyer, *Civil War Experiences,* 97.

7. Kidd, *Personal Recollections,* 164.
8. Ibid., 165.
9. Ibid., 164.
10. Meyer, *Civil War Experiences,* 97.
11. *Thirteenth Annual Reunion,* 50.
12. Wilson, *Under the Old Flag,* 1:370.
13. Oliver Otis Howard, *Autobiography of Oliver Otis Howard, Major General United States Army* (New York: Baker & Taylor, 1907), 2:29.
14. Meyer, *Civil War Experiences,* 97.
15. Sergent, *They Lie Forgotten,* 151.
16. Wilson, *Under the Old Flag,* 1:369.
17. Glazier, *Three Years in the Federal Cavalry,* 135.
18. Sergent, *They Lie Forgotten,* 151.
19. Meyer, *Civil War Experiences,* 97.
20. Glazier, *Three Years in the Federal Cavalry,* 134.
21. Kidd, *Personal Recollections,* 164.
22. John G. Barrett, *Sherman's March Through the Carolinas* (Chapel Hill: University of North Carolina Press, 1956), 214.
23. Alexander A. Lawrence, *A Present for Mr. Lincoln* (Macon, Ga: Ardivan Press, 1961), 183.
24. Starr, *Union Cavalry,* 1:417.
25. Lyman, *Meade's Headquarters,* 79.
26. Lewis, *Sherman: Fighting Prophet,* 405.
27. Charles S. Wainwright, *A Diary of Battle: The Personal Journals of Colonel Charles S. Wainwright,* ed. Allen Nevins (New York: Harcourt, Brace, & World, 1962), 265.
28. Howard, *Autobiography,* 2:29.
29. Wilson, *Under the Old Flag,* 1:369.
30. Kidd, *Personal Recollections,* 164.
31. Gregory J. W. Urwin, *Custer Victorious: The Civil War Battles of General George Armstrong Custer* (Rutherford, N.J.: Fairleigh Dickinson University Press, 1983), 55.
32. Ibid., 270.
33. Kidd, *Personal Recollections,* 165.
34. Starr, *Union Cavalry,* 1:417.
35. Wilson, *Under the Old Flag,* 1:371.
36. Preston, *History of the Tenth Regiment,* 46.
37. Davis, *Sherman's March,* 63.
38. Kidd, *Personal Recollections,* 233.
39. Monaghan, *Custer,* 168.
40. Camille Holt Hunt, "General Kilpatrick and His Men Arrive," in Jones, *When Sherman Came,* 296.
41. Glazier, *Three Years in the Federal Cavalry,* 163.
42. Monaghan, *Custer,* 151.
43. D. A. Kinsley, *Favor the Bold* (New York: Holt, Reinhart & Winston, 1967), 1:160.
44. Ibid.
45. Davis, *Sherman's March,* 82.
46. Kidd, *Personal Recollections,* 164.
47. Howard, *Autobiography,* 2:29.

48. *Thirteenth Annual Reunion,* 49–50.
49. Sergent, *They Lie Forgotten,* 150.

CHAPTER 7. JOE HOOKER

1. Shelby Foote, *The Civil War: A Narrative* (New York: Random House, 1958), 1:542.
2. Kenneth A. Hafendorfer, *Perryville: Battle for Kentucky* (Utica, Ky.: McDowell Publications, 1981).
3. Alexander F. Stevenson, *The Battle of Stones River Near Murfreesboro, Tennessee, December 30, 1862 to January 3, 1863* (Boston: James R. Osgood & Company, 1884).
4. Edward J. Stackpole, *Drama on the Rappahannock: The Fredericksburg Campaign* (Harrisburg, Pa.: Stackpole, 1957).
5. Walter H. Hebert, *Fighting Joe Hooker* (Indianapolis, Ind.: Bobbs-Merrill, 1944), 166.
6. Warner, *Generals in Blue,* 233–35.
7. Hebert, *Fighting Joe Hooker,* 180.
8. Starr, *Union Cavalry,* 1:329.
9. Ibid., 338.
10. Sifakis, *Who Was Who in the Union,* 393–94.
11. Official Records, ser. 1, vol. 25, pt. 2, 71–72.
12. Ibid., 82.
13. Ibid., 91.
14. Glazier, *Three Years in the Federal Cavalry,* 118.
15. Lewis, *Sherman: Fighting Prophet,* 405.
16. Glazier, *Three Years in the Federal Cavalry,* 139.
17. Ibid., 121.
18. King, "Civil War Career," 69.
19. Glazier, *Three Years in the Federal Cavalry,* 162.
20. Ibid., 163.
21. Edward J. Stackpole, *Chancellorsville: Lee's Greatest Battle* (Harrisburg, Pa.: Stackpole, 1958), 147.
22. Foote, *Civil War,* 2:262.
23. Official Records, ser. 1, vol. 25, pt. 1, 1089.
24. Official Records, ser. 1, vol. 25, pt. 2, 244.
25. Ibid., 274.
26. Official Records, ser. 1, vol. 25, pt. 1, 1074.
27. Glazier, *Three Years in the Federal Cavalry,* 177.
28. Ibid.
29. Ibid., 178.
30. Official Records, ser. 1, vol. 25, pt. 1, 1060.
31. Ibid., 1060–61.
32. Ibid., 1083–84.
33. Glazier, *Three Years in the Federal Cavalry,* 180.
34. Ibid., 181.
35. Moore, *Kilpatrick and Our Cavalry,* 49.
36. Glazier, *Three Years in the Federal Cavalry,* 181.
37. Moore, *Kilpatrick and Our Cavalry,* 50.

38. Glazier, *Three Years in the Federal Cavalry,* 182.

39. Ibid., 183.

40. Official Records, ser. 1, vol. 25, pt. 1, 1084.

41. Glazier, *Three Years in the Federal Cavalry,* 183.

42. Ibid.

43. Moore, "General Kilpatrick," *Sussex Independent,* 23 December 1881.

44. Official Records, ser. 1, vol. 25, pt. 1, 1084.

45. Glazier, *Three Years in the Federal Cavalry,* 184.

46. Ibid.

47. Official Records, ser. 1, vol. 25, pt. 1, 1084.

48. Ibid.

49. Glazier, *Three Years in the Federal Cavalry,* 185.

50. Sifakis, *Who Was Who in the Union,* 224.

51. Official Records, ser. 1, vol. 25, pt. 2, 452.

52. Ibid., 438.

53. Ibid., 463.

54. Comte de Paris, *History of the Civil War,* 3:118–21.

55. Official Records, ser. 1, vol. 25, pt. 2, 474.

56. Jay Luvaas, and Harold W. Nelson, eds., *The U.S. Army War College Guide to the Battles of Chancellorsville and Fredericksburg* (Carlisle, Pa.: South Mountain Press, 1988).

57. Official Records, ser. 1, vol. 25, pt. 1, 1072.

58. Starr, *Union Cavalry,* 1:368.

59. Sifakis, *Who Was Who in the Union,* 313–14.

60. Official Records, ser. 1, vol. 25, pt. 2, 584.

61. Ibid., 476.

62. Official Records, ser. 1, vol. 18, 360–61.

63. Ibid.

64. Ibid., 360.

65. Emory M. Thomas, *Bold Dragoon: The Life of J. E. B. Stuart* (New York: Harper & Row, 1986), 216.

66. Official Records, ser. 1, vol. 25, pt. 2, 538.

CHAPTER 8. BRANDY STATION

1. Samuel Carter III, *The Final Fortress: The Campaign for Vicksburg, 1862–1863* (New York: St. Martin's Press, 1980).

2. Samuel J. Martin, *The Road To Glory: The Life of Confederate General Richard S. Ewell* (Indianapolis, Ind.: Guild Press of Indiana, 1991), 173.

3. Official Records, ser. 1, vol. 25, pt. 2, 792.

4. Ibid., 538.

5. *New York Times,* 5 June 1863, 1.

6. Ibid.

7. Official Records, ser. 1, vol. 27, pt. 3, 33.

8. Preston, *History of the Tenth Regiment,* 82.

9. Marshall D. Krolick, "The Battle of Brandy Station," *Civil War Quarterly* 7 (Winter 1986): 56.

10. Official Records, ser. 1, vol. 27, pt. 3, 27–28.

11. Preston, *History of the Tenth Regiment,* 82.

12. Fairfax Downey, *Clash of Cavalry: The Battle of Brandy Station* (New York: David McKay Company, 1959), 88–89.

13. Krolick, "Battle of Brandy Station," 56.

14. Downey, *Clash of Cavalry*, 90.

15. Preston, *History of the Tenth Regiment*, 83.

16. Krolick, "Battle of Brandy Station," 58.

17. Official Records, ser. 1, vol. 27, pt. 1, 950.

18. Clark B. Hall, "The Battle of Brandy Station," *Civil War Times Illustrated* 29, no. 2 (May/June 1990): 35.

19. H. B. McClellan, *I Rode with Jeb Stuart: Life and Campaigns of Major General J. E. B. Stuart* (Bloomington: Indiana University Press, 1958), 265.

20. John W. Thomason Jr., *Jeb Stuart* (New York: Charles Scribner's Sons, 1930), 402.

21. Krolick, "Battle of Brandy Station," 60.

22. Mosby, *Memoirs*, 30.

23. Hall, "Battle of Brandy Station," 38.

24. Downey, *Clash of Cavalry*, 107.

25. Ibid.

26. McClellan, *I Rode with Jeb Stuart*, 270.

27. Burke Davis, *Jeb Stuart: The Last Cavalier* (New York: Rinehart & Company, 1957), 308.

28. Krolick, "Battle of Brandy Station," 63.

29. Hall, "Battle of Brandy Station," 39.

30. Hampton S. Thomas, *Some Personal Reminiscences of Service in the Cavalry of the Army of the Potomac* (Philadelphia: L. R. Hammersley, 1889), 9.

31. Preston, *History of the Tenth Regiment*, 85.

32. Official Records, ser. I, vol. 26, pt. 1, 950.

33. Ibid., 962.

34. Edward P. Tobie, *History of the First Maine* (Boston: First Maine Cavalry Association, 1887), 156.

35. Glazier, *Three Years in the Federal Cavalry*, 218.

36. Samuel H. Merrill, *Campaigns of the First Maine and First District of Columbia* (Portland, Maine: Bailey & Noyes, 1866), 109.

37. Tobie, *History of the First Maine*, 155.

38. Jedediah Hotchkiss, *Make Me a Map of the Valley: The Civil War Journal of Stonewall Jackson's Topographer*, ed. Archie P. McDonald (Dallas, Tex.: Southern Methodist University Press, 1973), 150.

39. Moore, *Kilpatrick and Our Cavalry*, 60.

40. Official Records, ser. 1, vol. 27, pt. l, 986.

41. Ibid., 950.

42. Ibid., 962.

43. Downey, *Clash of Cavalry*, 136–38.

44. Krolick, "Battle of Brandy Station," 64.

45. Official Records, ser. 1, vol. 26, pt. 1, 168–70.

46. Downey, *Clash of Cavalry*, 46.

47. Official Records, ser. 1, vol. 26, pt. 1, 169.

48. Ibid., 1045–46.

49. Judson Kilpatrick Deposition File.

50. Official Records, ser. 1, vol. 26, pt. 3, 105.

51. Downey, *Clash of Cavalry*, 124.

Chapter 9. Aldie

1. John W. Schildt, *Roads to Gettysburg* (Parsons, W. Va.: McClain Printing Company, 1978), 39.
2. Wilber Sturtevant Nye, *Here Come the Rebels!* (Baton Rouge: Louisiana State University Press, 1965), 71.
3. Official Records, ser. 1, vol. 27, pt. 1, 34.
4. Ibid., 35.
5. Clifford Dowdey, *Death of a Nation: The Story of Lee and His Men at Gettysburg* (New York: Alfred A. Knopf, 1958), 38.
6. Official Records, ser. 1, vol. 27, pt. 3, 172.
7. Ibid., 64.
8. Official Records, ser. 1, vol. 27, pt. 1, 962.
9. Comte de Paris, *History of the Civil War,* 3:493.
10. James Longstreet, *From Manassas to Appomattox* (Philadelphia: Lippincott, 1895), 341.
11. John J. Pullen, *The Twentieth Maine: A Volunteer Regiment in the Civil War* (Philadelphia: Lippincott, 1957), 84.
12. Glazier, *Three Years in the Federal Cavalry,* 226.
13. Official Records, ser. 1, vol. 27, pt. 1, 1052.
14. Official Records, ser. 1, vol. 27, pt. 2, 740.
15. Starr, *Union Cavalry,* 1:401.
16. *New York Times,* 22 June 1863, 1.
17. Official Records, ser. 1, vol. 27, pt. 2, 740.
18. *New York Times,* 20 June 1863, 1.
19. Official Records, ser. 1, vol. 27, pt. 2, 747.
20. Official Records, ser. 1, vol. 27, pt. 1, 972.
21. Tobie, *History of the First Maine,* 161.
22. Official Records, ser. 1, vol. 27, pt. 1, 975.
23. Tobie, *History of the First Maine,* 161.
24. *New York Times,* 20 June 1863, 1.
25. Glazier, *Three Years in the Federal Cavalry,* 228.
26. Official Records, ser. l, vol. 27, pt. 1, 171.
27. Ibid., 907.
28. Ibid., 171.
29. Official Records, ser. 1, vol. 27, pt. 2, 741.
30. Abner Hard, *History of the Eighth Cavalry Regiment, Illinois Volunteers* (Aurora, Ill.: Printed by the Regiment, 1868), 249–50.
31. Nye, *Here Come the Rebels!,* 180–81.
32. Official Records, ser. 1, vol. 27, pt. 1, 964.
33. Ibid., 965.
34. Ibid., 963.
35. Ibid., 964.
36. Ibid., 975.
37. Glazier, *Three Years in the Federal Cavalry,* 230.
38. Official Records, ser. 1, vol. 27, pt. 2, 689.
39. Official Records, ser. 1, vol. 27, pt. 1, 976.
40. Official Records, ser. 1, vol. 27, pt. 2, 689.
41. Official Records, ser. 1, vol. 27, pt. 1, 972.

42. Kidd, *Personal Recollections,* 122.

43. Glazier, *Three Years in the Federal Cavalry,* 231.

44. Official Records, ser. 1, vol. 27, pt. 1, 908.

45. Ibid., 909.

46. Official Records, ser. 1, vol. 27, pt. 3, 227.

47. Official Records, ser. 1, vol. 27, pt. 1, 920.

48. Ibid., 614.

49. Ibid., 615.

50. *New York Times,* 23 June 1863, 1.

51. Tobie, *History of the First Maine,* 169.

52. *New York Times,* 23 June 1863, 1.

53. Tobie, *History of the First Maine,* 169.

54. Ibid., 171.

55. *New York Times,* 23 June 1863, 1.

56. Ibid.

57. Official Records, ser. 1, vol. 27, pt. 1, 921.

58. Preston, *History of the Tenth New York,* 99.

59. Official Records, ser. 1, vol. 27, pt. 1, 912.

60. Ibid.

61. Ibid., 172.

62. Starr, *Union Cavalry,* 1:414.

63. Official Records, ser. 1, vol. 27, pt. 3, 349.

64. Official Records, ser. 1, vol. 27, pt. 1, 60.

65. Official Records, ser. 1, vol. 27, pt. 3, 334.

66. Official Records, ser. 1, vol. 27, pt. 1, 60.

67. Freeman Cleaves, *Meade of Gettysburg* (Norman: University of Oklahoma Press, 1960).

68. Starr, *Union Cavalry,* 1:416.

69. Official Records, ser. 1, vol. 27, pt. 1, 913.

70. Monaghan, *Custer,* 134.

CHAPTER 10. GETTYSBURG

1. Official Records, ser. 1, vol. 27, pt. 3, 376.

2. Warner, *Generals in Blue,* 148–49.

3. Monaghan, *Custer,* 151.

4. Sifakis, *Who Was Who in the Union,* 101.

5. John Gibbon, *Personal Recollections of the Civil War* (New York: G. P. Putnam's Sons, 1928), 129.

6. Official Records, ser. 1, vol. 27, pt. 3, 421.

7. Starr, *Union Cavalry,* 1:422.

8. Ted Alexander, "Gettysburg Cavalry Operations: June 27–July 3, 1863," *Blue and Gray* 7, no. 1 (October 1988): 21–22.

9. Fred L. Schultz, "A Cavalry Fight Was On," *Civil War Times Illustrated* 23 (February 1985): 44.

10. Ibid.

11. Alexander, "Gettysburg Cavalry Operations," 22.

12. Official Records, ser. 1, vol. 27, pt. 2, 692.

13. Clifford Dowdey, *Lee* (Boston: Little, Brown, 1965), 362.
14. Schultz, "A Cavalry Fight Was On," 44.
15. Ibid., 46.
16. Alexander, "Gettysburg Cavalry Operations", 26.
17. Official Records, ser. 1, vol. 27, pt. 1, 1008.
18. Schultz, "A Cavalry Fight Was On," 45.
19. Ibid.
20. Alexander, "Gettysburg Cavalry Operations," 26.
21. Schultz, "A Cavalry Fight Was On," 46.
22. William B. Edwards, *Civil War Guns* (Secaucus, N.J.: Castle Books, 1982), 150.
23. Official Records, ser. 1, vol. 27, pt. 2, 696.
24. Official Records, ser. 1, vol. 27, pt. 1, 1008.
25. Alexander, "Gettysburg Cavalry Operations," 27.
26. Judson Kilpatrick Pension File, RG 15, National Archives, Washington, D.C.
27. Official Records, ser. 1, vol. 27, pt. 1, 992.
28. Kinsley, *Favor the Bold,* 1:141.
29. Alexander, "Gettysburg Cavalry Operations," 30.
30. Ibid.
31. Ibid.
32. Urwin, *Custer Victorious,* 69.
33. Monaghan, *Custer,* 141.
34. Kinsley, *Favor the Bold,* 1:143.
35. Alexander, "Gettysburg Cavalry Operations," 30.
36. James S. Montgomery, *The Shaping of a Battle* (Philadelphia: Chilton Company, 1959), 87–127.
37. Alexander, "Gettysburg Cavalry Operations," 30.
38. Urwin, *Custer Victorious,* 72.
39. Official Records, ser. 1, vol. 27, pt. 1, 992.
40. Monaghan, *Custer,* 142.
41. Ibid., 144.
42. Official Records, ser. 1, vol. 27, pt. 1, 956.
43. Edwin B. Coddington, *The Gettysburg Campaign: A Study in Command* (New York: Charles Scribner's Sons, 1968), 524.
44. Official Records, ser. 1, vol. 27, pt. 1, 373.
45. Ibid.
46. Ibid.
47. Kathleen Georg Harrison, "Ridges of Grim War," *Blue and Gray* 5, no. 6 (July, 1988): 32.
48. Official Records, ser. 1, vol. 27 pt. 1, 1019.
49. H. C. Parsons, "Farnsworth's Charge and Death," in Buel and Johnson, *Battles and Leaders*, 3:394.
50. Ibid.
51. Ibid., 393.
52. Ibid., 394.
53. Ibid., 395.
54. Ibid.
55. Glenn Tucker, *High Tide at Gettysburg: The Campaign in Pennsylvania* (Indianapolis, Ind.: Bobbs-Merrill, 1958), 382.
56. John Purifoy, "Farnsworth's Charge and Death at Gettysburg," *Confederate Veteran* 32, no. 8 (August 1924): 308.

57. Ibid.
58. Parsons, "Farnsworth's Charge and Death," 395.
59. Purifoy, "Farnsworth's Charge," 308.
60. Ibid.
61. Edward Porter Alexander, *Military Memoirs of a Confederate: A Critical Narrative* (New York: Charles Scribner's Sons, 1907), 433.
62. Purifoy, "Farnsworth's Charge," 308.
63. Official Records, ser. 1, vol. 27, pt. 1, 993.
64. Ibid.
65. Ibid.
66. Ibid.
67. Starr, *Union Cavalry,* 1:441.

CHAPTER 11. BACK TO VIRGINIA

1. George Cary Eggleston, *The History of the Confederate War: Its Causes and Its Conduct* (New York: Sturgis & Walton Company, 1910), 2:149.
2. Wainwright, *A Diary of Battle,* 253.
3. Glazier, *Three Years in the Federal Cavalry,* 267.
4. Kidd, *Personal Recollections,* 166.
5. Starr, *Union Cavalry,* 1:444.
6. Official Records, ser. 1, vol. 27, pt. 1, 993.
7. John D. Imboden, "The Confederate Retreat From Gettysburg," in Buel and Johnson, *Battles and Leaders,* 3:424.
8. Official Records, ser. 1, vol. 27, pt. 1, 994.
9. Kidd, *Personal Recollections,* 169.
10. Starr, *Union Cavalry,* 1:448.
11. Official Records, ser. 1, vol. 27, pt. 2, 753.
12. Official Records, ser. 1, vol. 27, pt. 1, 994.
13. Ibid.
14. Official Records, ser. 1, vol. 27, pt. 2, 309.
15. James Arthur Lyon Fremantle, *The Fremantle Diary: Being the Journal of Lieutenant Colonel James Arthur Lyon Fremantle, Coldstream Guards, on His Three Months in the Southern States,* ed. Walter Lord (Boston: Little, Brown, 1954), 221.
16. Kidd, *Personal Recollections,* 172.
17. Glazier, *Three Years In the Federal Cavalry,* 270.
18. Kidd, *Personal Recollections,* 174.
19. Ibid.
20. Official Records, ser. 1, vol. 27, pt. 2, 701.
21. Kidd, *Personal Recollections,* 174.
22. Official Records, ser. 1, vol. 27, pt. 2, 702.
23. Kidd, *Personal Recollections,* 175.
24. Official Records, ser. 1, vol. 27, pt. 1, 935.
25. Official Records, ser. 1, vol. 27, pt. 3, 588.
26. Official Records, ser. 1, vol. 27, pt. 1, 935.
27. Coddington, *Gettysburg Campaign,* 554.
28. Charles Minor Blackford, *Letters from Lee's Army: Memoirs of Life In and Out of the Army of Virginia during the War Between the States,* ed. Susan Leigh Blackford (New York: Charles Scribner's Sons, 1947), 189.

29. Earl Schenck Miers, *The Web of Victory: Grant at Vicksburg* (New York: Alfred P. Knopf, 1957), 292–93.

30. Thomas, *Bold Dragoon,* 250.

31. Official Records, ser. 1, vol. 27, pt. 1, 925.

32. Ibid.

33. Ibid., 936.

34. Official Records, ser. 1, vol. 27, pt. 3, 602.

35. Starr, *Union Cavalry,* 1:458.

36. Kidd, *Personal Recollections,* 184–85.

37. Ibid., 185.

38. Ibid., 186.

39. Official Records, ser. 1, vol. 27, pt. 1, 990.

40. Ibid., 936–937.

41. Henry Heth, *The Memoirs of Henry Heth,* ed. James L. Morrison (Westport, Conn.: Greenwood Press, 1974), 179.

42. Official Records, ser. 1, vol. 27, pt. 1, 991.

43. Ibid., 990.

44. Ibid., 991.

45. Moore, *Kilpatrick and Our Cavalry,* 114.

Chapter 12. The Gunboat Expedition

1. Official Records, ser. 1, vol. 27, pt. 2, 877.

2. Iver Bernstein, *The New York City Draft Riots: Their Significance for American Society and Politics in the Age of the Civil War* (New York: Oxford University Press, 1990).

3. Official Records, ser. 1, vol. 27, pt. 2, 877.

4. Kinsley, *Favor the Bold,* 1:159.

5. Starr, *Union Cavalry,* 2:20.

6. Official Records, ser. 1, vol. 29, pt. 2, 75.

7. Ibid., 84.

8. Ibid., 90.

9. Official Records, ser. 1, vol. 29, pt. 1, 133.

10. Annie Jones File, RG 94, Special File 19. National Archives, Washington, D.C.

11. Official Records, ser. 1, vol. 29, pt. 2, 104.

12. Ibid., 106.

13. Ibid., 111.

14. Ibid., 112.

15. Glazier, *Three Years in the Federal Cavalry,* 316.

16. Boudrye, *Fifth New York Cavalry,* 74.

17. Glazier, *Three Years in the Federal Cavalry,* 316.

18. Ibid.

19. Official Records, ser. 1, vol. 29, pt. 1, 97.

20. Glazier, *Three Years in the Federal Cavalry,* 316.

21. Ibid., 318.

22. Official Records, ser. 1, vol. 29, pt. 1, 97.

23. Glazier, *Three Years in the Federal Cavalry,* 317.

24. Annie Jones File.

25. Ibid.

CHAPTER 13. BRANDY STATION REVISITED

1. William G. Piston, *Lee's Tarnished Lieutenant: James Longstreet and His Place in Southern History* (Athens: University of Georgia Press, 1987), 68.
2. Official Records, ser. 1, vol. 29, pt. 2, 172.
3. McClellan, *I Rode with Jeb Stuart,* 372–73.
4. Ibid., 373.
5. Official Records, ser. 1, vol. 29, pt. 1, 120.
6. Urwin, *Custer Victorious,* 96.
7. Monaghan, *Custer,* 160.
8. Official Records, ser. 1, vol. 29, pt. 1, 120.
9. Ibid., 121.
10. Ibid., 119.
11. Lyman, *Meade's Headquarters,* 17.
12. Urwin, *Custer Victorious,* 99.
13. Brian D. Kowell, "Pell-Mell Cavalry Chase," *America's Civil War* 5, no. 2 (July 1992): 43.
14. Cleaves, *Meade of Gettysburg,* 194.
15. James Lee McDonough, *Chattanooga: A Death Grip on the Confederacy* (Knoxville: University of Tennessee Press, 1984).
16. Fairfax Downey, *Storming of the Gateway: Chattanooga, 1863* (New York: David McKay, 1960), 141.
17. Douglas Southall Freeman, *Lee's Lieutenants: A Study in Command* (New York: Charles Scribner's Sons, 1942–44), 3:239.

CHAPTER 14. THE BUCKLAND RACES

1. Official Records, ser. 1, vol. 29, pt. 1, 380.
2. Ibid., 440.
3. Ibid.
4. Ibid., 381.
5. Ibid., 442.
6. Kidd, *Personal Recollections,* 207.
7. Millard K. Bushong, and Dean M. Bushong, *Fightin' Tom Rosser, C.S.A.* (Shippensburg, Pa.: Beidel Printing House, 1983), 60.
8. Kidd, *Personal Recollections,* 207.
9. Boudrye, *Fifth New York Cavalry,* 80.
10. Ibid.
11. Kidd, *Personal Recollections,* 207.
12. Ibid., 208.
13. Boudrye, *Fifth New York Cavalry,* 80.
14. Freeman, *Lee's Lieutenants,* 3:240.
15. William W. Hassler, *A. P. Hill: Lee's Forgotten General* (Richmond, Va.: Garrett and Massie, 1962), 179.
16. A. L. Long, *Memoirs of Robert E. Lee: His Military and Personal History, Embracing a Large Amount of Information Hitherto Unpublished* (New York: J. M. Stoddart & Company, 1886), 311.
17. Kowell, "Pell-Mell Cavalry Chase," 41.

18. Kidd, *Personal Recollections,* 212.
19. Kowell, "Pell-Mell Cavalry Chase," 43.
20. Ibid., 44.
21. Kidd, *Personal Recollections,* 214.
22. Ibid.
23. Ibid.
24. Official Records, ser. 1, vol. 29, pt. 1, 391.
25. Ibid., 382.
26. Ibid., 451.
27. Ibid.
28. Urwin, *Custer Victorious,* 109.
29. Kidd, *Personal Recollections,* 213.
30. Official Records, ser. 1, vol. 29, pt. 1, 382.
31. Kidd, *Personal Recollections,* 216.
32. Ibid., 219.
33. Kowell, "Pell-Mell Cavalry Chase," 72.
34. Ibid., 73.
35. Official Records, ser. 1, vol. 29, pt. 1, 387.
36. Ibid., 451.
37. Ibid., 387.
38. Kowell, "Pell-Mell Cavalry Chase," 73.
39. Official Records, ser. 1, vol. 29, pt. 1, 452.
40. Kowell, "Pell-Mell Cavalry Chase," 74.
41. Ibid.
42. Kidd, *Personal Recollections,* 226.
43. Starr, Union Cavalry, 2:30.
44. Kowell, "Pell-Mell Cavalry Chase," 74.
45. Official Records, ser. 1, vol. 29, pt. 1, 452.
46. Urwin, *Custer Victorious,* 112.

CHAPTER 15. A PLAN FOR GLORY

1. King, "Civil War Career," 161.
2. Ibid., 196.
3. Ibid.
4. Cleaves, *Meade of Gettysburg,* 203.
5. Official Records, ser. 1, vol. 29, pt. 1, 575.
6. Boudrye, *Fifth New York Cavalry,* 91.
7. Judson Kilpatrick Personal File.
8. Ibid.
9. Edward A. Pollard, *The Lost Cause: A New Southern History of the War of the Confederates, Comprising a Full and Authentic Account of the Rise and Progress of the Late Southern Confederacy—The Campaigns, Battles, Incidents, and Adventures of the Most Gigantic Struggle of the World's History* (New York: E. B. Treat & Co., 1866), 462.
10. Stanley F. Horn, *The Army of Tennessee: A Military History* (Indianapolis, Ind.: Bobbs-Merrill, 1941).
11. Kidd, *Personal Recollections,* 232–33.
12. Judson Kilpatrick Personal File.
13. Ibid.

14. Edward Skipworth, Rutgers University, New Brunswick, New Jersey, letter to author, 19 August 1992.

15. Wainwright, *A Diary of Battle,* 324.

16. Kidd, *Personal Recollections,* 228.

17. Official Records, ser. 2, vol. 4, 267.

18. William B. Hesseltine, *Civil War Prisons: A Study in War Psychology* (New York: Frederick Ungar, 1977), 87.

19. Ibid., 76.

20. Ibid., 89.

21. Virgil Carrington Jones, *Eight Hours Before Richmond* (New York: Henry Holt, 1957), 18–19.

22. Hesseltine, *Civil War Prisons,* 121.

23. Jones, *Eight Hours Before Richmond,* 20.

24. Richard E. Winslow, *General John Sedgwick: The Story of a Union Corps Commander* (Novato, Calif.: Presidio Press, 1982), 137.

25. Lyman, *Meade's Headquarters,* 68.

26. Butler, *Butler's Book,* 1051–52.

27. Official Records, ser. 1, vol. 33, 552.

28. Emory M. Thomas, "The Kilpatrick-Dahlgren Raid, Part I," *Civil War Times Illustrated* 16, no. 10 (February 1978): 8.

29. Official Records, ser. 1, vol. 33, 172–73.

30. Ibid., 171–72.

31. Jones, *Eight Hours Before Richmond,* viii.

32. Ibid.

33. Ibid., 29.

34. Ibid., 7–9.

35. Kidd, *Personal Recollections,* 234.

36. Jones, *Eight Hours Before Richmond,* 5.

37. Lyman, *Meade's Headquarters,* 76.

38. James O. Hall, "The Dahlgren Papers: A Yankee Plot to Kill President Davis," *Civil War Times Illustrated* 22, no. 7 (November 1983): 31.

39. Thomas, "Kilpatrick-Dahlgren Raid, Part I," 9.

40. Ibid.

41. Official Records, ser. 1, vol. 33, 170.

42. Ibid., 197.

43. Ibid., 183.

44. Merrill, *Campaigns of the First Maine,* 171.

45. W. H. Spira, "Kilpatrick's Richmond Raid," *History of the Seventeenth Regiment, Pennsylvania Volunteer Cavalry,* ed H. P. Moyer (Lebanon, Pa.: Sowers Printing Company, 1911), 233.

46. Ibid.

47. Official Records, ser. 1, vol. 33, 174.

Chapter 16. The Richmond Raid

1. Thomas, "Kilpatrick-Dahlgren Raid, Part I," 46.

2. Official Records, ser. 1, vol. 33, 181.

3. Jones, *Eight Hours Before Richmond,* 47.

4. Official Records, ser. 1, vol. 33, 182.

5. Ibid., 189.
6. Spira, "Kilpatrick's Richmond Raid," 234.
7. Ibid., 235.
8. Ibid.
9. Jones, *Eight Hours Before Richmond,* 48.
10. Spira, "Kilpatrick's Richmond Raid," 235.
11. Official Records, ser. 1, vol. 33, 189.
12. Ibid.
13. Merrill, *Campaigns of the First Maine,* 172.
14. Official Records, ser. 1, vol. 33, 189.
15. Spira, "Kilpatrick's Richmond Raid," 237.
16. Kidd, *Personal Recollections,* 244.
17. Official Records, ser. 1, vol. 33, 184.
18. Spira, "Kilpatrick's Richmond Raid," 238.
19. Official Records, ser. 1, vol. 33, 184.
20. Kidd, *Personal Recollections,* 246.
21. Official Records, ser. 1, vol. 33, 184.
22. Ibid., 192.
23. Ibid.
24. Ibid.
25. Ibid., 212.
26. Kidd, *Personal Recollections,* 249.
27. Ibid.
28. Tobie, *History of the First Maine,* 243.
29. Kidd, *Personal Recollections,* 249.
30. Official Records, ser. 1, vol. 33, 212.
31. Kidd, *Personal Recollections,* 250–51.
32. Spira, "Kilpatrick's Richmond Raid," 242.
33. Merrill, *Campaigns of the First Maine,* 177.
34. Official Records, ser. 1, vol. 33, 185.
35. Ibid., 201.
36. Kidd, *Personal Recollections,* 258.
37. Spira, "Kilpatrick's Richmond Raid," 243.
38. Official Records, ser. 1, vol. 33, 185.
39. Spira, "Kilpatrick's Richmond Raid," 243.
40. Ibid., 244.
41. Ibid., 245.
42. Emory M. Thomas, "The Kilpatrick-Dahlgren Raid, Part II," *Civil War Times Illustrated* 17, no. 1 (April 1978): 28.
43. Official Records, ser. 1, vol. 33, 195.
44. Thomas, "Kilpatrick-Dahlgren Raid, Part II," 27.
45. Official Records, ser. 1, vol. 33, 195.
46. Ibid., 196.
47. Spira, "Kilpatrick's Richmond Raid," 246.
48. Official Records, ser. 1, vol. 33, 186.
49. Spira, "Kilpatrick's Richmond Raid," 247.
50. Official Records, ser. 1, vol. 33, 193.
51. Spera, "Kilpatrick's Richmond Raid," 250.
52. Ibid., 251.
53. Ibid., 253.

54. Official Records, ser. 1, vol. 33, 182.
55. Ibid.
56. Ibid., 782.
57. Ibid., 183.
58. Ibid., 241.
59. Ibid.
60. Ibid.
61. Ibid., 242.
62. Ibid., 243.
63. Ibid., 1273.
64. William S. McFeely, *Grant: A Biography* (New York: W. W. Norton, 1981), 154.
65. Spira, "Kilpatrick's Richmond Raid," 257.
66. Official Records, ser. 1, vol. 33, 185.
67. Ibid.
68. Jones, *Eight Hours Before Richmond,* 112.
69. Official Records, ser. 1, vol. 33, 171.
70. Lyman, *Meade's Headquarters,* 79.
71. King, "Civil War," 179.
72. Ibid.

CHAPTER 17. THE DAHLGREN PAPERS

1. Official Records, ser. 1, vol. 33, 178.
2. Ibid., 180.
3. Ibid., 195.
4. Thomas, "Kilpatrick-Dahlgren Raid, Part II," 27.
5. Ibid.
6. Jones, *Eight Hours Before Richmond,* 82.
7. Thomas, "Kilpatrick-Dahlgren Raid, Part II," 28.
8. Ibid., 28–29.
9. Ibid., 29.
10. Jones, *Eight Hours Before Richmond,* 91.
11. Hall, "Dahlgren Papers," 31.
12. J. William Jones, "The Kilpatrick-Dahlgren Raid Against Richmond," *Southern Historical Society Papers* 13 (January–December 1885), 548.
13. Official Records, ser. 1, vol. 33, 178.
14. Ibid., 179.
15. Hall, "Dahlgren Papers," 33.
16. Thomas, "Kilpatrick-Dahlgren Raid, Part II," 31.
17. Official Records, ser. 1, vol. 33, 218.
18. Ibid., 222.
19. Ibid., 175.
20. Ibid., 176.
21. Jones, *Eight Hours Before Richmond,* 114.
22. Marsena Rudolph Patrick, *Inside Lincoln's Army: The Diary of Marsena Rudolph Patrick, Provost Marshall General, Army of the Potomac,* ed. David S. Sparks (New York: Thomas Yoseloff, 1964), 347.
23. Jones, *Eight Hours Before Richmond,* 128.
24. Official Records, ser. 1, vol. 33, 806.

25. Philip H. Sheridan, *Personal Memoirs of P. H. Sheridan, General United States Army* (New York: Charles L. Webster & Company, 1888), 1:352.

26. King, "Civil War Career," 196.

27. Official Records, ser. 1, vol. 33, 862.

28. Judson Kilpatrick Personal File.

29. Official Records, ser. 1, vol. 33, 178.

30. Ibid., 180.

CHAPTER 18. ATLANTA

1. Ulysses S. Grant, *Personal Memoirs of U. S. Grant* (New York: Charles L. Webster & Company, 1886), 2:130.

2. Lewis, *Sherman: Fighting Prophet,* 345.

3. Warner, *Generals in Blue,* 441–43.

4. Official Records, ser. 1, vol. 38, pt. 1, 115.

5. Ibid., 102.

6. William T. Sherman, *Memoirs of Gen. W. T. Sherman, Written By Himself* (New York: Charles L. Webster & Company, 1891), 2:32.

7. Official Records, ser. 1, vol. 38, pt. 1, 63.

8. W. W. Davis, "Initiation of the Georgia Campaign," *Confederate Veteran* 12, no. 2 (February 1904): 76.

9. Lewis, *Sherman: Fighting Prophet,* 357.

10. King, "Civil War Career," 198.

11. Sherman, *Memoirs,* 2:34.

12. Official Records, ser. 1, vol. 38, pt. 1, 64.

13. Polk Prince, "Polk Prince, Guthrie, Ky., Thinks He Shot Kilpatrick," *Confederate Veteran* 10, no. 4 (April 1902): 161.

14. Judson Kilpatrick Pension File.

15. Moore, *Kilpatrick and Our Cavalry,* 166.

16. Fred Harvey Harrington, *Fighting Politician: Major General Nathaniel P. Banks* (Westport, Conn.: Greenwood Press, 1970).

17. Howard P. Nash, *Stormy Petrel: The Life and Times of General Benjamin F. Butler, 1818–1893* (Rutherford, N.J.: Fairleigh Dickinson University Press, 1969).

18. William C. Davis, *The Battle of New Market* (Garden City, N.Y.: Doubleday, 1975).

19. Frank E. Vandiver, *Jubal's Raid: General Early's Famous Attack on Washington in 1864* (New York: McGraw-Hill, 1960).

20. William D. Matter, *If It Takes All Summer: The Battle of Spotsylvania* (Chapel Hill: University of North Carolina Press, 1988).

21. Noah André Trudeau, *Bloody Roads South: The Wilderness to Cold Harbor, May–June 1864* (Boston: Little, Brown, 1989).

22. McPherson, *Battle Cry of Freedom,* 742.

23. Official Records, ser. 1, vol. 36, pt. 2, 627.

24. Official Records, ser. 1, vol. 38, pt. 2, 60.

25. Johnston, *Narrative of Military Operations,* 318.

26. Official Records, ser. 1, vol. 38, pt. 2, 60.

27. Long, *Civil War Day By Day,* 518.

28. Sherman, *Memoirs,* 2:60.

29. Johnston, *Narrative of Military Operations,* 346.

30. Sherman, *Memoirs,* 2:70.

31. Benjamin P. Thomas, *Abraham Lincoln, A Biography* (New York: Alfred A. Knopf, 1952), 443.

32. John B. Hood, *Personal Experiences in the United States and Confederate States Armies* (New Orleans, La.: Hood Orphan Memorial Fund, 1880), 161.

33. Grant, *Personal Memoirs,* 2:167.

34. Moore, *Kilpatrick and Our Cavalry,* 166.

35. Ibid., 193.

36. Official Records, ser. 1, vol. 38, pt. 1, 858.

37. Samuel Carter III, *The Siege of Atlanta, 1864* (New York: Bonanza Books, 1973), 204.

38. William Key, *The Battle of Atlanta and the Georgia Campaign* (Atlanta, Ga.: Peachtree Publishers, 1981), 51–64.

39. Johnston, *Narrative of Military Operations,* 356.

40. Mary deForest Geary, *A Giant in Those Days: A Story about the Life of John White Geary* (Brunswick, Ga.: Coastal Printing Company, 1980), 194.

41. Carter, *Siege of Atlanta,* 239.

42. Howard, *Autobiography,* 2:16–26.

43. Carter, *Siege of Atlanta,* 253.

44. Ibid., 257.

45. Official Records, ser. 1, vol. 38, pt. 3, 953.

46. Official Records, ser. 1, vol. 38, pt. 2, 917.

47. Ibid., 762–63.

48. Carter, *Siege of Atlanta,* 258.

49. Official Records, ser. 1, vol. 38, pt. 2, 762.

50. Ibid., 858.

51. Sherman, *Memoirs,* 2:98.

52. Thomas L. Connelly, *Autumn of Glory: The Army of Tennessee, 1862–1865* (Baton Rouge: Louisiana State University Press, 1971), 435.

53. A. A. Hoehling, *Last Train from Atlanta* (New York: Bonanza Books, 1958), 317.

54. Official Records, ser. 1, vol. 38, pt. 5, 531.

55. Ibid., 530.

56. Ibid., 526.

57. Ibid., 548.

58. Sherman, *Memoirs,* 2:103.

59. Official Records, ser. 1, vol. 38, pt. 5, 581.

60. Ibid., 574.

61. Starr, *Union Cavalry,* 3:477.

62. Official Records, ser. 1, vol. 38, pt. 2, 858.

63. Official Records, ser. 1, vol. 38, pt. 5, 978.

64. Official Records, ser. 1, vol. 38, pt. 2, 858.

65. Starr, *Union Cavalry,* 3:477.

66. King, "Civil War Career," 206.

67. Official Records, ser. 1, vol. 38, pt. 2, 858.

68. Starr, *Union Cavalry,* 3:478.

69. Official Records, ser. 1, vol. 38, pt. 2, 858.

70. Ibid., 859.

71. Captain David Power Conyngham, *Sherman's March through the South, with Sketches and Incidents of the Campaign* (New York: Sheldan & Company, 1865), 205.

72. Official Records, ser. 1, vol. 38, pt. 2, 859.

73. Starr, *Union Cavalry,* 3:479.

74. Ibid., 480.

75. Ibid.

76. Official Records, ser. 1, vol. 38, pt. 2, 815.

77. Official Records, ser. 1, vol. 38, pt. 5, 628.

78. Ibid., 624.

79. Conyngham, *Sherman's March through the South,* 206.

80. Howard, *Autobiography,* 2:29.

81. Sherman, *Memoirs,* 2:104.

82. Official Records, ser. 1, vol. 38, pt. 2, 860.

83. Carter, *Siege of Atlanta,* 303.

84. Ibid., 306–7.

85. Official Records, ser. 1, vol. 38, pt. 2, 860.

86. Howell Purdue and Elizabeth Purdue, *Pat Cleburne, Confederate General* (Hillsboro, Tex.: Hill Junior College Press, 1973), 375.

87. Carter, *Siege of Atlanta,* 309.

88. Sherman, *Memoirs,* 2:108.

89. Key, *Battle of Atlanta,* 73.

90. Official Records, ser. 1, vol. 38, pt. 5, 777.

91. Sherman, *Memoirs,* 2:109–10.

92. Official Records, ser. 1, vol. 38, pt. 2, 861.

Chapter 19. The March to the Sea

1. Official Records, ser. 1, vol. 38, pt. 5, 777.

2. Sherman, *Memoirs,* 2:111.

3. Richard O'Connor, *Hood: Cavalier General* (New York: Prentice-Hall, 1949), 223.

4. John P. Dyer, *The Gallant Hood* (Indianapolis, Ind.: Bobbs-Merrill, 1950), 279.

5. Official Records, ser. 1, vol. 39, pt. 3, 94.

6. Richard M. McMurry, *John Bell Hood and the War for Southern Independence* (Lexington: University Press of Kentucky, 1982), 161.

7. Henry Stone, "Repelling Hood's Invasion of Tennessee," in Buel and Johnson, *Battles and Leaders,* 4:441.

8. Freeman Cleaves, *Rock of Chickamauga: The Life of General George H. Thomas* (Norman: University of Oklahoma Press, 1948), 243.

9. Official Records, ser. 1, vol. 39, pt. 3, 395.

10. Ibid., 162.

11. Starr, *Union Cavalry,* 1:8.

12. Official Records, ser. 1, vol. 39, pt. 2, 442.

13. Official Records, ser. 1, vol. 39, pt. 3, 104.

14. Ibid., 429.

15. Wilson, *Under the Old Flag,* 2:13.

16. Thomas A. Lewis, *The Guns of Cedar Creek* (New York: Harper & Row, 1988).

17. Official Records, ser. 1, vol. 39, pt. 3, 413.

18. Safikis, *Who Is Who in the Union,* 284.

19. Ibid., 12.

20. James Lee McDonough and Thomas L. Connelly, *Five Tragic Hours: The Battle of Franklin* (Knoxville: University of Tennessee Press, 1983), 18.

21. Sherman, *Memoirs,* 2:175.

22. Ibid.

23. Ibid.

24. Official Records, ser. 1, vol. 44, 362.

25. George Ward Nichols, *The Story of the Great March: From The Diary of a Staff Officer* (New York: Harper Brothers, 1865), 38.

26. Official Records, ser. 1, vol. 44, 413.

27. Ibid., 362.

28. Ibid., 66.

29. Howard, *Autobiography,* 2:74.

30. Louise Caroline Reese Cornwell, "General Howard Came at Tea Time," in Jones, *When Sherman Came,* 20.

31. Official Records, ser. 1, vol. 44, 363.

32. Howard, *Autobiography,* 2:72.

33. Morton R. McInvale, "All That Devils Could Wish For: The Griswoldville Campaign, November, 1864," *Georgia Historical Quarterly* 60, no. 2 (Summer 1976): 127.

34. Ibid., 128.

35. Charles E. Slocum, *The Life and Services of Major General Henry Warner Slocum, Officer in the United States Army: In the American Civil War in Different Military Campaigns Commander of Army Corps: Commander of Armies; Commander of District; Commander of Department; State and National Legislator; Citizen* (Toledo, Ohio: Slocum Publishing Company, 1913), 227–28.

36. Official Records, ser. 1, vol. 44, 363.

37. Conyngham, *Sherman's March through the South,* 256.

38. Davis, *Sherman's March,* 51.

39. Lewis, *Sherman: Fighting Prophet,* 455.

40. Official Records, ser. 1, vol. 44, 363.

41. John M. Gibson, *Those 163 Days: A Southern Account of Sherman's March from Atlanta to Raleigh* (New York: Coward-McCann, 1961), 57.

42. Conyngham, *Sherman's March through the South,* 280.

43. Official Records, ser. 1, vol. 44, 408.

44. Gibson, *Those 163 Days,* 57.

45. Davis, *Sherman's March,* 83.

46. Official Records, ser. 1, vol. 44, 363.

47. Ibid., 364.

48. W. W. Davis, "Kilpatrick's Spotted Horse," *Confederate Veteran* 14, no. 2 (February 1906): 62.

49. W. W. Davis, "Cavalry Service under General Wheeler," *Confederate Veteran* 11 no. 8 (August 1903): 353.

50. Official Records, ser. 1, vol. 44, 364.

51. Ibid., 409.

52. Ibid., 371.

53. Mary Elizabeth Massey, *Bonnet Brigades: American Women and the Civil War* (New York: Alfred A. Knopf, 1966), 239.

54. Official Records, ser. 1, vol. 44, 364.

55. Ibid., 365.

56. Ibid.

57. Ibid., 410.

58. Conyngham, *Sherman's March through the South,* 281.

59. Official Records, ser. 1, vol. 44, 365.

60. James Reston Jr., *Sherman's March and Vietnam* (New York: Macmillan, 1984), 76–77.

61. Official Records, ser. 1, vol. 44, 647.

62. Ibid., 365.

63. Gibson, *Those 163 Days,* 82.

64. Sarah Morgan, *The War-Time Journal of a Georgia Girl,1864–1865,* ed. Spencer B. King (Macon, Ga.: Ardivan Press,1960), 372–73.

65. Gibson, *Those l63 Days,* 85.

66. Official Records, ser. 1, vol. 44, 635.

67. Ibid., 706.

68. Ibid., 690.

69. Ibid., 372.

70. Ibid., 690.

71. Howard, *Autobiography,* 2:87.

72. Official Records, ser. 1, vol. 44, 705.

73. Ibid., 713.

74. Ibid., 708.

75. Ibid., 785.

76. McDonough and Connelly, *Five Desperate Hours.*

77. Stanley F. Horn, *The Decisive Battle of Nashville* (Knoxville: University of Tennessee Press, 1978).

78. Sherman, *Memoirs,* 2:231.

79. Moore, *Kilpatrick and Our Cavalry,* 194.

80. Ibid., 208–9.

81. Lewis, *Sherman: Fighting Prophet,* 651.

CHAPTER 20. SOUTH CAROLINA

1. Official Records, ser. 1, vol. 44, 785.

2. James Stacey, *History and Published Records of the Midway Congregational Church, Liberty County, Georgia* (Spartanburg, S.C.: Reprint Company, 1979).

3. Otis Amason, curator, Midway Church, Liberty County, Georgia, interview with author, 17 March 1993.

4. Joseph LeConte, *'Ware Sherman: A Journal of Three Months' Personal Experience in the Last Days of the Confederacy* (Berkeley: University of California Press, 1938), 30.

5. Mary Jones Mallard, "Kilpatrick's Cavalry . . . Their Conduct . . . Too Terrible To Be True," in Jones, *When Sherman Came,* 67.

6. John Stevens, "Personal Narrative of Sherman's Raid in Liberty County, Ga. Atrocities of the Enemy, Etc." (*Macon Telegraph & Messenger,* Hinesville, Georgia Public Library Archives Document), 2.

7. Ibid., 4.

8. Haskell Monroe, "Men Without Law: Federal Raiding in Liberty County, Georgia," *Georgia Historical Quarterly* 44, no. 2 (June 1960): 169.

9. Deposition of Eugene Eckels, Records, Letters, Telegrams, Reports, and Other Records Concerning the Conduct and Loyalty of Army Officers, War Department Employees and Citizens During the Civil War, RG 107, National Archives, Washington, D.C.

10. Moore, *Kilpatrick and Our Cavalry,* 209.

11. Davis, *Sherman's March,* 134.

12. Sherman, *Memoirs,* 2:271–2.

13. Rod Gregg, *Confederate Goliath: The Battle of Fort Fisher* (New York: Harper-Collins, 1991).

14. Davis, *Sherman's March,* 142.

15. Ibid., 141.

16. Howard, *Autobiography,* 2:114.

17. Barrett, *Sherman's March through the Carolinas,* 52.

18. Earl Schenck Miers, *The General Who Marched to Hell: Sherman and the Southern Campaign* (New York: Dorsett Press, 1990), 285.

19. B. H. Liddell Hart, *Sherman: Soldier, Realist, American* (New York: Dodd, Mead 1929), 359–60.

20. Deposition of Jane Dick, Records, Letters, Telegrams, Reports, and other Records Concerning the Conduct and Loyalty of Army Officers, War Department Employees and Citizens during the Civil War, RG 107, National Archives. Washington, D.C.

21. Official Records, ser. 1, vol. 47, pt. 1, 857.

22. Janet Hirt, "Morris Ford: Barnwell's Forgotten Battleground." Unpublished paper in Barnwell Public Library, Barnwell, S.C., 2.

23. William Hansford Duncan, *Barnwell People* (Barnwell, S.C.: Privately published, 1912–15), 18.

24. Mrs. Randolph Simms to her husband, 10 February 1865, Morris Collection, University of South Carolina, Columbia, South Carolina.

25. Ibid.

26. "Barnwell County Churches," 23. William Harris Manning Jr. Collection, Barnwell Public Library, Barnwell, South Carolina.

27. Mrs. Randolph Simms to her husband, 10 February 1865.

28. Reston, *Sherman's March and Vietnam,* 112.

29. Duncan, *Barnwell People,* 18–20.

30. "Sherman's Brutal Work of Sixteen Years Ago," *Barnwell Sentinel,* 10 February 1881.

31. Duncan, *Barnwell People,* 20.

32. Howard, *Autobiography,* 2:114.

33. Official Records, ser. 1, vol. 47, pt. 2, 351.

34. Official Records, ser. 1, vol. 47, pt. 1, 858.

35. Official Records, ser. 1, vol. 47, pt. 2, 382.

36. Ibid., 383.

37. Official Records, ser. 1, vol. 47, pt. 1, 879.

38. John P. Dyer, *Fightin' Joe Wheeler* (Baton Rouge: Louisiana State University Press, 1941), 217.

39. D. B. Morgan, "Incidents of the Fighting at Aiken, S.C.," *Confederate Veteran* 32, no. 8 (August 1924): 300.

40. Barrett, *Sherman's March through the Carolinas,* 57.

41. Ibid.

42. "Kilpatrick Made His Appearance Near Aiken," in Jones, *When Sherman Came,* 137.

43. Official Records, ser. 1, vol. 47, pt. 1, 858–59.

44. Official Records, ser. 1, vol. 47, pt. 2, 450.

45. Ibid.

46. Official Records, ser. 1, vol. 47, pt. 1, 859.

47. Dan Manville Hartley, "Do Not Show This Letter . . . ," *Barnwell People Sentinel,* 14 May 1970.

48. Ibid.

49. Joel Martin, auctioneer, Beaufort, South Carolina, interview with author, 22 July 1993.

50. Hartley, "Do Not Show This Letter . . ."

51. Hal Bridges, *Lee's Maverick General: Daniel Harvey Hill* (New York: McGraw-Hill, 1961), 271.

52. Don C. Seitz, *Braxton Bragg: General of the Confederacy* (Columbia, S.C.: State Company, 1924), 478.

53. Manly Wade Wellman, *Giant in Gray: A Biography of Wade Hampton of South Carolina* (New York: Charles Scribner's Sons, 1949), 165.

54. Nathaniel Cheairs Hughes Jr., *General William J. Hardee: Old Reliable* (Baton Rouge: Louisiana State University Press, 1965), 272.

55. Christopher Losson, *Tennessee's Forgotten Warriors: Frank Cheatham and His Confederate Division* (Knoxville: University of Tennessee Press, 1989), 244.

56. LeConte, *'Ware Sherman*, 81.

57. Conyngham, *Sherman's March through the South*, 311.

58. Official Records, ser. 1, vol. 47, pt. 2, 859.

59. Barrett, *Sherman's March through the Carolinas*, 98.

60. Official Records, ser. 1, vol. 47, pt. 2, 518.

61. Ibid., 533.

62. Ibid., 544.

63. Official Records, ser. 1, vol. 47, pt. 1, 860.

64. Ibid.

65. Official Records, ser. 1, vol. 47, pt. 2, 554.

66. Ibid.

67. Ibid., 591.

68. Ibid.

69. Conyngham, *Sherman's March through the South*, 310.

70. *A Checkered Life, Being a Brief History of the Countess Pourtales, Formerly Miss Marie Boozer of Columbia, S.C.* (Columbia, S.C.: Printed at the Office of the *Daily Phoenix*, 1878), 27–28.

71. Foster, "They Selected Our Home," 233–34.

72. Judson Kilpatrick Pension File.

73. John W. Dubose, "The Fayetteville (N.C.) Road Fight," *Confederate Veteran* 20, no. 2 (February 1912): 85.

Chapter 21. North Carolina

1. Noah A. Trudeau, *The Last Citadel: Petersburg, Virginia, June 1864–April 1865* (Boston: Little, Brown, 1991) .

2. Sherman, *Memoirs*, 2:290.

3. Johnston, *Narrative of Military Operations*, 372.

4. James L. McDonough, *Schofield: Union General in the Civil War and Reconstruction* (Tallahassee: Florida State University Press, 1972), 154–56.

5. Official Records, ser. 1, vol. 47, pt. 1, 861.

6. Ibid.

7. Ibid.

8. Ibid.

9. Ibid.

10. Ibid., 894.

11. Barrett, *Sherman's March Through the Carolinas,* 126.

12. E. L. Wells, "A Morning Call on General Kilpatrick," *Southern Historical Society Papers* 12 (January–December 1884): 126.

13. Ibid., 127.

14. Ibid.

15. Barrett, *Sherman's March through the Carolinas,* 128.

16. Wells, "A Morning Call," 128.

17. Ibid.

18. Conyngham, *Sherman's March through the South,* 356.

19. Lossing, *Pictorial History of the Civil War,* 3:497.

20. Davis, *Sherman's March,* 214.

21. DuBose, "Fayetteville (N.C.) Road Fight," 85.

22. Deposition of James H. Miller, Records, Letters, Telegrams, Reports, and Other Records Concerning the Conduct and Loyalty of Army Officers, War Department Employees and Citizens during the Civil War, RG 107, National Archives. Washington, D.C.

23. C. M. Calhoun, "Credit To Wheeler Claimed For Others," *Confederate Veteran* 20, no. 2 (February 1912): 82.

24. Barrett, *Sherman's March through the Carolinas,* 122.

25. Sherman, *Memoirs,* 2:295.

26. Ibid.

27. Davis, *Sherman's March,* 219.

28. Gibson, *Those 163 Days,* 203.

29. Ibid., 204.

30. Ibid.

31. Ibid., 205.

32. Barrett, *Sherman's March through the Carolinas,* 149.

33. Ibid.

34. Hughes, *General William J. Hardee,* 280–81.

35. Sherman, *Memoirs,* 2:301.

36. Davis, *Sherman's March,* 228.

37. Official Records, ser. 1, vol. 47, pt. 1, 24.

38. John W. Rowell, *Yankee Cavalrymen: Through the Civil War with the Ninth Pennsylvania Cavalry* (Knoxville: University of Tennessee Press, 1971), 235.

39. Official Records, ser. 1, vol. 47, pt. 1, 868.

40. Ibid., 25.

41. Ibid.

42. Ibid.

43. Ibid., 423.

44. Ibid., 1056.

45. Judith Lee Hallock, *Braxton Bragg and Confederate Defeat* (Tuscaloosa: University of Alabama Press, 1991), 252.

46. Official Records, ser. 1, vol. 47, pt. 1, 423.

47. Ibid., 862.

48. Gilbert E. Govan and James W. Livingood, *A Different Valor: The Story of General Joseph E. Johnston, C.S.A.* (Indianapolis, Ind.: Bobbs-Merrill, 1956), 357.

49. John M. Schofield, *Forty-Six Years in the Army* (New York: Century Company, 1897), 346.

50. Ibid., 863.

51. Ibid., 864.

CHAPTER 22. THE END OF THE WAR

1. Gibson, *Those 163 Days,* 233.
2. Official Records, ser. 1, vol. 47, pt. 2, 959.
3. Philip Van Doren Stern, *An End to Valor: The Last Days of the Civil War* (Cambridge, Mass.: Riverside Press, 1958), 107.
4. Henry W. Slocum, "Final Operations of Sherman's Army," in Buel and Johnson, *Battles and Leaders,* 4:754.
5. Allen P. Tankersley, *John B. Gordon: A Study in Gallantry* (Atlanta: Whitehall Press, 1955), 191.
6. Official Records, ser. 1, vol. 47, pt. 3, 123.
7. Nichols, *Story of the Great March,* 291.
8. Gibson, *Those 163 Days,* 242–43.
9. Bennett, *Sherman's March through the Carolinas,* 213.
10. Ibid.
11. Davis, *Sherman's March,* 253.
12. Nichols, *Story of the Great March,* 293.
13. Gibson, *Those 163 Days,* 240.
14. Bennett, *Sherman's March through the Carolinas,* 215.
15. Davis, *Sherman's March,* 254.
16. Bennett, *Sherman's March through the Carolinas,* 216.
17. Gibson, *Those 163 Days,* 247.
18. Ibid., 248.
19. Davis, *Sherman's March,* 255.
20. Gibson, *Those 163 Days,* 250.
21. Sherman, *Memoirs,* 2:346–47.
22. Wellman, *Giant in Gray,* 181.
23. Official Records, ser. 1, vol. 47, pt. 3, 207.
24. Ibid., 215.
25. Barrett, *Sherman's March through the Carolinas,* 229.
26. Deposition of Dr. R. Blacknall, Records, Letters, Telegrams, Reports, and Other Records Concerning the Conduct and Loyalty of Army Officers, War Department Employees and Citizens during the Civil War, RG 107, National Archives. Washington, D.C.
27. Deposition of James H. Miller.
28. Deposition of Mrs. Robert F. Morris, Records, Letters, Telegrams, Reports, and Other Records Concerning the Conduct and Loyalty of Army Officers, War Department Employees and Citizens during the Civil War, RG 107, National Archives. Washington, D.C.
29. Deposition of Dr. R. Blacknall.
30. Deposition of Jane Dick.
31. Official Records, ser. 1, vol. 47, pt. 3, 224.
32. Ibid., 225.
33. Sherman, *Memoirs,* 2:344.
34. Bradley T. Johnson, *A Memoir of the Life and Public Service of Joseph E. Johnston, Once the Quartermaster General of the Army of the United States and a General in the Army of the Confederate States of America* (Baltimore: R. H. Woodward & Company, 1891), 223.
35. Sherman, *Memoirs,* 2:348.
36. Nichols, *Story of the Great March,* 310.
37. Ibid., 311.

38. *Sussex Independent,* 13 January 1882.

39. Conyngham, *Sherman's March through the South,* 365.

40. Johnston, *Narrative of Military Operations,* 403.

41. Ibid.

42. Sherman, *Memoirs,* 2:350.

43. Ibid., 356–57.

44. Grant, *Personal Memoirs,* 2:516–17.

45. Wellman, *Giant in Gray,* 185.

46. Sherman, *Memoirs,* 2:368.

47. Deposition of Eugene Eckels.

48. Deposition of Jane Dick.

49. Deposition of Edmund Hill, Records, Letters, Telegrams, Reports, and Other Records Concerning the Conduct and Loyalty of Army Officers, War Department Employees and Citizens during the Civil War, RG 107, National Archives.Washington, D.C.

50. Deposition of Lieddy Garrett, Records, Letters, Telegrams, Reports, and Other Records Concerning the Conduct and Loyalty of Army Officers, War Department Employees and Citizens during Civil War, RG 107, National Archives. Washington, D.C.

51. Sergent, *They Lie Forgotten,* 150.

52. W. G. Caruthers, "More About Kilpatrick's Horses," *Confederate Veteran* 13, no. 10 (October 1905): 456.

53. Starr, *Union Cavalry,* 3:587.

54. Judson Kilpatrick Deposition File.

55. Ibid.

CHAPTER 23. AMBASSADOR TO CHILE

1. Charles Merriam Knapp, *New Jersey Politics during the Period of Civil War and Reconstruction* (Geneva, N.Y.: W. F. Humphrey, 1924), 149.

2. Ibid., 149–50.

3. Ibid., 152.

4. Ibid., 150–51.

5. Judson Kilpatrick to William H. Seward, 16 April 1866, Dispatches from U.S. Ministers to Chile, 1823–1906, RG 59, Microcopy 10, National Archives, Washington, D.C.

6. Judson Kilpatrick Deposition File.

7. Knapp, *New Jersey Politics,* 151.

8. Judson Kilpatrick Pension File.

9. Judson Kilpatrick to Hamilton Fish, 9 May 1870.

10. William H. Seward to Judson Kilpatrick, 16 November, 1865, Dispatches to U.S. Ministers to Chile, 1823–1906, RG 59, Microcopy 77, National Archives, Washington, D.C.

11. Judson Kilpatrick to William H. Seward, 31 July 1866.

12. Ibid.

13. Ibid.

14. Ibid.

15. *New York Citizen,* 23 June 1866.

16. Ibid.

17. Judson Kilpatrick to William H. Seward, 3 May 1866.

18. Ibid.

19. Ibid.
20. Ibid.
21. Ibid.
22. Ibid.
23. Ibid.
24. *Sussex Independent,* 20 January 1882.
25. Thomas McLeod Bader, "A Willingness to War: A Portrait of the Republic of Chile during the Years Preceding the War of the Pacific," (Ph.D. diss., University of California, 1967), 36–40.
26. William H. Seward to Judson Kilpatrick, 25 June 1866.
27. Judson Kilpatrick to William H. Seward, 13 July 1866.
28. Ibid.
29. Ibid.
30. Ibid.
31. Ibid.
32. Judson Kilpatrick to William H. Seward, 16 April 1866.
33. Judson Kilpatrick to William H. Seward, 2 October 1866.
34. Judson Kilpatrick to William H. Seward, 1 November 1866.
35. Gloria Vanderbilt, and Thelma Lady Furness, *Double Exposure: A Twin Autobiography* (New York: David McKay, 1958), 5.
36. *Sussex Independent,* 9 August 1978.
37. Judson Kilpatrick Pension File.
38. Judson Kilpatrick Deposition File.
39. Judson Kilpatrick to William H. Seward, 31 October 1867.
40. Judson Kilpatrick Pension File.
41. Judson Kilpatrick to William H. Seward, 20 March 1868.
42. *Sussex Independent,* 9 August 1878.
43. *New York World,* 25 September 1968.
44. Gideon Welles, *The Diary of Gideon Welles* (Boston: Houghton Mifflin, 1911), 3:437.
45. *New York Times,* 18 September 1868.
46. Judson Kilpatrick to William H. Seward, 26 September 1868.
47. Welles, *Diary of Gideon Welles,* 3:447.
48. Ibid.
49. *New York Times,* 3 November 1868.
50. Ibid.
51. Brian Steel Wills, *A Battle from the Start: The Life of Nathan Bedford Forrest* (New York: HarperCollins, 1992), 310.
52. Basil W. Duke, *Reminiscences of General Basil W. Duke, C.S.A.* (Garden City, N.Y.: Doubleday, Page & Co., 1911), 354.
53. Nash, *Stormy Petrel,* 248.
54. Leon Burr Richardson, *William Chandler, Republican* (New York: Dodd, Mead, 1940), 103.
55. Ibid.
56. *Sussex Independent,* 9 August 1872.
57. Welles, *Diary of Gideon Welles,* 3:527.
58. *Sussex Independent,* 29 August 1873.
59. Judson Kilpatrick to Hamilton Fish, 24 August 1869.
60. Judson Kilpatrick Pension File.
61. Hamilton Fish to Judson Kilpatrick, 17 March 1870.

62. Judson Kilpatrick to Hamilton Fish, 8 July 1870.

63. Judson Kilpatrick to Hamilton Fish, 9 May 1870.

64. *Sussex Independent,* 20 January 1882.

65. Judson Kilpatrick to Hamilton Fish, 22 September 1870.

66. L. E. Williams to H. H. Jackson, 23 September 1895. Cemetery Files, U.S. Military Academy Archives, West Point, New York.

Chapter 24. Farmer/Lecturer

1. *Sussex Independent,* 20 January 1882.

2. *Sussex Independent,* 12 May 1871.

3. *Sussex Independent,* 9 June 1871.

4. Ibid.

5. *Sussex Independent,* 1 September 1871.

6. *Sussex Independent,* 15 September 1871.

7. *Sussex Independent,* 20 September, 1871.

8. *Sussex Independent,* 15 September, 1871.

9. Ibid.

10. *Sussex Independent,* 10 November, 1871.

11. *Sussex Independent,* 8 March, 1872.

12. Claude M. Fuess, *Carl Schurz: Reformer* (New York: Dodd, Mead, 1932), 178.

13. Ibid., 188.

14. Ibid., 197.

15. *Sussex Independent,* 24 May 1872.

16. *New York Times,* 27 July 1872.

17. *Sussex Independent,* 9 August 1872.

18. Ibid.

19. *New York Times,* 2 August 1872.

20. *New York Times,* 7 August 1872.

21. Depositions, RG 107, National Archives. Washington, D.C.

22. *Sussex Independent,* 26 July 1872.

23. *Sussex Independent,* 12 December 1873.

24. *Sussex Independent,* 29 August 1873.

25. *Sussex Independent,* 14 February 1873.

26. *Sussex Independent,* 9 August 1878.

27. *Sussex Independent,* 24 January 1873.

28. *Sussex Independent,* 3 October 1873.

29. *Sussex Independent,* 20 June 1873.

30. *Sussex Independent,* 29 August 1873.

31. Eli Perkins, "Eli Perkins Talks of the War," *Confederate Veteran* 1, no. 7 (July 1893): 209.

32. Donald A. Sinclair, *A Bibliography: The Civil War and New Jersey* (New Brunswick, N.J.: Friends of the Rutgers University Library for the New Jersey Civil War Centennial Commission, 1961), 345.

33. Sergent, *They Lie Forgotten,* 151.

34. *Sussex Independent,* 20 January 1882.

35. *Sussex Independent,* 11 August 1876.

36. *Sussex Independent,* 17 November 1876.

37. *Sussex Independent,* 5 January 1877.

38. *Sussex Independent,* 19 January 1877.

39. *Sussex Independent,* 12 July 1878.

40. *Sussex Independent,* 26 July 1878.

41. *Sussex Independent,* 16 August 1878.

42. *Sussex Independent,* 30 August, 1878.

43. Ibid.

44. Ibid.

45. Ibid.

46. Ibid.

47. Ibid.

48. Ibid.

49. Ibid.

50. Ibid.

51. *Sussex Independent,* 6 September 1878.

52. *Sussex Independent,* 27 September 1878.

53. *Sussex Independent,* 1 November 1878.

54. *Sussex Independent,* 13 December 1878.

55. *Sussex Independent,* 27 January 1882.

56. J. S. Bliss Collection, E. S. Bird Library, Syracuse University, Syracuse, New York.

57. McFeely, *Grant: A Biography,* 478.

58. *New York Times,* 3 June 1880.

59. Ralph K. Andrist, ed., *The American Heritage: History of the Confident Years* (New York: American Heritage Publishing Company), 92–93.

60. *New York Times,* 9 June 1880.

61. Ibid.

62. Ibid.

63. Glenn Tucker, *Hancock the Superb* (Indianapolis, Ind.: Bobbs-Merrill, 1960), 300.

64. *Sussex Independent,* 24 September 1880.

65. *Sussex Independent,* 5 November 1880.

66. *Sussex Independent,* 27 January 1882.

67. *Sussex Independent,* 22 April 1881.

68. James G. Blaine to Judson Kilpatrick, 1 June 1881.

CHAPTER 25. THE END

1. Judson Kilpatrick Pension File.

2. Judson Kilpatrick to James G. Blaine, 2 August 1881.

3. James G. Blaine to Judson Kilpatrick, 1 June 1881.

4. Clements R. Markham, *The War Between Peru and Chile* (London: Sampson, Law, Marston, Searle, & Rivington, 1882), 84.

5. Ibid., 93–98.

6. Ibid., 259.

7. William F. Sater, *Chile and the War of the Pacific* (Lincoln: University of Nebraska Press, 1986), 209.

8. Warner, *Generals in Blue,* 245.

9. Herbert Millington, *American Diplomacy and the War of the Pacific* (New York: Columbia University Press, 1948), 88.

10. Louisa Kilpatrick for Judson Kilpatrick to James G. Blaine, 30 August 1881.
11. Judson Kilpatrick to James G. Blaine, 13 September 1881.
12. Judson Kilpatrick to James G. Blaine, 28 September 1881.
13. *Sussex Independent,* 27 January 1882.
14. *Sussex Independent,* 20 January 1882.
15. Judson Kilpatrick to James G. Blaine, 2 December 1881.
16. *Sussex Independent,* 20 January 1882.
17. Judson Kilpatrick Pension File.
18. Sergent, *They Lie Forgotten,* 151.

Epilogue

1. Judson Kilpatrick Pension File.
2. Vanderbilt and Furness, *Double Exposure,* 4.
3. Barbara Goldsmith, *Little Gloria . . . Happy At Last* (New York: Alfred A. Knopf, 1980), 120.
4. Ibid., 467.
5. Ibid., 45.
6. Ibid., 48.
7. Ibid., 106.
8. Vanderbilt and Furness, *Double Exposure,* 58.
9. Ibid., 127.
10. Goldsmith, *Little Gloria,* 68–69.
11. Vanderbilt and Furness, *Double Exposure,* 129.
12. Goldsmith, *Little Gloria,* 136.
13. Ibid., 155.
14. Ibid., 275–77.
15. Ibid., 61.
16. Ibid., 73.
17. Ibid., 123.
18. Ibid., 135.
19. Vanderbilt and Furness, *Double Exposure,* 165–66.
20. Ibid., 273.
21. Goldsmith, *Little Gloria,* 291.
22. Ibid., 524.

Selected Bibliography

PRIMARY SOURCES

Manuscripts/Official Documents

Bliss, J. S. Collection. E. S. Bird Library, Syracuse University.

Cemetery Files. United States Military Academy Archives, West Point, N.Y.

Dispatches to United States Ministers to Chile, 1823–1906. RG 59. National Archives, Washington, D.C.

Dispatches from United States Ministers to Chile, 1823–1906. RG 59. National Archives, Washington, D.C.

Jones, Annie File. RG 94. Special File 19. National Archives, Washington, D.C.

Kilpatrick, Judson. Deposition. RG 94. National Archives, Washington, D.C.

Kilpatrick, Judson. Pension File. RG 15. National Archives, Washington, D.C.

Kilpatrick, Judson. Personal File. RG 94. National Archives, Washington, D.C.

Library of Congress, Photoduplication. Washington, D.C.

Manning, William Harris Jr. Collection. Barnwell Public Library, Barnwell, S.C.

Merit Collection. Carolina Collection. University of South Carolina, Columbia, S.C.

Official Register of the Officers and Cadets of the United States Military Academy. West Point, N.Y.: U.S. Military Academy, June 1857.

Records, Letters, Telegrams, Reports, and Other Records Concerning the Conduct and Loyalty of Army Officers, War Department Employees and Citizens during the Civil War. RG 107. National Archives, Washington, D.C.

Special Collections Division. United States Military Academy Library, West Point, N.Y.

U.S. War Department. *Atlas to Accompany the Official Records of the Union and Confederate Armies.* Washington, D.C., 1891–95.

U.S. War Department. *The War of the Rebellion: A Compilation of the Official Records of the Union and Confederate Armies.* 127 vols. and index. Washington, D.C., 1880–1901.

Regimental Histories

Boudrye, Louis N. *Historic Records of the Fifth New York Cavalry, First Ira Harris Guards: Its Operations, Marches, Raids, Scouts, Engagements, and General Services during the Rebellion of 1861–1865.* Albany, N.Y.: J. Munsell, 1868.

Davenport, Alfred. *Camp and Field: Life of the Fifth New York Volunteer Infantry*. New York: Dick & Fitzgerald, 1879.

Glazier, Willard. *Three Years in the Federal Cavalry*. New York: R. H. Ferguson & Co., 1874.

Hard, Abner. *History of the Eighth Cavalry Regiment, Illinois Volunteers*. Aurora, Ill.: Printed by the Regiment, 1868.

Merril, Samuel H. *Campaigns of the First Maine and First District of Columbia*. Portland, Me.: Bailey & Noyes, 1866.

Meyer, Henry C. *Civil War Experiences Under Bayard, Gregg, Kilpatrick, and Custer.* New York: Raulson & Newberry, 1911.

Moyer, H. P., ed. *History of the Seventeenth Regiment, Pennsylvania Volunteer Cavalry*. Lebanon, Pa.: Sowers Printing Company, 1911.

Preston, Noble D. *History of the Tenth Regiment of Cavalry, New York State Volunteers*. New York: D. Appleton Company, 1892.

Pullen, John J. *The Twentieth Maine: A Volunteer Regiment in the Civil War.* Philadelphia: Lippincott, 1957.

Pyne, Henry R. *The History of the First New Jersey Cavalry*. Trenton, N.J.: J. A. Beecher, Publisher, 1871.

Rowell, John W. *Yankee Cavalrymen: Through the Civil War with the Ninth Pennsylvania Cavalry*. Knoxville: University of Tennessee Press, 1971.

Tobie, Edward P. *History of the First Maine*. Boston: First Maine Cavalry Association, 1887.

Printed Correspondence and Diaries

Blackford, Charles Minor. *Letters from Lee's Army: Memoirs of Life In and Out of the Army of Virginia during the War Between the States*. Edited by Susan Leigh Blackford. New York: Charles Scribner's Sons, 1947.

Fremantle, James Arthur Lyon. *The Fremantle Diary: Being the Journal of Lieutenant Colonel James Arthur Lyon Fremantle, Coldstream Guards, on His Three Months in the Southern States*. Edited by Walter Lord. Boston: Little, Brown, 1954.

Hotchkiss, Jedediah. *Make Me a Map of the Valley: The Civil War Journal of Stonewall Jackson's Topographer*. Edited by Archie P. McDonald. Dallas, Tex.: Southern Methodist University Press, 1973.

King, Spencer B., ed. *The War-Time Journal of a Georgia Girl, 1864–1865*. Macon, Ga.: The Ardivan Press, 1960.

LeConte, Joseph. *'Ware Sherman: A Journal of Three Months' Personal Experience in the Last Days of the Confederacy*. Berkeley: University of California Press, 1938.

Lyman, Theodore. *Meade's Headquarters, 1863–1865: The Letters of Colonel Theodore Lyman from the Wilderness to Appomattox*. Edited by George R. Agassiz. Boston: The Atlantic Monthly Press, 1922.

Patrick, Marsena Rudolph. *Inside Lincoln's Army: The Diary of Marsena Rudolph Patrick, Provost Marshall General, Army of the Potomac*. Edited by David S. Sparks. New York: Thomas Yoseloff, 1964.

Russell, William Howard. *My Diary North and South*. 2 vols. Boston: T. O. H. P. Burnham, 1863.

Wainwright, Charles S. *A Diary of Battle: The Personal Journals of Colonel Charles S. Wainwright*. Edited by Allen Nevins. New York: Harcourt, Brace & World, 1962.

Welles, Gideon. *The Diary of Gideon Welles*. 3 vols. Boston: Houghton Mifflin, 1911.

Memoirs, Reminiscences, and Recollections

A Checkered Life, Being a Brief History of the Countess Pourtales, Formerly Miss Marie Boozer of Columbia, S.C. Columbia, S.C.: Printed at the Office of the *Daily Phoenix,* 1878.

Alexander, Edward Porter. *Military Memoirs of a Confederate: A Critical Narrative.* New York: Charles Scribner's Sons, 1907.

Averell, William Woods. *Ten Years in the Saddle: The Memoirs of William Woods Averell, 185–1862.* Edited by Edward K. Eckert and Nicholas J. Amato. San Rafael, Calif.: Presidio Press, 1978.

Blackford, W. W. *War Years with Jeb Stuart.* New York: Charles Scribner's Sons, 1945.

Buel, Clarence C., and Robert J. Johnson, eds. *Battles and Leaders of the Civil War.* 4 vols. New York: The Century Company, 1884–87.

Butler, Benjamin F. *Butler's Book.* Boston: A. M. Thayer & Company, 1892.

Conyngham, Capt. David Power. *Sherman's March through the South with Sketches and Incidents of the Campaign.* New York: Sheldan & Company, 1865.

Duke, Basil W. *Reminiscences of General Basil W. Duke, C.S.A.* Garden City, N.Y.: Doubleday, Page & Company, 1911.

Gibbon, John. *Personal Recollections of the Civil War.* New York: G. P. Putnam's Sons, 1928.

Grant, Ulysses S. *Personal Memoirs of U. S. Grant.* 2 vols. New York: Charles L. Webster & Company, 1886.

Heth, Henry. *The Memoirs of Henry Heth.* Edited by James L. Morrison. Westport, Conn.: Greenwood Press, 1974.

Hood, John B. *Personal Experiences in the United States and Confederate States Armies.* New Orleans, La.: Hood Orphan Memorial Fund, 1880.

Howard, Oliver Okis. *Autobiography of Oliver Otis Howard, Major General United States Army.* 2 vols. New York: The Baker & Taylor Company, 1907.

Johnston, Joseph Eggleston. *Narrative of Military Operations Directed during the Late War Between the States.* New York: D. Appleton & Company, 1874.

Jones, Katharine M., ed. *When Sherman Came: Southern Women and the "Great March."* Indianapolis, Ind.: Bobbs-Merrill, 1964.

Kidd, James H. *Personal Recollections of a Cavalryman with Custer's Michigan Cavalry Brigade in the Civil War.* Iona, Mich.: Sentinel Printing Company, 1908.

Long, A. L. *Memoirs of Robert E. Lee: His Military and Personal History, Embracing a Large Amount of Information Hitherto Unpublished.* New York: J. M. Stoddert & Company, 1886.

Longstreet, James. *From Manassas to Appomattox.* Philadelphia: Lippincott, 1895.

McClellan, George B. *McClellan's Own Story.* New York: Charles L. Webster & Company, 1886.

———. *Report on the Organization and Campaigns of the Army of the Potomac: To Which Is Added an Account of the Campaign in Western Virginia, with Plans of Battle-Fields.* New York: Sheldon & Company Publishers, 1864.

McClellan, H. B. *I Rode with Jeb Stuart: Life and Campaigns of Major General J. E. B. Stuart.* Bloomington: Indiana University Press, 1958.

Moore, James. *Kilpatrick and Our Cavalry: Comprising a Sketch of the Life of General Kilpatrick with an Account of the Cavalry Raids, Engagements, and Operations under His Command, from the Beginning of the Rebellion to the Surrender of Johnston.* New York: Hurst & Company, 1865.

Mosby, John S. *The Memoirs of Colonel John S. Mosby.* Bloomington: Indiana University Press, 1959.

Schofield, John M. *Forty-Six Years in the Army.* New York: The Century Company, 1897.

Sheridan, Philip H. *Personal Memoirs of P. H. Sheridan, General U.S. Army.* 2 vols. New York: Charles L. Webster & Company, 1888.

Sherman, William T. *Memoirs of Gen. W. T. Sherman, Written By Himself.* 2 vols. New York: Charles L. Webster & Company, 1891.

Thomas, Hampton S. *Some Personal Reminiscences of Service in the Cavalry of the Army of the Potomac.* Philadelphia: L. R. Hammersley, 1889.

Vanderbilt, Gloria, and Thelma Lady Furness. *Double Exposure: A Twin Autobiography.* New York: David McKay Company, 1958.

Wilson, James H. *Under the Old Flag.* 2 vols. New York: D. Appleton & Company, 1912.

Newspapers and Magazines

America's Civil War.
Barnwell (S.C.) Sentinel.
Blue and Gray Magazine.
The Civil War Quarterly.
Civil War Times Illustrated.
Confederate Veteran Magazine.
Georgia Historical Quarterly.
Macon (Ga.) Telegraph & Messenger.
New York Citizen.
New York Herald.
New York Times.
New York World.
Southern Historical Society Papers.
Sussex (N.J.) Independent.

SECONDARY SOURCES

Books

Andrist, Ralph K., ed. *The American Heritage: History of the Confident Years.* New York: American Heritage Publishing Company, n.d.

Barrett, John G. *Sherman's March through the Carolinas.* Chapel Hill: University of North Carolina Press, 1956.

Bernstein, Iver. *The New York City Draft Riots: Their Significance of American Society and Politics in the Age of the Civil War.* New York: Oxford University Press, 1990 .

Bridges, Hal. *Lee's Maverick General: Daniel Harvey Hill.* New York: McGraw-Hill, 1961.

Bushong, Millard K., and Dean M. Bushong. *Fightin' Tom Rosser, C.S.A.* Shippensburg, Pa.: Beidel Printing House, 1983.

Carter, Samuel, III. *The Final Fortress: The Campaign for Vicksburg, 1862–1863.* New York: St. Martin's Press, 1980.

———. *The Siege of Atlanta, 1864.* New York: Bonanza Books, 1973.

Catton, Bruce. *The Army of the Potomac.* 3 vols. Garden City, N.Y.: Doubleday, 1952.

Chambers, Lenoir. *Stonewall Jackson.* 2 vols. New York: William Morrow, 1959.

Cleaves, Freeman. *Meade of Gettysburg.* Norman: University of Oklahoma Press, 1960.

———. *Rock of Chickamauga: The Life of General George H. Thomas.* Norman: University of Oklahoma Press, 1948.

Coddington, Edwin B. *The Gettysburg Campaign: A Study in Command.* New York: Charles Scribner's Sons, 1968.

Comte de Paris. *History of the Civil War in America.* 4 vols. Philadelphia: Porter & Coates, 1875.

Connelly, Thomas L. *Autumn of Glory: The Army of Tennessee, 1862–1865.* Baton Rouge: Louisiana State University Press, 1971.

Cullen, Joseph. *The Peninsula Campaign, 1862.* Harrisburg, Pa.: Stackpole, 1973.

Daniels, Pamela, and Kathy Weingarten. *Sooner or Later.* New York: W. W. Norton, 1982.

Davis, Burke. *Jeb Stuart: The Last Cavalier.* New York: Rinehart & Company, 1957.

———. *Sherman's March.* New York: Random House, 1980.

Davis, William C. *Battle at Bull Run.* Garden City, N.Y.: Doubleday, 1977.

———. *The Battle of New Market.* Garden City, N.Y.: Doubleday, 1975.

———. *Duel between the First Ironclads.* Garden City, N.Y.: Doubleday, 1975.

Dowdey, Clifford. *Death of a Nation: The Story of Lee and His Men at Gettysburg.* New York: Alfred A. Knopf, 1958.

———. *Experiment in Rebellion.* Garden City, N.Y.: Doubleday, 1946.

———. *Lee.* Boston: Little, Brown, 1965.

———. *The Seven Days: The Emergence of Lee.* Boston: Little, Brown, 1964.

Downey, Fairfax. *The Clash of Cavalry: The Battle of Brandy Station.* New York: David McKay Company, 1959.

———. *Storming of the Gateway: Chattanooga, 1863.* New York: David McKay Company, 1960.

Dufour, Charles. *The Night the War Was Lost.* Garden City, N.Y.: Doubleday, 1960.

Duncan, William Hansford. *Barnwell People.* Barnwell, S.C.: Privately Published, 1912–15.

Dyer, John P. *Fightin' Joe Wheeler.* Baton Rouge: Louisiana State University Press, 1941.

———. *The Gallant Hood.* Indianapolis, Ind.: Bobbs-Merrill, 1950.

Eckenrode, H. J., and Bryan Conrad. *James Longstreet: Lee's War Horse.* Chapel Hill: University of North Carolina Press, 1936.

Edwards, William B. *Civil War Guns.* Secaucus, N.J.: Castle Books, 1982.

Eggleston, George Cary. *The History of the Confederate War: Its Causes and Its Conduct.* 2 vols. New York: Sturgis & Walton Company, 1910.

Eisenschiml, Otto. *The Celebrated Case of Fitz John Porter: An American Dreyfus Affair.* Indianapolis, Ind.: Bobbs-Merrill, 1950.

Foote, Shelby. *The Civil War: A Narrative.* 3 vols. New York: Random House, 1958.

Freeman, Douglas Southall. *R. E. Lee: A Biography.* 4 vols. New York: Charles Scribner's Sons, 1934.

Fuess, Claude M. *Carl Schurz: Reformer.* New York: Dodd, Mead, 1932.

Geary, Mary deForest. *A Giant in Those Days: A Story About the Life of John White Geary.* Brunswick, Ga.: Coastal Printing Company, 1980.

Gibson, John M. *Those 163 Days: A Southern Account of Sherman's March from Atlanta to Raleigh.* New York: Coward-McCann, 1961.

Goldsmith, Barbara. *Little Gloria . . . Happy At Last.* New York: Alfred A. Knopf, 1980.

Govan, Gilbert E., and James W. Livingood. *A Different Valor: The Story of General Joseph E. Johnston, C.S.A.* Indianapolis, Ind.: Bobbs-Merrill, 1956.

Gregg, Rod. *Confederate Goliath: The Battle of Fort Fisher.* New York: HarperCollins, 1991.

Hafendorfer, Kenneth A. *Perryville: Battle for Kentucky.* Utica, Ky.: McDowell Publications, 1981.

Hallock, Judith Lee. *Braxton Bragg and Confederate Defeat.* Tuscaloosa: University of Alabama Press, 1991.

Hamilton, James. *The Battle of Fort Donelson.* New York: Thomas Yoseloff, 1968.

Harrington, Fred Harvey. *Fighting Politician: Major General Nathaniel P. Banks.* Westport, Conn.: Greenwood Press, 1970.

Hart, B. H. Liddell. *Sherman: Soldier, Realist, American.* New York: Dodd, Mead, 1929.

Hassler, William W. A. *P. Hill: Lee's Forgotten General.* Richmond, Va.: Garrett & Massie, 1962.

Haythornthwaite, Philip. *Uniforms of the Civil War.* New York: Sterling Publishing Company, 1990.

Herbert, Walter H. *Fighting Joe Hooker.* Indianapolis, Ind.: Bobbs-Merrill, 1944.

Henry, Robert Selph. *The Story of the Confederacy.* Indianapolis, Ind.: Bobbs-Merrill, 1931.

Hesseltine, William B. *Civil War Prisons: A Study in War Psychology.* New York: Frederick Ungar, 1977.

Hoehling, A. A. *Last Train from Atlanta.* New York: Bonanza Books, n.d.

Horn, Stanley F. *The Army of Tennessee: A Military History.* Indianapolis, Ind.: Bobbs-Merrill, 1941.

Hughes, Nathaniel Cheairs, Jr. *General William J. Hardee: Old Reliable.* Baton Rouge: Louisiana State University Press, 1965.

Johnson, Bradley T. *A Memoir of the Life and Public Service of Joseph E. Johnston, Once the Quartermaster General of the Army of the United States and a General in the Army of the Confederate States of America.* Baltimore: R. H. Woodward & Company, 1891.

Jones, Virgil Carrington. *Eight Hours Before Richmond.* New York: Henry Holt, 1957.

Kajencki, Colonel Francis C. *Star on Many a Battlefield: Brevet Brigadier General Joseph Karge in the American Civil War.* Rutherford, N.J.: Fairleigh Dickinson University Press, 1980.

Key, William. *The Battle of Atlanta and the Georgia Campaign*. Atlanta, Ga.: Peachtree Publishers Limited, 1981.

Kinsley, D. A. *Favor the Bold*. 2 vols. New York: Holt, Rinehart & Winston, 1967.

Knapp, Dr. Charles Merriam. *New Jersey Politics during the Period of Civil War and Reconstruction*. Geneva, N.Y.: W. F. Humphrey, 1924.

Lawrence, Alexander A. *A Present for Mr. Lincoln*. Macon, Ga.: The Ardivan Press, 1961.

Lewis, Lloyd. *Sherman: Fighting Prophet*. New York: Harcourt, Brace, 1932.

Lewis, Thomas. *The Guns of Cedar Creek*. New York: Harper & Row, 1988.

Long, E. B., and Barbara Long. *The Civil War Day By Day: An Almanac, 1861–1865*. New York: Doubleday, 1971.

Lossing, Benson J. *Pictorial History of the Civil War*. 3 vols. Philadelphia: Douglas McKay, 1866.

Losson, Christopher. *Tennessee's Forgotten Warriors: Frank Cheatham and His Confederate Division*. Knoxville: University of Tennessee Press, 1989.

Luvaas, Jay, and Harold W. Nelson, eds. *The U.S. Army War College Guide to the Battles of Chancellorsville and Fredericksburg*. Carlisle, Pa.: South Mountain Press, 1988.

Markham, Clements R. *The War Between Peru and Chile*. London: Sampson, Law, Marston, Searle, & Rivington, 1882.

Martin, Samuel J. *The Road To Glory: The Life of Confederate General Richard S. Ewell*. Indianapolis, Ind.: Guild Press of Indiana, 1991.

Massey, Mary Elizabeth. *Bonnet Brigades: American Women and the Civil War*. New York: Alfred A. Knopf, 1966.

Matter, William D. *If It Takes All Summer: The Battle of Spotsylvania*. Chapel Hill: University of North Carolina Press, 1988.

McDonough, James Lee. *Chattanooga: A Death Grip on the Confederacy*. Knoxville: University of Tennessee Press, 1984.

———. *Schofield: Union General in the Civil War and Reconstruction*. Tallahassee: Florida State University Press, 1972.

McDonough, James Lee, and Thomas L. Connelly. *Five Tragic Hours: The Battle of Franklin*. Knoxville: University of Tennessee Press, 1983.

McFeely, William S. *Grant: A Biography*. New York: W. W. Norton, 1981.

McMurry, Richard M. *John Bell Hood and the War for Southern Independence*. Lexington: University Press of Kentucky, 1982.

McPherson, James M. *Battle Cry of Freedom: The Civil War Era*. New York: Oxford University Press, 1988.

Miers, Earl Schenck. *The General Who Marched to Hell: Sherman and the Southern Campaign*. New York: Dorsett Press, 1990.

———. *The Web of Victory: Grant at Vicksburg*. New York: Alfred A. Knopf, 1957.

Miller, Francis Trevelyan, ed. *The Photographic History of the Civil War*. 10 vols. New York: The Review of Reviews Company, 1911.

Millington, Herbert. *American Diplomacy and the War of the Pacific*. New York: Columbia University Press, 1948.

Monaghan, Jay. *Custer: The Life of General George Armstrong Custer*. Boston: Little, Brown, 1959.

Montgomery, James S. *The Shaping of a Battle*. Philadelphia: Chilton Company, 1959.

Murfin, James V. *The Gleam of Bayonets: The Battle of Antietam and Robert E. Lee's Maryland Campaign, 1862.* New York: Thomas Yoseloff, 1965.

Nash, Howard P. *Stormy Petrel: The Life and Times of General Benjamin F. Butler, 1818–1893.* Rutherford, N.J.: Fairleigh Dickinson University Press, 1969.

Nichols, George W. *The Story of the Great March: From the Diary of a Staff Officer.* New York: Harper & Brothers, 1865.

Nolan, Alan T. *The Iron Brigade: A Military History.* New York: Macmillan, 1961.

Nye, Wilber Sturtevant. *Here Come the Rebels!* Baton Rouge: Louisiana State University Press, 1965.

O'Connor, Richard. *Hood: Cavalier General.* New York: Prentice-Hall, 1949.

Phisterer, Frederick. *New York in the War of the Rebellion, 1861–1865.* 5 vols. Albany, N.Y.: J. B. Lyon Company, 1912.

Piston, William G. *Lee's Tarnished Lieutenant: James Longstreet and His Place in Southern History.* Athens: University of Georgia Press, 1987.

Pollard, Edward A. *The Lost Cause: A New Southern History of the War of the Confederates, Comprising a Full and Authentic Account of the Rise and Progress of the Late Southern Confederacy—The Campaigns, Battles, Incidents, and Adventures of the Most Gigantic Struggle of the World's History.* New York: E. B. Treat & Co., 1866.

Potter, David M. *The Impending Crisis, 1848–1861.* New York: Harper & Row, 1976.

Purdue, Howell, and Elizabeth Purdue. *Pat Cleburne, Confederate General.* Hillsboro, Tex.: Hill Junior College Press, 1973.

Richardson, Leon Burr. *William Chandler, Republican.* New York: Dodd, Mead, 1940.

Sandberg, Carl. *Abraham Lincoln: The War Years.* 4 vols. New York: Harcourt, Brace & World, 1936.

Sater, William F. *Chile and the War of the Pacific.* Lincoln: University of Nebraska Press, 1986.

Schaff, Morris. *The Spirit of Old West Point, 1858–1862.* Boston: Houghton Mifflin, 1907.

Schenck, Martin. *Up Came Hill: The Story of the Light Division and Its leaders.* Harrisburg, Pa.: Stackpole, 1958.

Schildt, John W. *Roads to Gettysburg.* Parsons, W. Va.: McClain Printing Company, 1978.

Sears, Stephen W. *George B. McClellan: The Young Napoleon.* New York: Ticknor & Fields, 1988.

Sergent, Mary Elizabeth. *They Lie Forgotten: The United States Military Academy, 1856–1861, Together with a Class Album for the Class of May, 1861.* Middletown, N.Y.: The Prior King Press, 1986.

Seitz, Don C. *Braxton Bragg: General of the Confederacy.* Columbia, S.C.: The State Company, 1924.

Sifakis, Stewart. *Who Was Who in the Union: A Comprehensive, Illustrated Biographical Reference to More Than 1,500 of the Principal Union Participants in the Civil War.* New York: Facts On File, 1988.

Sinclair, Donald A. *A Bibliography: The Civil War and New Jersey.* New Brunswick, N.J.: Friends of Rutgers University Library for the New Jersey Civil War Centennial Commission, 1961.

Slocum, Charles E. *The Life and Services of Major General Henry Warner Slocum, Officer in the United States Army in the American Civil War in Different Military Campaigns*

Commander of Army Corps; Commander of Armies; Commander of District; Commander of Department; State and National Legislator; Citizen. Toledo: The Slocum Publishing Company, 1913.

Snell, James P. *The History of Sussex and Warren Counties, New Jersey.* Philadelphia: Everts & Peck, 1881.

Stacey, James. *History and Published Records of the Midway Congregational Church, Liberty County, Georgia.* Spartanburg, S.C.: The Reprint Company, 1979.

Stackpole, Edward J. *Chancellorsville: Lee's Greatest Battle.* Harrisburg, Pa.: Stackpole, 1958.

———. *Drama on the Rappahannock: The Fredericksburg Campaign.* Harrisburg, Pa.: Stackpole, 1957.

———. *From Cedar Mountain to Antietam: August–September 1862.* Harrisburg, Pa: Stackpole, 1959.

Starr, Stephen Z. *The Union Cavalry in the Civil War.* 3 vols. Baton Rouge: Louisiana State University Press, 1979.

Stern, Philip Van Doren. *An End to Valor: The Last Days of the Civil War.* Cambridge, Mass.: The Riverside Press, 1958.

Stevenson, Alexander F. *The Battle of Stones River Near Murfreesboro, Tennessee, December 30, 1862 to January 3, 1863.* Boston: James R. Osgood & Company, 1884.

Sword, Wiley. *Shiloh: Bloody April.* New York: William Morrow, 1974.

Tankersley, Allen P. *John B. Gordon: A Study in Gallantry.* Atlanta, Ga.: The Whitehall Press, 1955.

Tanner, Robert G. *Stonewall in the Valley: Thomas J. "Stonewall" Jackson's Shenandoah Valley Campaign, Spring 1862.* New York: Doubleday, 1976.

Taylor, Emerson G. *Gouverneur Kemble Warren: The Life and Letters of an American Soldier, 1830–1883.* Boston: Houghton Mifflin, 1932.

Thirteenth Annual Reunion of the Association of the Graduates of the United States Military Academy at West Point, June 12, 1882. Philadelphia: Times Printing House, 1882.

Thomas, Benjamin P. *Abraham Lincoln, A Biography.* New York: Alfred A. Knopf, 1952.

Thomas, Emory M. *Bold Dragoon: The Life of J. E. B. Stuart.* New York: Harper & Row, 1986.

Thomason, John W., Jr. *Jeb Stuart.* New York: Charles Scribner's Sons, 1930.

Trudeau, Noah André. *Bloody Roads South: The Wilderness to Cold Harbor, May–June, 1864.* Boston: Little, Brown, 1989.

———. *The Last Citadel: Petersburg, Virginia, June 1864–April 1865.* Boston: Little, Brown, 1991.

Tucker, Glenn. *Hancock the Superb.* Indianapolis, Ind.: Bobbs-Merrill, 1960.

———. *High Tide at Gettysburg: The Campaign in Pennsylvania.* Indianapolis, Ind.: Bobbs-Merrill, 1958.

Urwin, Gregory J. W. *Custer Victorious: The Civil War Battles of General George Armstrong Custer.* Rutherford, N.J.: Fairleigh Dickinson University Press, 1983.

Vandiver, Frank E. *Jubal's Raid: General Early's Famous Attack on Washington in 1864.* New York: McGraw-Hill, 1960.

Warner, Ezra J. *Generals in Blue: Lives of the Union Commanders.* Baton Rouge: Louisiana State University Press, 1964.

Webb, Alexander S. *The Peninsula: McClellan's Campaign of 1862.* New York: Charles Scribner's Sons, 1881.

Wellman, Manly Wade. *Giant in Gray: A Biography of Wade Hampton of South Carolina.* New York: Charles Scribner's Sons, 1949.

Wert, Jeffry. *Mosby's Rangers.* New York: Simon & Schuster, 1990 .

Wills, Brian Steel. *A Battle from the Start: The Life of Nathan Bedford Forrest.* New York: HarperCollins, 1992.

Winslow, Richard E. *General John Sedgwick: The Story of a Union Corps Commander.* Novato, Calif.: Presido Press, 1982.

Articles in Newspapers/Journals

Alexander, Ted. "Gettysburg Cavalry Operations: June 27–July 3, 1863." *Blue and Gray* 6, no. 1 (October 1988).

Calhoun, C. M. "Credit To Wheeler Claimed For Others." *Confederate Veteran* 20, no. 2 (February 1912).

Carr, Joseph B. "Operations of 1861 About Fort Monroe." In vol. 2 of *Battles and Leaders of the Civil War,* edited by Clarence C. Buel and Robert J. Johnson. New York: The Century Company, 1884–87.

Caruthers, W. G. "More about Kilpatrick's Horses." *Confederate Veteran* 13, no. 10 (October 1905).

Cornwell, Louise Caroline Reese. "General Howard Came at Tea Time." In *When Sherman Came: Southern Women and the "Great March,"* edited by Katharine M. Jones. Indianapolis, Ind.: Bobbs-Merrill, 1964.

Crawford, Frank. "Your Charlie." *Civil War Times Illustrated* 31, no. 6 (January/February 1993).

Davis, W. W. "Cavalry Service under General Wheeler." *Confederate Veteran* 14, no. 2 (February 1906).

———. "Initiation of the Georgia Campaign." *Confederate Veteran* 12, no. 2 (February 1904).

———. "Kilpatrick's Spotted Horse." *Confederate Veteran* 14, no. 2 (February 1906).

Dubose, John W. "The Fayetteville (N.C.) Road Fight." *Confederate Veteran* 20, no. 2 (February 1912).

Foster, J. H. "They Selected Our Home for General Kilpatrick's Headquarters." In *When Sherman Came: Southern Women and the "Great March,"* edited by Katharine M. Jones. Indianapolis, Ind.: Bobbs-Merrill, 1964.

Hall, Clark B. "The Battle of Brandy Station." *Civil War Times Illustrated* 29, no. 2 (May/June 1990).

Hall, James O. "The Dahlgren Papers: A Yankee Plot to Kill President Davis." *Civil War Times Illustrated* 22, no. 7 (November 1983).

Harrison, Kathleen Georg. "Ridges of Grim War." *Blue and Gray* 5, no. 6 (July 1988).

Hartley, Dan Manville. "Do Not Show This Letter . . ." *Barnwell People Sentinel,* 14 May 1970.

Hunt, Camille Holt. "General Kilpatrick and His Men Arrive." In *When Sherman Came: Southern Women and the "Great March,"* edited by Katharine M. Jones. Indianapolis, Ind.: Bobbs-Merrill, 1961.

Imboden, John D. "The Confederate Retreat From Gettysburg." In vol. 3 of *Battles and Leaders of the Civil War,* edited by Clarence C. Buel and Robert J. Jonnson. New York: The Century Company, 1884–87.

Jones, J. William. "The Kilpatrick-Dahlgren Raid Against Richmond." *Southern Historical Society Papers* 13 (January to December 1885).

"Kilpatrick Made His Appearance Near Aiken." In *When Sherman Came: Southern Women and the "Great March,"* edited by Katharine M. Jones. Indianapolis, Ind.: Bobbs-Merrill, 1964.

Kowell, Brian D. "Pell-Mell Cavalry Chase." *America's Civil War* 5, no. 2 (July 1992).

Krolick, Marshall D. "The Battle of Brandy Station." *The Civil War Quarterly* 7 (December 1986).

Mallard, Mary Jones. "Kilpatrick's Cavalry . . . Their Conduct . . . Too Terrible To Be True." In *When Sherman Came: Southern Women and the "Great March,"* edited by Katharine M. Jones. Indianapolis, Ind.: Bobbs-Merrill, 1964.

McInvale, Morton R. "All That Devils Could Wish For: The Griswoldville Campaign, November 1864." *Georgia Historical Quarterly* 60, no. 2 (Summer 1976).

Monroe, Haskell. "Men Without Law: Federal Raiding in Liberty County, Georgia." *Georgia Historical Quarterly* 44, no. 2 (June 1960).

Moore, J. Owen. "General Kilpatrick: A Brief Biography." *The Sussex Independent,* 23 December 1881–20 January 1882.

Morgan, D. B. "Incidents of the Fighting at Aiken, S.C." *Confederate Veteran* 32, no. 8 (August 1924).

Parsons, H. C. "Farnsworth's Charge and Death." In vol. 3 of *Battles and Leaders of the Civil War,* edited by Clarence C. Buel and Robert J. Johnson. New York: The Century Company, 1884–87.

Perkins, Eli. "Eli Perkins Talks of the War." *Confederate Veteran* 1, no. 7 (July 1893).

Prince, Polk. "Polk Prince, Guthrie, Ky., Thinks He Shot Kilpatrick." *Confederate Veteran* 10, no. 4 (April 1902).

Purifoy, John. "Farnsworth's Charge and Death at Gettysburg." *Confederate Veteran* 32, no. 8 (August 1924).

Schultz, Fred L. "A Cavalry Fight Was On." *Civil War Times Illustrated* 23, no. 10 (February 1985).

"Sherman's Brutal Work of Sixteen Years Ago." *Barnwell Sentinel,* 10 February 1881.

Slocum, Henry W. "Final Operations of Sherman's Army." In vol. 4 of *Battles and Leaders of the Civil War,* edited by Clarence C. Buel and Robert J. Johnson. New York: The Century Company, 1884–87.

Spira, W. H. "Kilpatrick's Richmond Raid." In *History of the Seventeenth Regiment, Pennsylvania Volunteer Cavalry,* edited by H. P. Moyer. Lebanon, Pa.: Sowers Printing Company, 1911.

Stevens, John. "Personal Narrative of Sherman's Raid in Liberty County, Ga. Atrocities of the Enemy, Etc." *Macon Telegraph & Messenger.*

Stone, Henry. "Repelling Hood's Invasion of Tennessee." In vol. 4 of *Battles and Leaders of the Civil War,* edited by Clarence C. Buel and Robert J. Johnson. New York: The Century Company, 1884–87.

Thomas, Emory M. "The Kilpatrick-Dahlgren Raid, Part I." *Civil War Times Illustrated* 16, no. 10 (February 1978).

——. "The Kilpatrick-Dahlgren Raid, Part II." *Civil War Times Illustrated* 17, no. 1 (April 1978).

Wells, E. L. "A Morning Call on General Kilpatrick." *Southern Historical Society Papers* 12 (January–December 1884).

Unpublished Materials

Papers and Dissertations

Badar, Thomas McLeod. "A Willingness to War: A Portrait of the Republic of Chile during the Years Preceding the War of the Pacific." Ph.D. diss., University of California, 1967.

Hirt, Janet. "Morris Ford: Barnwell's Forgotten Battleground." Barnwell (S.C.) Public Library.

King, George W. "The Civil War Career of Hugh Judson Kilpatrick." Ph.D. diss., University of South Carolina, 1969.

Interviews/Letters

Otis Amason, curator, Midway Church, Liberty County, Georgia. Interview with author, 17 March 1993.

Therese A. Erskine, Sussex County Library, Newton, New Jersey. Letter to author, 13 August 1992.

Joel Martin, auctioneer, Beaufort, South Carolina. Interview with author, 22 July 1993.

Edward Skipworth, Rutgers University, New Brunswick, New Jersey. Letter to author, 19 August 1992.

Susan Walker, United States Military Academy Archives, West Point, New York. Letter to author, 15 June 1992.

Index

317